Considering Class

Studies in Critical Social Sciences Book Series

Haymarket Books is proud to be working with Brill Academic Publishers (www.brill.nl) to republish the *Studies in Critical Social Sciences* book series in paperback editions. This peer-reviewed book series offers insights into our current reality by exploring the content and consequences of power relationships under capitalism, and by considering the spaces of opposition and resistance to these changes that have been defining our new age. Our full catalog of *SCSS* volumes can be viewed at https://www.haymarketbooks.org/series_collections/4-studies-in-critical-social-sciences.

Series Editor
David Fasenfest, Wayne State University

Editorial Board
Eduardo Bonilla-Silva (Duke University)
Chris Chase-Dunn (University of California–Riverside)
William Carroll (University of Victoria)
Raewyn Connell (University of Sydney)
Kimberlé W. Crenshaw (University of California–LA, and Columbia University)
Heidi Gottfried (Wayne State University)
Karin Gottschall (University of Bremen)
Alfredo Saad Filho (University of London)
Chizuko Ueno (University of Tokyo)
Sylvia Walby (Lancaster University)
Raju Das (York University)

CONSIDERING CLASS

Theory, Culture and the Media
in the 21st Century

Edited by
Deirdre O'Neill
Mike Wayne

Haymarket Books
Chicago, IL

First published in 2017 by Brill Academic Publishers, The Netherlands.
© 2017 Koninklijke Brill NV, Leiden, The Netherlands

Published in paperback in 2018 by
Haymarket Books
P.O. Box 180165
Chicago, IL 60618
773-583-7884
www.haymarketbooks.org

ISBN: 978-1-60846-103-5

Trade distribution:
In the U.S. through Consortium Book Sales, www.cbsd.com
In the UK, Turnaround Publisher Services, www.turnaround-uk.com
In Canada, Publishers Group Canada, www.pgcbooks.ca
All other countries, Ingram Publisher Services International, ips_intlsales@ingramcontent.com

Cover design by Jamie Kerry and Ragina Johnson.

This book was published with the generous support of Lannan Foundation and the Wallace Action Fund.

Printed in United States.

10 9 8 7 6 5 4 3 2 1

Library of Congress Cataloging-in-Publication Data is available.

Contents

List of Illustrations   VII
Notes on Contributors   IX

1   Introduction   1
      Deirdre O'Neill and Mike Wayne

PART 1
Class Theory

2   Class and the Classical Marxist Tradition   15
      Joseph Choonara

3   Social Class and Education   31
      Dave Hill

4   Marxist Class Theory: Competition, Contingency and Intermediate Class Positions   51
      Jonathan Pratschke

5   Class Segregation   68
      Danny Dorling

6   The 'Secret' of the Restoration: Increased Class Exploitation   93
      Maurizio Donato and Roberto Taddeo

7   Exploitation, Oppression, and Epistemology   114
      Holly Lewis

PART 2
Class and Culture

8   Peasants, Migrants and Self-Employed Workers: The Masks that Veil Class Affiliation in Latin America: The Argentine Case   133
      Marina Kabat and Eduardo Sartelli

9   Capitalism, Class and Collective Identity: Social Movements and
    Public Services in South Africa   149
    Adrian Murray

10 On Intellectuals   166
    Deirdre O'Neill and Mike Wayne

11 The British Working Class Post-Blair Consensus: We Do Not Exist   185
    Lisa Mckenzie

12 From Class Solidarity to Cultural Solidarity: Immigration, Crises,
    and the Populist Right   198
    Ferruh Yılmaz

13 Recovering the Australian Working Class   217
    Tony Moore, Mark Gibson and Catharine Lumby

PART 3
Class and the Media

14 'Everything Changes. Everything Stays the Same': Documenting
    Continuity and Change in Working Class Lives   237
    Anita Biressi

15 Ghettos and Gated Communities in the Social Landscape of
    Television: Representations of Class in 1982 and 2015   255
    Fredrik Stiernstedt and Peter Jakobsson

16 Class, Culture and Exploitation: The Case of Reality TV   273
    Milly Williamson

17 Class Warfare, the Neoliberal Man and the Political Economy of
    Methamphetamine in *Breaking Bad*   288
    Michael Seltzer

18 'The Thing Is I'm Actually from Bromley': Queer/Class
    Intersectionality in *Pride* (2014)   303
    Craig Haslop

Index   317

List of Illustrations

Figures

5.1	Social class residential segregation in Britain, all ages, 2001	71
5.2	Social class financial segregation in Britain, 2011	74
5.3	Changes in financial segregation in Britain 1968–2005	76
5.4	The segregation of political belief by area in Britain 1981–2015	77
5.5	The English geography of class segregation in education, 2005	82
5.6	Social mobility, income inequality and education mobility, selected countries, 2008–2009	83
5.7	Rising and then falling income inequalities, all countries, 1200–2000	85
5.8A	Inequality in wealth, international, GDP, 2002	86
5.8B	Inequality in food international, undernourishment, 2002	86
5.9	Inequality in income in Britain, top 1%, 1918–2011	87
5.10	Inequality in income in Britain, GINI, 1961–2008	89
6.1	Employment in advanced economies (average annual growth)	96
6.2	Part-time employment, percent of population	96
6.3	Annual hours worked per worker in OECD countries	97
6.4	Annual hours worked per person, most recent years	98
6.5	Labour productivity trends in European Union and United States of America	101
6.6	Labour productivity (levels) in G7	101
6.7	Hours worked per employee (rates of change) in US and EU	102
6.8	Real hourly wages in USA (1933–2012)	104
6.9	Share of labour compensation in GDP at current national prices for United States	107
6.10	Productivity and wages	109
14.1	Ray provides a historical perspective in the film	246
14.2	Interviewees reflect on the past outside the Royal Bank of Scotland which was rescued by taxpayers following the 2007–2008 crash	247
14.3	Angie fears for her children's future	249
14.4	Collective cast curtain call	250

Tables

3.1	The office for national statistics classification of occupations	33
5.1	An example of segregation by race and class in Britain: Medical school	79
5.2	Class residential segregation in Britain, 1997–2005 (%)	90

6.1   Labour productivity trend in OECD countries   100
15.1 The social classes as represented on television in 1982 and 2015   263
15.2 Occupations among persons on television in 2015   264
15.3 Gender among different social classes in the television output in 1982 and 2015   265
15.4 Nationality among different social classes in 1982 and 2015   266
15.5 Social classes in different types of television output 1982 and 2015   267
15.6 The class composition of reality television in 2015   267

Notes on Contributors

Anita Biressi
is Professor of Media and Society at the University of Roehampton, London. Her research interests include documentary and popular factual programming, feminist media studies and social class. She is the co-author of *Class and Contemporary British Culture* (Palgrave, 2013).

Joseph Choonara
is working on a PhD at Middlesex University, focusing on class, precarity and insecurity in the UK. He is a member of the editorial board of *International Socialism*, a columnist on *Socialist Review* and the author of *Unravelling Capitalism: A Guide to Marxist Political Economy* (Bookmarks, 2009).

Maurizio Donato
is a Researcher in Political Economy currently working in the Department of Law at the University of Teramo, Italy. His main research interest is to analyze the dynamics of the crisis and its impact on the working class from a Marxian perspective. He also likes to work with non-academic co-authors.

Danny Dorling
is the Halford Mackinder Professor of Geography at the University of Oxford. He grew up in Oxford and went to University in Newcastle upon Tyne. He has worked in Newcastle, Bristol, Leeds, Sheffield and New Zealand. His work concerns issues of housing, health, employment, education, inequality and poverty—and cartography. His most recent books include *Injustice* (Policy Press, 2015), *Inequality and the 1%* (Verso, 2014) and *A Better Politics* (London Publishing Partnership, 2016).

Mark Gibson
is Head of Communications and Media Studies at Monash University, Australia. He has research interests in suburban cultures, cultural and creative industries, media practices and class. He is author of *Culture and Power—A History of Cultural Studies* (Bloomsbury Academic, 2007) and, until recently, editor of *Continuum—Journal of Media and Cultural Studies*.

Craig Haslop
is a Lecturer in Media in the department of Communication and Media at the University of Liverpool. His main research interests are representations of 'lad

culture' in the media including sociological analysis of the intersections of masculinity, sexuality and class on social media platforms. He is also researching British and US cult television including its promotional cultures, textual class politics and queer sensibilities.

Dave Hill
is a Marxist academic and political activist, focusing on issues of neoliberalism, neo-conservatism, capitalism, class, 'race', resistance and socialist/Marxist education. He edits the *Journal for Critical Education Policy Studies* (www.jceps.com). He fought 13 local, Parliamentary and Euro-elections and was an elected regional trade union leader. He has recently been tear-gassed on Left demonstrations in Ankara and Athens. He is Emeritus Professor at Anglia Ruskin University, Chelmsford. He co-organises the annual ICCE, International Conference on Critical Education (icce-vii.weebly.com).

Peter Jakobsson
is a Researcher at Södertörn University and Senior Lecturer at Beckmans University College of Design. He has published on issues such as media law, copyright, class, and media production. Recent publications include 'Watching television from a distance: class, genre and reality television' in *Media, Culture & Society* and 'At the intersection of commons and market: negotiations of value in open-sourced cultural production' in *International Journal of Cultural Studies*.

Marina Kabat
is a researcher at the University of Buenos Aires and at CONICET (National Council for Scientific and Technological Research). She is a specialist in work organization, labor conflicts, and collective labor agreements; she has also studied contemporary unemployment and the occupied factories movements in Argentina. She is also a head researcher at the CEICS and a political activist.

Holly Lewis
is the author of *The Politics of Everybody: Feminism, Queer Theory, and Marxism at the Intersection* (Zed Books, 2016). She teaches in the Department of Philosophy at Texas State University.

Catharine Lumby
is Professor of Media at Macquarie University and former Foundation Director of the Journalism and Media Research Centre at UNSW and Foundation

Chair of the Media and Communications Department at the University of Sydney. She has been the recipient of nine ARC grants and has conducted large research projects for organisations as diverse as Google Australia, the National Rugby League, the Australian Communication and Media Authority and the Australian Sports Commission. Her research focuses on ethics, gender, class and media.

Lisa Mckenzie
is a working class academic and Lecturer in Practical Sociology at Middlesex University. She researches issues of social inequality and class stratification through ethnographic research. Lisa brings an unusual and innovative approach to research bringing the academic world and local community together. She is the author of *Getting By, Estates, Class and Culture in Austerity Britain* (Policy Press, 2015).

Tony Moore
is Associate Professor in the School of Media, Film and Journalism where he is Director of the Communications and Media Studies Graduate Program. Tony's research interest includes Australian history, artistic bohemia, media activism, class and radical political and cultural movements. Recent works include *Dancing with Empty Pockets* (Murdoch Books, 2012), a history of Australian bohemia, and *Death or Liberty* (Murdoch Books, 2010), a book and international TV documentary about British and Irish political prisoners exiled as convicts to Australia.

Adrian Murray
is a PhD Candidate in the School of International Development and Global Studies at the University of Ottawa. His research explores the experiences of organised labour and social movements in opposing and developing alternatives to the neoliberal restructuring of public services, particularly in Southern Africa. He is also a researcher and activist in the international movement to defend public services and is an active trade unionist.

Deirdre O'Neill
is a working class lecturer and filmmaker. Her forthcoming book *Film as a Radical Pedagogical Tool* (Routledge, 2017) explores the way a radical pedagogy of film grounded in the experiences and everyday realities of the working class can provide a starting point for a critical engagement with and a materialist understanding of how society is organised. She is the co-director (with Mike Wayne) of the feature length documentary *The Condition of the Working Class* (2012)

(www.conditionoftheworkingclass.info) and the forthcoming *The Acting Class* (www.theactingclass.info).

Jonathan Pratschke
is a Research Fellow in Economic Sociology at the University of Salerno in Southern Italy. His research interests are centred on the nature and consequences of uneven development at varying spatial scales, with a focus on poverty, inequalities and labour markets. He has published widely on these themes, including recent articles on Marxist state theory (*World Review of Political Economy*, 2015) and socio-spatial inequalities (*Environment and Planning B: Planning and Design*, 2014).

Eduardo Sartelli
is a College teacher at the University of Buenos Aires—Argentina and the Academic director of the Center for Studies and Research in Social Sciences (Centro de Estudios e Investigación en Ciencias Sociales—CEICS). He is a specialist in Argentine economy and working class history and a political activist. He edits the Marxist journal *Razón y Revolución*.

Michael Seltzer
is a Professor at Oslo and Akershus University College of Applied Sciences. He researches heroin and methamphetamine addicts in therapeutic communities, merchant sailors at sea and on land, lorry drivers, families in therapy and social workers. He is the editor of *Listening to the Welfare State* (Ashgate) and author of articles in *The Social History of Alcohol and Drugs, Journal of Groups in Addiction and Recovery, International Journal of Self-Help and Self-Care, Nordic Social Work Research, Journal of Family Therapy, Family Process*, and *Current Anthropology*.

Fredrik Stiernstedt
is a senior lecturer in Media and Communication Studies at Södertörn University, Sweden. His research interests concern media work and labour, media, law and policy and media and social class. His most recent publication is the article 'Watching reality from a distance: class, genre and reality television' published in *Media, Culture & Society* (online first) in 2016.

Roberto Taddeo
worked in the electricity sector. He is a political activist involved for several years in the struggles of the unemployed. At present, he is active in the movements of opposition to war and militarism. His main field of interest is the

study of the capitalist domination over wage workers in different parts of the world.

Mike Wayne
is a Professor in Screen Media at Brunel University. He has written widely on the politics and ideology of film, television and the media. He is the co-director (with Deirdre O'Neill) of the feature length documentary *The Condition of the Working Class* (2012) and the forthcoming *The Acting Class*. Wayne has written widely on Marxist cultural theory. His most recently published book is *Red Kant: Aesthetics, Marxism and the Third Critique* (Bloomsbury, 2014).

Milly Williamson
teaches film and television studies at Brunel University. She has recently published a monograph *Celebrity: Capitalism and the Making of Fame* (Polity, 2016). She conducts research into the political economy of celebrity culture, formations of class in celebrity and gender and celebrity.

Ferruh Yılmaz
is Associate Professor in the Communication Department at Tulane University, USA. Before becoming an academic, he worked as a journalist for a number of news organizations in Britain, Denmark and Turkey including the BBC World Service and Danish Broadcasting Corporation (DR) and *Cumhuriyet* (a Turkish daily newspaper). He also worked as information officer at the Board for Ethnic Equality (Denmark) in the late 1990s. His latest publication is *How the Workers Became Muslim: Immigration, Culture, and Hegemonic Transformation in Europe* (University of Michigan Press, 2016).

CHAPTER 1

Introduction

Deirdre O'Neill and Mike Wayne

The retreat from class as a powerful explanatory optic and basis for political action has occurred at a time when what used to be called the 'class war', propagated by capital and the rich, has never been more extensive and ambitious. Through a class optic, categories like profit and poverty, investment and insecurity, competition and unemployment, share dividends and wages, creditors and debtors, commodification and anomie, are inextricably interconnected. Equally interconnected, from a class perspective, are the empirical phenomena of a world of evident unreason, the world which a class analysis tries to make sense of: food banks in some of the richest countries in the world, whole economies at the mercy of unaccountable financial forces, corporations engaging in environmental despoliation, resource wars and migration, developers driving the poor out of city centres to get their hands on property assets, public services privatised, public revenues poured into private pockets, the working classes abandoned, the middle classes beginning to join them: class joins the dots, conceptually and politically.

Yet joining the dots is not a widespread activity in a period of historical defeat and retrenchment. Scholarly interest, scholarly concerns, the fashionable theories, what's 'hot' and what's not, turn away from class theory and class explanations. The fragments loom large, the totality disappears. The gap, the chasm even between the objective situation—that is theoretically persuasive and empirically demonstrable—and the diminishing of class as a self-consciously lived, practiced way of seeing and understanding the world at a popular level, is central to the crisis. For both theoretical and popular consciousness tend to take the form of pragmatic adaption to the dominant ways of conceiving our situation and trajectory. The trends, the directions are not seen as historically contingent and in principle alterable, but permanent and fixed. Worse, the facts on the ground become celebrated as the norms by which we *ought* to live. Are we not better human beings for being flexible, adaptable and quick-witted enough to surf the roiling seas of the market economy, than those rather lazy bathers who used to paddle around in the social democratic pond of yesteryear?

Yet the gulf between the objective situation and the retreat from class as a methodological explanatory framework and political practice, can only result in one of those historical 'corrections' that will jolt us into a very bad place indeed. Before we get there (if we have not already arrived) we need to stop the retreat from class and make the evidence based case patiently but firmly, that to disavow a major structural feature of our world, is not conducive for happy historical outcomes. Class-deniers, like climate change deniers, risk a rendezvous with the 'objective situation' that will be more unpleasant and painful than if we acknowledge the situation and try and do something positive to change it.

This means in the first instance challenging the retreat, the scepticism, the all-too-easy formulations by scholars that are keen to shuffle class off into some historical museum. Joseph Choonara's opening essay in Part 1 is a robust defence of the objective necessity of class relations within capitalism. If there is capital, there must also be workers, and this holds good irrespective of particular contractual arrangements, types of work or industry, the particular development of the productive forces or the particular level of struggle or consciousness at any given moment. What workers do, what the composition of workers are (for example in terms of gender or ethnicity), what technologies they work with, all change. But this change does not abolish the class relation itself. Yet the question of consciousness about that class relation haunts the hopes of the socialist imagination and returns again and again, in one form or other, in the essays gathered here. While class as structure, economic imperatives, relations and systemic contradictions (the 2007–8 crash) remains vivid, and while the relatively homogenous class actors at the top have conducted their war on the majority with great skill, co-ordination and sophistication, class as a lived reality, practiced by those on the receiving end of these dynamics and actions, has diminished and fragmented as many of the industries and patterns of work have altered under capitalism's own special kind of 'permanent revolution'. A working class conscious of its position has been unable to take up the latent possibilities of the situation and turn the objective features of the system into objective actions against the system; has been unable in short to become a historical subject, a 'class for itself' as Marx put it.

'Marx believed' writes Dave Hill, that:

> the proletariat and bourgeoisie (workers and capitalists respectively) are in *objective conflict* with each other: the former are materially exploited by the latter whether they *subjectively* know it or not, or whether they like it or not.

Education, the case study that Hill explores, is indeed one of the most important sites where consciousness of the society we grow up in is first forged.

Educational institutions supply the labour-market with the next generation of workers with the right skills, aptitudes and just as importantly, attitudes adjusted to accept the employer-employee relationship on terms best suited to the employer. This requires a broader 'knowledge' about society that is also in many ways characterised by absence, ignorance and acceptance of present social and institutional arrangements. Critical thinking is not high up on the agenda of educational institutions and it is a major contradiction within all the educational organs of society that the development of knowledge and understanding must ideally be kept within certain bounds. Of course educational institutions as Hill points out are sites of struggle between conflicting models of education, some more liberating and less oppressive than others. But situating education within the broader class relations of capitalist society is a sober reminder that in many ways, the problems within the education system, many of which are acknowledged by mainstream politicians and media, are signs that the education system is actually working as it should be, for example how education reproduces class stratification between the working classes and the middle classes.

The whole question of the middle class and their relationship to the working class has certainly been a key problem within Marxist class theory. The middle class pose one aspect of a general problem concerning the complex internal differentiation of classes. In terms of the middle class their role as managers and supervisors (co-ordination and control for example) while still being technically workers exchanging their labour for a wage, has complicated and muddied the binary class model of Marxist analysis. There is a strand of Marxist theory which has argued that the key role of the middle class is ideological. Jonathan Pratschke is rather sceptical of this argument and instead suggests that in addition to their co-ordination and control roles, they should also be conceived as key to product innovation and corporate strategising within a system based on intra-class competitive struggle between capitals in the labour-market. This is part of Pratschke's attempt to bridge the gap between Marxist class theory, which is often formulated at a quite high level of abstraction, and the more concrete analysis of trends in labour markets, educational participation and social mobility associated with the middle class professions. Choonara also calls for more research into labour markets.

Danny Dorling's analysis of class segregation is a model of theoretically informed and empirically rich analysis of how class works in Britain to divide, to skew wealth and opportunities and status (especially in relation to the labour market). Unlike many sociological analyses of class, Dorling has a historical and global perspective that de-natures class patterns, linking them to political trends and choices. Dorling situates his analysis within an international perspective on trends in global inequality and in the context of a very sick capitalist political economy internationally, inequality is growing and social mobility stalling. Dorling writes of the rich, rather than 'capital', but the rich are merely the grateful and greedy personifications of those more abstract trends that critical political economy analyses. Segregation also has a profound impact on knowledge and culture:

> In Britain, and it can also be argued in the US, the implications of this rising segregation have been a growth in ignorance across the board: ignorance of poverty for the rich, ignorance by the poor of the true value of riches held by the few, and more and more people seeing themselves as average, while fewer are near to average.

Class as a category requires us to stretch our mind across disciplines (political economy, history, sociology, politics, cultural and media studies) and to operate at different levels of abstraction—a point made by Pratschke and demonstrated by the move to different levels of abstraction at which the essays in this volume operate. With Maurizio Donato and Roberto Taddeo's essay, we move back 'up' a level of abstraction, mapping, with empirical evidence, the struggles over value at a global level. For Donato and Taddeo, the 'secret' by which the international bourgeoisie has managed to secure a growing mass of profits and a slowdown in the falling rate of profit in the 'years of restoration' is the intensification and extension of exploitation. The historical context of the extraction of absolute surplus value typical of the primitive stages of accumulation has been combined with the typical methods of extraction of relative surplus value: technological innovations that reduce the average social work time needed to produce one unit of a commodity. As Donato and Taddeo show, globally productivity has risen while real wages have fallen.

When class is not dismissed altogether, the dominant way in which the concept is used, is highly problematic. Again and again our contributors critique class models based primarily on income and consumption, that have static a-historical assumptions underpinning them and that tend to break the link between accumulation at one pole and dispossession at the other end, or to put it another way, tend to obscure the causal forces that are responsible for outcomes. Holly Lewis reminds us of Marx's essential insight about the mystification embedded in the rational form of the wage-relation. The shifting salience of class as a political and methodological optic and the ability to uncouple various oppressions from class analysis, is in part determined by the way structurally, within capitalism, class relations are typically less visible than other relations or identities, precisely because the extraction of surplus value is at its core economically pumped out rather than *reliant* on (as opposed to opportunistically making use of) forms of force or irrational discrimination (e.g. racism, sexism). As Lewis puts it: "Capitalism, ... grows through the expropriation of the free labourer through a mathematical ratio between surplus value and socially necessary labour time." It is all so technical, rational, contractual, legal, atomised and fair-seeming that tracking the flow of value upwards seems to go against modernity itself. The very structures of capitalism pose difficult epistemological and political problems.

Part 2 of this book, dedicated to exploring the cultural question in more detail begins again with a orthodox and robust defence of a Marxist definition of class. Sartelli and Kabat dissect some of the ways a version of E.P Thompson's work has been reworked in a Latin American context, paying particular attention to their own country of Argentina. They show the problematic nature of the dismissal of class analysis in the scholarly literature, news media and State policies and discourses. Alternative conceptions based around 'migrants', 'slaves', 'peasants' and 'self-employed' are used in ways that are analytically dubious and ideologically suspect. Yet turning a more adequate analysis of a situation into a political reality returns us once more to the question of class consciousness: how classes move from being mere existence to subjective self-knowledge as a class for itself. While culture may be national, local and even 'sub-cultural', and while it may be penetrated by the forces of commodification, as Holly Lewis rightly argues, the development of class consciousness also always develops within and on the terrain of culture, in relation to other categories such as race, nation and gender and requires patient political organising if it is to be fostered.

Adrian Murray's essay transfers many of the issues that Satelli and Kabat engage with around rival conceptions of the working class in conditions of 'under-development' to Cape Town, South Africa. Like them he finds that class remains an objectively valid category in understanding the life experiences of the exploited majority. Murray however offers a detailed ethnographic case study of the organisational work going on within a 'social movement' that is struggling to turn that objective reality into something subjectively grasped in class terms and acted on by the participants in the process. Influenced by E.P. Thompson's work, the central argument of Murray's chapter is that the "translation and production of knowledge by organic, movement intellectuals and the molecular, catalytic work done by organisers in working class homes, workplaces and communities ... are at the core of a dynamic process of becoming at the heart of class formation." For Murray the concrete work of organising cannot be displaced by a focus on mobilisation alone (the traditional focus of 'social movement' theory and practice). Prioritising mobilisation (of the already politicised) relies on a limited understanding of class and social change and retains the focus on elite social movement politics that has dominated much traditional scholarship and contemporary movement practice.

The role of intellectuals, the question of education that politicises, the relative positions of the working class and middle class in the public sphere as actors who can make their voices heard, frame debates, set agendas and so forth, connect Murray's essay with O'Neill and Wayne's contribution on intellectuals. In the UK, neoliberalism has seen the social democratic bases for working class subject formation, dismantled. The public sphere where decisions are made and discussed, in the media, education and politics, have been occupied completely by a middle class dedicated to managerialist approaches to public life and market focused insistence on competitive individualism that removes the potential for collective action. What Nancy Fraser calls 'counter publics', a necessary riposte to the exclusionary tactics of those who dominate the official public sphere, where oppositional agendas, interests and identities can be articulated, need to be reconstructed. The growing gap between liberalism, of both its economic and social variety, and the working class, has provided a space for the 'oppositional' politics of a populist Right, that has no answers to the problems they diagnose, because they remain committed to one model or another of the same broken system. In this context O'Neill and Wayne reconstruct the philosophical basis for democratic intellectual practice in the work of Marx and Gramsci, both of whom make reflexive awareness of the role of the intellectual within the social division of labour central to their transformative vision. Elaborating on Gramsci's discussion of the different types or models of intellectuals and the way they implement the relationships between knowledge and power, O'Neill and Wayne examine the role of the hegemonic and counter-hegemonic intellectual in the contemporary era and the relations that the working and middle classes have to these models. They argue that digital media has opened up spaces for a broader range of class voices to assume the social function of being an intellectual and to challenge the liberal-conservative spectrum of thought within the dominant media. The development of organic counter-hegemonic intellectuals from the working class is a prerequisite for progressive social change.

Some sense of how important counter-hegemonic working class intellectuals are can be glimpsed (by their absence) in Lisa Mckenzie's essay. The English working class are on the receiving end of the most brutal economic and political forces, with even less protection than workers in other parts of Britain and which have profound disorganising effects. Mckenzie draws on long-term ethnographic research into working class communities in London and Nottingham, with a particular focus on the experiences and perspectives of working class women. She picks up on an argument made by Bev Skeggs about how the question of 'value' has been simultaneously turned into an individual question (which lets a failing capitalist system off the hook) and measured by purely financial criteria. This has for example driven the gentrification of London and the displacement of working class communities. Mckenzie's contribution is story-based: built around the lives and experiences of those at the sharp end of neoliberalism and she shows how conceptions of 'community' underpin working class lives and are under assault. Such conceptions are the bases for a future counter-hegemonic resistance against those currently winning the class war. Yet the political disorganisation of the Left in England is an ongoing disaster for those strata of the working class most exposed and with the least political and organisational protection against the forces of State and capital ranged against them. Mckenzie offers vivid case-studies of social and moral injustice and the counter-productive stupidity of the class system. Her essay counts the cost of contemporary capitalism in a language that capital itself simply no longer recognises or registers.

The shift from public and collective moral values to individual ones and the shift to individual ones that stress the financial value of individuals, is one part of the hegemonic struggle around moral and political values that is being conducted by neoliberalism. Another dimension of neoliberalism's assault has been this paradoxical sleight of hand: if everything has become available as a commodity, if everything has a financial value primarily and some assessment of whether this financial value is 'worth it', we have also seen a massive culturalisation of problems which uncouple effects from socio-economic causalities. Here the individualisation of moral values is blown up to a culturalisation built around 'us' and 'them', with the dividing line being built very much between 'Western values' and 'Muslims' as well as other 'threats' (migrants in general for example). This has provided the terrain on which a Right-wing populism is now flourishing.

Like Lisa Mckenzie, Ferruh Yılmaz tells us a story, but in this instance it is autobiographical rather than the product of ethnographic research. Yılmaz's story is one where a national culture strongly inflected by working class values that had accepted him into Denmark in his late teens, had become years later a national culture defined by cultural values which now placed him as 'Muslim', rather than a member of the working class. As he notes: "The focus had moved away from class that brought immigrants and native Danes together around common class interests despite cultural differences, to culture that brought cultural (religious, ethnic, racial) differences to the forefront." This process has been a familiar one in Europe and the US and may be read as part of the dominant hegemonic system attempting to reframe its own failures in ways that divides the working class and displaces its antagonism away from the system and the elites within it. In this is has been aided by the 'official' social democratic Left which has abandoned the working class and the language of class analysis, leaving the field wide open to the populist Right in times of crisis. Yılmaz suggests that this shift has a very fundamental ontological basis. This articulates a widespread view on the Left that perhaps things have changed irreversibly with theoretical and political consequences that thrust us into a substantively new historical situation. Undoubtedly there are great difficulties sifting through the complex relationships between class, culture and politics, and as Yılmaz argues neither a straight-forward return to at least some of the older positions on class will suffice, but neither is a rush to embrace identity politics going to work. As Yılmaz points out, even gay politics has been recently articulated to right-wing nationalistic anti-Muslim positions. We may also add, that liberalism has been openly 'classist' following such events as Britain voting to leaving the EU or Donald Trump's election as US President, both of which are seen by liberalism as powered by a racist, ignorant, nationalistic working class. Conversely, an older language of class politics did frequently marginalise or downplay other forms of oppression (based on race, gender, sexuality and so forth). The theoretical complexities involved in reconciling these tensions and re-articulating a vision of society that can forge the right kind of solidarities are linked to very high political stakes in the current conjuncture. A liberalism that automatically equates class with an agenda hostile to the claims of race, gender and sexuality really needs to examine its own repressions.

How international the trends towards the disorganisation and symbolic annihilation of the working class are, is illustrated by the essay from Tony Moore, Mark Gibson and Catharine Lumby. As they show, what they call the 'civic potency' of working class culture(s) has been de-recognised in academia, politics and policy discourse. The latter has moved to re-classify social inequality using other terms such as 'social exclusion', a policy drift that the New Labour government in the UK also excelled at in the early part of the 21st century. One of the consequences of this way of framing divisions in society was to make the culture of the excluded responsible for their exclusion, and that the task was to 'include' them without changing anything in society. The only thing that had to be changed was the culture of the excluded it seemed. Likewise, the Australian Labor Party, even earlier than the British Labour Party, began to uncouple itself from its working class base and the authors chart the specific dynamics and patterns of that trajectory within the Australian context, but one which again has strong echoes of what has been happening to social democratic parties of the Left elsewhere. A similar story of class receding from view is told in relation to Australian Cultural Studies. In wanting to revive the relevance of class for politics, policy-making and cultural studies, Moore et al, like Yılmaz, argue that the substantive economic, social and cultural changes of the last several decades need to be recognised. There can be no simple return to class as it was perhaps once imagined. They advocate a more culturally differentiated model of class and one which stresses the potential for cultural agency to avoid functionalism. As with O'Neill and Wayne, Moore et al stress the possibilities of digital media and cultural practices as one important site where cultural, and the beginnings of political, self-determination may emerge.

The whole question of continuity and change and of the importance of working class access to the means of cultural production, takes us into Anita Biressi's essay that begins Part 3 of the book. Here the essays focus on specific media practices and representations, discussing how class in particular, but also in relation to other identities, intersects with the politics of representation. Biressi is sympathetic to the critiques of abstract and overly homogenised conceptions of class. Such conceptions came not only from the Left. They continue to be widely circulated by media organisations that deal with simplistic class typologies that at once indicate that class remains alive in the popular imaginary but often cast as out of date/dying/a residual threat or comforting nostalgia. Such representations are indicative of broader attitudes and policies that contribute to the 'hidden injuries of class'. Biressi explores how O'Neill and Wayne's 2012 feature documentary *The Condition of the Working Class*, uses a cultural project to deconstruct some of the simplistic typologies of class in broader circulation (both 'positive' and 'negative') and give them a more complex, historical inflection that is both vividly individual and grounded in collective, shared experiences. Biressi concludes that *The Condition of the Working Class* is in significant ways, outside the western documentary tradition with its focus on the formation of collective agency, knowledge and memory—but what then of the dominant media and their representations of class? This is the question that the remaining essays in Part 3 analyse, with a focus on television and film.

A detailed content analysis of the dominant media and its representations of class, using Swedish television as a case study, is offered by Fredrik Stiernstedt and Peter Jakobsson. Comparing their results with an earlier study of class on Swedish television in 1982 they find again both continuities and some significant differences. The authors offer a useful sketch of broader changes and continuities in class relations and composition that connects with Choonara's opening contribution, before going on to discuss their results. Their quantitative analysis discovers some expected but still nonetheless shocking skews in the televisual representation of class. Only 11% of the total number of persons they could codify in class terms belonged to the working class while 70% were middle class and 19% were upper class. Given that Swedish social statistics suggest that the working class makes up 48% of the population, their findings tells us an awful lot about wider social relations of power and the dominant cultural norms influencing representation. Within that small underrepresented figure of 11% they find television has registered changes in the gender and ethnic/national composition of the Swedish working class. The authors also find wider social changes being internalised in televisual discourse in another less positive way: where the working class do appear, it is no longer in the genres of news and factual reportage (where they have been "eradicated") but in the genre of reality television. This may be taken to summarise and symbolically naturalise the big neoliberal drive to push the working class out of the public sphere in terms of politics and consign them to a much more individualised and privatised cultural ghetto.

It is the genre of reality television, focusing on the UK and the US, which is the subject of Milly Williamson's essay. This offers us a much more detailed analysis of the political economy of reality television than Stiernstedt and Jakobsson had space for. The genre is typical—in the sense meant by Lukács—in that it exemplifies the leading socio-economic forces within the industry and helps drive them. De-regulation, commercialisation, concentration of ownership, the internationalisation of formats and the drive to find cost-effective programming that could attract the sort of demographics advertisers are interested in (especially young people) converge in the reality television genre. The multichannel environment has been good for the advertisers on which commercial television depends (Stiernstedt and Jakobsson find that one-fifth of the output on Swedish television is advertising). Multichannel television has driven down costs by increasing competition, but this is bad for programmers. Williamson's political economic analysis of the genre shows how reality television has helped programmers slash labour costs because its on-screen talent is paid either nothing or next to nothing. But as Williamson argues, this did not solve the contradictions of contemporary television's economic base, but it has led to increased exploitation—in both the strictly Marxist economic sense of that term and in a broader moral sense (treating people badly). Williamson does also usefully restate exactly where and why the Marxist concept of exploitation is applicable and where it is not.

The extraordinarily popular American television series *Breaking Bad* has won plaudits for its portrayal of middle class drug king Walter White. Michael Seltzer however situates its representation of drugs and class in a more critical context, as a production of neoliberal values and attitudes and an ideologically formulaic commodity aestheticising the reality of drug addiction in the US. It is not coincidental that the main point of identification for 'upscale' audiences is a middle class character. Echoing Stiernstedt and Jakobsson's essay, Seltzer notes that the working class are massively underrepresented on American television. While *Breaking Bad* does embed the action amongst the working class criminal underground, it shows little sympathy for the victims of the drug, methamphetamine, that Walter White deals in. Seltzer deconstructs the series' decontextualisation of methamphetamine use, its individualisation of the issue and the resulting contraction of empathy towards those suffering from drug addiction. By providing the political economy of methamphetamine and filling in the absences within the series itself, Seltzer provides a new context within which to evaluate the series' "victim-blaming framing" which is indeed part of the broader culture of neoliberalism.

If Stiernstedt and Jakobsson, Williamson and Seltzer all offer compelling arguments and evidence of the way cultural forms and representational practices may uncritically internalise and reproduce the dominant political-moral patterns of the society around them, it would be wrong to assume that this is always the case. Because that wider culture is contested and the wider political economy at the very least throws up anxiety (and oftentimes resistance) due to its remorseless uncontrolled changes, its inequality generating effects and severe contradictions, we would expect to find spaces within popular culture that articulate more critical, questioning perspectives. It is in this light that we turn to our final essay in this volume by Craig Haslop. He explores the intersection between class and gay identity in relation to the popular film *Pride* (2014) about the UK Miners' Strike in 1984–5 and the support they received from the Lesbian and Gays Support The Miners (LGSM) group. Haslop uses the film to explore how the experiences of being gay are differentially inflected by class identity, or conversely, how class identity can be differentially inflected by sexual orientation. He notes for example how gay culture has become increasingly commodified and implicitly underpinned by a middle class cultural identity. British films exploring the intersection of class and gay sexuality have been few in number, but in some ways *Pride* can be seen as a more conventional (and problematic) attempt to deal with complex identity formations that *My Beautiful Laundrette* engaged with at the same time that *Pride* is set. Haslop explores the way the film does this by a series of comparisons between metropolitan London and a rural Welsh village, a series of journeys by both the LGSM and the miners and their wives back and forth between these spaces, as well as some eye for the internal differentiations within the rural working class village and London (repressed middle class Bromley vs the working class figure of Mark Ashton for example). Haslop also introduces an autobiographical element, grounding the question of class, as others have done in this volume, in the important but often marginalised question of 'experience'. He notes that shifts in class identity (from working to middle class for example) can also be thought of in terms of 'intersectionality'. While the film can be criticised for being schematic in some ways, what it is probing and recollecting is interesting, significant and should not be dismissed. On the question of class, it may be thought in some sense as exploring the hole in our symbolic maps for thinking about class, given the radical transformations in the composition, work and technologies associated with the working class since the Miners' Strike. And on the question of building those solidarities between class and other identities, as has been discussed above, in the context of a resurgent populist Right, this has never been more urgent.

PART 1

Class Theory

CHAPTER 2

Class and the Classical Marxist Tradition

Joseph Choonara

Introduction

Some point around 2013, according to data from the International Labour Organization, a historic landmark was reached. For the first time, wage labourers constituted a majority of the global labour force, amounting to some 1.6 billion people (ILO 2013). This symbolic milestone might be seen to confirm Karl Marx's prognosis in *The Communist Manifesto* that "the bourgeoisie … produces, above all, its own grave-diggers". However, the sentence that follows in the *Manifesto*, "Its fall and the victory of the proletariat are equally inevitable," has increasingly been contested, not simply within mainstream political discourse but also on the radical left (Marx 1977, 231). As early as the mid-1980s, Ellen Meiksins Wood felt moved to write *The Retreat from Class*, decrying the rise of post-Marxism as a return to the kind of perspectives Marx criticised among the German left intelligentsia of the 1840s. According to the introduction to the second edition, published a decade later, in the subsequent wave of "post-left theories … there is even less room for class politics than there was in post-Marxism" (Wood 1998, xiv). A couple of years later, *Empire*, the first in a trilogy of works by Antonio Negri and Michael Hardt, appeared, popularising ideas that had gestated among Italian autonomist Marxists since the crisis of the *operaismo* movement in the 1970s (Hardt and Negri 2001; Wright 2002):

> In a previous era the category of the proletariat centred on and was at times effectively subsumed under the *industrial working class*, whose paradigmatic figure was the male mass factory worker … Today that working class has all but disappeared from view … it has been displaced from its privileged position in the capitalist economy … [U]nder the category of the proletariat we understand *all* those exploited by and subject to capitalist domination … Some labour is waged, some is not; some labour is restricted to within the factory walls, some is dispersed across the unbounded social terrain; some labour is limited to eight hours a day and forty hours a week, some expands to fill the entire time of life.
> HARDT and NEGRI 2001, 52–53

Their emphasis on the breakdown of the capital-labour relationship in traditional workplaces leads Hardt and Negri to focus on a new political subject, the multitude, consisting of practically anyone engaged in any form of creative activity. This position does not seek to invalidate traditional Marxist claims about class so much as to relegate them to a historical proposition. So too with a second strand of left thinking, which emphasises the emergence of a 'precariat' of insecure workers. This conception gained currency in the English-speaking world with the publication in 2011 of Guy Standing's *The Precariat: The New Dangerous Class*. For Standing, the vanishing epoch of the working class was characterised by:

> A society consisting mostly of workers in long-term, stable, fixed-hour jobs with established routes of advancement, subject to unionisation and collective agreements, with job titles their fathers and mothers would have understood, facing local employers whose names and features they were familiar with.
> STANDING 2011, 6

To these strands of criticism we could add works by Eric Hobsbawm, Ernesto Laclau and Chantal Mouffe, André Gorz, Manuel Castells, Slavoj Žižek and Paul Mason to name just a few (Hobsbawm 1978, Laclau and Mouffe 2014, Gorz 1982, Castells 2000a, Žižek 2012, Mason 2015). The argument here is that there are important elements of the classical Marxist notion of class that are ignored or misconstrued by recent radical left writers. We have to return to Marx to assess the validity or otherwise of the retreat from class.

Relations of Production

Marx never set out his view on class in a single work. One of his plans for *Capital* did include a book on wage-labour, but this never materialised; the third volume of the published text famously finishes with a "title: *Classes*. Forty lines, then silence" (Lebowitz 2003, 27–50; Althusser and Balibar 1971, 193). Nonetheless, it is possible to reconstruct a consistent account of class from the totality of Marx's writing.

Class, for Marx, arises out of the *relations of production*, a category that begins to emerge in *The German Ideology*, co-authored with Frederick Engels around 1846. Initially Marx and Engels speak of production in a given nation involving a combination of "productive forces" and "internal and external intercourse". A given "mode of production" gives rise to and is characterised by "the real process of production" consisting of both material factors and social relations (Marx and Engels 1974, 57–58). While, at this stage, the term *intercourse* is used, rather than *relations of production*, we get, in embryonic form, a vision of historical development that will be refined in later works, involving a succession of forms of intercourse promoting and then acting as "fetters" on the forces of production (Marx and Engels 1974, 87).

This process of refinement is clear in Marx's polemic against the German revolutionary Karl Heinzen, penned a year or so after *The German Ideology*:

> Since *private property* ... consists in the totality of the *bourgeois* relations of production ... since all these bourgeois relations of production are class relations ... a change in, or even the abolition of, these relations can only follow from a change in these classes and their relationships with each other, and a change in the relationship of classes is a historical change, a product of social activity as a whole ....
> MARX 1976, 337

Relations of production are here explicitly linked both to the control of property and to class relations. The developing account of forces and relations of production culminates in the famous preface to *A Contribution to the Critique of Political Economy*:

> In the social production of their existence, men inevitably enter into definite relations, which are independent of their will, namely relations of production appropriate to a given stage in the development of their material forces of production ... At a certain stage of development, the material productive forces of society come into conflict with the existing relations of production or—this merely expresses the same thing in legal terms—with the property relations within the framework of which they have operated hitherto. From forms of development of the productive forces these relations turn into their fetters.
> MARX 1981, 20–21

Marx's account only makes sense if the broad range of concrete relationships through which workers are organised in workplaces are considered, along with technology, as an element in the *forces of production*. This category, for Marx, denotes the capacity of a society to produce in order to satisfy historically determined needs (Marx 1991, 959). The relations of production are a much narrower set of relationships, consisting of two species. The first are the antagonistic relations of exploitation:

> The specific economic form in which unpaid surplus labour is pumped out of the direct producers determines the relationship of domination and servitude, as this grows directly out of production itself and reacts back on it in turn as a determinant. On this is based the entire configuration of the economic community arising from the actual relations of production, and hence also its political form.
>
> MARX 1991, 927

The other species of relations of production are those governing the effective control (and usually ownership) of the means of production. Under capitalism, in contrast with, say, feudalism, control of the means of production rests almost exclusively with the capitalist class. Labourers can only access these by entering into a wage relation with capital. It should be added that ownership of the means of production is not collective among capitalists. Competition, which is "the inner *nature of capital*, appearing in and realised as the reciprocal interaction of many capitals with one another" is inherently a part of the relations of production (Marx 1993, 414).

A looser notion of the relations of production leads to the idea that changes to the production process can reconfigure the class structure willy-nilly. Negri and Standing both tend to fetishise particular phases in the history of the working class, associated with a particular stage of the development of the forces of production. In Negri's case, the benchmark is the Italian factory struggle of the 1970s; in Standing's case, the world of the long boom following the Second World War, which created employment conditions that existed only for a brief period in the history of capitalism and have never existed across most of the globe.

Some of the post-Marxists explicitly collapse relations of production into the forces of production. So Castells argues:

> Technology is embodied in technical relationships, which are socially conditioned ... In principle ... it could be assigned primarily to the process of production, in which we could then distinguish social relationships of production, and technical relationships of production, as proposed in the Marxian model, and as I had proposed in my own work. I now think this is questionable ... In the last analysis, the networking of production leads to the blurring of class relationships ... production-based, social classes, as constituted, and enacted in the Industrial Age, cease to exist in the network society.
>
> CASTELLS 2000b, 8–9, 18

Hardt and Negri write: "Production becomes indistinguishable from reproduction; productive forces merge with relations of production" (Hardt and Negri 2001, 385). In both cases the result is a kind of technological determinism in which changes to production methods translate into a sidelining of a supposedly 'traditional' proletariat.

The importance of Marx's account of relations of production is that, while the forces of production can change dramatically over the life-course of a mode of production, it is nonetheless possible to speak of a set of "relations of production corresponding to [a] specific and historically determined mode of production" (Marx 1991, 1018). If, as I shall argue, the most important shared capacities and interests of classes arise out of the relations of production, and the way they interact with the forces of production, we should expect these to be preserved *despite* the real changes to capitalism in recent decades.

The Special Class

Following Hal Draper, we can consider the features making the working class a "special class" (Draper 1978, 33–48). First, the "proletariat is the only class that has the social weight and power to carry through the abolition of the old order and to build a new society" (Draper 1978, 46). This is true in the sense that the working class in advanced capitalist societies constitutes the numerical majority. More fundamentally, capitalism's relations of production compel it not simply to create a working class but to imbue it with power due to "the strategic role of the indispensable services performed by the proletariat in keeping society going" (Draper 1978, 46–47).

It is this *interdependence* of capital and labour that distinguishes exploitation from oppression. To be oppressed on the grounds of gender or race does not imbue the oppressed with any particular power; exploitation does. Stoppages, strikes and workplace occupations are all evidence of the working class mobilising this power. The dependence of capital on labour holds regardless of whether workers are involved in producing goods or services. Either can involve the appropriation of unpaid surplus-labour to generate surplus-value (the source of profits), a point acknowledged by Marx with regard to private education:

> Capitalist production is not merely the production of commodities, it is, by its very essence the production of surplus-value ... If we may take an example from outside the sphere of material production, a schoolmaster

> is a productive worker when, in addition to belabouring the heads of his pupils, he works himself into the ground to enrich the owner of the school. That the latter has laid out his capital in a teaching factory, instead of a sausage factory, makes no difference to the relation.
> MARX 1990, 644

It is noteworthy, given recent debates, that Marx chooses a field in which "knowledge" is involved. There is no reason in principle why Marx's political economy, and hence his class analysis, cannot be extended into these areas (Carchedi 2012, 183–207).

The dependence of capital on labour is most obvious when workers directly generate surplus-value or in, for instance, the financial sector where they are essential to the appropriation of surplus-value generated elsewhere in the system. However, the role that the state has come to play in capitalist production (and reproduction) also imbues large numbers of public sector workers with considerable power. The disruption involved in shutting down publically-run transport networks, waste disposal services or schools are examples. The public sector strikes of 2011 cost British industry an estimated £500 million, primarily by forcing parents to make alternative arrangements for their children (HM Treasury, 2011).

A second consequence of capitalist development is the formation of a *collective* class. Collectivisation takes two forms. First, capitalism is a largely urban system that experiences a pressure to agglomerate within cities (Harvey 2006, 417–418). Fear of the "mob" in cities such as Paris or London long predates industrialisation. However, under capitalism, urbanisation has become, for the first time in world history, the norm, another historic landmark, this one reached in 2007 according to the United Nations (UN-Habitat 2006, iv).

This form of concentration dovetails with a more fundamental form, namely the concentration of workers within workplaces. While this process begins in the early stages of manufacturing, it is the utilisation of machinery on a large scale that really revolutionises production. Mechanisation of the labour process has contradictory impacts on the collectivisation of labour. At first, as greater quantities of capital are mobilised and the scale of production expands, and as firms swallow up their rivals, the number of workers mobilised in workplaces generally grows. However, mechanisation can also lead to the replacement of workers with machinery. This does not automatically entail a reduction of workplace size. If the overall expansion of capital is more rapid than the increase in its organic composition (the ratio of investment in machinery and raw material to investment in labour power), or if capital is being centralised in fewer hands, workplaces can still expand. If this is not the case, though, we might expect the workplaces in a particular industry to decline in size.

This has indeed occurred in many fields of manufacturing. However, this has not necessarily diminished the strength of groups of workers still employed. Indeed, the use of "just in time" methods across production networks spanning continents can imbue relatively small groups of workers with extraordinary strategic power (Dunn 2011, 68). The "surplus population" produced by accumulation in particular fields of employment also "becomes, conversely, the lever of capitalist accumulation", offering the potential for new fields of production to open up and draw labourers into them (Marx 1990, 784). Marx cites the railways as an example, but the century and a half since has seen many more instances, notably the growth of the service sector generally across advanced capitalist countries since the Second World War.

What is surprising over the past few decades is not that some workplaces have diminished in size while others have grown, but rather how stable the distribution of workplace size seems to have been. In the US, between 1980 and 2007, the percentage of employees in workplaces with over 100 employees fell by just 1 percent from 46 percent to 45 percent (Dunn 2011, 67). Given the decline in the size of many manufacturing workplaces this suggests the emergence of a range of big service sector workplaces. Half the US labour force is today in workplaces comparable in size to the cotton mills of Lancashire during the great Chartist agitation of the 1840s, which generally employed around 100 or 200 labourers.

A third consequence of the rise of capitalism is that workers are placed in a *homogenous position relative to capital*. This is, it should be stressed, not absolute homogeneity. Workers can occupy quite different positions in the labour process and work within entirely different labour processes. Fortunately absolute homogeneity is not necessary. It is sufficient that the working class have the potential to recognise the simple fact that they face a common situation of exploitation by a common enemy.

The combination of collectivisation and relative homogeneity tends to close off individual solutions. Crudely, the peasantry could rise up, seize the lord's land, divide it up, and each farm a plot individually. There is no analogous solution if workers take over a supermarket, car plant or hospital.

The fourth point is that capitalism creates a propensity to struggle. As Draper points out, this does not rest on a particular view of society. "The working class moves towards class struggle insofar as capitalism fails to satisfy its economic and social needs and aspirations, not insofar as it is told about struggle by Marxists" (Draper 1978, 42).

Ultimately these struggles can break the bounds of capitalist society and herald the emergence of a new form of society. As Draper puts it: "The thrust of the proletariat's organised struggle persistently tends to go outside the framework of bourgeois institutions and ideas" (Draper 1978, 42). This is true even though the organisations of workers may be led by reformist leaders who seek to constrain the struggles within the limits afforded by capitalism and even if many workers enter struggle on the basis of attempting to win reforms. That the aspirations held by workers cannot ultimately be satisfied within the confines of capitalist society again reflects the relations of production of capitalism. The potential for those living under the system to realise their historically determined needs is consistently undercut by the class relations of capitalism—the production relations of capital have, in a real sense, become "fetters" on the development of society.

Militancy and Consciousness

For those of us living in societies experiencing a long lull in class struggle it is important to remind ourselves that the working class demonstrates a persistence of militancy surpassing that of any other exploited class historically. While peasant revolts and slave rebellions were known in previous epochs, they tended to be occasional eruptions threatening the social order. Under capitalism, strikes, occupations and demonstrations feature regularly in almost any country. Revolutions or revolutionary situations, though less common, have occurred somewhere within the system in every decade of the 20th and 21st centuries.

Accompanying this is a persistence of organising of some form or other. As Draper points out, "Workers are taught organisation not by their superior intelligence or by outside agitators, but by the capitalists ... Capitalism has no choice about teaching its workers the wonders of organisation and labour solidarity, because without these the system cannot operate" (Draper 1978, 41). In carrying through their struggles, workers are compelled to form organisations on class lines. "The basic function of class organisation is struggle, present or potential, reality or threat. The very notion of an organisation, like a trade union, which is inherently hospitable to members of one class only, and which is inherently weakened until it achieves the organisation of the entire class as such, is a notion that fits no bourgeois ideology" (Draper 1978, 42).

In this account it is not a case of achieving a level of organisation and then embarking on the class struggle. On the contrary, organisation tends to flow from the needs of, and actuality of, struggle. The same applies to the development of class consciousness. Consider the succinct theorisation of contradictory consciousness offered by Antonio Gramsci:

> The active man-in-the-mass has a practical activity, but no theoretical consciousness of his practical activity, which nonetheless involves understanding the world in so far as it transforms it. His theoretical consciousness can indeed be historically in opposition to his activity. One might almost say that he has two theoretical consciousnesses (or one contradictory consciousness): one which is implicit in his activity and which in reality unites him with all his fellow-workers in the practical transformation of the real world; and one, superficially explicit or verbal, which he has inherited from the past and uncritically absorbed.
> GRAMSCI 1998, 333

The uncritical absorption of ideas can be best understood as a consequence of the alienation experienced by the worker. Capitalism confronts workers as a set of apparently naturalised, immutable relations (Perlman 1990). It is under those conditions that the "ideas of the ruling class" can become "the ruling ideas", even where they run counter to the interests of the majority (Marx and Engels 1974, 64). Yet, Gramsci suggests, such ideas are never the totality of consciousness; they always exist in tension with ideas that reflect the objective interests of workers.

The combination of these two contradictory conceptions of the world can lead to a paralysis that "does not permit any action", resulting in "passivity", but this is not a static state of affairs. First, as Gramsci notes, there is a distinction between "normal times" and "exceptional" ones. Prolonged periods of crisis—political or economic—disrupt the coherence of ruling class ideology and along with it the complex, contradictory sedimentation of ideas forming the "common sense" of the working class (Gramsci 1998, 326–328, 345–346).

Second, the experience of struggle leads to the transformation of consciousness: "[E]very 'spontaneous' movement contains rudimentary elements of conscious leadership" (Gramsci 1998, 197). In other words, the development of militancy and organisation is what Draper helpfully describes as a process of *maturation* (Draper 1978, 52–56). The converse of this is that periods of setback and demoralisation may lead to regression. Following the defeats suffered by the working class movements in most advanced capitalist countries from the late 1970s onwards, there has been a long period of capitalist restructuring in which new potential class forces have developed with little or no direct experience of open class struggle—especially sustained, successful class struggle.

However, there is no objective reason why new groups of workers created by contemporary capitalism cannot acquire the militancy of older groups. Indeed, we have seen this process develop in embryo over recent years. Consider the now venerable arguments, dating back at least to the 1950s, regarding the emergence of large groups of "white-collar", middle-class professionals. C Wright Mills includes in his "white-collar mass" three groups: "schoolteachers, salespeople ... and assorted office workers" (Mills 1956, 64). Taking teachers as an example, we can see how militancy among this group has proliferated in recent decades, achieving a geographical spread "far greater than was the case historically for the textile or automobile industries" (Silver 2003, 115). Whatever special factors obfuscated teachers' shared interest with the wider working class or encouraged identification with other classes have substantially broken down. An early observer of this process in the UK, Stephen Ball, traces it back to the education reforms that began at the end of the 1960s leading to greater emphasis on regulation and control of the labour process:

> In this historical process the immediate work experience of the teacher is undergoing a significant shift from that approximating a classical, if limited, professionalism towards that of technical labourer... Increasingly teachers see it to be in their interests to oppose the measures introduced by management in specific instances and to be "in opposition" to management in general terms.
> BALL 1988, 292

Ball sees these factors as underlying the build-up to the industrial action by teachers in 1985–6. A more recent two-year study of teachers by Bob Carter and Howard Stevenson (2012) shows that the experience of educational reform under subsequent Labour governments saw further work intensification, a strengthening of managerial control and a decline of autonomy. The analogy between teaching factories and sausage factories, made by Marx, is not lost on many contemporary teachers.

None of this is to ignore the presence of divisions in the working class. The argument is simply that, in the long-run, capitalism tends to exert unifying pressures on the proletariat that can push groups who did not do so to identify themselves with the wider working class movement. It is this pressure that will ultimately lead to new explosions of working class struggle, likely centred on new working class forces forged by contemporary capitalism.

Employment Relations

Employment relations are formed in the context of class relations. Within Marxist theory, labour-power is identified as a commodity, but, as Marx notes, a "peculiar commodity" (Marx 1990, 274). Labour-power, unlike most commodities, is reproduced outside the capital-labour relation and is sold, not outright, but only for a period of time in exchange for a wage. In addition, unfortunately for the capitalist, the worker also accompanies their labour-power into the workplace, and must be subjected to managerial discipline if the capitalist is going to receive the full benefit of their market transaction.

Managerial relations in large firms typically involve delegation by the capitalist, to managers and supervisors "who command during the labour process in the name of capital" (Marx 1990, 450). As Guglielmo Carchedi points out, managers perform two functions. One is actually a function of collective labour, namely the work of "coordination and unity of the labour process" (Carchedi 1977, 63), something that would hypothetically be necessary even in a world free from antagonistic social relations. Managers also perform a second function, "the global function of capital", which involves "control and surveillance":

> Labour must be performed regularly, properly and continuously. The worker must not ill-use or damage the machines; must not waste raw materials; must not only reproduce his own labour power but must also produce surplus value, by working for a time longer than that contained in his wage, etc. Of particular importance is that since the quantity produced is a function of both the length of the working day and of the intensity of labour, it is necessary that the labourer works with the average degree of intensity.
>
> CARCHEDI 1977, 63

Managers and supervisors form bureaucratic hierarchies combining to different degrees these two functions. Near the base of this hierarchy, we could expect low-level supervisors to sometimes side with workers against capital; near the top we would expect a greater propensity to side with capital. In this analysis, the participants in the hierarchy are best seen as a series of layers pulled between the two main classes of capitalist society, rather than a coherent class with distinctive interests. These groupings, the economic basis of the "new middle class" are "only identifiable in terms of contradiction" (Carchedi 1977, 167).

Turning to the market side of the employment relationship, there is a dearth of literature from a classical Marxist perspective. Ben Fine, in one of the few serious theoretical treatments of the issue, offers a number of insights. The reproduction of labour-power outside the capital-labour relationship involves the creation of systems of provision and consumption that "vary not only with income but also with a range of other socioeconomic variables such as age, region, household composition, etc". The "shifting differentiation in consumption can lead to differentiation of wages as these are consolidated within the labour market" (Fine 1998, 181, 185). Alongside this "supply side" structuring of the labour market, there is a distinctive Marxist approach to the "demand side". Across an economy there will both be a distribution of labour between sectors, reflecting the social division of labour, and particular divisions of labour within workplaces. These two divisions of labour interact in complex ways that are not "reducible by a technological imperative alone to the nature of the tasks themselves". For instance, vertical integration and disintegration may coexist, as rival firms seek to "guarantee markets up or downstream" or seek to reduce their capital requirement and "exert competitive pressure on fragmented suppliers". Within firms themselves, there can be competing imperatives towards specialisation of labour or towards generalisation in which workers undertake a wider range of tasks. Mechanisation and automation may interact with these tendencies, further differentiating the workforce (Fine 1998, 177–179). In addition, the processes structuring labour markets cannot be reduced simply to "the narrow economic arena defined by production, distribution and exchange". The process of "social reproduction encompasses a wide range of factors ... such as sexism, racism, trade unionism, etc.," each interacting with economic reproduction in particular ways to generate labour market reproduction (Fine 1998, 108, 192–193). From all this, Fine draws a crucial conclusion:

> [L]abour markets are different from one another, not only in outcomes in the sense of rewards in the form of wages, conditions and careers, but also in the way in which they are structured and reproduced. There is no single labour market, although labour markets are intimately connected to one another, and no single generally applicable labour market theory. Whilst it is possible to identify appropriate abstract analytical principles, how they apply will differ across labour markets. This simple, even elementary insight appears to have been implicitly rejected by the vast majority of the literature.
> FINE 1998, 5

If Fine is correct, then we need a concrete examination of particular labour markets, rather than sweeping claims of an endless rise in precarity or straightforward generalisation from the most marginal workers. This leads to a second, related, sense in which many radical left conceptions of the labour market might be misleading. As Kevin Doogan puts it, "the labour market is not only an imperfect conduit through which new employment relations might be transmitted, it also acts as an insulator against the pressures for institutional changes imputed to technological development and capital mobility"

(Doogan 2009, 113). The labour performed by labour-power is always of a dual nature, creating new use-values as "concrete labour" as well as creating value as "abstract labour" (Marx 1990, 131–137). The concrete, determinant qualities of labour are specific to particular labour processes and have to be reproduced accordingly. As Doogan writes: "While one set of market pressures is generated by the immediate requirements of production ... there is another set of reproductive imperatives that impact upon the labour market." Changes to labour markets will reflect both pressures. Furthermore, "in contrast to the irrationality engendered by neoliberal compliance with market forces, the reproductive requirements of capitalism confer a greater sense of rationality and order, demand long-term planning for current and future needs" (Doogan 2009, 98, 112). Capitalists and state managers are not indifferent to the problems of establishing a reliable, suitably skilled supply of labour and the retention of the correct forms of labour-power.

For all the claims of Standing and others, the proportion of the labour force in the UK with temporary contracts has been stable at about 6 percent for three decades. A great deal has been written in the UK on the rise of 'zero-hours contracts', which offer no guaranteed hours of employment. According to the Labour Force Survey (LFS), about 801,000 people—one in 40 of the workforce—have such a contract for their main job in the UK. A more detailed look at the LFS data shows that these contracts are overwhelmingly concentrated in just five areas: 'hotels', 'restaurants', 'beverage serving', 'residential care for the elderly and disabled' and 'social work without accommodation for the elderly and disabled'. The first three of these areas are disproportionately undertaken by students, who make up, for instance, about half of those serving beverages, and these have long been highly casualised forms of work. Their widespread use in areas of social care is in this sense more striking. However, use of zero-hours contracts does not seem to have generalised more widely across the labour force. There is no reason to assume that they will, nor is the growth of zero-hours contracts unstoppable. In April 2016, McDonald's announced it was offering all of its UK staff the option of moving off these contracts; in July 2016, when KFC were found by a journalist to be using zero-hours contracts they swiftly acted to rectify what they saw as an "administrative error" (Ruddick 2016; Farrow 2016). Again, a concrete analysis of particular areas of the economy where such contracts are used and a strategy to force employers to concede contracts guaranteeing hours are more useful than sweeping generalisation.

There is little evidence of the employment relation in general becoming more transitory in countries such as the UK. Data from the General Household Survey shows that, on average, employees in Great Britain could by 2007 expect their job to last 16 years, roughly the same as in 1975. Doogan has shown that the phenomenon of increasing employment stability under neoliberalism holds for many advanced capitalist countries (Doogan 2009).

There are instances where capital can benefit from rendering labour more precarious, as has sometimes happened in low-skilled areas of retail or food serving where staff turnover is relatively high, as well as in some areas of social care and in tertiary education in the UK, where non-permanent employment runs at levels three times higher than in the labour force as a whole. However, there are powerful countertendencies that mean that, in many cases, labour remains relatively secure in its employment, but faces other attacks—on conditions of employment, pay, autonomy in the workplace or control of the labour process, for instance. Often workers risk not so much being shunted out of good jobs as being stuck in increasingly lousy ones.

Conclusion

Marxism offers a distinctive approach to class, envisaging it as bound up with the relations of production, which give rise to particular capacities and interests. It is these, rather than the existence of particular types of workers—the textile workers of the 1840s, the engineers of the Great Unrest or the car workers of 1968—that create the potential for a collective challenge to capitalism.

The particular level of combativity at any given moment does not indicate either the scale of the working class or its potential power. Class forces must mature, and, in particular, they do so through struggle. Fortunately, in the long run, they tend to be impelled towards struggle by the workings of capitalism itself. It is in this sense that Marx argues in *The Holy Family*: "The question is not what this or that proletarian, or even the whole of the proletariat at the moment *considers* as its aim. The question is *what the proletariat is*, and what, consequent on that *being*, it will be compelled to do" (Marx 1956, 53).

The classical Marxist tradition does not stop at identifying the particular capacities and interests of workers. It also provides a basis on which labour markets can be theorised. This theorisation, critically, sees the relationship between capital and labour as one of two-way dependence, in which workers have potential power over their employers, challenging a vision of ever-growing marginalisation that have become pervasive on the left.

This rich and subtle tradition deserves to be applied to the complexities of contemporary capitalism. Sadly, the rejection of what generally amounts to a crude caricature of Marx's own theory risks erasing the hard-won insights of classical Marxism from radical left class analysis.

References

Althusser, L. and Balibar, É. (1971) *Reading Capital.* New York: Pantheon.
Ball, S.J. (1988) Staff Relations during the Teachers' Industrial Action: Context, Conflict and Proletarianisation. *British Journal of Sociology of Education* 9 (3): 289–306.
Carchedi, G. (1977) *On the Economic Identification of Social Classes.* London: Routledge.
Carchedi, G. (2012) *Behind the Crisis: Marx's Dialectics of Value and Knowledge.* Chicago: Haymarket Books.
Carter, B. and Stevenson, H. (2012) Teachers, workforce remodelling and the challenge to labour process analysis. *Work, Employment & Society*, 26 (3): 481–496.
Castells, M. (2000a) *The Rise of the Network Society.* Oxford: Blackwell Publishing.
Castells, M. (2000b) Materials for an exploratory theory of the network society. *The British Journal of Sociology* 51 (1): 5–24.
Doogan, K. (2009) *New Capitalism? The Transformation of Work.* Cambridge: Polity.
Draper, H. (1978) *Karl Marx's Theory of Revolution, Volume II: The Politics of Social Classes.* New York: Monthly Review Press.
Dunn, B. (2011) The New Economy and Labour's Decline: Questioning Their Association. In: Serrano, M., Xhafa, E. and Fichter, M. (eds) *Trade Unions and the Global Crisis.* Geneva: ILO.
Farrow, A. (2016) "KFC's Finger Lickin' Zero Hours Lies Exposed", Socialist Worker 26 July, 2016. Available at: https://socialistworker.co.uk/art/43121/KFCs+finger+lickin+zero+hours+lies+exposed.
Fine, B. (1998) *Labour Market Theory: A Constructive Reassessment.* London: Routledge.
Gorz, A. (1982) *Farewell to the Working Class: An Essay on Post-Industrial Socialism.* London: Pluto Press.
Gramsci, A. (1998) *Selections from the Prison Notebooks.* London: Lawrence and Wishart.
Hardt, M. and Negri, A. (2001) *Empire.* Cambridge, Massachusetts: Harvard University Press.
Harvey, D. (2006) *The Limits to Capital.* London: Verso.
HM Treasury (2011) Estimating the impact on GDP of a strike in the public sector. Available at: https://www.whatdotheyknow.com/request/breakdown_of_500_million_estimat.
Hobsbawm, E. (1978) The Forward March of Labour Halted? *Marxism Today*, September: 279–86.
ILO (2013) Key Indicators of the Labour Market (eight edition).
Laclau, E. and Mouffe, C. (2014) *Hegemony and Socialist Strategy: Towards a Radical Democratic Politics.* London: Verso.
Lebowitz, M. (2003) *Beyond Capital: Marx's Political Economy and the Working Class.* Houndmills: Palgrave Macmillan.

Marx, K. (1976) Moralising Criticism and Critical Morality. In: *Karl Marx and Frederick Engels, Collected Works, volume 6*. New York: International Publishers.

Marx, K. (1977) The Communist Manifesto. In: McLellan D. (ed) *Karl Marx: Selected Writings* Oxford: Oxford University Press.

Marx, K. (1981) *A Contribution to the Critique of Political Economy*. London: Lawrence and Wishart.

Marx, K. (1990) *Capital, volume one*. London: Penguin.

Marx, K. (1991) *Capital, volume three*. London: Penguin.

Marx, K. (1993) *Grundrisse*. London: Penguin.

Marx, K. and Engels, F. (1956) *The Holy Family or Critique of Critical Critique*. Moscow: Foreign Languages Publishing House.

Marx, K. and Engels, F. (1974) *The German Ideology*. London: Lawrence and Wishart.

Mason, P. (2015) *PostCapitalism: A Guide to our Future*. London: Allen Lane.

Mills, C.W. (1956) *White Collar: The American Middle Classes*. New York: Oxford University Press.

ONS (2013) Graduates in the UK Labour Market 2013. Available (consulted 11 July, 2016) at: http://www.ons.gov.uk/employmentandlabourmarket/peopleinwork/employmentandemployeetypes/articles/graduatesintheuklabourmarket/2013-11-19.

Perlman, F. (1990) Introduction: Commodity Fetishism. In: Rubin, I.I. *Essays on Marx's Theory of Value*. Montreal: Black Rose.

Ruddick, G. (2016) McDonald's Offer Staff the Chance to Get Off Zero-hours Contracts. *Guardian*. 15 April, 2016. Available at: https://www.theguardian.com/business/2016/apr/15/mcdonalds-offer-staff-the-chance-to-get-off-zero-hours-contracts.

Silver, B.J. (2003) *Forces of Labour: Workers' Movements and Globalization since 1870*. New York: Cambridge University Press.

Standing, G. (2011) *The Precariat: The New Dangerous Class*. London: Bloomsbury Academic.

UN-Habitat (2006) *State of the World's Cities 2006/7*. Nairobi: United Nations Human Settlements Programme.

Wood, E.M. (1998) *The Retreat from Class: A New 'True' Socialism*. London: Verso.

Wright, S. (2002) *Storming Heaven: Class Composition and Struggle in Italian Autonomist Marxism*. London: Pluto Press.

Žižek, S. (2012) The Revolt of the Salaried Bourgeoisie. *London Review of Books* 34 (2): 9–10.

CHAPTER 3

Social Class and Education

Dave Hill

> The history of all hitherto existing society is the history of class struggles ... Our epoch ... has simplified the class antagonisms .... into two great hostile camps. into two great classes directly facing each other: Bourgeoisie and Proletariat.
> MARX and ENGELS (1848)

⁂

Introduction

In this chapter I discuss the relationship between social class, society and education. The perspective adopted is Marxist. Firstly I discuss social class and how it is measured. Then I present some of the main concepts of Marxist social class analysis. I will then show how these concepts relate to education, referring to the work of Bourdieu, Althusser, Bowles and Gintis, and, in the UK, work by Bernstein and by Duffield and her co-writers. Finally I differentiate between two types of Marxist analysis—Structuralist neo-Marxism and Culturalist neo-Marxism.

What is Social Class and How is it Measured?

What social class are you? What social class were the people you went to school with, or work or study with? One classification, social class, is generally recognised as having particular significance. Social class is generally recognised as both reflecting and causing major social, economic, and cultural differences in, for example, income, wealth, status, education, and lifestyle. Income (pay packet, salary, and dividends) and wealth (what we own, such as housing, shares, money in the bank, and possessions) reflect our social class position. However, not only does social class *reflect* such social differences, it also *causes* them. Our social background, social class, social class-related ways in which we present ourselves tend to affect the ways in which we are treated by teachers, by the police, by friends, by employers, by sexual partners, and by many others in society. As with racism and sexism, this can take the form of *personal discrimination*—positive or negative stereotyping, labelling and expectation. It can also take the form of *structural discrimination*—taking place on a systematic, repetitive, embedded nature within particular social structures such as schooling, housing, employment, credit agencies, police, armed forces.

In the education system there are different social class-related;

- patterns of educational attainment (such as reading age, SATs scores, number of GCSE passes, entry into higher education)
- patterns of teaching methods (or pedagogy) used by teachers for different social classes
- 'hidden curricula'
- formal (subject) curricula (to an extent, despite the existence of a National Curriculum in schools)
- job destinations

Of course, not all sons and daughters of the upper class go into higher education and subsequently take up jobs with high social status, a high degree of power over others, and a high income. And not all the children of semi-skilled or unskilled workers leave school or further education at the age of 16 or 18, and work in low-status and low-paid jobs. But most do.

The official, governmental, classifications shown in Table 3.1, have been used for the census since 2001 (Office for National Statistics, 2016).

These types of classification are clearly useful. Positions within this wealth/income/status hierarchy clearly do have important correlation, with for example, health, diet, conditions at work, years of healthy life, age of death, and educational attainment. However, I will critique such classifications later in the essay.

Reports by organisations such as The Joseph Rowntree Foundation (2016; Social Market Foundation, 2015) testify to the depths of poverty, low pay and reduction in welfare benefits in the UK. In the words of an *Independent* headline 'Britain's divided decade: the rich are 64% richer than before the recession, while the poor are 57% poorer'. (see Hill et al., 2016)

To take only one correlation, these widening gaps in income and wealth in Britain (and, in other countries such as the USA), since the 'Bankers' crisis of 2008 and the subsequent years of 'Immiseration Capitalism' (Hill, 2012a,

TABLE 3.1 *The office for national statistics classification of occupations.*

Class	Title
1	Professionals; Employers, Administrators and Managers employing 25 or more people (e.g. doctor, lawyer, scientist, company director)
2	Associate Professionals; Employers, Administrators and Managers employing fewer than 25 people (e.g. supervisor, nurse, sales manager, laboratory technician)
3	Intermediate Occupations in Administrative, Clerical, Sales and Service Work (e.g. secretary, nursery nurse, salesman [sic], computer operator)
4	Self-Employed Non-Professionals (e.g. plumber, driving instructor)
5	Other Supervisors, Craft and Related Workers (e.g. factory foreman [sic], joiner)
6	Routine Occupations in Manufacturing and Services (e.g. Lorry driver, traffic warden, assembly line worker).
7	Elementary Occupations (e.g. fast-food waiter [sic], supermarket cashier, cleaner, labourer)
8	Never Worked, Unemployed, Long-term Sick

SOURCE: OFFICE FOR NATIONAL STATISTICS 2016.

2013) characterised and caused by the decline in services, welfare and labour benefits, result in the poor dying even earlier on average than the rich. Under 'Austerity Capitalism' "the gap between the life-spans of rich and poor people in England and Wales is increasing for the first time in almost 150 years" (Pells 2016). And there are huge social class differences in years of healthy life. In London:

> Women living in Richmond can look forward to 72 years of "healthy life"-compared with just 54 for women in Tower Hamlets. That equates to people in the East End's most deprived borough losing almost a year for every stop on the District line that links them to Richmond. The difference is only slightly less for men—with 70 healthy years for those in Richmond, compared with 55 in Tower Hamlets'.
>
> LYDALL and PRYNN, 2013

Marxist Analysis of Social Class

It was Karl Marx (1818—1883) more than anyone else who developed a comprehensive theory about the relationship between social class and social structures, in particular the relationship between social classes in capitalist society. In a capitalist economy the means of production (raw materials, machinery and so on) and the means of distribution (such as transport) and exchange (such as finance companies and banks) are concentrated into a few hands- actually, into fewer and fewer hands. The vast majority are forced to sell their labour power in order to survive. Workers are paid only a proportion of the value they create in productive labour. The capitalist mode of production is a system of exploitation of one class (the working class) by another (the capitalist class). It is the Labour -Capital Relation, *the economic relations of production.*

For Marx this class exploitation and domination are reflected in *the social relations of production.* These are how people relate to each other—for example relationships between 'bosses' and senior management, supervisors/foremen/women/middle management and, for example, shop floor workers in factories, finance companies, telesales centres, offices and schools.

A condensed definition of social class is that,

> Classes are large groups of people differing from each other by the place they occupy in a historically determined system of social production, by their relation (in most cases fixed and formulated by law) to the means of production, by their role in the social organisation of labour, by the dimensions of the share of the social wealth of which they dispose and their mode of acquiring it.
> LENIN 1965, 421

Marx believed that the proletariat and bourgeoisie (workers and capitalists respectively) are in *objective conflict* with each other: the former are materially exploited by the latter whether they *subjectively* know it or not, or whether they like it or not.

Furthermore, the state acts, to a major degree, in the interests of the ruling class. In Marx and Engels's words in *The Communist Manifesto*, "(T)he executive of the modern state is essentially a committee for managing the common affairs of the whole bourgeoisie" (Marx and Engels 1848). Currently, that is, in the interests of the ruling capitalist class. To refer to Althusser's concepts (1971), ideological state apparatuses (ISAS) (such as the education system and the mass media) and the repressive state apparatuses (RSAS) (such as the police, the law, the army) seek to ensure the continuation and enforcement of the current (capitalist) system.

Marxists believe that the point is not simply to describe the world but to change it, in Marx's words, "The philosophers have only interpreted the world, in various ways; the point is to change it" [1845]. Class-consciousness does not follow automatically or inevitably from the objective fact of economic class position. Marx's *The Poverty of Philosophy* [1847] distinguishes between a 'class-in-itself' (an objective determination relating to class position) and a 'class-for-itself' (a subjective appreciation of class consciousness). *The Communist Manifesto* [1848] explicitly identifies "the formation of the proletariat into a class" as the key political task facing the communists. In *The Eighteenth Brumaire of Louis Napoleon* [1852] Marx observes,

> In so far as millions of families live under economic conditions of existence that divide their mode of life, their interests and their cultural formation from those of the other classes and bring them into conflict with those classes, they form a class.
> MARX [1852] 1974: 239

The process (and conceptual category) which links economic and social class is that of *class consciousness*. The class conflict arising from class consciousness and class struggle is fundamental to understanding economic, political and educational change. It is also fundamental in understanding why some social classes of children and students do, on average, so very much better than others.

It is in periods of extreme class differentiation, periods of the intensification of the extraction of surplus value—profit—from the labour power of workers, that more and more workers perceive, subjectively, the objective nature of their exploitation. There is now, unlike pre-the 'Bankers Crisis' of 2008, a wide understanding and appreciation of the 99% being ruled and fooled and exploited by the 1%.

In the introductory quotation to this chapter Marx refers to two mutually antagonistic classes in capitalist society, the proletariat (working class) and the bourgeoisie (the capitalist class). However, social class, for Marx, is not simply monolithic, nor is it static. Under capitalist economic laws of motion the working class, and indeed, the capitalist class, is constantly decomposed and reconstituted due to changes in the forces of production, technological changes in the type of work. New occupations, such as telesales and computing have come into existence, others, such as coal mining, manufacturing and other manual working class occupations, decline. Within the capitalist class there has been a change from the mill owner, the factory owner, to Chief Executives of national and global corporations- together with their owners and (other) major shareholders.

There are manifestly different layers, or strata among the working classes. Skilled workers, (if in work, and particularly in full-time, long-term work), in general have a higher standard of living than semi-skilled or unskilled workers, those in 'the precariat'- (Standing, 2014) for example on zero-hours contracts, or unemployed workers. Whatever their stratum, or 'layer' in the working class, however, Marxists assert that there is a common identity of interest between these strata.

Marx never completed his writing on social class (Rikowski, 2002), and did at various times refer to other classes. Marx and Engels, in various writings (e.g. Marx and Engels, 1848; Marx, 1852), referred to a fourth class, the 'lumpenproletariat', people who live in poverty, an underclass, a rabble proletariat. However, in Marxist sociology there are two types of middle class described: firstly, the old middle class or petit bourgeoisie, such as shopkeepers, and, secondly, as from the mid-twentieth century, the new middle class, of professional workers, often state workers such as health and education professionals.

Marx wrote of the 'petit bourgeoisie' (e.g. Marx and Engels, 1848), and various subsequent Marxists from Pannekoek have analysed this 'middle class' (e.g. Pannekoek, 1909), a class standing between capital and labour, the old middle class, or petit bourgeoisie. And, since the 1960s, Marxist sociologists, pre-eminently Erik Olin Wright (e.g. 1989, 2002) have identified, analysed and categorised the 'new middle class', the growth of a professional and managerial stratum, such as supervisors, personal managers, teachers, lecturers in further and higher education, local government workers and so forth. These are 'between capital and labour' in the sense that while being entirely dependent on capital, whether in the shape of the national or local state, or in the shape of private companies/ corporations, they exercise *supervisory functions* over the working class. Teachers or supervisors or office managers are not capitalists—they do not themselves take profit from the surplus value extracted from working class labour. Nor are they working class in this specific, particular sense- in the sense that they do not have surplus value directly extracted from their own labour. For many sociologists and analysts they are 'a new middle class', occupying a contradictory class location (e.g. Wright, 1989).

However, many such supervisory, health and education professional workers have a consciousness of status in which they place themselves above other, especially manual, sectors of the working class. On the other hand, their conditions of work and pay have resulted in a degree of proletarianisation—loss of autonomy, loss of status, loss of pay and also loss of jobs and job security. Many of 'the new middle class' identify with the aims and values of the working class.

For many Marxists, adopting a binary notion of class (e.g. Kelsh and Hill, 2006) the 'new middle class' workers are defined as part of working class. The 'two class' or 'binary' or 'classical Marxist' model of class in capitalist society, is that there are basically two classes in society—those who sell their labour, the working class on the one hand, and the capitalist class- those who buy workers' labour and labour power, on the other.

Criticisms of Marxist Social Class Analysis

There are a number of objections to Marxist social class analysis put forward by rival sociological theories such as Weberian analysis, Functionalism and Postmodernism.

1   *Social Class and Individualism*
First, some say 'we are all individuals, why can't we treat people simply as individuals?' A Marxist objection to this criticism is that this ignores or denies the well substantiated patterns of treatment and ways in which we relate to others in the employment and educational processes. It ignores the social relationships we have with our employers/employees, our teachers, what Marx called *'the social relations of production'*, the power relations of patterns of control or deference between bosses, managers and workers. It also ignores the different relationships we have to 'the means of production', what Marx called *'the economic relationships of production'*. Do we own the bakery or the factory, or the school, or the bank,—either as outright owner, senior manager such as CEO (Chief executive Officer, with shares), or major shareholder—or are we employed by the owner(s)?

2   *Social Class and Post-Fordism/Post-Modernism*
Secondly, there is rejection of class as an anachronistic, outdated category which is no longer relevant in the context of a society which has become 'classless'—as, for example, claimed by the former Conservative British Prime Minister, John Major. A similar claim was made in 2013: "David Cameron rejected criticisms that the country was run by a private school-educated elite by arguing 'what counts is not where you come from, it is where you are going'" (Butler 2016). Since the consumer boom of the 1950s, they claim, and since social mobility—moving from one class to another—has been made easier by the expansion of higher education since 1960s, people are less imprisoned (or liberated) by their class—'anybody can become anything they want'.

These theorists argue that the disappearance of class has resulted from cultural changes occurring as a result of economic changes such as the transition from an assembly line mass production/ limited consumer choice ('Fordist') to a specialist production ('post-Fordist') economy. Their claim is that *relations of production* have been superseded in political, educational and social importance by *relations of consumption*; that we live in a postmodern and post Fordist society and economy—there is no mass production assembly line culture, no longer mass production and no mass consumption any more. Instead there are myriad ways of working, types of work, types of product, types of consumption, brand names, niches in the market. The social and cultural order organised around class has been replaced, they allege, by a 'new order' based on individual rights, social mobility, job mobility, geographical mobility, consumer choice, lifestyle choice, choice over sexual identity and type of sexuality. However, whether individuals work in computer- and consumer-driven niche production, their relationship to the means of production is essentially the same.

3 *Social Class and Identity*

Postmodernists suggest that class identity and affiliation are outdated concepts, that people no longer identify themselves by their social class, or if they do, it is one, not a hugely important, self-identifier. Postmodernist accounts of identity, of a fragmented, de-centred subjectivity became fashionable and dominant in the 1990s. They object to the Marxist project of class struggle on the grounds that it denies or suppresses the facts of 'social difference'. For some decades now, academic neo-Marxism, and Radical Left political activity have significantly departed from this exclusivity, and recognised and embraced the importance of non-social class movements, both in academic writing and on the streets, in demonstrations.

4 *Nomenclature*

In Britain, *official* classifications of social class are based, not only on income, but Weberian notions of status and associated consumption patterns and lifestyles. Thus for Weberian sociologists, some classes are 'higher' and some lower' than others. There is a 'gradation' from top to bottom, with those at the top having 'more' or something (income, wealthy, education, power) than the group or class immediately below them, and so on and so on until the group or class at the bottom of this gradational hierarchy has the least, of income, wealth, education, power, or whatever combination.

Issues of nomenclature—what we call people—are crucial in understanding the nature of social class. For example, the use of the terms 'upper class' and 'lower class' can set out not simply a description of a group's/ class' place on a ladder of possession, but also a justification for the existence of differentiated social classes, and indeed, a moral hierarchy. Such a 'gradational' classification says very little about the relationship between these classes. For Marxists, class is a relational concept (Wright 1978).

5   *Hiding Class*
Such classifications ignore, indeed hide, the existence of the capitalist class—that class which dominates society economically and politically. This class owns the means of production (and the means of distribution and exchange). These consumption- based patterns mask the existence of the super-rich and the super-powerful—the ruling class, the 1%, or the 0.1%. In the Registrar-General's classification, the mega-rich capitalists such as Richard Branson, Sir Philip Green, Mike Ashley and property owners such as the Duke of Westminster are placed in the same class as, for example, university lecturers, journalists and solicitors.

A related criticism of consumption based classifications is that, by segmenting the working class, they both (a) hide the existence of the working class and (b) serve a purpose of 'dividing and ruling' the working class. Such classifications hide and work to inhibit or disguise the common interests of these different groups. They serve to inhibit the development of a common (class) consciousness against the exploiting capitalist class. In a similar way, Marxists note that the promotion of ethnic or 'racial' divisions between black and white workers, between women and men and between heterosexuals and homosexuals, between public sector workers and private sector workers, between the employed and those on benefits, also serves to weaken the solidarity and 'muscle' of the working class.

Marxists recognise that sex or 'race' exploitation is very widespread. However, in contrast to the exploitation of women and particular minority ethnic groups, Marxists go on to note the fundamental nature of class exploitation in capitalist economy. Social class exploitation is seen as basic and necessary to the continuation of capitalism. Capitalism can (and may) survive with sex and 'race' equality—indeed, for neo-liberals these are desirable attributes of an economy and education/training system—but to conceive of equality between different social classes in a capitalist economy and society is impossible. Capitalism is defined as the exploitation of one class by another.

This is not to trivialise the issue of identity and of identity politics, either in the micro-sphere of day-to-day personal existence, delight and dismissal, or in the macro- sphere of structural forms of positive and negative discrimination. Social class is clearly only one of a range of possible identifications and one which is sometimes less immediately 'obvious' than, for example, those of gender or 'race' or religion or fashion. However, for millions, the duality 'worker/boss' is not at all abstract. The 2015 British Attitudes Social Survey found that 60% of Britons regard themselves as working class (Butler, 2016). In Hill, 2009, I discuss the interrelationships between 'race' and class, noting that rich women and bourgeois blacks have, in important respects, an easier life than working class populations, whatever their ethnicity, sex, sexuality.

A range of sociologists, politicians and political theorists and postmodernist social theorists have challenged socialist and Marxist analysis and socialist solidaristic, egalitarian educational and political programmes. Many seek to bury Marxism and socialism and egalitarianism, claiming that 'the class struggle is over', that society which is not characterised any more by such old-fashioned struggles as those of workers against bosses, or of the working class against the ruling capitalist class.

Such arguments gloss over and hide the fundamentally antagonistic *relationship* between the two main classes in society, the working class and the capitalist class. In Marxist analysis, as noted above, the working class includes not only manual workers but also millions of white-collar workers—such as bank clerks and supermarket checkout operators, as well, whose conditions of work are, in many ways, similar to those of manual workers. While it may be of sociological interest to be informed of, for example, the different leisure pursuits of different occupational groups, research based on occupational hierarchies tells us little, if anything about the relationship between social classes, which, Marxists argue, is based fundamentally on conflict. This conflict is not just 'class war from below', workers on strike, for example. Class war takes place from above as well as below, with the ruling capitalist class holding and using the levers of power, using the ideological and repressive apparatuses of the state to weaken organisations of actual or potential working class power such as trade unions, as during the Miners' Strike in Britain of 1984–5.

Marxist Theory and Education

With respect to schooling and education, what are the detailed explanations for working class under-achievement in schools and in education that follow from the above analyses? Who is to blame? What, therefore, should be the locus and the focus of policy?

- Should the blame be attached to the individual child, as lazy or individually unintelligent?

SOCIAL CLASS AND EDUCATION 41

- Should the blame be spread more widely, attached to the working class itself—(its 'defective culture' and child-rearing patterns, its supposed attitude to life such as the demand for 'immediate gratification', or its 'defective genetic pool')?
- Should the blame be attached to individual schools and individual 'ineffective' teachers? Will the problem of differential social class achievement be sorted out by naming and shaming and improving ineffective schools and going along with the 'Effective Schools' Movement, improving school management and performance, appointing 'superheads'?
- Or is the problem a larger one, that of (capitalist) society itself—that schools' formal curriculum and the hidden curriculum are deliberately geared to failing most working class children, and to elevating, middle- and upper-class children above them? In other words, is the problem with the way society is organised, organised around the exploitation of the working classes by the ruling capitalist class with the assistance—willing or unwilling—of teachers?

Marxists would accept the final one of the above explanations. Reproduction theorists (Structuralist neo-Marxists, looking at the power of the capitalist economic structure to heavily affect education and social structures) and analysts agree that this is, largely, what schools do. However, unlike Functionalists, rather than welcoming this ideological hegemonising, this use of schools by the ruling capitalist class to reproduce society culturally, economically and ideologically, Marxists critique it and regard it as immoral and in need of radical change.

Below, I give examples of Structuralist neo-Marxist theorists, or theorists working broadly within this tradition such as Bourdieu, and seek to explain a number of their key concepts.

- Bourdieu (1976, 1990; Bourdieu and Passeron, 1997) and his theory of Schooling as Cultural Reproduction, and his concepts of Habitus, Cultural Capital and Symbolic Violence, whereby schools recognise and reward middle-class / upper class knowledge, language, body language, and diminish and demean working class and some minority ethnic cultures.
- Bernstein (1977) and his theory of class specific Language Codes, whereby schools privilege and reward middle-class so-called 'Elaborated Language' and devalue and demean working class so-called 'Restricted Language', and his theory that there are significant social class differences in curriculum and pedagogy (Bernstein, 1977) validated by Duffield et al. (Brown et al., 1997; Duffield 1998a, b).

- Bowles and Gintis' (1976) theory of Schooling as Economic Reproduction, whereby 'The Correspondence Principle' explains the way in which the hidden curriculum of schools reproduces the social (and economic) class structure of society within the school, training school students for different economic and social futures on the basis of their social and economic pasts—their parental background.
- Althusser (1971) and his theory of Schooling as Ideological Reproduction, whereby schooling as an Ideological State Apparatus (ISA) works to persuade children that the status quo is fair and legitimate, and if that doesn't work- then schools also function as a Repressive State Apparatus (RSA), disciplining and punishing what they regard as unacceptable 'deviance' or non-conformity/ rebellion.

The concepts of culture and cultural capital are central to Bourdieu's analysis of how the mechanisms of cultural reproduction functions within schools. For Bourdieu the education system is not at all meritocratic. Its major function is to maintain and legitimate a class-divided society. In his analysis, schools are middle-class institutions run by and for the middle class. Cultural reproduction, for Bourdieu, works in three ways.

Firstly, it works through the formal curriculum and its assessment. The curriculum and examinations serve to confirm the advantages of the middle-class while having the appearance of being a free and fair competition. They clearly privilege and validate particular types of 'cultural capital', the type of elite knowledge that comes naturally to middle- and, in particular, upper-class children, but which is not 'natural' or familiar to non-elite children and school students. Therefore, at the same time, and as a consequence, it disconfirms, rejects, invalidates the cultures of other groups, both social class groups and ethnic minority and immigrant groups.

Secondly, cultural reproduction works through the hidden curriculum. This second type of cultural capital is 'knowing how', how to speak to teachers, not only knowing about books, but also knowing how to talk about them. It is knowing how to talk with the teacher, with what body language, accent, colloquialisms, register of voice, grammatical exactitude in terms of the 'elaborated code' of language and its associated habitus, body posture, or way of behaving.

> In a number of social universes, one of the privileges of the dominant, who move in their world as a fish in water, resides in the fact that they need not engage in rational computation in order to reach the goals that best suit their interests. All they have to do is follow their dispositions

which, being adjusted to their positions, 'naturally' generate practices adjusted to the situation.

BOURDIEU 1990, 108–109

For Bourdieu, and for Stephen Ball (2003) and sociologists in general, children and teenagers bring their social class backgrounds into school with them (as well as, of course, other aspects of their subjectivities). And, as Ball (2003) points out, "[W]ithin the educational system almost all the authority remains vested in the middle classes. Not only do they run the system, the system itself is one which valorises middle rather than working class cultural capital." Some ways of being and behaving, language, clothing, body language, and attitudes and values are not viewed quite as tolerantly or supportively by teachers as are others. Some pupils/students tend to be regarded as suitable subjects for exclusion, if not from school itself then from academic success. Teenagers attending schools in 'challenging'—that is, poor—areas tend to be labelled and stereotypes, and to be guided into different work futures than those attending the suburban schools in wealthy areas or the most prestigious of private schools, Benenden or Eton. Some are trained/educated to rule, others to supervise, others to serve.

Thirdly, cultural reproduction works, in Britain, through the separate system of schooling for the upper and upper middle classes, nearly all of whom send their children to private (independent) schools. The Joseph Rowntree Foundation (e.g. 2016) regularly show how Britain is a deeply divided society, indeed, an increasingly class-divided country, characterised by class distinctions. In particular, the system of secondary education exemplifies and reproduces class differentiation, which is rigidly separated into a flourishing, lavishly-funded private sector, as compared to demoralised, underfinanced public sector, itself divided into schools in wealthy areas and those in inner urban / inner-city areas.

As part of social class-based differentiation between schools via 'the hidden curriculum', there is ample evidence that the pedagogies—the teaching and learning methods used by teachers and pupils—vary according to the pupils' social class. Sally Brown, Sheila Riddell and Jill Duffield's research involved following two classes in each of four Scottish schools through their first two years of secondary education, observing 204 lessons. Their findings were that children in the two working class schools spent between 3 and 6 per cent of their time in English class discussion compared with 17 to 25 per cent in the middle-class schools. They observed that pupils in predominantly working-class secondary schools appear to be given many more time-consuming reading and writing tasks than children in middle-class schools and have less opportunity for classroom discussions (Brown et al., 1997; Duffield 1998a, b).

In many ways this can be seen to replicate the findings of Bernstein's work on what are 'acceptable' and what are 'unacceptable' language codes within the school and educational settings. Bernstein's central concern was with the social class based reproductive nature of the curriculum, and the hidden curriculum, of schools, the different pedagogies used for working class and middle class pupils/ students (Bernstein 1977).

Schools play a major role in reproducing educational, social, cultural and economic inequality. For Bowles and Gintis (1976), it is the 'hidden curriculum' rather than the actual 'formal' or subject curriculum, of the school/further/higher education system which is crucially important in providing capitalism with a workforce which has the personality, attitudes and values which are most useful. The educational system helps integrate youth into the economic system through a structural correspondence between its social relations and those of production. The structure of social relations in education develops the types of personal demeanour, modes of self-presentation, self-image, and social-class identifications which are the crucial ingredients of job adequacy. Specifically, the social relationships of education—the relationships between administrators and teachers, teachers and students, students and students, and students and their work—replicate the hierarchical division of labour (Bowles and Gintis 1976). They suggest that different levels of education feed workers into different levels within the occupational structure. Furthermore, at each level of the certification process, they showed that, regardless of similar qualifications, job destination was class-related.

Althusser's analysis of schooling was concerned with a specific aspect of cultural reproduction, namely, ideological reproduction. He suggested that schools are concerned with the reproduction, the recycling of what is regarded as 'common sense'—in particular, with an acceptance of current capitalist, individualistic, inegalitarian, consumerist society and economy. This 'common sense', as for example propagated by the MSM (Mainstream Media) is to be contrasted with what Gramsci called 'good sense'- of seeing through the capitalist and Mainstream media propaganda.

How does the school function as an ISA? Althusser suggests that what children learn at school is 'know-how':

> children at school also learn the 'rules' of good behaviour, rules of respect for the socio—technical division of labour and ultimately the rules of the order established by class domination. The school takes children from

every class at infant-school age, and then for years in which the child is most 'vulnerable', squeezed between the family state apparatus and the educational state apparatus, it drums into them, whether it uses new or old methods, a certain amount of 'know-how' wrapped in ideology in its pure state.

ALTHUSSER 1971, 104–105

Two Types of Marxist Analysis

Culturalist or Humanist neo-Marxist theorists since the 1980s and 1990s see rather more space for resistance to the dominant politics and culture, and to many of the messages within the National Curriculum (and pedagogy) than did theorists within the more deterministic Structuralist neo-Marxism of the 1970s such as Althusser, Bourdieu, and Bowles and Gintis. They criticise the Structuralist neo-Marxist for focusing on the way in which the capitalist economic structures 'determine' state policy, with the capitalist state 'inevitably' reproducing the capitalist system within and through education.

Culturalist neo-Marxist writers suggest that teachers and schools can make a difference, that they can work to, and have some degree of success in promoting, an ideology, understanding of, and commitment to, for example, antiracism and anti-sexism. They emphasise the degree of 'relative autonomy' that teachers in classrooms, and individual schools, and Departments of Education, and governments can have in relation to the demands of Capital, what capitalists, the large corporations, would like them to do. As such they refute what they see as the pessimism and determinism and fatalism of the Structuralist neo-Marxists, and stress the power of human agency, the power of people to intervene and to change history.

Having recognised validity in the above Culturalist (Gramscian) analysis, or 'Resistance Theory', I do consider that the particular concepts of Althusser, Bourdieu, and Bowles and Gintis are valid and illuminating. In particular this seems to be the case with respect to the National Curriculum and to the restructuring of other education state apparatuses, such as Initial Teacher Education and to the restructuring of education in general.

Deborah Kelsh and I (Kelsh and Hill, 2006) present a detailed critique of Culturalist Marxism, for example that of Michael W. Apple, and his neo-Weberian analysis of class. We criticise Apple, and others, "who have participated in the conversion of the Marxist concept of class to a descriptive term by culturalizing it -pluralizing it and cutting its connection to the social relations of exploitation that are central to capitalism". We argue that "[T]he Marxist concept of class ... is marginalized and trivialized by the revisionist left discourses." We continue:

> As the revisionist left now uses class, the term 'social class' refers to social divisions, social strata, that are effects of market forces that are understood to be (relatively) autonomous from production practices, that is, from the social relations of capitalism that are the relations of exploitation between labor and capital.
> KELSH and HILL 2006, 4–5

Although he acknowledges the significance of class as a key variable in the perpetuation of educational inequality, Apple has nevertheless remained a trenchant critic of 'traditional' Marxists for their overtly 'economistic' and 'deterministic' analyses of schooling', accusing an unspecified 'mid-Atlantic' group (by whom he was referring to Peter McLaren, Mike Cole, Dave Hill, Paula Allman, Glenn Rikowski and co-thinkers) of being Marxist fundamentalists (Apple, 2006) and he was, in turn replied to, by Glenn Rikowski (2006).

Conclusion

Pro-capitalists, neoliberals, neoconservatives and postmodernists explain recent developments in education in very different ways from Marxists. Postmodernists explain contemporary developments in society and the restructuring of schooling and education systems, such as that brought about by the 1988 Education Reform Act in England and Wales, and the marketisation of and fragmentation of the schooling system through diversity in types of schools, as reflecting the increased diversity of society, the increased position and self-perception of people as consumers. And, with their hyper-individualism, they would welcome individual merit pay/ Performance Related Pay, that is, individualised pay bargaining instead of collective/ trade union pay bargaining, that has now been introduced for teachers in England (Hill et al., 2016). Capitalist educators, and privatisers, see the scope and actuality of profit through this niche marketing, as well as through privatisation of education, and its ancillary support services and functions.

The Marxist interpretation, whether Culturalist neo-Marxist or Structuralist neo-Marxist, is very different. These changes are seen as rendering the schooling and education systems as more locked into and more supportive of the current requirements of capitalism. In England and Wales, the Conservative 'reforms' of 1988, continued in essence by 'New Labour' governments of Tony

Blair (1997–2007) and Gordon Brown (2007–2010), as well as the Conservative-Liberal Democrat Coalition of 2010–15, and the Conservative government since 2015, are seen as reinforcing economic, ideological and cultural reproduction in support of the status quo of social class exploitation. (In Hill, 2001, I discuss the varying ideological analyses of education policy in England).

I do think that Culturalist neo-Marxists have two major theoretical, and thereby, political agitational and organisational flaws. Firstly, they are too starry-eyed about the 'relative autonomy' of teachers and schools and education state apparatuses, and about the possibility of major change through the education system. With 'human agency', with human resistance, and with collective class consciousness and action, Marxists would argue, then, although there are major difficulties, people can successfully struggle to change events and systems—at micro-levels and at societal levels. In this struggle for social justice the ideological state apparatuses of education can play an important role. But educational change, to mis-quote Basil Bernstein (1970), cannot compensate for or overthrow (capitalist) society.

Secondly, I do think that Culturalist Marxists, or neo-Marxists, and, in the political field, reformists and social democrats, downplay, indeed, subvert and impede, class analysis and class struggle. We are faced with the actualisation of the capitalist dream for education, to produce and reproduce a hierarchically skilled and unequally rewarded labour force that is socially and politically quiescent and integrated with no dissonance or resistance, into capitalism. The strategy, in the USA, in England, is the same at various times, to rubbish and underfund the state school system, then propose vouchers/ pre-privatisation (e.g. Academy Schools and Free Schools in England, enforcing individualised pay bargaining/ merit pay/ Performance Related Pay for teachers, ending tenure/ secure contracts for teachers, and the suppression of critical thought, critical pedagogy and critical teachers.

Anti-hegemonic, socialist, Marxist struggle, must take place in arenas outside the classroom, school and education apparatus, and needs analysis, activism, organisation, party, (socialist/ Marxist) programmes (see Hill, 2012b, 2017). And that analysis must be a Marxist class analysis. This is a revolutionary Marxist programme, to replace, overcome, overthrow, go beyond capitalism, to abolish the Labour—Capital relation, to progress into a Socialist Society.

References

Althusser, L. (1971) Ideology and ideological state apparatuses. *Lenin and Philosophy and Other Essays*. London: New Left Books.

Apple, M. (2006) Review Essay: Rhetoric and reality in critical educational studies in the United States. *British Journal of Sociology of Education* 27 (5): 679–687.

Ball, S.J. (2003) *Class Strategies and the Educational Market: the Middle Classes and Social Advantage*. London, Routledge/Falmer.

Bernstein, B. (1970) Education cannot compensate for society. *New Society* 26th February.

Bernstein, B. (1977) Class and pedagogies: visible and invisible. In Bernstein, B., *Class, codes and control, vol. 3*. London: Routledge and Kegan Paul, 16–156.

Bourdieu, P. (1976) The school as a conservative force in scholastic and cultural inequalities. In: Dale, R. et al. *Schooling and Capitalism*. London: Routledge and Kegan Paul.

Bourdieu, P. (1990) *In Other Words: Towards a Reflexive Sociology*. Stanford, California: Stanford University Press.

Bourdieu, R. and Passeron, J. (1977) *Reproduction in Education, Society and Culture*. London: Sage Publications.

Bowles, S. and Gintis, H. (1976) *Schooling In Capitalist America*. London: Routledge and Kegan Paul.

Brown, S., Riddell, S., Duffield, J. (1997) Classroom approaches to learning and teaching: the social class dimension. Paper delivered to the ECER (European Educational Research Association) Annual Conference, Seville, Spain.

Butler, P. (2016) Most Britons regard themselves as working class, survey finds. *The Guardian*, 29 June. Available at: https://www.theguardian.com/society/2016/jun/29/most-brits-regard-themselves-as-workingclass-survey-finds.

Duffield, J. (1998a) Unequal opportunities or don't mention the (class) war. Paper to the Scottish Educational Research Association (SERA) Conference, Dundee.

Duffield, J. (1998b) Learning experiences, effective schools and social context. *Support for Learning*, 13(1): 3–8.

Harvey, D. (2005) *A Brief History of Neoliberalism*. Oxford, England: Oxford University Press.

Hill, D. (2001) State Theory and The Neo-Liberal Reconstruction of Schooling and Teacher Education: A Structuralist Neo-Marxist Critique of Postmodernist, Quasi-Postmodernist, and Culturalist Neo-Marxist Theory. *The British Journal of Sociology of Education*. 22 (1): 137–157.

Hill, D. (2009) Culturalist and Materialist Explanations of Class and 'Race': Critical Race Theory, Equivalence/ Parallelist Theory and Marxist Theory. *Cultural Logic: an electronic journal of Marxist Theory and Practice*. Available at: http://clogic.eserver.org/2009/2009.html.

Hill, D. (2012a) Immiseration Capitalism, Activism and Education: Resistance, Revolt and Revenge. *Journal for Critical Education Policy Studies*, 10 (2). Available at: http://www.jceps.com/index.php?pageID=article&articleID=259.

Hill, D. (2012b) Fighting Neo-Liberalism with Education and Activism. *Philosophers for Change*. 1 March. Available at: https://philosophersforchange.org/2012/02/29/fighting-neo-liberalism-with-education-and-activism/.

Hill, D., (ed.) 2013 *Immiseration Capitalism and Education: Austerity, Resistance and Revolt*. Brighton: Institute for Education Policy Studies.

Hill, D. (2017) The Role of Marxist Educators Against and Within Neoliberal Capitalism. *Insurgent Scripts*, January. New Delhi: Insurgent Scripts. Available at: http://insurgentscripts.org/the-role-of-marxist-educators-against-and-within-neoliberal-capitalism/.

Hill, D., Lewis, C., Maisuria, A. Yarker, P. and Hill, J. (2016) Conservative Education Policy Reloaded: Policy, Ideology and Impacts in England. *Journal for Critical Education Policy Studies* 14 (3). Available at: http://www.jceps.com/wp-content/uploads/2016/12/14-3-1-1.pdf.

Joseph Rowntree Foundation, 2016. *We can solve poverty*. Available at: www.jrf.org.uk/solve-uk-poverty.

Kelsh, D. and Hill, D. (2006) The Culturalization of Class and the Occluding of Class Consciousness: The Knowledge Industry in/of Education. *Journal for Critical Education Policy Studies*, 4 (1). Available at: http://www.jceps.com/index.php?pageID=article&articleID=59.

Lenin, V.I. (1965) A great beginning. In: Lenin, V.I., *Collected Works, vol. 29*. Moscow: Progress Publishers.

Lydall R. and Prynn, J. 2013. London's rich get 18 more healthy years. *Evening Standard*. 18 September. Available at: http://www.standard.co.uk/news/health/london-s-rich-get-18-more-healthy-years-8824143.html.

Marx, K. [1845] *Theses on Feuerbach*. Available at: https://www.marxists.org/archive/marx/works/1845/theses/.

Marx, K. [1847] *The Poverty of Philosophy*. Available at: https://www.marxists.org/archive/marx/works/1847/poverty-philosophy/.

Marx, K. [1852] *The Eighteenth Brumaire of Louis Bonaparte*. Available at: https://www.marxists.org/archive/marx/works/download/pdf/18th-Brumaire.pdf.

Marx, K. and Engels, F. [1848] *The Communist Manifesto*. Available at: https://www.marxists.org/archive/marx/works/1848/communist-manifesto/.

Office for National Statistics (ONS) (2016) The National Statistics. Socio-economic Classification. London: ONS. Available at: https://www.ons.gov.uk/methodology/classificationsandstandards/otherclassifications/thenationalstatisticssocioeconomicclassificationnssecrebasedonsoc2010.

Pannekoek, A. (1909) The New Middle Class. *International Socialist Review*. October 1909. Available at: https://www.marxists.org/archive/pannekoe/1909/new-middle-class.htm.

Pells, R., 2016. Life expectancy gap between rich and poor widening for first time in 150 years. *The Independent,* 3 May. Available at: http://www.independent.co.uk/news/uk/home-news/life-expectancy-gap-between-rich-poor-widening-first-time-in-150-years-men-women-a7010881.html.

Rikowski, G. (2002) After the manuscript broke off: thoughts on Marx, social class and education. A paper prepared for the British Sociological Association Education Study Group Meeting, King's College London, 23rd June. Available at: http://www.leeds.ac.uk/educol/documents/00001931.htm.

Rikowski, G. (2006) In Retro Glide. *Journal for Critical Education Policy Studies* 4 (2) Available at: http://www.jceps.com/index.php?pageID=article&articleID=81.

Social Market Foundation, 2015. *Wealth in the Downturn: Winners and Losers examine wealth and debt in the period since the recession to uncover who has really won and lost since 2008.* London: Social market Foundation. Available at: http://www.smf.co.uk/events/wealth-in-the-downturn-winners-and-losers/.

Standing, G. (2014) *The Precariat, the new Dangerous Class.* London: Bloomsbury.

Wright, E.O. (1989) *The Debate on Classes.* London: Verso.

Wright, E.O. (2002) A Framework of Class Analysis in the Marxist Tradition. In: Wright, E.O. (ed.) *Alternative Foundations of Class Analysis.* Available at: http://www.ssc.wisc.edu/~wright/Found-all.pdf.

CHAPTER 4

Marxist Class Theory: Competition, Contingency and Intermediate Class Positions

Jonathan Pratschke

Introduction

Understanding the nature and role of social class divisions in a society dominated by the capitalist mode of production is a complex undertaking and one that requires continuous theoretical elaboration. Classical Marxism provides a framework for undertaking this task—which is arguably as important today as it was in Marx's time. Marxist theory comprises an evolving and integrated set of ideas which must be continually reformulated in order to take account of historical change and theoretical developments in relation to specific issues. By providing a coherent overview of class relations, Marxism can help to overcome the fragmentation of empirical research—particularly evident in the current period—and generate stimulating research questions.

The main argument that I will make is that the Marxist approach to theorising class involves the development and deployment of a special kind of explanatory framework. Its capacity to explain the social world is central to Marxism's emancipatory potential and its orientation towards political praxis. Marxists aim to explain social phenomena (such as female labour market participation, forms of racism and discrimination, educational and health inequalities, etc.) by identifying the causal mechanisms that give rise to them. These explanations take into account the ways in which the social world is stratified and the capacity of social actors to react to and transform their environment, which is related reflexively to their ideas.

Capital accumulation exerts a particularly profound influence in capitalist societies, and this is why class processes are given particular weight in Marxist accounts (Resnick and Wolff 2006). This does not involve a reduction of non-class to class processes, but entails linking a given outcome to these class processes via a set of mediating mechanisms. As far as cultural processes are concerned, a strength of Marxism is its ability to shed light on contradictions and conflicts, showing how ideas and practices change and develop over time (Harvey 2012; Williams 2005). Other theoretical programmes have difficulties dealing with these dynamic aspects of cultural forms, and tend to treat them as either a support for static structures or as an irrational and indecipherable irruption within social life (Callinicos 2006). The most influential contemporary strands of research on class offer little more than pragmatic empirical typologies (MacKenzie 1982; Gubbay 1997; Morris and Scott 1996), which can identify inequalities but have limited capacity to explain their origins.

Marxist class theory must also engage with broader debates and in this chapter I will address the argument that epochal change in the present historical period is leading to the emergence of a 'new capitalism', 'network society' or 'post-industrial society' in which class is increasingly irrelevant (Beck 2013; Castells 2004; Sennett 2006). I follow Doogan (2009) in associating these notions of systemic transformation with the ascent of neoliberalism. Indeed, the identification of neoliberalism as a global political project which unites core components of the capitalist class is itself an important achievement of Marxism and a good example of how Marxist class analysis can integrate cultural, political and economic processes within a powerful explanatory account (Doogan 2009; Harvey 2005).

One of the paradoxes of recent decades is that the neoliberal class offensive has coincided with the abandonment of class-based theories by a substantial part of the Left and by many social scientists. Indeed, after more than twenty years of neoliberalism, the academic study of social class appears increasingly incongruous. Many mainstream scholars argue that this is due to its irrelevance, emphasising notions of epochal change, individualisation and social fragmentation, as noted above. However, the available evidence points in the other direction, towards the continuing relevance of class and continuity of labour market structures and processes (Smith 2000; Becker and Hadjar 2013; Doogan 2009; Jemielniak 2010).

In the following sections, I will discuss four themes which are fundamental to the study of social class within Marxism. The first relates to the specific character of Marxism as a theory of society, including what is generally described as its 'stratified realist ontology'. The second describes how social class processes relate to the production and distribution of value. The third refers to competition between rival capitals (and blocs of capital) and the last one involves the labour market and its links to class. In the course of this discussion, I will draw on the notion of 'functions of capital' (Carchedi 1991) in the aim of providing a more solid theoretical grounding for the 'intermediate' classes that are situated between capital and labour.

Explanation in Marxism

One way of identifying the specificities of Marxist class theory is by using the concepts provided by Critical Realist philosophy of science (Bhaskar 1998; Brown, Fleetwood, and Roberts 2002). It has proved useful in other areas of Marxist theory to formalise Marx's method by using Bhaskar's approach to Critical Realism (cf. Callinicos 2006). I will limit the discussion here to the following issues: (1) ontological stratification; (2) emergence; and (3) the relationship between structure and agency.

Starting with the first point, Marxist class theory is based on a stratified ontology, whereby reality is viewed as comprising distinct levels and the objects of scientific inquiry are the generative mechanisms which give rise to the phenomena of interest (Archer 1995). The principle of ontological depth implies that these generative mechanisms are not all situated at the same level—some are more fundamental than others—and most outcomes of interest are influenced by a multiplicity of mechanisms. As a result of their complex, hierarchical structure, social mechanisms are not always (or even typically) self-evident. Theoretical work is thus required in order to describe how they operate, as social actors may or may not be aware of their existence (even if they experience their effects).

Marx's method is informed by analogous ontological commitments and his method is an attempt to grasp the complex structure of social reality (Sayer 1979). Guided by the available evidence, the Marxist theorist develops an account of fundamental mechanisms and then integrates additional ones in an iterative fashion to obtain a progressively richer and more adequate account (Carter and New 2004). The only limits to this process are those imposed by reality itself, as the recalcitrant and obstinate judge of theoretical adequacy. Critical Realism—like all forms of realism—acknowledges the absence of any final form of theoretical adjudication, whilst defending the possibility of treating well-supported theories as descriptions of really-existing structures or processes (Psillos 2009).

This implies that class processes may be involved in a multiplicity of generative mechanisms which operate at different levels. Mobilising the resources of class theory is thus about identifying mechanisms which are causally efficacious in a given context, whilst integrating them in a coherent way to create powerful explanations. For example, women's labour market participation may be influenced by a range of class-related processes regarding reproduction, gender ideologies, strategies for maximising profits, labour market segmentation, strategies for family survival and so on. Class-related processes are thus plural and multifaceted, and can be mediated and shaped by other processes or mechanisms which are related to gender, ethnicity, legal status and other attributes.

Marxist class theory is not just about categorising individuals into classes, but involves developing an account of how a specific outcome might have emerged through the joint effects of various processes. Marxist theory does not simply posit the existence of classes but shows how individuals are caught up in or 'thrown into' relationships by capital in its incessant pursuit of profit. It is thus simultaneously a theory of social structure and a theory of historical change in social forms, relationships and institutions. To speak of the 'members of a specific class' represents a short-hand way of indicating how social actors are incorporated into the social structure via fundamental class processes. Most importantly, positions in the social structure are associated with specific capacities, constraints, roles and relationships which shape their experiences, ideas, identities, language, attitudes, bodies and behaviour in complex but determinate ways.

The second theme, referred to by Bhaskar as 'emergence', aims to capture the nature of the relationship between processes, mechanisms and phenomena that are situated at different levels of social reality. Any given outcome cannot be 'reduced' to mechanisms operating at a deeper level, as each level has its own emergent properties (Bhaskar 2008). This suggests that there can be no single theoretical formulation of the relationship between class and culture, for example, as any cultural form will require a specific kind of explanation. As a materialist (as opposed to idealist) theory, Marxism seeks explanations for changing ideas and cultural practices in the conditions of existence of social actors. The Marxist critique of neoliberalism focuses on the class actors who promote it, its class-based impacts and the ways in which it is shaped by struggles between different classes or fractions. This approach entails a careful study of the economic and political effects of ideologies as well as exploring their social bases.

It is possible, using these concepts, to reformulate one of the enduring problems in class analysis, which regards the binary opposition between structure and agency. Rather than positing a reciprocal relationship between structure and agency, or collapsing one into the other, it becomes clear that social structure should be seen as preceding any given action (Archer 2004). Structures can thus impose limits, and agency can either reproduce or transform structures in a 'tensed' process (Archer 1995). The possibility of transformation (either deliberate or unintended) is consequently inherent in an open social world, but presupposes specific forms of collective as well as individual agency. Marxism provides a theoretical model of transformative collective agency and seeks to identify its conditions of possibility, against the backdrop of capitalist class relations. The fundamental processes of capitalism generate social class roles and relationships which are an archetypal example of social structure; different kinds of action can be studied against this backdrop. The ability of financial capitalists to promote a neoliberal agenda, for example, is facilitated by the distinctive class-related capacities they possess, whilst the ability of workers to oppose this is influenced by their own class position and related capacities and constraints.

Fundamental Class Processes

Marxist class theory cuts across common-sense and official classifications of occupations which are based on status or sector ('white-collar employment', 'service work', 'professionals', 'atypical employment', etc.). Most Marxists construct their account of social classes around Marx's description of the relations of production and his labour theory of value (Carchedi 1991). The latter is essential in order to understand exploitation, to theorise the different stages of capitalism, to analyse the crisis tendencies of capitalism and to study the state and imperialism. As Gubbay (1997, 78) observes, classes are "locations in the overall flow of value within the generation, appropriation and allocation of surplus value."

At the most basic level of abstraction (often referred to as 'capital in general'), the only classes that can be identified are the capitalist class and the working class. This implies abstracting from the complexities generated by competition and imagining a much simpler economic system characterised by a single capitalist enterprise.[1] This is why Marxism is often described as providing a dichotomous model of social class. At the next level of abstraction (which is generally referred to as 'many capitals'), it is possible to imagine a multiplicity of capitalist firms engaged in competition, which enables us to focus on the relationship between competition and class, to introduce notions of uneven and combined development, to develop an idea of the state and to distinguish between the petty bourgeoisie and the capitalist class. However, it is only when we reach the next level of abstraction (which we might refer to as that of the 'historical period') that we can identify the prevailing forms of the capitalist firm and state, which is essential in order to fully define social classes.

---

1   Rather than repeating well-known arguments here, the reader is invited to consult any good summary of Marx's account of accumulation in Volume One of *Capital* (such as, for example, Braverman 1998; Callinicos and Harman 1987; Carchedi 1991; Harvey 2010).

It should therefore be noted that classes, in the Marxist account, are integrated into the overall theoretical framework in different ways and at different levels of abstraction. There is no fixed number of classes and no pre-determined way of deploying class concepts in concrete analysis.

There is broad agreement amongst Marxists on a number of important aspects of class theory, such as the possibility for capitalist commodities to take the form of services as well as physical goods (e.g. Braverman 1998). This is reinforced by the understanding that the working class is not limited to productive workers and includes those who perform unproductive labour in retailing, banking, marketing and other sectors (but see Poulantzas 1978). Moreover, most Marxists do not limit the composition of the capitalist class to legal ownership of the means of production, but also include salaried CEOs and their equivalents (e.g. Ehrenreich and Ehrenreich 1979). For most Marxists, the petty bourgeoisie is a distinct class that comprises artisans, shopkeepers, independent farmers, self-employed professionals and other truly autonomous workers (Ehrenreich and Ehrenreich 1979). Skills are generally seen as qualifying the value of labour power and consequently influencing pay and conditions for both manual and non-manual workers (e.g. Carchedi 1991).

On this basis, Marxists identify the working class as comprising individuals who are forced to sell their labour-power in order to survive and who work under the control of capital. There is little consensus, however, regarding the class position of 'intermediate' groups like middle or lower managers, professionals, technicians and supervisors. I will therefore focus on this issue in the remainder of this chapter. The most influential theory of these employees relies on the 'service class' idea, which was developed by a non-Marxist (John Goldthorpe) on the basis of writings by an Austrian Marxist, Karl Renner. In Renner's formulation, the service class included various kinds of white-collar workers performing unproductive labour, who were distinguished from the working class as much by their 'code of service' as by their indirect relationship to accumulation (Renner 1978). Renner further characterised members of the service class by their relatively stable and predictable career trajectories within bureaucratic organisations. Goldthorpe took over this distinction between the 'service contract' and the 'labour contract', arguing that members of the service class are "typically engaged in the exercise of delegated authority or in the application of specialist knowledge and expertise" (Goldthorpe 1982, 169).

There are a number of other ways of theorising the class location of this heterogeneous group of employees. One is to define them as a 'Professional-Managerial Class', following Ehrenreich and Ehrenreich (1979), who argue that this consists of "salaried mental workers who do not own the means of production and whose major function in the social division of labour may be described broadly as the reproduction of capitalist culture and capitalist class relations" (12). It includes teachers, social workers, psychologists, journalists and other figures "who are directly concerned with social control or with the production and propagation of ideology" (ibid.). Another possibility is to rely on the notion of 'contradictory class locations', which Poulantzas (1975), Wright (1976) and Callinicos (1987) use when describing the class situation of employees who participate in the extraction of surplus value from productive workers, whilst being simultaneously dominated by capital. The idea that intermediate occupational groups embody a combination of characteristics associated with different classes is at the core of this approach:

> Polarised between the bourgeoisie and the proletariat are those professional, managerial and administrative employees who occupy what the American Marxist Erik Olin Wright has called 'contradictory class locations'. This group, who live by selling their labour-power but perform functions on behalf of capital in the process of production, form what I shall call the 'new middle class'.
> CALLINICOS 1987, 17–18

None of these approaches provides a satisfactory definition of the class location of these intermediate groups. The 'service class' concept relies on the idea that capital trusts and rewards employees who carry out particularly delicate or sensitive tasks within the firm. This is certainly a theoretical possibility, but is far from being a necessary condition. For example, it is not clear why capital must reward and trust, rather than using some other combination of strategies. In fact, there is evidence that capital does not always reward and trust managers and professionals, regardless of the delicate or discretionary nature of their tasks (Edwards 2000). Moreover, many workers carry out 'delicate' tasks which require the exercise of 'discretion'. Scholars have also observed that 'service class' careers are not always confined to internal labour markets and may involve performance assessment and contractual arrangements rather than trust and permanent employment. Thus, without specifying the nature of the 'delicate tasks' performed by members of the service class, and consequently linking these with capital accumulation, it is impossible to provide a determinate account of their class position.

The Professional-Managerial Class theory is more ambitious, but attributes to professionals a problematic and one-dimensional role in the conscious manipulation and coercion of the working class which is not (and probably cannot be) demonstrated. More generally, attempts to define class position by reference to ideological function or role tend to lead to a static, tautological structuralism which cannot account for class conflict, contingency and subjectivity and which reduces or eliminates the autonomy of the cultural sphere. Turning to Wright and Callinicos, it is difficult to find anything truly contradictory in the role of managers and experts, on either theoretical or empirical grounds. The fact that they receive a salary in exchange for their work does not qualify them as members of the working class, and similar arguments can be made about professionals: the fact that they tend to have a high level of autonomy does not automatically make them bourgeois or petty bourgeois, as this applies to many work roles under capitalism. The notion of contradictory class locations is also questionable to the extent that it implies that individuals are distributed between the opposing poles of 'capital' and 'labour', grouped together in a class whose fuzzy boundaries can only be identified arbitrarily. For example, Callinicos (1987) has difficulty assigning occupational groups like teachers, nurses and laboratory technicians to either the middle class or the working class, and his theory provides little guidance. Thus, to affirm that a given employee or group of employees occupies a 'contradictory class location' implies a high level of indeterminacy, with a consequent fall in explanatory power.

A more differentiated, determinate and defensible derivation of the class position of these intermediate employee roles is possible. Starting with managers, it is relatively straightforward and perfectly in line with Classical Marxism to argue that they operate 'on behalf of capital', whilst being distinct from the capitalist class.[2] Thus, managers exercise delegated authority over workers and other subordinate employees in a determinate role of coordination and control; they do not occupy a contradictory class location simply because they receive a salary for doing so.

The second step in the argument is to realise that professionals cannot be assimilated *tout court* to this managerial role, as if control over knowledge were in some way analogous to control over labour. It is necessary, therefore, to unpack the different roles that lie behind the 'professional' label and to avoid illicit generalisations. It is then possible to identify a second group of employees who—like managers—act on behalf of capital. They do so by developing and implementing innovations in products and processes with a view to increasing the profitability of the firm. These two roles—that of the manager and that of the innovator or expert—are analytically and historically separable, although they may overlap in practice. The concept of 'functions of

---

[2] Managers have interests which are not always aligned with those of capital, not least because they have an interest in keeping their jobs, whilst capitalists may, in certain circumstances, have an interest in 'delayering' them.

capital' is useful here, as these intermediate positions correspond to two broad challenges facing capital: to coordinate and control labour and to remain competitive within product markets. Managers are often involved in carrying out both of these functions, but are defined by their role in coordinating and exerting control over labour, whilst their expert advisers are involved in carrying out the second function. This approach allows us to distinguish between the main components of the middle class without introducing arbitrary distinctions, illicit generalisations, inconsistencies or other theoretical weaknesses. It has greater explanatory power than its rivals and does not rely on rigid models of career prospects or 'trust'.

There are also many skilled and qualified employees who do not act on behalf of capital in these ways. It is appropriate to consider these individuals skilled workers, whilst noting that their labour market situations can vary greatly. Indeed, capital is compelled, by competition, to draw on many different kinds of labour. Some forms of skilled labour cannot be subsumed under capital via the purchase of labour-power at its value and its consumption within a labour process under direct capitalist control (cf. Gupta 1980; Murray 2004; Vercellone 2007). This means that within the general category of skilled labour, there are always workers with advantageous conditions of employment due to their capacity to avoid direct control (for example, highly-skilled computer programmers). In certain cases, this is due to the fact that self-employment is a viable and lucrative alternative to paid employment, whilst in other cases it is due to the nature of the work itself or a result of effective formal or informal organisation.

Concrete analyses of intermediate groups and occupations must therefore refer to a wider range of generative mechanisms, going beyond formal class position. Wright suggests that high professional employees often have a 'petty bourgeois shadow class', given that they are not actually forced to sell their labour power, but "choose to sell their labour power over self-employment because it is their preference" (Wright 1989, 334). He assigns these employees *en masse* to the middle class, based on his 'intuitions'.[3] In theoretical terms, however, it is more coherent to consider the possibility of classifying at least some 'professionals' as skilled labourers, if they are not in self-employment, do

---

3 "In some sense or other they are 'middle class' and thus a conceptual justification for identifying their non-working class location is needed" (Wright 1989, 332). Aronowitz also suggests that trained scientific/technical employees cannot "credibly be described as either traditional proletarians or capitalists" (2003, 3), and MacKenzie (1982) provides some further discussion of the role of 'intuitions' and 'common sense' in class theory.

not have managerial responsibilities in relation to workers and are not expert advisers to capital.

To recapitulate, it is possible to distinguish between capitalists and workers at the highest level of abstraction, whilst at lower levels it is possible to identify both the petty bourgeoisie and an intermediate (middle) class which acts on behalf of capital or carries out functions of capital. This class is subdivided into 'managers' (who coordinate and control) and 'experts' (who innovate and advise). These functions are closely linked, as control and innovation are fundamental, inter-related components of the capitalist labour process. It seems justifiable to use the term 'new middle class' to refer to these two groups, reserving the term 'old middle class' for the petty bourgeoisie, in line with current useage. The working class, in turn, is conventionally and quite appropriately sub-divided into groups with low skills, average skills and high skills.[4]

Competition and Class

It is necessary, at this point, to clarify the role of competition in relation to Marxist class theory. As I noted at the outset, Marx's account of capitalism hinges around the twin axes of capitalism as a mode of production: the 'vertical' relationship between classes and the 'horizontal' relationship between rival capitals. The latter gives rise to the mechanisms which determine the value of commodities, the socially-necessary labour time for their production and generate pressures to innovate and expand production (Callinicos 1995). It is thus one of the main sources of the structured antagonism and social conflict in the relationship between capital and labour. Competition is also a multi-scalar phenomenon with effects at different levels. The original idea presented here is that the class position of many intermediate employees must be theorised by reference to their role in the competitive struggle between rival capitals and blocs of capital.

State decisions and policies are linked in various ways to the competitiveness of national/regional capital (Pratschke 2015). At the international level, state spending and decisions play an important role in shaping competitive accumulation (Brenner 2006; Desai 2013). More efficient/effective state

---

[4] For Marxists, average skills are those required by the average worker in a given branch of production at a given moment in time. This means that there can be variations across sectors in how skills are evaluated, which suggests that skill levels should be defined in relation to the labour process as well as the attributes of the worker.

processes—including health and welfare provision, education/skills, etc.—enable specific national/regional capitals to gain a larger share of total surplus value. This capitalist nexus is secured by direct lobbying and influence and, more fundamentally, by the way financial flows constrain political decision-making (cf. Pratschke 2015). This binds the political executive and élite to the capitalist class and places the managers of state departments and corporations in an analogous role to their private-sector counterparts. Experts and advisers in the public sector also play an equivalent role to their private-sector counterparts, as innovators in search of competitive advantage at various levels. On this basis, it is possible to argue that competition is related to class processes in both the private and public sectors via the pressures it places on the cost and productivity of labour.

A large number of public employees are involved in the education, health and welfare systems, which are involved in the reproduction of labour at various levels of skill. The state was historically central to the constitution of the working class and continues to play a fundamental role in the reproduction of classes and class relations (Doogan 2009). This includes the organisation of state labour processes which involve the skilled labour of teachers, health professionals, civil servants and other employees. As in the private sector, these employees should be considered part of the working class, to the extent that they are not involved in managing other people's labour and are not employed as expert advisers.[5] When divorced from specific social roles, in other words, technical knowledge, practical ability and specialist training can only alter the skill level of labour power. As a consequence, the advantages associated with these skills are always vulnerable to deskilling or other kinds of management strategies. The social roles described above—involving managers and advisers—are associated with sharp class boundaries because of the ways in which they shape work relationships, identities, opportunities and rewards. Members of the 'new middle class' can maintain and often improve their position by identifying with specific capitals and by seeking to ensure that surplus value is extracted from the labourers and realised in the sphere of exchange. Workers, by contrast, can typically only improve their situation by identifying with each other and by organising collectively.

---

5 Some state employees carry out specific social functions (police, judges, etc.) which must be analysed in their own terms, for example by referring to the relationship between class divisions, conflict and state repression. To effectively theorise these roles, the relationship between class, social function and capital accumulation needs to be further elaborated, although this goes beyond the scope of this chapter.

The Labour Market and the Labour Process

As noted earlier, Marxist class analysis is based on Marx's account of the nature of the capitalist labour process and associated ideas regarding the structuring of social roles in the production and distribution of surplus value. By contrast, Weberian approaches to social class tend to ignore what happens within the labour process, basing their accounts on market situations. In this sense, the two perspectives are diametrically opposed. In Marxism, class positions are sometimes described as a 'structure of empty places', shaped by the requirements of capitalist production. This is a useful initial definition, but has the effect of radically divorcing class processes from the labour market, which may become a limitation.

Capital draws on various forms of labour power through specific kinds of labour markets, which means that in concrete terms, labour market experiences are constitutive of class. Indeed, the historical emergence of the working class was itself conditional upon the institution of the labour market, and the management of various kinds of labour reserves maintains this link. So class should not be confined to the labour process, as there are important links between the labour market and the labour process which are not merely contingent but are bound up with class.

Secondly, the notion of an 'empty structure of places' tends to mystify the reproduction of classes and class society, which is a fundamental aspect of class itself. The class processes that drive the production and distribution of surplus value are also implicated in the development of policies for the reproduction of labour power and skills via state or corporate welfare, migration policies, subsidies and so on. Although social reproduction is always a problematic and contradictory affair, it is of vital importance to the capitalist class and has a significant effect on labour markets (Doogan 2009). The nature of capital accumulation thus influences both production and reproduction via a series of interlocking processes, whereby the mediated membership of a class influences an individual's labour market situation, which in turn influences the individual's prospects of recruitment to a particular class. So rather than seeing social mobility as forming classes, in the Weberian mould, or denying that labour market phenomena have any relevance to them, we should perhaps look at classes themselves through the prism of capitalist production/reproduction.

Thirdly, skills are closely related to the functioning of labour markets, and it is largely through competition for different kinds of labour-power that the cost of skilled labour can rise above that of generic labour. When specific skills are in short supply, capitalists must compete for workers who possess these skills.

This is obviously an advantageous situation for the workers concerned (as long as it lasts). The most obvious way of reducing the cost of skilled labour-power is to produce or 'import' more of it, but any attempt to solve one type of skills shortage is likely to exacerbate others, and there will always be skill shortages in some areas—particularly during periods of employment growth. This does not mean that skills define classes (which leads to theoretical contradictions), but it does imply that the market dynamics of skill require concrete analyses which go beyond abstract definitions of class.

The supply of skilled labour is strongly influenced by the education system, and the very definition of 'average' skills has shifted over time due to the secular trend of increasing average educational attainments in successive age cohorts. The expansion of higher education is driven by a multiplicity of factors, including the demand for skilled labour, whilst the expansion of state-funded education has had the effect of reducing the value of specific forms of skilled labour. This is a contradictory process, as the shift to third-level qualifications for jobs in nursing, early years teaching, physiotherapy, radiology and so on implies their 'professionalisation', whilst the expansion of these courses (and of higher education more generally) suggests that this may not translate into higher relative earnings.

Fourthly, it is important to appreciate that the 'deep structure' of labour markets is shaped by various aspects of these class processes, including not only skills but also the reproduction of labour-power, the mobilisation of labour reserves and class struggles over various aspects of these processes. As Doogan (2009) points out, capital continues to need skilled labour-power and makes considerable investments in welfare, pensions and other benefits in order to recruit and retain the workers that it needs. This suggests that 'precarious' or 'contingent' employment is problematic for capital, in many cases, and not just for labour, and confirms that class theory is a crucial resource when seeking to understand contemporary capitalism.

Finally, any benefits that accrue to the new middle class, in the form of salaries and conditions, are due to similar processes and should not be treated as a reward for their loyalty in carrying out 'delicate' tasks. Capitalism is a competitive system, and there is no mechanism by which capital as a whole might decide to reward a specific category of employee, regardless of its effects. Thus, it is more appropriate to explain higher salaries (where these are actually observed) by referring to competition. As far as managers and experts are concerned, higher average salaries are 'socially necessary' in order to prevent them from going to work for a rival. In place of the harmonious notion of 'reward for loyalty and discretion', we should perhaps refer to the 'competitive struggle to retain key employees'. One of the effects of this kind of competition (and the other labour market mechanisms discussed earlier) is to superimpose a finely-grained hierarchy of salaries and status upon the underlying class divisions. The class system is thus characterised by both continuous hierarchy (in terms of wages) and sharp social divisions (in class terms), and once again it is competition in the labour market that mediates between these two forms.

Conclusion

As I have sought to show in this chapter, Marxist class theory can make a distinctive contribution to the analysis of the social structure of capitalist societies. In order to appreciate its potential, it is necessary to understand the specificities of Marxism as a scientific research programme, which I summarised using concepts derived from Critical Realism. Marxism involves a special kind of explanatory framework, and must be assessed on this basis. This facilitates the resolution of a series of objections and difficulties that have hampered Marxist class theory in the past, and leads to useful reformulations of various aspects of the classical approach.

Amongst Marxists who adhere to this tradition, the question of how to theorise intermediate employees continues to create difficulties. I have tried to overcome some of these difficulties by showing that social classes can be theorised at different levels of abstraction and by emphasising the importance of specifying the underlying mechanisms that link classes to the accumulation process.

Of the various arguments made in the chapter, the most original involves the link between capitalist competition and class, including the definition of an intermediate class which operates on behalf of capital—either within a capitalist firm or within the state—to promote its competitiveness vis-à-vis rival capitals and to expand market share. By integrating the horizontal axis of capitalist competition within class theory, therefore, it is possible to develop a coherent theoretical account of intermediate class positions which can accommodate both private sector and state labour processes. This involves abandoning attempts to theorise the 'new middle class' by reference to contradictory class locations, trust or ideological role. All such attempts appear destined to fail, as they rely on arbitrary distinctions, illicit generalisations or rigid tautologies. The alternative approach presented here draws on the notion of 'functions of capital' to identify two intermediate class fractions between capital and labour, alongside the petty bourgeoisie, comprising 'managers' and 'expert aides', who together constitute the 'new middle class'.

When Marxist class theory is reformulated in this way, it becomes clear that concrete explanations must inevitably make reference to a multiplicity of mechanisms. This means that class position is not the only determinant of incomes, work relationships, status, attitudes and behaviours, which is an obvious but crucial statement. It is clear, at the same time, that considerable theoretical work is required in relation to all of the issues raised in this chapter, from the theory of capitalist competition to the analysis of labour market structures and processes. By providing a relatively brief but broad overview, I hope to have brought this task into focus, whilst emphasising the need to continuously develop new ideas within the framework provided by the classical Marxist tradition.

References

Archer, M.S. (1995) *Realist Social Theory: The Morphogenetic Approach*. Cambridge and New York: Cambridge University Press.

Archer, M.S. (2004) *Being Human: The Problem of Agency*. Cambridge: Cambridge University Press.

Aronowitz, S. (2003) *How Class Works: Power and Social Movement*. New Haven: Yale University Press.

Beck, U. (2013) Why "class" Is Too Soft a Category to Capture the Explosiveness of Social Inequality at the Beginning of the Twenty-First Century. *The British Journal of Sociology* 64 (1): 63–74. doi:10.1111/1468-4446.12005.

Becker, R., and Hadjar, A. (2013) "Individualisation" and Class Structure: How Individual Lives Are Still Affected by Social Inequalities. *International Social Science Journal* 64 (213–14): 211–223. doi:10.1111/issj.12044.

Bhaskar, Roy. (1998) *The Possibility of Naturalism*. Third Edition. London: Routledge.

Bhaskar, R. (2008) *A Realist Theory of Science*. London and New York: Routledge.

Braverman, H. (1998) *Labor and Monopoly Capital: The Degradation of Work in the Twentieth Century*. 25th anniversary ed. New York: Monthly Review Press.

Brenner, R. (2006) *The Economics of Global Turbulence: The Advanced Capitalist Economies from Long Boom to Long Downturn, 1945–2005*. London: Verso.

Brown, A., Fleetwood, S., and Roberts, J.M. (2002) *Critical Realism and Marxism*. London; New York: Routledge.

Callinicos, A. (1987) The "New Middle Class" and Socialist Politics. In *The Changing Working Class: Essays on Class Structure Today*, edited by Alex Callinicos and Chris Harman, 13–52. London: Bookmarks.

Callinicos, A. (1995) *Theories and Narratives: Reflections on the Philosophy of History*. Cambridge: Polity.

Callinicos, A. (2006) *The Resources of Critique*. Cambridge and Malden: Polity.
Callinicos, A. and Harman, C. (1987) *The Changing Working Class: Essays on Class Structure Today*. London: Bookmarks.
Carchedi, G. (1991) *Frontiers of Political Economy*. London; New York: Verso.
Carter, B., and New, C. (2004) *Making Realism Work: Realist Social Theory and Empirical Research*. London; New York: Routledge.
Castells, M., ed. (2004) *The Network Society: A Cross-Cultural Perspective*. Cheltenham, UK; Northampton, MA: Edward Elgar Pub.
Desai, R. (2013) *Geopolitical Economy: After US Hegemony, Globalization and Empire*. London: Pluto.
Doogan, K. (2009) *New Capitalism*. Cambridge: Polity.
Edwards, P. (2000) Late Twentieth Century Workplace Relations: Class Struggle Without Classes. In: Crompton R., Devine F., Savage M., and Scott J. (eds.) *Renewing Class Analysis*, 141–164. Oxford: Blackwell.
Ehrenreich, B., and Ehrenreich, J. (1979) The Professional-Managerial Class. In: Walker P., (ed) *Between Labor and Capital*, 5–45. Boston: South End Press.
Goldthorpe, J.H. (1982) On the Service Class, Its Formation and Future. In: Gidden A., and MacKenzie G., (eds) *Social Class and the Division of Labour: Essays in Honour of Ilya Neustadt*, 162–185. Cambridge: Cambridge University Press.
Gubbay, J. (1997) A Marxist Critique of Weberian Class Analyses. *Sociology* 31 (1): 73–89.
Gupta, D. (1980) Formal and Real Subsumption of Labour under Capital: The Instance of Share-Cropping. *Economic and Political Weekly* 15 (39): 98–106.
Harvey, D. (2005) *A Brief History of Neoliberalism*. Oxford: Oxford University Press.
Harvey, D. (2010) *A Companion to Marx's Capital*. London: Verso.
Harvey, D. (2012) *Rebel Cities: From the Right to the City to the Urban Revolution*. London: Verso.
Jemielniak, D. (2010) *The New Knowledge Workers*. New Horizons in Management. Cheltenham and Northampton, MA: Edward Elgar.
MacKenzie, G. (1982) Class Boundaries and the Labour Process. In: Gidden A., and MacKenzie G., (eds) *Social Class and the Division of Labour: Essays in Honour of Ilya Neustadt*, 63–86. CAMbridge: Cambridge University Press.
Morris, L. and Scott, J. (1996) 'The Attenuation of Class Analysis: Some Comments on G. Marshall, S. Roberts and C. Burgoyne, "Social Class and the Underclass in Britain in the USA"'. *The British Journal of Sociology* 47 (1): 45–55. doi:10.2307/591115.
Murray, P. (2004) The Social and Material Transformation of Production by Capital: Formal and Real Subsumption in Capital, Volume I. In: Bellofiore R. and Taylor N. (eds) *The Constitution of Capital: Essays on Volume I of Marx's Capital*, 243–273. Houndmills, Basingstoke: Palgrave.
Poulantzas, N. (1975) *Classes in Contemporary Capitalism*. London: New Left Books.
Poulantzas, N. (1978) *Political Power and Social Classes*. London: Verso.

Pratschke, J. (2015) Clearing the Minefield: State Theory and Geopolitical Economy. *World Review of Political Economy* 6 (4): 459–481.

Psillos, S. (2009) *Knowing the Structure of Nature: Essays on Realism and Explanation*. Basingstoke: Palgrave Macmillan.

Renner, K. (1978) The Service Class. In: Bottomore T. and Goode P. (eds) *Austro-Marxism*, Oxford: Oxford University Press.

Resnick, S.A., and Wolff, R.D. (eds) (2006) *New Departures in Marxian Theory*. London: Routledge.

Sayer, D. (1979) *Marx's Method: Ideology, Science, and Critique in Capital*. Hassocks, Sussex: Harvester Press.

Sennett, R. (2006) *The Culture of the New Capitalism*. The Castle Lectures in Ethics, Politics, and Economics. New Haven: Yale University Press.

Smith, T. (2000) *Technology and Capital in the Age of Lean Production: A Marxian Critique of the 'New Economy'*. New York: State University of New York Press.

Vercellone, C. (2007) From Formal Subsumption to General Intellect: Elements for a Marxist Reading of the Thesis of Cognitive Capitalism. *Historical Materialism* 15 (1): 13–36.

Williams, R. (2005) *Culture and Materialism: Selected Essays*. London and New York: Verso.

Wright, E.O. (1976) Class Boundaries in Advanced Capitalist Societies. *New Left Review* 98: 3–41.

Wright, E.O. (1989) *The Debate on Classes*. London; New York: Verso.

CHAPTER 5

Class Segregation

Danny Dorling

Introduction

This essay concentrates on the causes, outcomes and implications of social and geographical segregation by class, using the example of how social geography has changed in Britain since around 1968, and putting these changes into a wider geographical and historical context. (Northern Ireland is not included for numerous reasons, not least because it has a special and very different recent history of segregation.) Here I argue that the antecedents of the current growth in class segregation in Britain can be seen as early as the mid-1960s especially in voting records from around that time onwards. Figure 5.4, below, shows the first tiny increase in this form of segregation to have occurred in 1964. Compared to 1960s racial segregation and rioting in the US, what was happening in the UK was almost imperceptible change, but it was slow and steady change in one particular direction. By the end of the 1970s, economic polarisation was following that earlier rise in political segregation. This led to rising social polarisation, seen most clearly in rising spatial segregation between tenures and within the British housing market during the 1980s. The same occurred in the US. Poorer areas became residualised, while in rich areas house prices began to soar upwards, stumbled briefly in 1989, and then took off again.

During the 1990s wealth inequalities continued to grow, and next came consequential and huge rises in health inequalities. In the UK, this is what increasing class segregation resulted in. In the US, race may have been more important. In mainland Europe, no similar great rises in segregation were measured, and in some rich nations, processes of equalisation were taking place during this same period (Dorling 2012). In the UK for a few years in the early 2000s, it looked as if the rising segregation might be ending, but that again was just a stumble. The overall outcome has been increasingly 'different strokes for different folks' growing up in different neighbourhoods.

---

* Acknowledgements: An expanded version of this essay was first published in 2014 in the book *Social-spatial segregation: Concepts, processes and outcomes*, edited by Christopher D. Lloyd, Ian Shuttleworth and David Wong. Our thanks to the publisher, Policy Press and to Danny Dorling, for their permission to use this shorter version.

In Britain, and it can also be argued in the US, the implications of this rising segregation have been a growth in ignorance across the board: ignorance of poverty for the rich, ignorance by the poor of the true value of riches held by the few, and more and more people seeing themselves as average, while fewer are near to average. But that could be about to end, not with a bang, but with the hiss of wealth slowly but surely escaping out the value of assets, which themselves depend on segregation for their value: housing and land.

The Geography of Class Segregation

To be segregated is to be separated for part of the time. There are many ways in which such separation is possible, but it must always involve physical separation at some point to be geographical segregation. Boys can be segregated from girls in separate schools, even if it is almost impossible for them not to mix in families (Fuller et al. 2005). Servants and the upper classes can be segregated between floors of a country house, even if they must mix in that house for the service to occur. If people are completely segregated, between living in Myanmar and Thailand, for example, then they may be considered not as segregated, but as simply living in completely separate areas. For another example of where separation is not segregation: men on Mount Athos are not segregated from women, they are completely separated—no women are ever allowed on to the land of Mount Athos (see della Dora 2011).

Conversely, people who are taught together at school and who play together out of school are only segregated into different families, not castes or classes. Segregation is about mixing only part of the time, enough for the lack of mixing the rest of the time to be of lasting importance. In very mixed neighbourhoods, children play after school with other children outside of their families. Here, there is even less segregation than in areas where almost all children do not go to the nearest school to their home. The same can be true if adults from otherwise different social groups mix in workplaces, but also during recreation outside of work, on holiday or through where they shop. Segregation tends to be least at the start and end of life. In Sheffield, UK, there is only one maternity unit where almost all babies are born, and one city mortuary for any bodies to be held where anyone who has not been in the care of a doctor is taken.

The time during which people are segregated can be very long, and the amount of mixing that occurs can be very slight, but still enough for the segregation to be evident. People have only to mix ever so slightly to know that they are segregated. For example, people can spend almost all of their childhood living in areas where other people (*not* like them) do *not* live. They might only occasionally come across someone from a different social class, for instance, when a dignitary visits their estate, or they go to the doctor's. Alternatively, the farm labourers on the country estate of a very rich child might be the poorest of people that child ever sees, she rarely mixes with them, but she knows she is different because she sees them and occasionally hears them talking. While these two are extreme examples, it is worth asking much more generally just how differentiated lives in Britain and similar countries are today (Wilson and Keil 2008). In the US, race plays a larger part again. This further complicates the pictures of geographical segregation. Elsewhere, one religious group may see itself as above another, even if it is not always economically more prosperous.

Britain (excluding Northern Ireland) is useful to study because social class is so much more important than most other factors such as race or religion. Figure 5.1 (below) makes one attempt to show just how much the norms of British society alter by where people in Britain live. It is based on 2001 Census data. When the 2011 Census is released it will be possible to determine the extent to which the polarisation shown in Figure 5.1 has risen or fallen. Later in this chapter the changes since the 1971 Census, and from a little before even that time, are discussed. For now, Figure 5.1 divides the country into 1,282 areas of equal population size and colours each area by one of 15 shades. The shading of the areas is done according to what is normal in each place. The two extreme places are described below: first, the worst-off place, and then the best-off, and then the average place. In each case the number of disadvantages and then advantages are counted up using the following numerals in brackets: (1), (2) ... to (7). That is why these seven numbers appear oddly placed in brackets in each of the next three paragraphs—you need to count them up. You have to count to appreciate the depths of segregation.

In the worst-off places in Britain, *most* (1) infants live in a family where there is no car, and that is the case for all children living in these areas under the age of five. *Most* (2) children of school age live in families with almost no spare wealth, they would inherit almost nothing if their parents were to die, and this is the case for the majority of children in all the streets around them—it is simply normal. Here (3) *less than* a fifth of young adults will go to university, often as few as one in ten. If they go, they will rarely return. Of those adults who work (4), *the majority* work in a job that is described as either unskilled or semi-skilled. Often these jobs require a great deal of skill, for instance, making lunch for 200 youngsters at a school, but this is given the understated title 'dinner lady', with an equally understated pay packet, belying the skill required in the job. Between the ages of 40 and 59 in these areas (and also for people much older and younger), *most* (5) people live in housing owned by the council or a housing association and rent. Between the ages of 60 to 74, *most* (6) describe

CLASS SEGREGATION 71

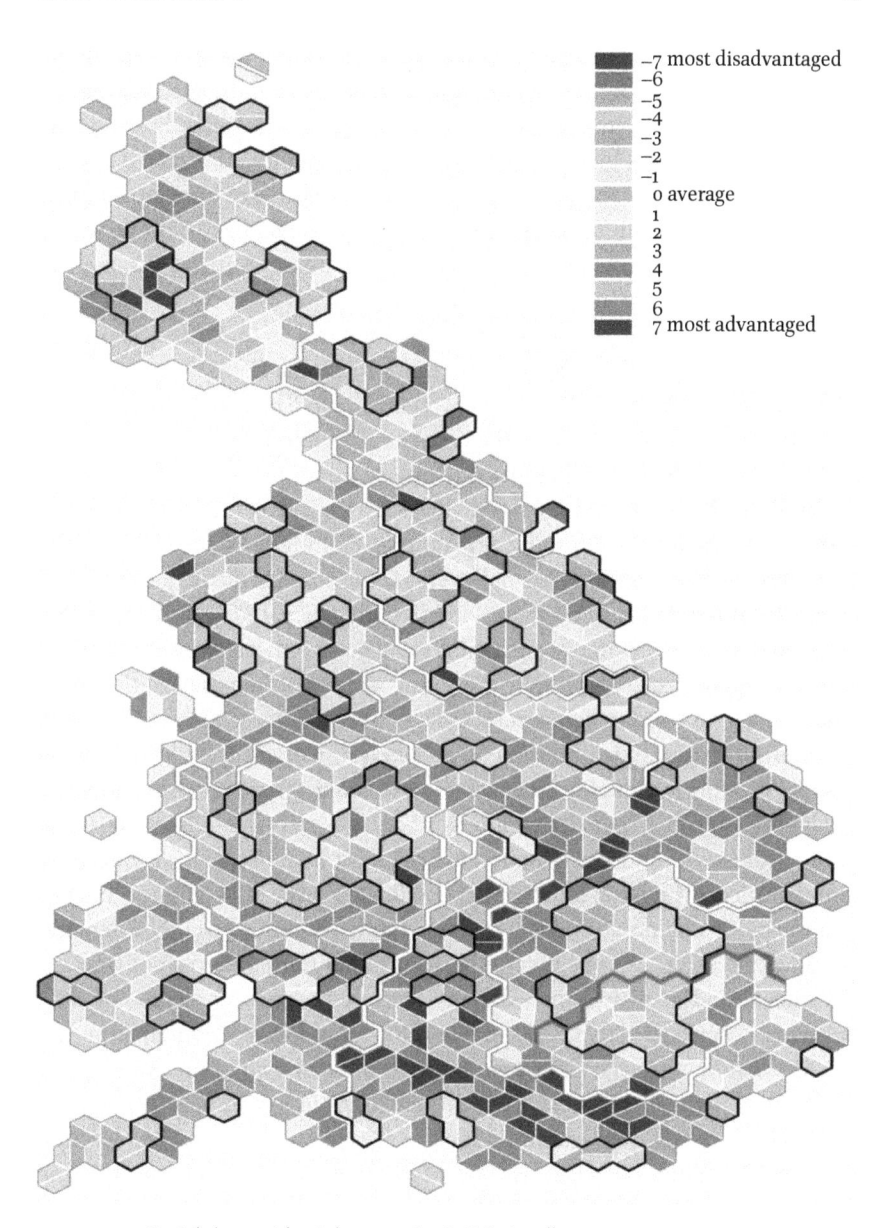

FIGURE 5.1 *Social class residential segregation in Britain, all ages, 2001.*
Note: This is a cartogram showing every parliamentary constituency in Britain as a hexagon with roughly similar populations and hence sizes. The divisions within each constituency are also shown by dividing each in half and colouring the two halves separately.
SOURCE: DORLING 2011.

their health as poor, because it is poor. *Most* (7) die under the age of 80. All the areas where all seven of these conditions are true are coloured darkest red.

In contrast to the most disadvantaged areas just described, in the many areas coloured darkest blue, the very opposite is most often the case. If you are reading this chapter—and you are British—you are likely to have grown up in the kind of place about to be described, a very unusual place, but one where what is nationally unusual is locally usual. If you are not British the same still applies, unless you are from a very equal country such as Norway, Japan, Denmark or the Netherlands, places where we can guess so much less about you from just knowing within that country where you come from.

In the best-off places in Britain *most* (1) infants live in a family where there are two or more cars and that is the case for all children living in these areas under the age of five. Most parents can almost always just hop in the car with their toddler. *Most* (2) children of school age in this type of area live in families with so much spare wealth that they would each inherit £54,000 and usually a lot more, if their parents were to die. This is the case for the majority of children in all the streets around them—it is simply normal to be rich here. Here (3) *more than* 40 per cent of young adults will go to university by age 19, often almost all go by age 30, especially the young women. When they go they then tend to move to London before returning to areas like these to have their own children. Of those adults who work (4) *the majority* work in a job that is grandly described as professional or management. Inflated salaries at the top end of the labour market means that some workers are overvalued. Many of those in the professions and management are seen, for instance, as receiving good remuneration for talking tough about 'leadership' over long paid-for lunches in an expenses-paid culture. In contrast, many workers whose jobs demand considerable skills, responsibility and commitment are undervalued and are not understood as possessing skills. *All* work requires some degree of skill, but what is currently labelled as highly skilled and low skilled may in future be seen as rather arbitrary. Between the ages of 40 and 59 in these areas, and much older and younger, *most* (5) people are living in homes they by now own outright—they hold property. Between the ages of 60 to 74, *most* (6) describe their health as good, because it is good. *Most* (7) die well over the age of 83, the women often in their nineties. All these areas where all seven of these conditions is true are coloured darkest blue.

So what is it to be 'normal', to live in a 'normal' area? Well, there is nothing normal about being normal in a highly class-segregated society. Most people are not normal but it is normal to be either better-off than average or worst-off—polarisation is the norm. Should you want to check whether the neighbourhood you live in is normal, then ask around and ensure that: (1) *most* children live in a family that has just one car; (2) *most* children of school age live in families with a little spare wealth so that average inheritances on sudden death of both parents would be £20,000–54,000—here, (3) *between* a fifth and two-fifths of young adults will go to university. Of those adults who work (4) *the majority* work in a job that is described in a 'levelling' way as either skilled manual or lower professional. Between the ages of 40 and 59 in these areas, (5) *most* people are renting privately and after that, the next largest group are paying a mortgage. Between the ages of 60 to 74, (6) *most* describe their health as fair. The average life expectancy (7) is around 80, 81 or 82 in all of these areas, although individuals in these areas are, of course, more varied in exactly when they die. Where all seven of these conditions is true, those areas are coloured grey. If you happen to be British and this fits your area and you also fit these boundaries, you are very unusual—you are normal. If you are not British, ask someone you know where they come from in Britain, and whether it mattered in terms of who they are now.

Figure 5.1 is a map of the spatial manifestation of growing social class segregation. In countries where car use is determined much more by need than by wealth, car users are more often found in the countryside, not among the affluent. In a highly class-segregated society you have access to many cars if you have much money. Your home has many rooms if you have much money, not if you have many people who need to sleep there. In Figure 5.1, each hexagon is a Westminster parliamentary constituency. These are the areas used to elect Members of Parliament (MPs). Each has been placed in the map so as to be as close to its original neighbours as possible. Each is also split in half along a line that best divides the poorer half of each constituency from its richer half. Often these two sides of each area will be quite similar. When that is the case the two halves tend to be coloured the same shade. However, sometimes there are great differences within a parliamentary constituency and this mapping technique helps to reveal some of that, as well as give the more populous cities the space they deserve in the overall impression gained.

Next, in Figure 5.2, is a non-geographical image of British society. All but one of the figures in this chapter are taken from the book, *Fair Play*, which allows me to avoid having to go into details about the sources or give many references to data and explanations of the statistics behind the figures. If you want to know more, go to the source. Carry on reading here if you want to hear an argument not interrupted by too much detail. So let's consider this particular image of British society, and ask how we got here.

Is this image fair, is it true, and are only half the population normal? Well, the figure for a quarter being poor and a tenth being very poor is very commonly quoted. About a quarter of people, especially children, do not have what

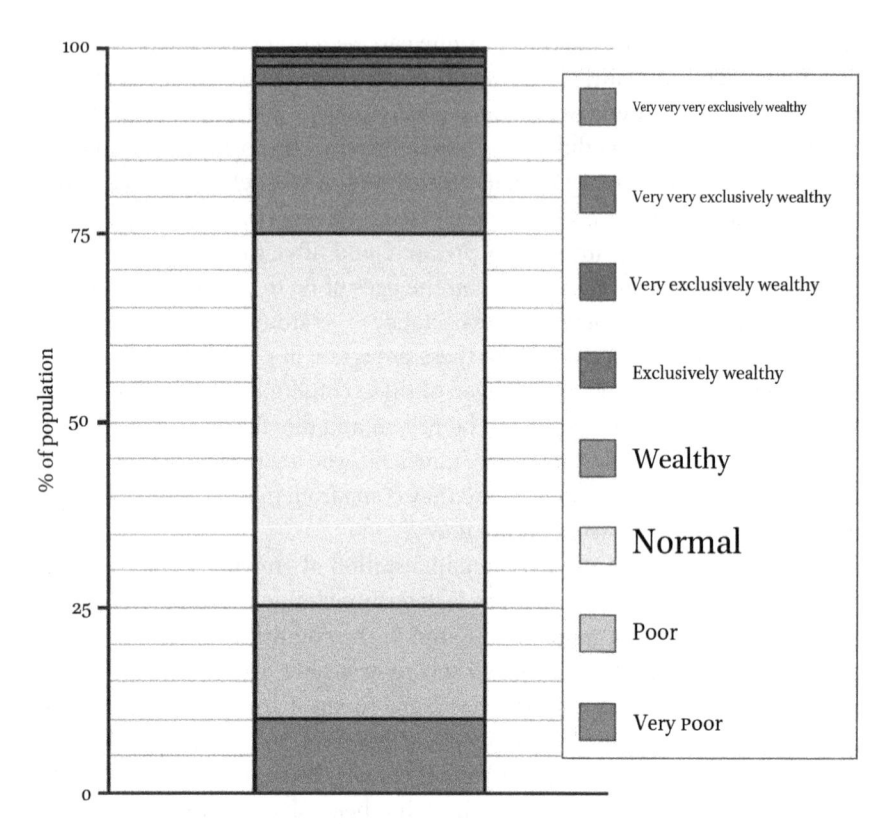

FIGURE 5.2 *Social class financial segregation in Britain, 2011.*
SOURCE: DORLING 2011, 162.

most people consider as essentials. They are unable to afford to take a holiday once a year, unless they stay at a family (such as grandparents') or friend's home. However, the image shown in Figure 5.2 is not based on actual numbers; it is more indicative than empirical, but it may well ring true. That is because just as about a quarter of us are poor (and rising), and a tenth of us are very poor (and rising rapidly), so, too, about a quarter of us are asset rich (and today will be much more so if we brought a home in the South East or London before 2005) and about a tenth are exclusively rich.

The statistics just quoted can simply be read off the chart below—Figure 5.3 is based on actual data rather than being schematic. But whether the numbers are based on reams of survey data, or are just how an academic says they see the world as being, the extent to which you believe the pictures you are about to be presented with might well depend as much on what you bring to this chapter as on what is within it. That is because, in a highly-divided class system, we all tend to have quite different but often firmly held views.

As inequality has risen in Britain, it has closed down much of the concern for others. One newspaper headline writer got it spot on in 2008: "As the middle classes feel the pain of comparison with the super-rich, we lose all enthusiasm for the common good" (Russell 2008). Then, in late 2011 it was revealed, using data from the British Social Attitudes Survey, that as British class segregation rose further: "Private education perpetuates a form of 'social apartheid' and has given rise to a political class drawn from a 'segregated elite' that does not understand or share the views of most people, the annual British Social Attitudes Survey warns on Wednesday" (Ramesh 2011). When the differences between people's life chances were falling, from the 1920s through to the late 1970s, these apartheid attitudes became less chilling. Only the last decade of these falls is shown in Figure 5.3 below.

The poor in Figure 5.3 are people excluded from the norms of society, with 'excluded' being as defined by the majority of the population. The exclusively rich are also defined in this way. The asset rich have substantial monies. If they were to drop dead today they would be liable for inheritance tax. In fact, less than a third of them ever pay that tax as they tend to spend most of their assets before death. In contrast the 'core poor' will hardly ever have held assets of any value. They are people seen as poor whether their assets, income or their own views are taken into account. They are poor by any definition.

How did we come to be so divided and why did the arrows shown in Figure 5.3 start to separate from 1980 onwards? One suggestion is that the separation in living standards followed another separation—an economic separation in life chances—and that separation itself followed a separation of beliefs and prejudices. Figure 5.4, shown next, provides data that backs up this point.

To understand Figure 5.4, you need to know that the Conservative (Tory) Party is Britain's most successful political party, the party that has held office the most times since 1920, and the one that has not much changed its identity. You also need to understand that a segregation index measures how geographically concentrated a group is, irrespective of how large that group is. Were Tory voters spread in the same way as the rest of the voters, so as to be found in equal proportion in every area of the country, the index would be 0 per cent. Were they all to be found in areas exclusively occupied by them (that is, other areas occupied exclusively by other groups), then the index would be 100 per cent. The index is the proportion that would have to move to other areas to spread the Tory voters around in the same way as the other voters. The areas used here are Westminster parliamentary constituencies, the smallest areas for which votes are revealed.

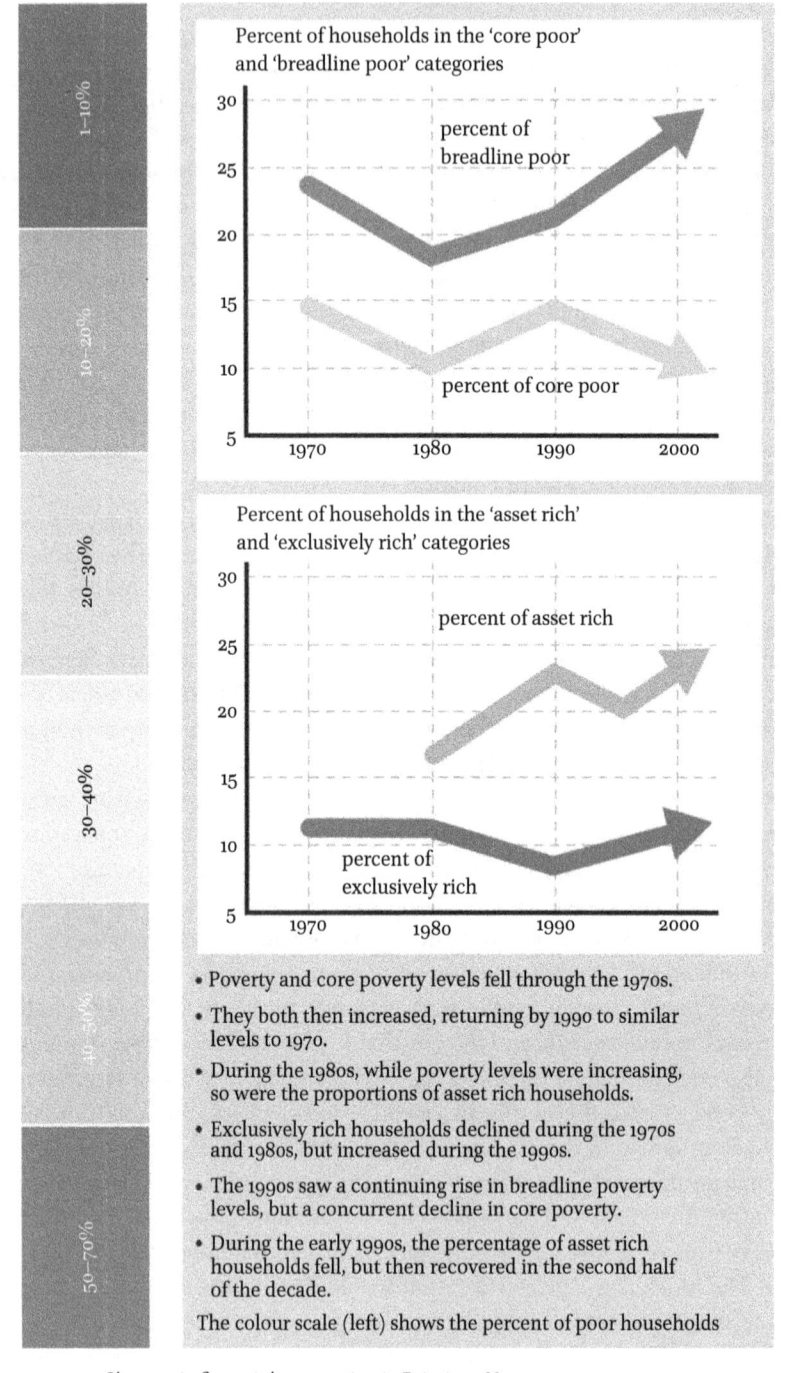

Percent of households in the 'core poor' and 'breadline poor' categories

Percent of households in the 'asset rich' and 'exclusively rich' categories

- Poverty and core poverty levels fell through the 1970s.
- They both then increased, returning by 1990 to similar levels to 1970.
- During the 1980s, while poverty levels were increasing, so were the proportions of asset rich households.
- Exclusively rich households declined during the 1970s and 1980s, but increased during the 1990s.
- The 1990s saw a continuing rise in breadline poverty levels, but a concurrent decline in core poverty.
- During the early 1990s, the percentage of asset rich households fell, but then recovered in the second half of the decade.

The colour scale (left) shows the percent of poor households

FIGURE 5.3 *Changes in financial segregation in Britain 1968–2005.*
SOURCE: DORLING 2011.

CLASS SEGREGATION

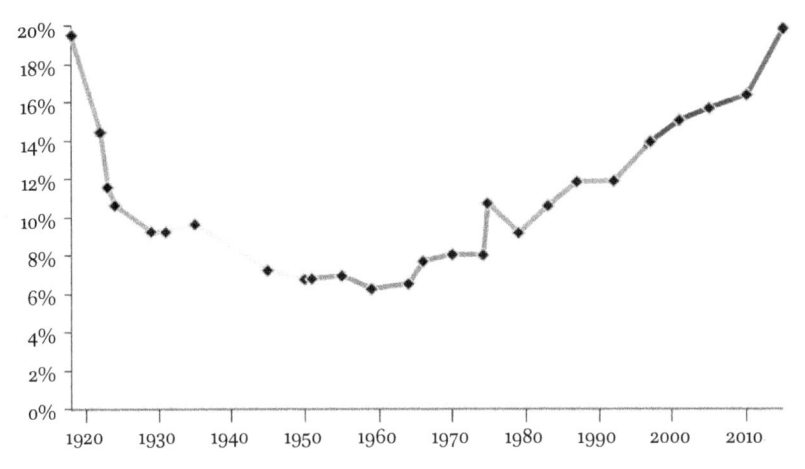

[Graph showing segregation index from 1920 to ~2015, declining from ~20% in 1920 to a low around 1960, then rising back to ~20% by 2015]

SOURCE: DRAWN INITIALLY IN DORLING, D. (2006) 'CLASS ALIGNMENT RENEWAL': *THE JOURNAL OF LABOUR POLITICS*, VOL. 41, NO. 1, P. 849, SHOWING THE SPATIAL SEGREGATION INDEX. UPDATED IN DORLING, D. (2013) CRISES AND TURNING POINTS: THE PIVOTS OF HISTORY, *RENEWAL*, 21, 4, PP. 11–20.

The Segregation Index of Conservative voters in Britain*, 1885–2015

Election	Concentration	Election	Concentration
1885	7.11%	1951	6.77%
1886	5.53%	1955	6.93%
1892	5.81%	1959	6.24%
1895	4.70%	1964	6.51%
1900	4.39%	1966	7.69%
1906	6.67%	1970	8.04%
1910 Dec	6.24%	1974 Feb	8.01%
1910 Jan	7.91%	1974 Oct	10.72%
1918	19.30%	1979	9.17%
1922	14.44%	1983	10.59%
1923	11.57%	1987	11.84%
1924	10.62%	1992	11.88%
1929	9.24%	1997	13.94%
1931	9.23%	2001	15.05%
1935	9.65%	2005	15.69%
1945	7.21%	2010	16.40%
1950	6.74%	2015	19.89%

*Northern Irish seats are not included.

FIGURE 5.4 *The segregation of political belief by area in Britain 1981–2015.*
Note: The statistic being measured is the segregation index of Conservative votes across all British seats at each general election. The proportion is the minimum number of votes who would have to be moved across constituency boundaries to ensure that within each parliamentary constituency the Conservatives received exactly the same share of the vote.
SOURCE: DORLING 2015.

Figure 5.4 shows the minimum number of Tory voters who have to be moved between parliamentary constituencies for an equal number to be allocated to every area. It is a segregation index. Tory segregation was at an all-time high in the strange 'Khaki Election' of 1918.[1] That segregation rate then fell, stumbling upwards only slightly in 1935 before falling again, right through to 1959. Where one lived in Britain mattered less and less for how one voted, but then something changed.

In 1963 Bob Dylan's worldwide hit 'Blowin' in the Wind' was released, and became one of the theme tunes of the American Civil Rights Movement. However, and in hindsight, things were blowing in another direction than that which Dylan imagined, in both the US and the UK. In 1964 there was a tiny rise in Tory voting segregation. It jumped up two years later in 1966, jumped again in October 1974, fell back with Margaret Thatcher's landslide in 1979, but then rose and rose and rose. South East England became progressively more and more Conservative as the rest of Britain went the other way. That political polarisation began before the other forms of polarisation we can measure by diverging health outcomes or rising economic inequalities. And it is hard not to think it is important that these events occurred in this order. By 2015 political segregation in the UK was greater than it had been at the previous 1918 peak.

Class segregation can rise as other forms of segregation fall. Civil rights were won in Britain as well as in the US from the mid-1960s onwards. Partly to try to mitigate some of the shame of imposing greater immigration controls Race Relations Acts of Parliament were passed to try and ensure greater fair play. More importantly, societal attitudes changed from extreme racism being very normal in the 1970s to it being a social gaff to be obviously racist by the 2000s.

Table 5.1, below, illustrates how class is many times more important than race in influencing one set of life chances, the chance of any individual child entering medical school. Someone from Social Class I (professional) parents is 6.76/0.28 = 24 times more likely to go to medical school than someone whose parents are unskilled. Someone who is Black and of Social Class I has 6.20/4.93 = 25.8 per cent higher chance than someone who is White. There are,

---

[1] The 1918 general election was known the khaki elections, due to the importance of demobilised soldiers, often still in uniform. A very large number of Liberal and Tory MPs stood on the same 'ticket'. They were literally issued a coupon by Lloyd George and the Conservative leader Bonar Law as candidates who had agreed to support the pair and hence Conservative voting may have appeared more segregated than it was as Conservatives could choose to vote for a coupon Liberal in many areas rather than a Conservative without a ticket or one unlikely to win locally. Almost a hundred years later the Conservative and Liberal party are again in coalition.

CLASS SEGREGATION

TABLE 5.1 *An example of segregation by race and class in Britain: Medical school.*

Ethnic group	% of UK population	% of medical school admissions	Selection ratio[a]	% of admissions from social classes I and II	Overall	I	II	III non-manual	III manual	IV	V
					\multicolumn{7}{c}{Standardised admission ratio by social class[b]}
Asian	4.2	25.5	0.55	60.5	6.07	41.73	5.41	3.83	3.29	3.56	5.15
Bangladeshi	0.5	0.9	0.40	48.0	1.80	9.82	1.27	1.89	NC	1.93	6.00
Indian	1.7	13.8	0.63	74.0	8.12	72.32	7.96	3.17	4.68	2.78	0.18
Pakistani	1.3	4.5	0.62	39.0	3.46	NC	5.29	3.71	2.71	2.25	3.08
Chinese	0.3	2.0	0.45	68.0	6.67	54.55	6.01	NC	9.02	2.86	NC
Other	0.4	4.3	0.51	73.6	10.75	127.05	3.63	6.96	NC	4.76	NC
Black	2.0	1.9	0.36	82.8	0.95	6.2	1.75	0.16	0.64	0.07	NC
African	0.9	1.4	0.34	70.0	1.56	12.25	1.63	0.24	1.83	0.37	NC
Caribbean	1.0	0.3	0.44	78.3	0.30	0.78	0.75	0.10	0.25	NC	NC
Other	0.1	0.2	0.39	100.0	2.00	18.18	3.92	NC	NC	NC	NC
White	92.2	67.6	0.52	79.5	0.73	4.93	1.22	0.27	0.32	0.13	0.05

TABLE 5.1 *An example of segregation by race and class in Britain: Medical school.* (cont.)

Ethnic group	% of UK population	% of medical school admissions	Selection ratio[a]	% of admissions from social classes I and II	Standardised admission ratio by social class[b]				
					Overall	I	II	III non-manual	III manual	IV	V

Ethnic group	% of UK population	% of medical school admissions	Selection ratio[a]	% of admissions from social classes I and II	Overall	I	II	III non-manual	III manual	IV	V
Other	0.6	3.0	0.6	72.6	5.00	53.64	2.67	2.38	4.71	1.21	NC
Not known	0.2	2.0	0.40	NA	10.00	9.82	1.27	1.89	NC	1.93	6.00
Total	100	100	0.63	72.5	1.00	6376	1.38	0.41	0.42	0.28	0.20

SOURCE: DORLING 2011, 124.
a Selection ratio = admissions as a proportion of applications
b Some ratio are high as the ratios are based on very small denominations
NA = Data not available. NC = Not calculated because there were no pupils in the subgroup.

of course, far fewer Social Class 1 Black children. Class differences are almost 100 times higher than race differences, as 24 times is 2,500 per cent.

The class segregation involved in access to higher education is huge, with these multiples of thousands of percentages at the extremes. In contrast, the geographical inequalities can appear much less, as shown in Figure 5.5 below. However, this figure includes everyone going to university, not just those going to medical school, and it also includes everyone from every class, not just the two extremes. The metropolitan North, the Black Country (an area of the English West Midlands north and west of Birmingham and south and east of Wolverhampton), the East End of London (within area 38 shown in the figure) and the Norfolk coast fair worse, while the golden bowl of the North Western Home Countries (including Buckinghamshire, Hertfordshire, Berkshire and Surrey), coupled with parts of Cheshire and North Yorkshire, fare best. Underlying the map in Figure 5.5 are class differences in educational chances, but also other effects, such as a low number of immigrants harming overall chances for particular areas. Immigrants tend to have more 'get up and go', and so areas such as London do better despite more poverty at its heart.

Figure 5.5 contains both a normal map showing the rate at which people aged 18 and 19 go to university from each county in England, and a population cartogram, inset, of the same areas showing the same rates, but with the circles drawn in proportion to population, not land area. A relatively small area in population terms, such as North Yorkshire (area number 6) is over-emphasised on the normal map. The large majority of those going to university from each area shown in Figure 5.5 are middle class before they go. Almost all are middle class once they have gone, although many continue to identify with working class origins long after having passed through the middle class-making machine—that is the modern university.

Before taking too seriously the idea that universities provide social class changing opportunities, it is worth noting that, on average, from the poorest 20 per cent of wards in the country, only 4 children out of a class of 30 used to go to university. The New Labour government did improve that statistic, by a (deceptively) massive 25 per cent. That rise appears high in per cent terms but is small in absolute effect, because it amounted to only 1 extra child in each class of 30 children from poorer areas going to university by the time Labour left power. They invested a huge amount of money across the country's schools, some of which did improve the services provided to children in those schools in the worse-off areas. They started an Educational Maintenance Allowance scheme, much more of which found its way to those areas, and helped young people stay on at school at ages 16 and 17. Most importantly they encouraged universities to become less discriminating to working class children.

As a result, by 2010, instead of 4 out of 30 children from the poorest fifth of areas going to university, 5 out of 30 went. Although a 25 per cent increase on a low number is not necessarily a huge influx, New Labour claim this as one of their greatest achievements (Dorling 2011, 147). It certainly angered some people on the political right who thought that too many of these children were being allowed into universities. The right-wing press has often claimed that 'dumbing down' was occurring. Only in a country as socially divided as the UK could the provision of an additional university place for the 5th most able child in a class of 30 children be seen as dumbing down. But before becoming too

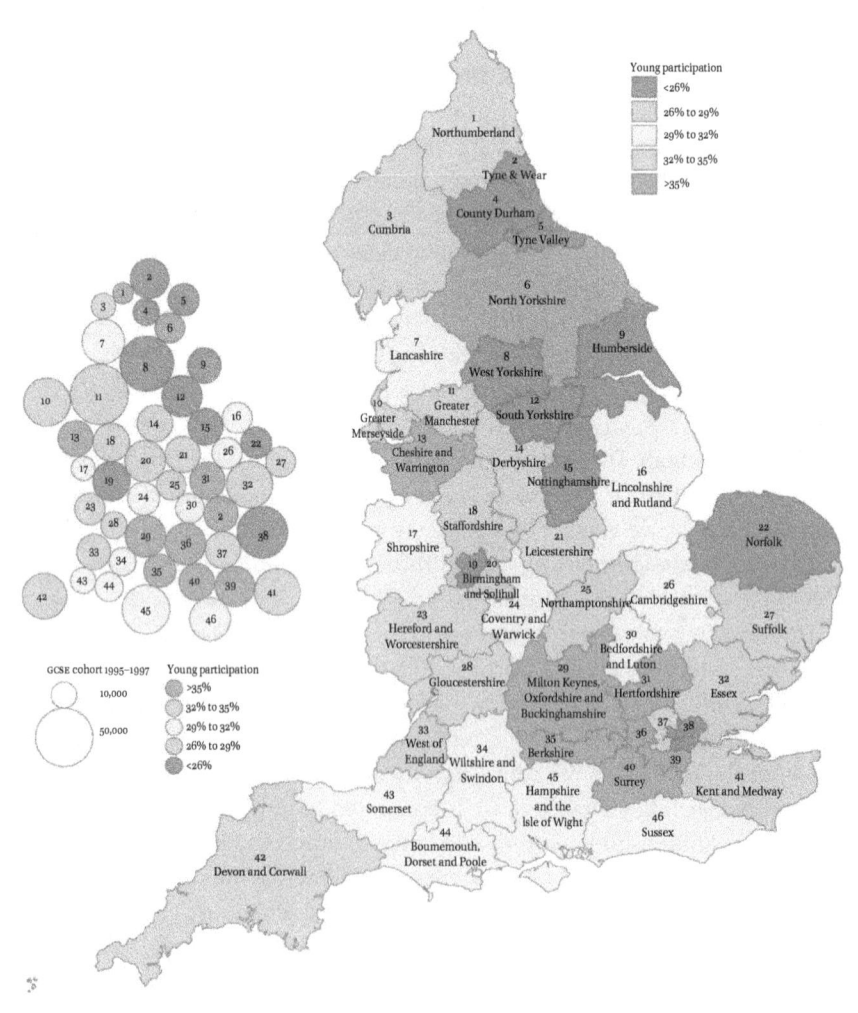

FIGURE 5.5 *The English geography of class segregation in education, 2005.*
SOURCE: DORLING 2011, 143.

caught up in these slight changes in slight chances, it is worth sitting back and considering how the UK compares to other countries when it comes to income inequality, social mobility and educational mobility.

Figure 5.6 provides a summary that essentially implies that the UK has a very rigid class structure, high income inequality and little mobility between income groups, but that all this is not the fault of its education systems (the education system actually provides more mobility than that in Norway or Germany). It is just that children in Britain start off far more unequal in the first place, and the education system can, in general, only do a little to alleviate that. The axis labelled 'income immobility' in the figure is a measure of social mobility that compares how easy it is to predict the income of an adult from that of their parents when their parents were the same age. Brazil has the lowest social mobility and Denmark the highest.

The rigidity of the UK class system is thus comparable to the rigidity of society in the US. Social mobility is even lower and income inequality even higher in the US than in the UK. Because in the dim and distant past (about 150 years ago and more) these inequalities were much lower in the US for people who were not slaves or their children a myth of opportunity emerged in the US which has remained. This was also substantiated by the US being an actual

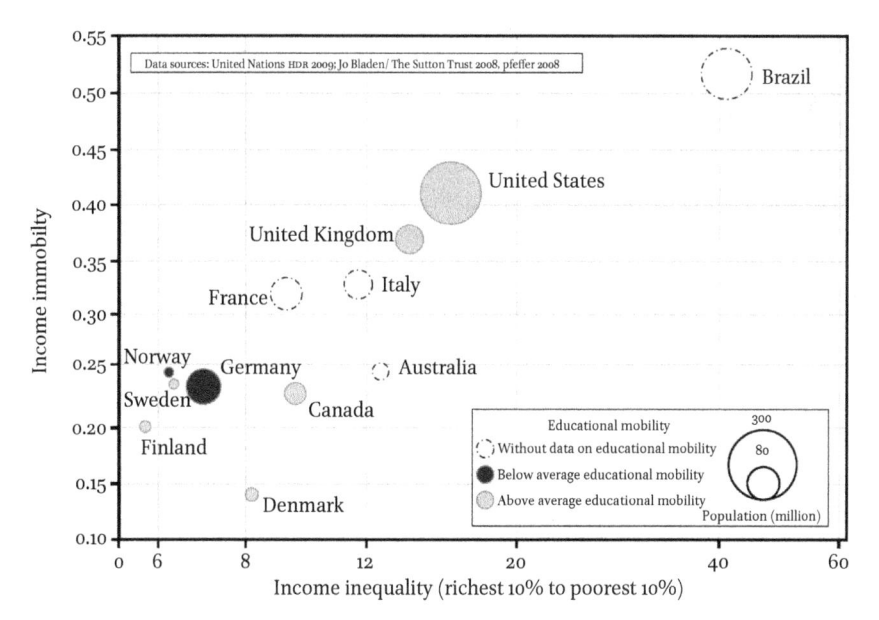

FIGURE 5.6 *Social mobility, income inequality and education mobility, selected countries, 2008–2009.*
SOURCE: DORLING 2011, 158.

destination of great upwards mobility for people emigrating from Europe at the time, and for a few decades later. The US high school system, a largely comprehensive and nationalised state education system, also helps maintain a sense of some fairness in a land of very low opportunities. However, what Figure 5.6 also shows is that in comparison to the only non-rich world country shown, opportunities for more equality in income and social mobility are far higher in the US than in Brazil.

Worldwide income inequalities have been growing, creating a new kind of global class divide. This is illustrated in Figure 5.7 which shows how, compared to world average household income, incomes in first Europe and then North America and then Japan pulled away and upwards, leaving the Near East, South America and Eastern Europe behind the average. In recent decades the Far East and China have seen average incomes rise to join this average group, leaving Northern and South-eastern Africa behind, areas joined by a rising but previously more impoverished India (made relatively much poorer from 1800 onwards with colonialism and continuing to rise). Central Africa continues to plummet in relation to the world average, incomes falling to a tenth of that average by the turn of the millennium, in contrast to nearer 10 times the average in the most affluent places.

One trend worth pointing out in Figure 5.7 is the lost decade for the Japanese at the very end of the period (the big dip in the line for Japan). This has now become two lost decades, and it looks as if North America and Europe may also be about to lose decades. In terms of worldwide class/income divides this is a reduction in global inequality. The extent to which the world is currently unequal in terms of income distribution is illustrated in Figures 5.8a and 5.8b below. These global inequalities are now having a great effect on class segregation within Britain. As the income gap between continents and regions has grown over time, for instance, between Greater India (India defined according to its 1900 old borders) and Western Europe, people migrating into Western Europe from many parts of the Indian subcontinent would, on average, find themselves entering British society at a lower and lower initial entry point. In contrast, as North America rose from being well below the global average income earning economy in 1600, surpassing Western Europe in the 1850s, immigrants to Britain from the US from then on would tend to enter far higher up in the British class hierarchy. The greatest concentration of American-born children in Britain is now found around Hyde Park and Mayfair in London. Figures 5.8a and 5.8b illustrate why the relationships between particular groups of people entering Britain from particular countries tend to be as they are.

CLASS SEGREGATION 85

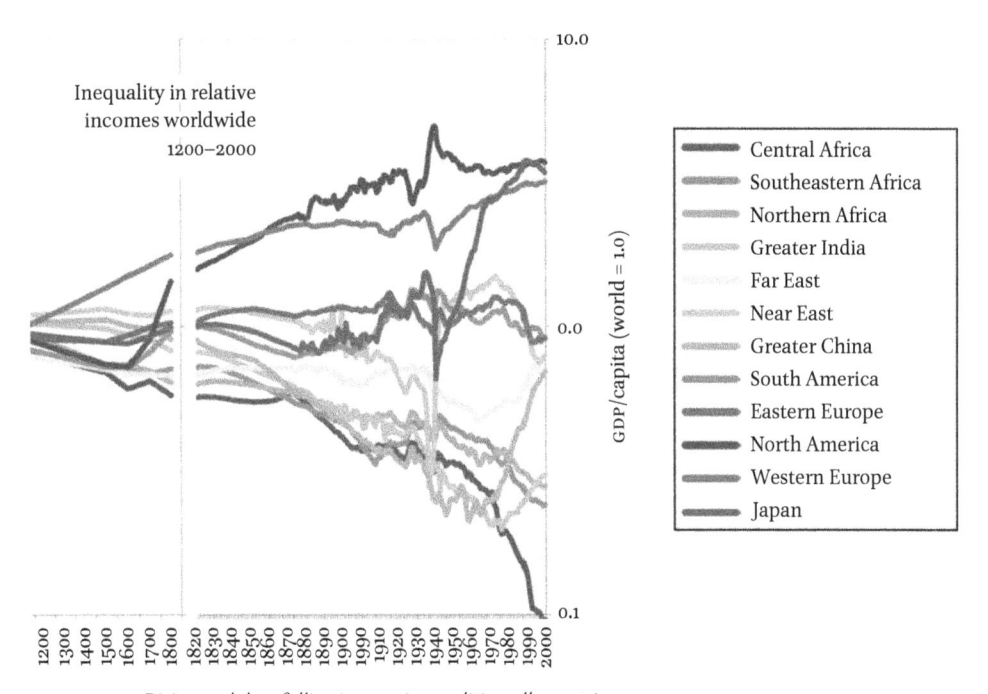

FIGURE 5.7 *Rising and then falling income inequalities, all countries, 1200–2000.*
SOURCE: DORLING 2011, 323.

There is great inequality within many countries, and so just because someone arrives from one particular country, this does not directly imply that they are either rich or poor, but in aggregate, different immigrant groups tend to be slotted into the class structure at particular points because of these (until recently) growing global divides. The two figures that make up Figure 5.8 (a and b) are both population cartograms. Each country is drawn with its area made to be proportional to the values being mapped.

The world is hugely unequal, and that inequality has been growing for centuries. As a result, just three areas dominate the cartogram of global GDP: North America, Western Europe and Japan/China. These countries form the three circles of wealth in Figure 5.8a above. The particular kind of class segregation found within Britain today is as a result of its position on the edge of one of those circles. Poorer countries tend to have far greater inequalities.

Figure 5.8b shows the world shaped by poverty, in this case poverty as revealed through the numbers of people who are undernourished. Inequalities in most of the countries drawn large here tend to be far greater than those

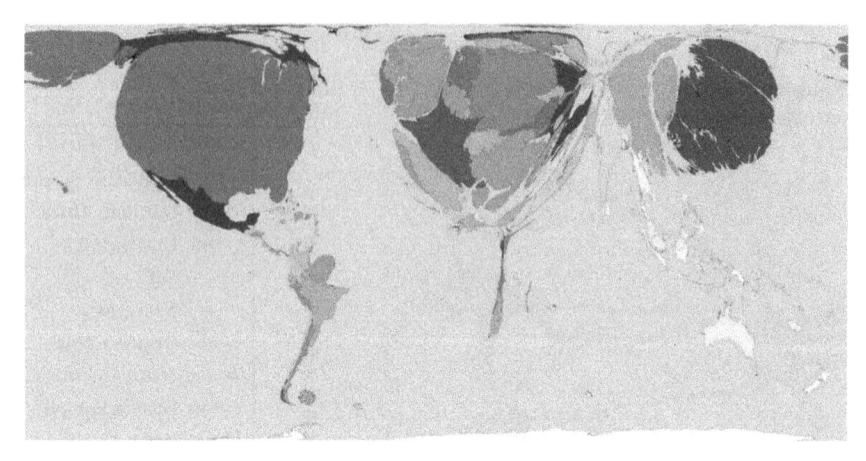

FIGURE 5.8A   *Inequality in wealth, international, GDP, 2002.*
SOURCE: DORLING 2011,135.

FIGURE 5.8B   *Inequality in food international, undernourishment, 2002.*
SOURCE: DORLING 2011, 135.

found within the richer countries. Income inequalities between people are found to be lowest in Cuba and China (note that the data were for 2002) and highest in South Africa and Brazil. The most unequal of the rich countries can also be seen in the map of undernourishment as millions are still going hungry in the US. Compare Eastern Europe to the UK to see one reason why there has been migration into the lower parts of the British class hierarchy from Eastern Europe in recent years. And look at how Eastern Europe has fared economically since 1989 (see Figure 5.7).

CLASS SEGREGATION 87

It takes a greatly divided world for immigration status to become so linked to class at the top and bottom of the class scale, but it also takes the country into which immigrants are entering to be highly divided for there to be extra places at the bottom and top of that scale to be populated. Figure 5.9 shows how the proportion of all income received by the best-off 1 per cent in Britain fell from 1918 through to 1979 and then rose relentlessly. The best-off 1% took a greater and greater share of national income almost every year from 1979 through to 2014 by which time their share had both risen to 15% and was rising faster than in any earlier year according to HMR estimates. After paying tax, about a third of their income, their share of total national income rose from 8.2% in 2012–13 to 9.8% in 2013–14 (Wintour 2014). Note that Figure 5.9 is based on a different data series which considers inequalities between households which are greater still. It fell like this in most countries, but then only rose as high again in a few countries, particularly in the UK and US. In the UK it is currently rising rapidly back to its 1918 peak as average incomes are falling in relation to inflation and incomes at the top are continuing to climb rapidly. Taxation now mutes the inequalities a little, but in the past it was used to mute them far more. Today the highest earning 1% of individuals pay about a third of all their income in tax reducing their take-home share from around 15% to just under 10%. Income tax rates were much higher for most of the period when income inequalities were falling. High taxation of very high incomes helped deter greed.

Guardian journalist and former newspaper editor Peter Wilby asked the obvious question about all this in May 2011:

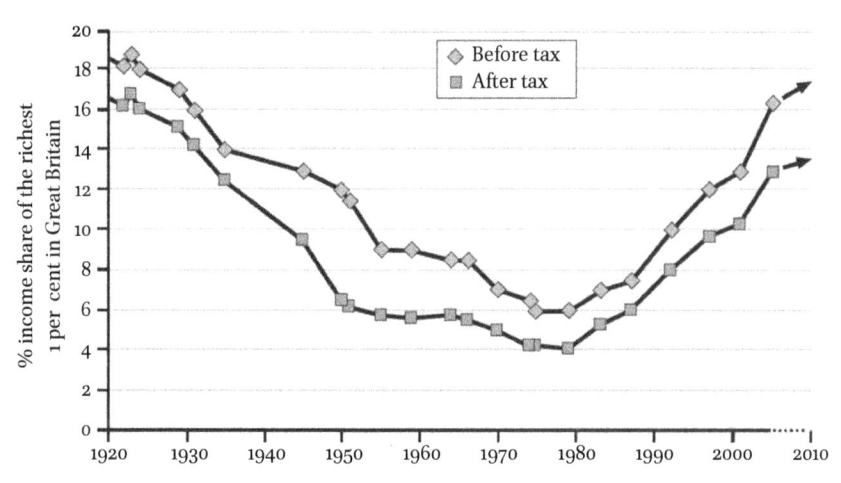

FIGURE 5.9 *Inequality in income in Britain, top 1%, 1918–2011.*
SOURCE: DORLING 2011, 70.

> Why aren't we more angry? Why isn't blood running, metaphorically at least, in the streets? Evidence of how the rich prosper while everyone else struggles with inflation, public spending cuts and static wages arrives almost daily. The Institute for Fiscal Studies reports that last year incomes among the top 1% grew at the fastest rate in a decade. According to the Sunday Times Rich List, the top 1,000 are £60.2bn better off this year than in 2010, bringing their collective wealth close to the record pre-recession levels.
>
> WILBY, 2011

He concluded:

> This generation of the middle classes has internalised the values of individualist aspiration, as zealously propagated by Tony Blair as by Margaret Thatcher. It does not look to the application of social justice to improve its lot. It expects to rely on its own efforts to get ahead and, crucially, to maintain its position. As psychologists will tell you, fear of loss is more powerful than the prospect of gain. The struggling middle classes look down more anxiously than they look up, particularly in recession and sluggish recovery. Polls show they dislike high income inequalities but are lukewarm about redistribution. They worry that they are unlikely to benefit and may even lose from it; and worse still, those below them will be pulled up sufficiently to threaten their status. This is exactly the mindset in the US, where individualist values are more deeply embedded. Americans accepted tax cuts for the rich with equanimity. Better to let the rich keep their money, they calculated, than to have it benefit economic and social inferiors.

In other affluent countries people think in different ways to the British who have become habituated to high levels of inequality over a long time. If you were born after 1989 then you have known nothing else. Figure 5.10 shows how abruptly inequalities rose in Britain during the 1980s.

High income inequality means high and rising inequalities in wealth and growing poverty, but poverty for other people if you do not live in poor areas. As the rich become more and more segregated from the poor in Britain rising poverty affects their daily lives less and less. This is easily illustrated if the fortunes of people living in the seats of 1997 Labour Cabinet ministers are compared to the fortunes of those living in the seats of the then Conservative Shadow Cabinet. Labour was traditionally the political party of the poor in Britain and the Conservatives were the party of the rich. For every 100 people

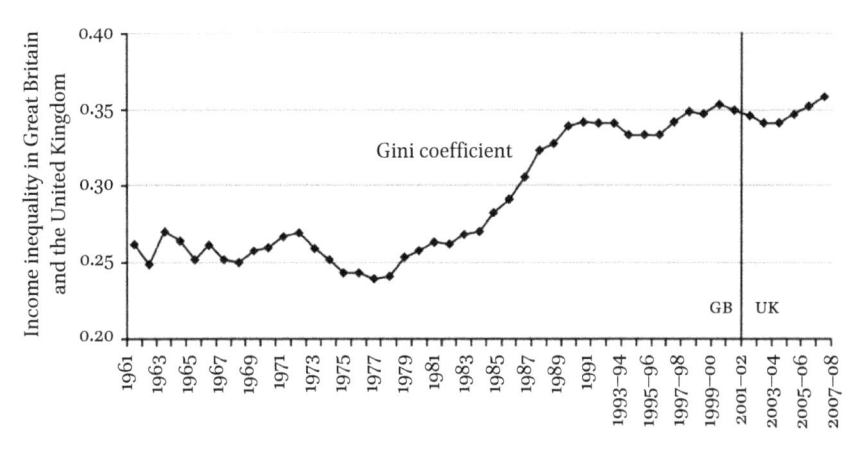

FIGURE 5.10 *Inequality in income in Britain, GINI, 1961–2008.*
SOURCE: DORLING 2011, 69.

who were poor in 1991 in those Conservative strong holds, 197 were poor in traditional Labour areas. That rose to 201 by 2001.

Much more dramatic was the move away of wealth from Labour areas between 1991 and 2001. For every 100 people who were wealthy in Conservative areas in 1991, 29 were wealthy in Labour areas. That fell to 22 by 2001. All this is shown in Table 5.2, as are the numbers of intermediate areas. Labour came to power in the face of high and rising inequalities, including those measured by income and wealth, and hence, growing class segregation. Initially it muted slightly the previous Conservative administration's celebration of inequality, partly because its ministers were still finding their feet and sorting out trouble-makers from among the back benches. Labour policies on education did reduce gaps a little, but in general they allowed division to continue to grow, and the spatial outcomes reflect that.

Conclusion

Almost all affluent societies in the world are less class-ridden than Britain. The segregation of people by social class in Britain is so acute that we tend to think of it as normal. Just as a White American in 1950s Mississippi might have thought it normal to eat in a Whites-only cafe and to sit at the front of the bus and never socialise with Black Americans so, in class-segregated Britain, we are increasingly tending to 'stick to our own'. We have schools for our social class, universities for our social class (or no university), jobs for our social class,

TABLE 5.2 *Class residential segregation in Britain, 1997–2005 (%).*

Constituencies grouped by the political post held by the MP elected for each seat immediately after the 1997 General Election	Cabinet Minister	Government Minister (non-cabinet)	Government Backbench	Non-Tory Opposition (Lib Dem/PC/SNP)	Conservative Backbench	Conservative Shadow Cabinet
Breadline poor latest estimates (at time of publication this was 2001)	201%	178%	133%	127%	103%	100%
Breadline poor 1991 estimates	197%	173%	127%	125%	101%	100%
Asset wealthy latest estimates (at time of publication this was 2001)	22%	26%	61%	84%	107%	100%
Asset wealthy 1991 estimates	29%	39%	76%	94%	119%	100%

SOURCE: DORLING 2011, 20.

housing estates, holidays, clothes, hobbies, even jokes for one social class and not another. And all this is becoming more and more established, but it is also becoming more noticed and resented by many.

In Japan, over the course of the last 20 years, housing and land prices have been falling every year (Allen 2011; Nakaya 2011). Close to the heart of the British class system is land and the wealth stored in housing. At one point recently, half of all personal wealth in Britain was held in the form of housing equity, but only by the minority who own property or the shrinking group who were purchasing it. That proportion has now fallen as, outside of London and the South East, housing and land values have been falling. When the property bubble finally bursts it tends, as the Japanese experiences have shown, to carry on deflating year after year. If we come together in future in Britain, it is more likely to be with a long, slow, hissing sound, as the land and housing markets gradually lose momentum, rather than with a bang. It is possible to imagine one can hear that noise beginning today, but to be sure that class segregation is reducing, wait until there is any evident sign of the value of property in London falling, and those falls being sustained; at present there is precious little sign of that.

References

Allen, K. (2011) Will UK property prices weather a new recession? *The Guardian*. London, 9 October.

Della Dora, V. (2011) *Imagining Mount Athos*. Virginia: University of Virginia Press.

Dorling, D. (2006) Class alignment renewal. *The Journal of Labour Politics*. 14 (1): 8–19.

Dorling, D. (2011) *Fair Play*. Bristol: Policy Press.

Dorling, D. (2012) *The no-nonsense guide to equality*. Oxford: New Internationalist.

Dorling, D. (2015) *Injustice*. Bristol: Policy Press.

Fuller, A., Beck, V. et al. (2005) *Employers, young people and gender segregation*. EOC Working Paper Series (number 28). London, Equal Opportunities Commission.

Nakaya, T. (2011) Personal communication. And see: http://tochi.mlit.go.jp/english/land/01-02_21k.pdf. See page 25 headed by 'Nationwide accumulated land price changes'.

Ramesh, R. (2011) Private schools fuel division in society, politics and pay, says study, *The Guardian*. London, 7 December.

Russell, J. (2008). Inequality is closing down our concern for others: As the middle classes feel the pain of comparison with the superrich, we lose all enthusiasm for the common good, *The Guardian*. London, 18 January.

Wilby, P. (2011). Anxiety keeps the super-rich safe from middle-class rage, *The Guardian,* London, 18 May.

Wilson, D. and Keil, R. (2008) The real creative class. *Social and Cultural Geography.* 9 (8) : 841–847.

Wintour, P. (2014) Labour reveals tax data showing UK economic growth "only helps top 1%". *The Guardian,* 13 May, http://www.theguardian.com/politics/2014/may/13/labour-tax-data-showsgrowth-helps-top-1-percent.

CHAPTER 6

The 'Secret' of the Restoration: Increased Class Exploitation

Maurizio Donato and Roberto Taddeo

> Within the capitalist system all methods for raising the social productivity of labour are put into effect at the cost of the individual worker [...] All means for the development of production undergo a dialectical inversion so that they become a means of domination and exploitation of the producers; they distort the worker into a fragment of a man, they degrade him to the level of an appendage of a machine, they destroy the actual content of his labour by turning it into a torment, they alienate from him the intellectual potentialities of the labour process [...], they transform his life into working-time, and his wife and child beneath the wheels of the juggernaut of capital. But all methods of the production of surplus-value are at the same time methods of accumulation, and every extension of accumulation becomes, conversely, a means for the development of these methods. It follows therefore that in proportion as capital accumulates, the situation of the worker be his payment high or low must grow worse.
>
> KARL MARX, *Das Kapital: Kritik der politischen Ökonomie* (1992, 799)

∴

Introduction

Following Marxist theory, the mass of surplus value in a given period of time is obtained by multiplying the number of workers by the surplus value rate.[1] So, the total number of workers employed (or the total number of hours worked) is the first step we have to take in order to analyze the dynamics of the exploitation of the global working class.

---

1 Following Marx, we identify the surplus value rate with the level of exploitation of labour (Karl Marx, 1993a, 275).

We place exploitation at the center of our analysis because we believe that the increase in surplus value has been the peculiar characteristic, the secret of the 'years of restoration'.[2]

We will try to show how the new working class[3] emerging from three decades of restoration is more numerous, despite rumours concerning the alleged 'end of the working class', is more 'global', with a greater relative weight of the newly industrialized countries, and characterized by levels of productivity that was not matched by an equivalent upward trend of wages: this means more exploitation, more surplus value as a global mass, and as a rate.

According to International Labour Office data (ILO 2014) in 1991 there were 2.2bn people globally working and producing value (and surplus value); in 2014 there were 3.3bn: as a result the global workforce has risen by 1bn in the last 23 years. In absolute terms, between 1991 and 2007 global employment grew at an annual rate of 1.7%, though since the outbreak of the financial crisis, the pace has slowed to 1.2% per annum.

The employment trend is more pronounced in the industrial sector and this indicates that, in the global economy, not only are there more employees, but more industrial workers, a reconfigured working class. In a dualistic—or at least heavily layered—capitalistic mode of production, the increase of exploitation has occurred in different ways both in the dominant countries[4] and in the countries dominated by imperialism. A figure makes clear the centrality and importance of the new geography drawn by the relocation of the transnational chains of value: just over 10% of the global labour force is working in the old industrialized countries; as we will see the new working class propels not only capital accumulation, but also the trend of global wages.

In the 1990's the process of industrialization in many countries once predominantly agricultural has made a big leap forward assuming a size and significance of historic proportions. The new international division of labour[5] is the result of a thirty year dynamic that has disrupted the world market with important consequences for the global trend of employment and wages. In the old industrialized countries employment and relative wages have fallen, but the other side of this enormous process of relocation of international production has been—as is inevitable—the creation of a new young section of the international working class, mainly in Asia and particularly in China.

---

2 The reference is to the *Historical materialism* conference *Revolution and Restoration,* Rome, 17-18-19 September 2015.
3 New in terms of its geographical composition as well as the workers' countries of origin.
4 For a definition of dominant States and States dominated by imperialism, see G. Pala (1999, 63).
5 See on this issue, Donato M. and Pala G. (1999, 70–74).

A considerable part of the growth of this new labour force has been determined by the trend toward relocation of many manufacturing activities from the mature capitalist countries. This phenomenon in part explains the (relative) decrease of employment in the industrial sectors of these countries. But it did not occur only because of this trend otherwise we would have a compensation and a zero balance in the number of employed, while globally there was an employment growth rate of about 50%. The displacement of entire productive sectors to emerging countries stimulated the creation of new production, both to feed the outsourced factories and government spending, and to meet the new local demand caused by the growth of the local working class and of the other social classes with their new needs.

In mature capitalist countries, the labour force has radically changed. Together with the transformations in the spatial sense of the value chains, the process of production and valorization has involved the technological restructuring and reorganization of work processes. Many activities previously carried out within a single company or even in the same plant have been outsourced. We are referring not only to stages of industrial production, but also—and, perhaps, above all—to service activities, ranging from logistics to general administration, from security to trade. When these activities were carried out within companies, they were considered industrial in statistics, while at present this does not appear to be the case. If the statistics took account of the 'global value chains', much employment would still be part of 'industry'. Bearing in mind this observation, we can hypothesize that the reduction of employment recorded in mature capitalist countries is actually less pronounced than might be indicated by official statistics; it is rather more correct to observe that the new employment conditions are different from the past in its qualitative characteristics, first of all in relation to its insecurity and flexibility.

So, total employment (Figure 6.1) grew globally, but, if we consider instead the rates of growth of the employment in the advanced economies, the picture is somewhat different: the employment trend is decreasing, and this phenomenon is common to the main economic areas, from the '80s to the present, though with some differences.

Working Hours, Flexibility and Job Insecurity

Before analyzing some statistics related to the trend of the hours worked, some preliminary considerations. When we observe the decline in hours worked, it is difficult to determine in advance whether the reduction is due to a crisis situation, or—as in the case of many more or less developed countries—to a widespread use of part-time work (Figure 6.2).

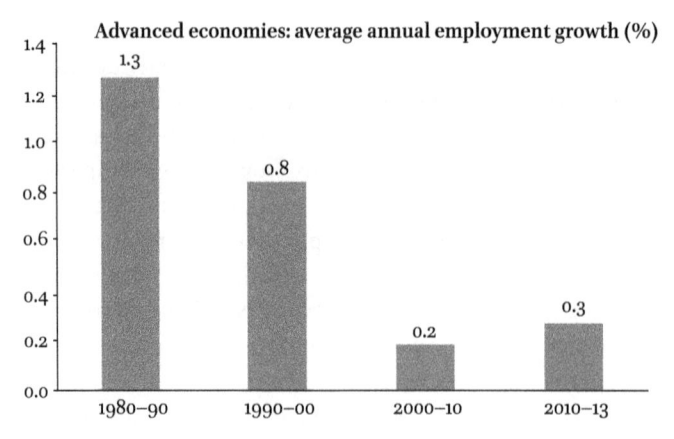

FIGURE 6.1 *Employment in advanced economies (average annual growth).*
SOURCE: INTERNATIONAL LABOUR ORGANIZATION.

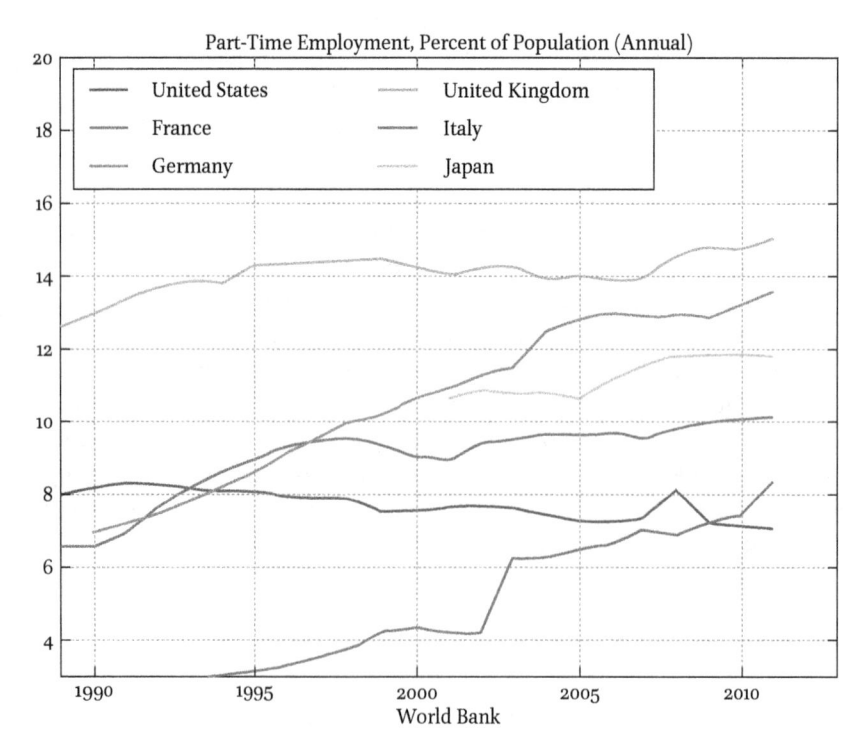

FIGURE 6.2 *Part-time employment, percent of population.*
SOURCE: WORLD BANK.

THE 'SECRET' OF THE RESTORATION 97

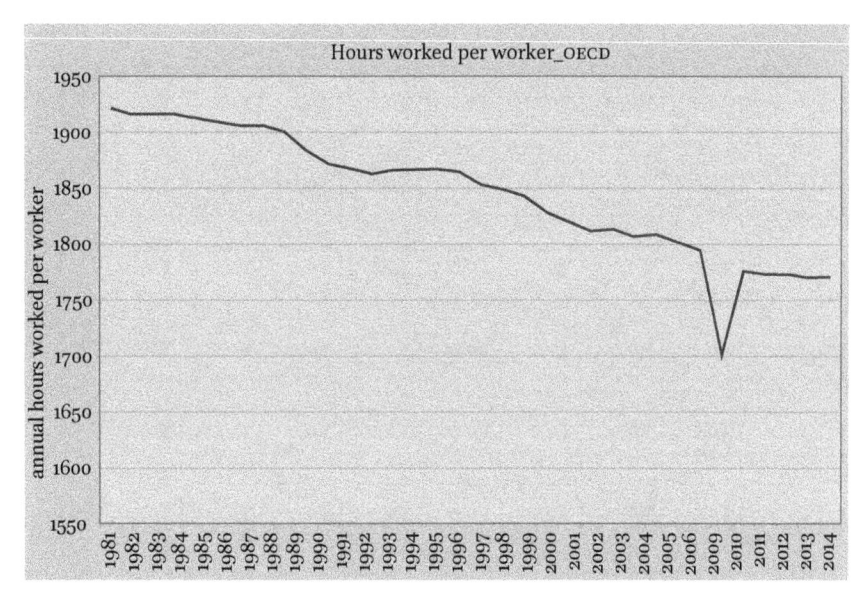

FIGURE 6.3 *Annual hours worked per worker in OECD countries.*
SOURCE: AUTHOR ELABORATIONS ON OECD DATA.

In general terms, the annual hours worked per worker in all the OECD countries in the period 1981–2014 are decreasing. There was an initial period of slow decline (the 80s), a second—short one—characterized by a more marked decline, followed by a period in which—in the presence of a recession—the hours worked per worker slightly rose. In the second half of the 1990s the hours worked continue to decline, until the outbreak of the great depression, after which the trend seems to stabilize. Overall, the hours worked annually per worker (Figure 6.3) fell in 33 years by about 7%.

Again, we must underline the difference between the different countries in relation to their level of development, their position in the hierarchy of the international division of labour and the more or less recent spread of the industrialization processes. As indicated by the International Labour Office, (ILO 2011, 7) it is not easy to compare the working hours between countries because of different methods of calculation used, but even with this warning it seems to us that the data indicates a clear negative difference in hours worked in economically weaker countries. This difference is confirmed by the comparison with the years preceding and subsequent to 2009 (Figure 6.4).

In the newly industrialized countries, the management of working time is usually very elastic and, even in the face of legal schedules which do not differ much from those of more developed countries, these can be modified on the

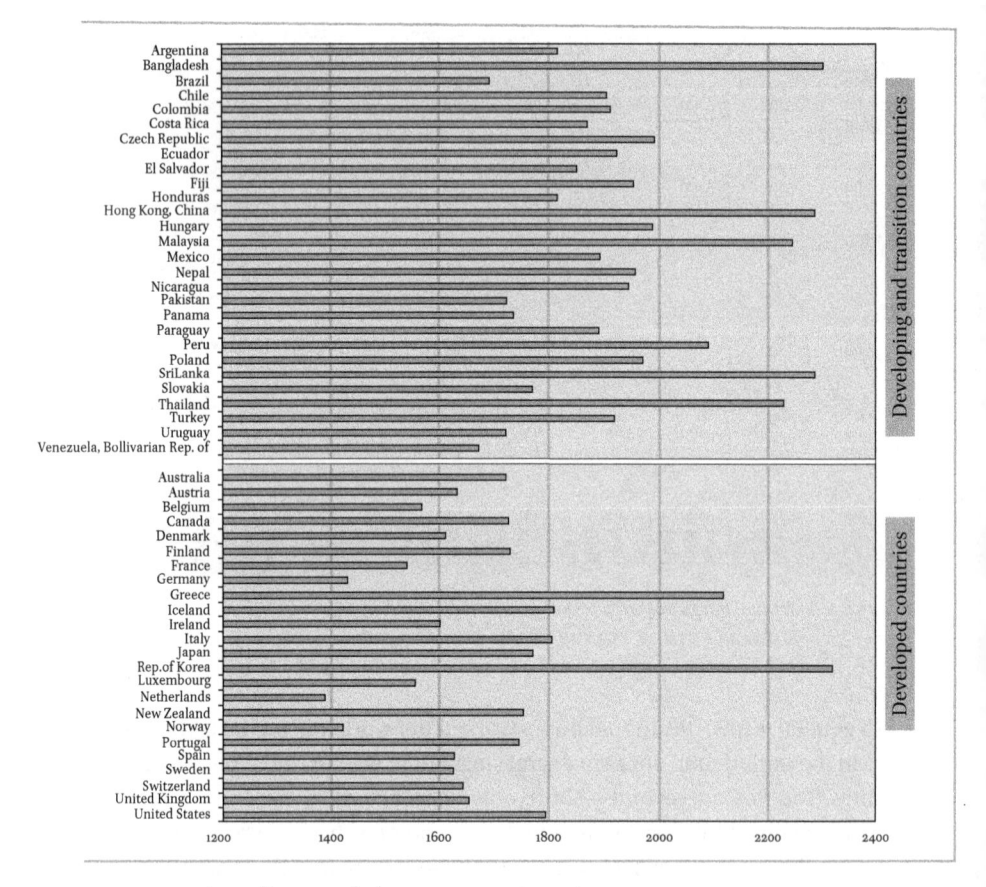

FIGURE 6.4 *Annual hours worked per person, most recent years.*
SOURCE: ILO 2011.

basis of company agreements and especially through the extensive use of overtime. In this way, the actual working hours in these countries range between 10 and 12 hours a day, not counting the additional regulations permitted by local legislation.

In the countries with the highest capitalist development there has been a long-term trend toward a gradual reduction of working hours, as officially prescribed by law and collective labour agreements. The long phase of growth following World War II, the huge productivity gains achieved, the organization and solidarity of the working class, reinforced by the fall in unemployment, have resulted in significant reductions in working time. But with the crisis of accumulation, the rise of neo-liberalism and the effects of relocation, the strength of the working class has been greatly weakened, so in the period referred to as 'the years of Restoration' this historical trend towards the reduction of working time has weakened and in some cases reversed.

In the years from 1990s to now, various methods have been used to break down the rigidities in the use of labour and of working time. The exemption of compliance with collective agreements on working hours, the weakening of the bodies responsible for collective bargaining and its decentralization, the timetable of flexible work that ties the duration and the concentration to production needs, the spread of individual contracts through which it is possible to impose exceptions to collective bargaining (Hermann 2015, 159).

The result has been a massive transformation in the use of the workforce, with unprecedented flexibility and variability: overtime, bank hours, the possibility of exceeding the weekly or monthly schedule with subsequent recovery, reduction of breaks, etc. The main innovation introduced in the '80s and '90s to demolish the rigidity of working hours has been the spread of night work and work on weekends. If previously this type of performance was required only in those categories in which the emergency services performed or the physical demands of production required a continuous cycle activities (hospitals, steel industry, chemical), currently it has spread to various fields of production and services, without technical reasons and with considerably negative impact on workers' health and psycho-physical equilibrium.

For capitalists, the opportunity to use different shifts even at night has many advantages, as it allows them to increase the velocity of circulation of capital by amortizing the cost of fixed capital in less time and to use the labour force more intensively. In addition to these measures, the more intensive use of the labour force has been obtained with various other methods. The introduction of new technologies and machinery together with a different organization of work, have made workers more dependent on a production process in which the machines dictate the timing and intensity of work performance. In this way, the command on the labour force has been significantly strengthened, but the decrease of idle time also results—as usually happens in a typical capitalistic contradiction—in a faster obsolescence of machines.

So, although there has been in previous years a significant reduction of working hours, not only has this trend halted, but in the meantime the hours worked have become more dense and more functional to the needs of production: this means a more intense use of the workforce. As a result, both the workers of the least developed countries and those of developed countries have seen their conditions worsen and an increase in the amount of surplus value extracted.

We agree with the definitions of absolute and relative surplus value provided by Marx in *Capital* Volume One, according to which the surplus-value produced by prolongation of the working day, is called absolute surplus-value and the surplus-value arising from the curtailment of the necessary labour-time, and from the corresponding alteration in the respective lengths of the two components of the working day, is called relative surplus-value. In this sense, the best way for capitalists to increase surplus value is to focus on relative surplus value, because the extraction of absolute surplus value is constrained within natural limits. However it is also to be noted in the 'thirty years of restoration', due to the limits encountered in the extraction/creation of relative surplus value, capitalists were also forced to resort to the old but always valid weapon of absolute surplus value. With all its limitations, an indirect indicator of relative surplus value can be represented by productivity (Table 6.1), while an indicator of absolute surplus value can be represented by the hours worked.

In the OECD countries, the (log of) labour productivity, measured at constant prices and in terms of purchasing power, had a generally declining trend, albeit with differences between areas and periods (Figure 6.5).

It is worth pointing out that we are not claiming that productivity—measured in absolute levels—has fallen; it has actually increased: instead,

TABLE. 6.1 *Labour productivity trend in OECD countries.*

	1970–1980	1980–1990	1990–1995	1995–2000	2000–2007	2007–2013
Austria	n.d	n.d	n.d	1,803	1,855	0,672
Belgium	4,235	2,078	2,441	1,513	1,278	-0,063
Denmark	3,361	2,570	2,721	1,321	1,200	0,506
France	3,986	2,985	2,001	2,185	1,432	0,586
Germany	3,778	2,314	2,504	1,952	1,503	0,466
Greece	n.d	n.d	0,276	3,010	2,504	-0,802
Italy	4,082	1,803	2,092	1,017	0,074	-0,043
Japan	4,264	4,117	2,146	2,004	1,597	0,856
Luxembourg	2,306	3,519	1,696	2,587	0,728	1,288
Netherlands	3,859	1,723	0,901	1,826	1,332	0,000
Portugal	3,583	2,057	2,215	1,643	1,256	0,968
Spain	4,760	2,769	1,936	0,114	0,441	1,753
United Kingdom	2,863	2,155	2,817	2,153	2,216	-0,186
United States	1,523	1,562	1,223	2,389	2,053	1,127

SOURCE: OECD PRODUCTIVITY STATISTICS, CONSTANT PRICES PPP.

THE 'SECRET' OF THE RESTORATION 101

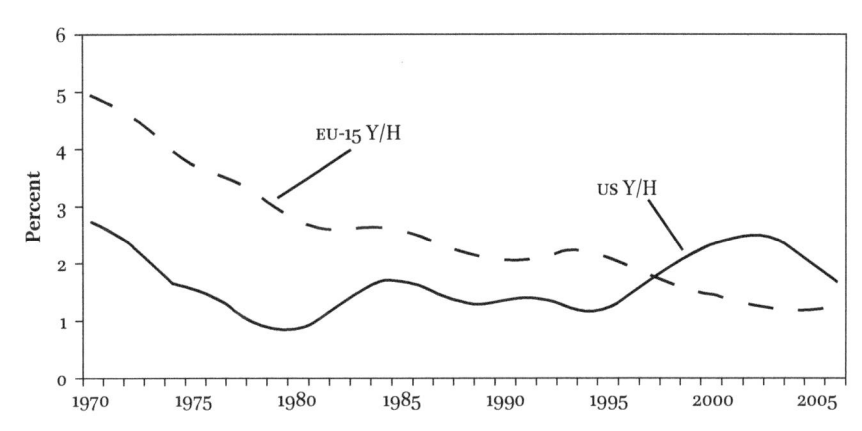

FIGURE 6.5 *Labour productivity trends in European Union and United States of America.*
SOURCE: OECD.

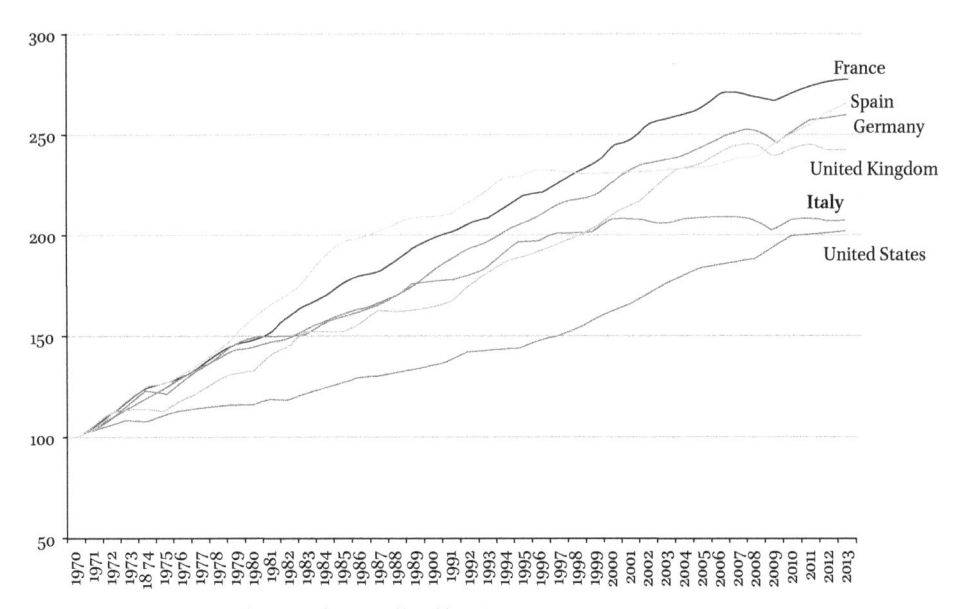

FIGURE 6.6 *Labour productivity (levels) in G7.*
SOURCE: OECD PRODUCTIVITY STATISTICS, CONSTANT PRICES.

despite the increase in terms of levels, its rate of change has decreased. Below (Figure 6.6) we show the dynamics of labour productivity in terms of levels.

Now, the question is: in the same period when the rates of change of labour productivity tended to decline, what happened to the hours worked?

The hours worked per employee (Figure 6.7) were decreasing at the beginning of the 1970s. Afterwards, they fell by less, both in EU and in USA. In the

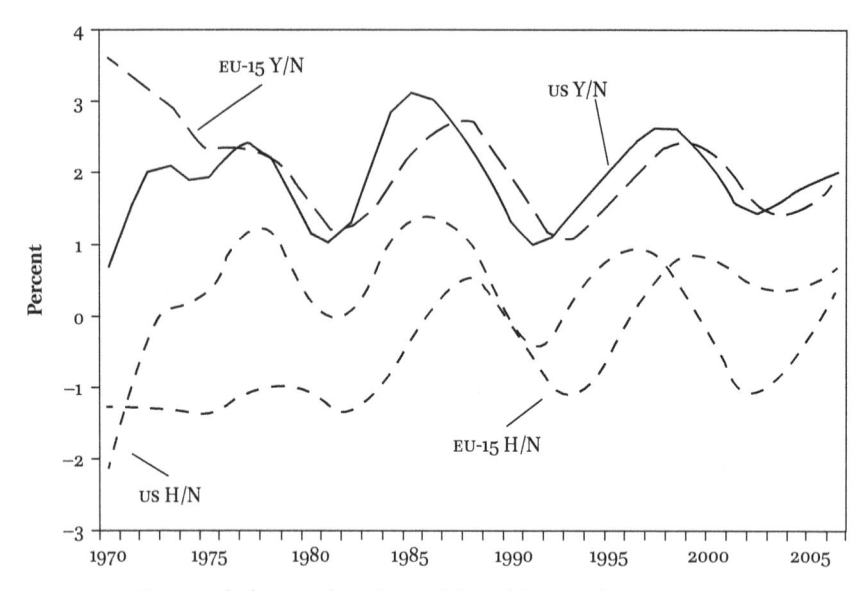

FIGURE 6.7 *Hours worked per employee (rates of change) in US and EU.*

mid '80s (the beginning of the 30 years of restoration) they start to grow, more in the USA than in the EU. In the mid-1990s there is a further reduction but in recent years we can observe a new rise. As a general trend, it is a rising trend, just the opposite of productivity, again with some differences in cyclical terms.

It is noteworthy that, while in the USA hours worked begin to decline almost as productivity—and thus profitability—were rallying, in Europe the hours worked initially stagnate and then continue to grow (after the burst of the speculative bubble, this also happens in USA) while productivity—in terms of rates of change—continues to decline. We can then argue that hours worked and productivity are moving in the opposite directions: when the rate of change of productivity is not satisfying, the hours worked increase.

Wages, Unemployment and the Industrial Reserve Army

A further confirmation of the stratified character of capitalism can be illustrated by the official statistics on employment/unemployment. The ILO estimated that the global unemployment rate in 2014 amounted to just under 6% of the total labour force, distinguishing eight areas or regions; the one in which the unemployment rate is the highest (twice the average) is the so-called MENA region (Middle East and North Africa); the group of developed economies—especially EU countries—has an unemployment rate above the average, the same percentage of the countries of Sub—Saharan Africa and of Central and South—Eastern Europe; the lower unemployment rate is registered in the countries of the South Asian region, a little lower than that of the countries of Southeast Asia and Pacific and East Asia, while the level of unemployment in Latin America and the Caribbean is slightly above average.

When the working conditions worsen, the overall strength of the working class is weakened and it becomes relatively more difficult to obtain wage increases and overall improvements in the standard of living mainly because of the threat represented by unemployment. Therefore, according to ILO Global Wage Reports, one of the most obvious consequences of the growth of the industrial reserve army is the trend towards stagnation of wages. Again keeping in mind the differences between areas, we see that—at least in this last cycle—the growth rate of wages is low worldwide, almost in line with the growth rate of world GDP. Keeping in mind the start at lower levels, the leaders of this moderate growth are the wages of the workers employed in factories of the newly industrialized countries, while the wage of the workers in the 'centre' stagnates or decreases because of the weakening of unions, zero hour and minimum wage contracts.

The flat wage trend in a typically imperialist country (Mishel, Goulf and Bivens 2015; Mishel and Shierholz 2013) is evidenced by the data on the dynamics of the real hourly wages of USA workers between 1933 and 2012 (Figure 6.8).

After a long period of wage increases, corresponding to the growth stage of the accumulation of capital, by the end of the 70s wages had stopped growing. Among the explanations offered by the economists for such a flat dynamic, some propose the lack of flexibility, in this case the rigidity of wages (Akerlof, Dickens and Perry 1996). Wages do not grow enough in the positive phases of the cycle because they do not decrease enough during the recessions (Daly and Hobijn 2015). A different explanation concerns the changes in the composition of employment: the wage—which is assumed to be linked to productivity— does not increase because of growth in the services sector, characterized by the widespread use of precarious work and atypical employment contracts, as well as from a low productivity (Chagny and Husson 2014). The explanation that we propose, that does not neglect the changes in the employment composition, is rooted in the relationship that exists—in the capital accumulation cycle— between wages and unemployment.

The trend of capital accumulation—despite the growth in employment— also produces an increase of the industrial reserve army, as predicted by

Real Hourly Wages, 1933–2012

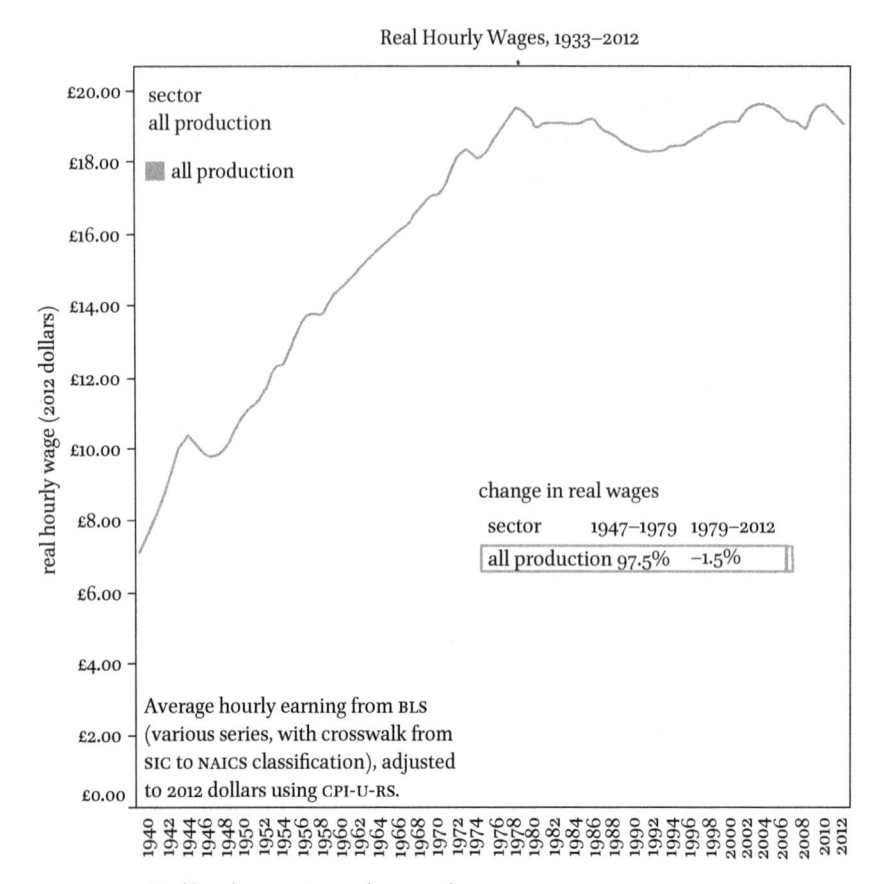

FIGURE 6.8 *Real hourly wages in USA (1933–2012).*

Marx in the description of the general law of capitalist accumulation. If we analyze the official statistics, we find an unemployment rate relatively stable and before the crisis even decreasing, but we must consider that the official statistics considers employed also those with a very precarious and discontinuous employment, while not considered unemployed those who are discouraged from seeking employment. The neoliberal policies, especially in the more developed countries, have weakened all the residual regulations which guaranteed a relative rigidity of the labour market, causing the growth of employment previously considered 'atypical' and a radical challenge to the normal and regular job.

Apart from the labour regulations, the industrial reserve army growth is mainly the result of rising productivity (in terms of absolute levels, not of rates of change) achieved through the use of new technologies and machinery.

The ongoing technological revolution, aimed at reducing the amount of work necessary to reproduce the value of labour power, continuously makes unnecessary an increasing proportion of workers. The expansion of production certainly creates an additional demand for labour to be employed, but, because of the growing productivity and of the higher organic composition inevitably linked to it, the demand for new jobs becomes less elastic in relation to the amount of invested capital. This trend—which is a general feature of capitalism—has increased in these last decades, so much so that even in periods of relative economic recovery, the unemployment rate has failed to drop significantly.

In the emergent countries, apart from the consequences of productivity which in terms of percentage growth has been higher than that of developed countries, we must add the expulsion of huge amounts of peasants from the countryside expanding the population in urban slums. This part of the population, violently pushed into poverty and available as a reserve for capital accumulation needs, is often used temporarily in the informal sector and in home-working. Its existence, functional to the needs of capitalist production during high phases of the cycle, also acts as blackmail toward the industrial army of active workers, exerting pressure to keep wages under control.

With regard to wages, the international condition of the working class is highly stratified. Despite the wages of the workers living in the developing countries increasing in recent years at a higher rate than that of workers of the Western countries, the gap is still significant. In 2013, the global average wage was roughly equal to US $1,600 (expressed in Purchasing Power Parity, PPP); however, it is a value that hides very marked differences, since the average wage in the developed economies oscillates around $3,000 US (PPP) compared with a level of approximately $1,000 in the emerging countries. Considering the case of two particularly significant countries, the average wage in the United States, measured in PPP$, is more than triple to the one prevailing in China, although this difference seems to be slowly decreasing over time. As for the EU, the unit labour costs[6] varies from 4 to 40 euro; according to a study by Confindustria Balkans (Sanfey, Milatovic and Kresic 2016, 18) in 2012, the average monthly wage in Romania is 350 Euros, a bit higher than Albania; the average wage paid to workers from Eastern Europe is just over 400 euro, about three times less than the prevailing average wage in Italy. Summing up, the wage differentials are still relevant in terms of level (Ashenfelter 2012), the overall trend is toward convergence, but its pace is slowing (Belser 2011).

---

6   Unit labour costs (according to OECD, Glossary of Statistical Terms) measure the average cost of labour per unit of output and are calculated as the ratio of total labour costs to real output.

Productivity, Relative Wage and Labour Share

Attention in recent years to changes in income distribution (Milanovic 2012, Picketty 2014, Deaton 2015) can now be framed correctly, that is, considering the growing inequalities as a result of the radical changes that have occurred in the capitalist mode of production and not as the cause of the crisis. It should be noted that, for Marx, the word 'misery' does not mean absolute poverty, for he stated on a number of occasions that the immiseration of the working class would have grown, even with nominal wages growing. From this emerges the importance of the concept of 'relative wage'. Marx introduces this concept in 'Wage Labour and Capital', one of his early lectures on economics dating from 1847. In Section IV Marx distinguishes three definitions of the wage: first, it is the amount of money that the worker receives from his employer which he calls 'nominal wages' and which we would now call 'money wages'; second, we can consider the actual amount of goods and services which at any time this amount of money will buy, i.e. the 'real wages'; but:

> Wages are determined above all by their relations to the gain, the profit, of the capitalist. In other words, wages are a proportionate, relative quantity. Real wages express the price of labour-power in relation to the price of commodities; relative wages, on the other hand, express the share of immediate labour in the value newly created by it, in relation to the share of it which falls to accumulated labour, to capital.
> MARX 1978, 63–64

From this, it follows that relative wages (i.e., the labour share in GDP) can fall even though real wages have risen. Most of those who accuse Marx of having believed that capitalism would reduce the working class to starvation have failed to understand this key distinction, which he took from Ricardo, between relative wages and real wages. It is the relative wage that mattes and the relative wage tends to decline.

All over the world, the labour share has declined globally since the early 1980s. This decline has been pervasive, from the largest liberal economies of the world to all Scandinavian countries, where labour unions and Welfare States have been traditionally strong. The labour share declined also, though less, in many emerging countries like China, India, and Mexico. As for the size of the decline, the ILO/OECD (2015, 3–4) estimates for G20 countries plus Spain are in the order of 9 percentage points—from 65 to 56%—departing from the '60s. For the growth scholars of the University of Groningen, at least in reference to

THE 'SECRET' OF THE RESTORATION 107

the US economy (Figure 6.9), the decrease of the relative share of wages would begin in the early 70s.

Among the hypotheses proposed to explain this decline, Frey and Osborne (2015, 3) recognize that:

> The economic benefits of recent technological developments are not being widely shared. Productivity had increased globally but real median wages have stagnated in many OECD countries leading to significant declines in labour's share of GDP.

For Karabarbounis and Neiman (2014) there has been a relative decrease in the price of investment goods relative to that of the consumer goods, and this is a consequence of technological change. The increase in productivity, achieved in particular thanks to the technological innovations incorporated in the machines system, is associated with an increase of the production obtained in a given labour time. But, even if a higher productivity manifested itself through an increase of use values obtained with the same working hours, it does not determine any increase in its exchange value per unit; the total value of the mass of commodities will be higher, but the amount of value added from labour, that is the only source of new value creation, does not increase.

A working day of 8 hours will have the same value before and after the rise in productivity, as soon as these hours become the new average of the socially necessary labour time in a given productive branch and will have the same value of 8 hours worked in an industry with a different organic composition. The manufacturing sectors with the most modern machinery and innovative

FIGURE 6.9 *Share of labour compensation in GDP at current national prices for United States.*
SOURCE: UNIVERSITY OF GRONINGEN, UNIVERSITY OF CALIFORNIA, DAVIS

technologies, and so with a higher organic composition, appropriates a larger amount of value subtracting shares of product and therefore of value to the capitalists who have not innovated.

The most important result of the increase in productivity is related to its effects on the reduction of labour time needed to produce the commodities which thus lower their unit value. The generalized productivity increase has an effect on all commodities including those contained in the commodities necessary to the reproduction of the labour force. Therefore, even if the workers get the same amount of use values or even a larger share than the one received before the increase in productivity, the total working time of these commodities has decreased and with it their value. In the working day of an employee, the labour time required to produce the equivalent of her wage decreases, which increases the share of surplus labour and therefore of surplus value that the employer can extract. Since the lengthening of the working day is impossible beyond certain physical limits, this mechanism becomes the main instrument under mature capitalism to increase the mass of surplus value and its rate. This is the reason why there is an obsessive attention to increasing productivity on the part of the capitalist class, not because—as many economists and academics claim—this would increase the amount of value added by each individual worker.

But the introduction of new machinery, the use of advanced technologies generally also allows for increasing the intensity of labour, which is reflected in greater tension (work pace), condensation (saturation), less porosity (downtime) which can be added to the extension of the duration of the working day.[7] The more intensive use of the labour force produces, for the same working hours, a greater amount of value and this, without prejudice to the value of the labour force, allows it to increase the amount of surplus labour and thus of surplus value which capitalists can appropriate. Since the intensification of labour also causes an increase in the amount of commodities produced, it becomes difficult to distinguish how much of more use values is the result of technical innovations and new machinery and how much is the result of more intense use of the labour force.

---

7   In his Foundations of the Critique of Political Economy (Grundrisse, Notebook VII—The Chapter on Capital) Marx addresses the problem of the contradiction between the lower nominal duration of the working day and its increased real intensity: *"surplus population (from this standpoint), as well as surplus production, is a condition for this* [here the antithetical form]. *the tendency of capital is, of course, to link up absolute with relative surplus capital; hence greatest..."* https://www.marxists.org/archive/marx/works/1857/grundrisse/ch15.htm.

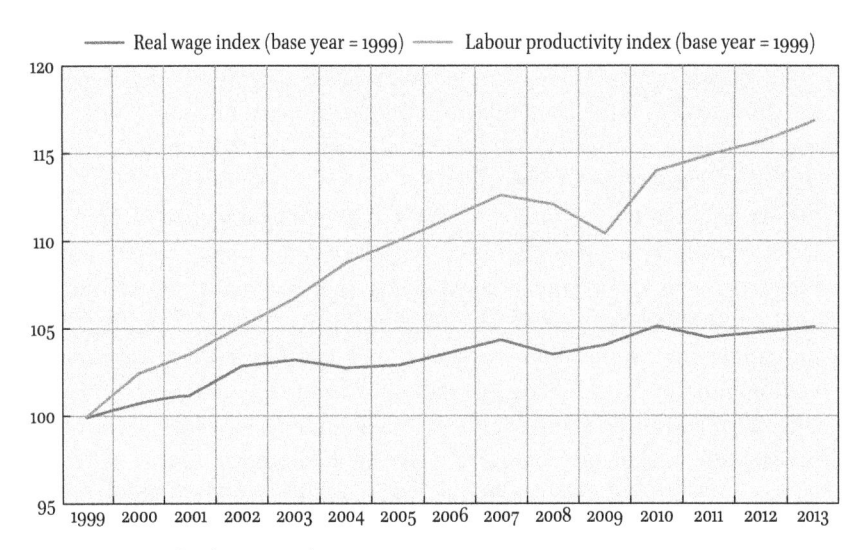

FIGURE 6.10 *Productivity and wages.*
Note: Labour productivity is defined as GDP per employed person and uses GDP in constant 2005 PPP$ for all countries. G20 advanced economies include: Australia, Canada, France, Germany, Italy, Japan, the Republic of Korea, the United Kingdom and the United States. Both indices are based on a weighted average of all the countries in the group that takes into account labour productivity and the size of paid employment.
SOURCE: ILO STAFF ESTIMATION, USING DATA FROM THE ILO GLOBAL EMPLOYMENT TRENDS REPORTS AND THE ILO GLOBAL WAGE DATABASE, REVISED AND UPDATED.

Apart from temporary changes, and keeping in mind the foregoing observations, the productivity revealed by the statistical data (measured as a ratio of value added and hours worked) can give only an indirect indication of the increase in the workers' exploitation (see Figure 6.10).

Final Remarks: An Endless Restoration and a Global Working Class

The transformations that occurred in the international economy in recent decades have a precise meaning: a big counter-offensive by capital against the international working class, that produced a greater proletarianization of the world population with an expansion of the production base but also a growth of the industrial reserve army. This is an epochal change that has led to not only a globalization of trade but of the same world-scale production. The expansion of the base of capital accumulation has increased the total numbers of workers in the industrial sectors by 50%, i.e. a mass of 230 million extra workers from which to extract surplus value. Even without considering the rate of exploitation of these workers and its influence on the average general rate of profit, we can say that the mass of profit was significantly extended by providing a break to a gasping economy.

The extension of the labour force has focused mainly on emerging and developing countries. In these countries, wage conditions, working hours and intensity of use of the labour force are worse than those that capitalists are able to impose on the workers of the most developed countries. The relocation occurred mainly in labour-intensive sectors, or specialized intermediate parts of the final product in which, based on current technologies, the labour component still constitutes a significant part. The building of new plants has taken place using the latest technologies, and the same happened to the organizational methods of production so that, especially in the factories directly controlled by multinational firms, the working methods were not very different from the existing ones in the western countries of the same productive sector.

In Marxian terms, we can say that there was a significant increase in the rate of surplus labor and thus of surplus value. Indeed, both the reduction in the cost of the workforce as the lengthening of work hours, as well as its more intense use, results in an increase of the surplus labor time with respect to that necessary to reproduce the value of labor power. In addition, relocation, as well as the increasing use of the immigrant labor force in the developed capitalist countries, has increased the bargaining power of the capitalists through the threat of moving production sites or to use more blackmailed immigrant labor, in order to worsen the conditions in terms of wages, working hours and other important regulatory aspects.

Thus the attack on workers, starting with the Thatcher governments in the UK and Reagan presidency in the US in the 1980s, affected not only the working conditions and wages, but has gradually scaled back all the assurances won with hard struggles: from health care to the pension provisions, from direct and indirect tax increases to the cost of education; nothing was overlooked in significantly reducing indirect wages which represents a decisive component of real wages. Furthermore, the opportunity to import cheap goods from the newly industrialized countries led to a reduction in the price of commodities necessary for the reproduction of the labor force and therefore to the labor time necessary to reproduce its value.

These mechanisms, together with the increase—albeit at a decreasing rate—of productivity, have resulted in a reduction of the value of labor power and therefore an increase in the surplus labor time and surplus value which the capitalists have been able to appropriate. To the capitalist, it is irrelevant that the reduction in the value of the commodities necessary to the reproduction of labor power is realized through a general increase in productivity or because the workers who produce these commodities are paid a minimum wage: what matters is achieving the goal, the increase in the exploitation rate obtained by the growth of relative surplus value.

With the change in the balance of power between the classes, the capitalists have succeeded in putting a stop to the historical trend of the legal reduction of the working hours in the most developed countries—trends which in many cases have been reversed—introducing the criterion of flexibility in the workplace, widespread insecurity and employment volatility. We have thus witnessed the return to the typical methods for increasing the absolute surplus value, that have increased even more the rate of exploitation, including in relation to industrial workers in the more developed countries. The old typical methods of extraction of absolute surplus value are not a mere return to the past however; rather, they represent the result of the enormous development reached by productive forces and productivity. In most developed countries, the organic composition of capital in the main productive sectors has reached very high levels, beyond which it is difficult to go except with exorbitant costs and diminishing returns. A typical capitalistic contradiction anticipated by Marx: the more it is reduced to a minimum part of the working day necessary to reproduce the value of labor power, the lower the increase of surplus value obtained through an increase in productivity. Surplus value increases, though not at the same rate as productivity dynamics.[8]

The new industrial revolution that is shaping through the use of artificial intelligence and the massive use of robotics, will not produce an exit from the current crisis, but rather an amplification of the contradictions of capitalism.

---

[8] "The larger the surplus value of capital before the increase of productive force, the larger the amount of presupposed surplus labour or surplus value of capital; or, the smaller the fractional part of the working day which forms the equivalent of the worker, which expresses necessary labour, the smaller is the increase in surplus value which capital obtains from the increase of productive force. Its surplus value rises, but in an ever smaller relation to the development of the productive force. Thus the more developed capital already is, the more surplus labour it has created, the more terribly must it develop the productive force in order to realize itself in only smaller proportion, i.e. to add surplus value—because its barrier always remains the relation between the fractional part of the day which expresses necessary labour, and the entire working day. It can move only within these boundaries. The smaller already the fractional part falling to necessary labour, the greater the surplus labour, the less can any increase in productive force perceptibly diminish necessary labour; since the denominator has grown enormously. The self-realization of capital becomes more difficult to the extent that it has already been realized." (Marx 1993b, 340).

References

Akerlof, G.A., Dickens, W.T., and P.G.L. (1996) The Macroeconomics of Low Inflation, *Brookings Papers on Economic Activity*, 1. Available at: https://www.brookings.edu/wp-content/uploads/1996/01/1996a_bpea_akerlof_dickens_perry_gordon_mankiw.pdf.

Ashenfelter, O. (2012) Comparing Real Wage Rates. *Presidential Adress delivered at the one hundred twenty-fourth meeting of the American Economic Association*, January 7, Chicago.

Belser, P. (2011) Global wage trends: The great convergence?, *Global Labour Column*, 53.

Chagny, O. and Husson, M. (2014) Looking for an 'optimal wage regime' for the Euro zone. *IRES France*. Available at: http://www.ires-fr.org/images/files/Documents Travail/DdT01.2015/DdT01.2015.pdf.

Daly, M.C. and Hobijn B. (2015) Why Is Wage Growth So Slow? *FRBSF Economic Letter* January 5.

Deaton, A. (2015) La grande fuga. Salute, ricchezza e origini della disuguaglianza, *italian edition,* Bologna, *il Mulino.*

Donato, M. and Pala G. (1999) La catena e gli anelli. Divisione internazionale del lavoro, capitale finanziario e filiere di produzione, Napoli, *La Città del Sole.*

Federal Reserve Economic Data. Share of Labour Compensation in GDP at Current National Prices for United States. Available at: https://fred.stlouisfed.org/series/LABSHPUSA156NRUG.

Frey, C.B. and Osborne M.A. (2015) Technology at Work, The Future of Innovation and Employment. Citi GPS, Oxford Martin School. Available at: http://www.oxfordmartin.ox.ac.uk/downloads/reports/Citi_GPS_Technology_Work.pdf.

Hermann, C. (2015) *Capitalism and the Political Economy of Work Time.* London: Routledge.

International Labour Organization/OECD (2015), The Labour Share in G20 Economies. *Report prepared for the G20 Employment Working Group Antalya, Turkey, 26–27 February 2015.* Available at: https://www.oecd.org/g20/topics/employment-and-social-policy/The-Labour-Share-in-G20-Economies.pdf.

International Labour Organization (2014) *Global Employment Trends 2014.* Geneva: ILO. Available at: http://embargo.ilo.org/global/research/global-reports/global-employment-trends/2014/WCMS_233953/lang--en/index.htm.

International Labour Organization (2011) *Working time in the twenty-first century. Report for discussion at the Tripartite Meeting of Experts on Working-time Arrangements,* 17–21 October, Geneva. Geneva: ILO. Available at: http://www.ilo.org/wcmsp5/groups/public/---ed_protect/---protrav/---travail/documents/publication/wcms_161734.pdf.

Karabarbounis, L. and Nieman B. (2014), The Global Decline of the Labor Share, *The Quarterly Journal of Economics*, 129 (1): 61–103.

Marx, K. (1992) *Capital* Vol. I. London: Penguin.
Marx, K. (1993a) *Capital* Vol. III. London: Penguin.
Marx, K. (1993b) *Grundrisse. Foundations of the Critique of Political Economy*. London: Penguin.
Marx, K. (1978) *Lavoro salariato e capitale*. Roma: Newton Compton.
Milanovic, B. (2012) *Chi ha e chi non ha*. Bologna: il Mulino.
Mishel, L. Gould, E. and Bivens, J. (2015) Wage Stagnation in 9 Charts. *Economic Policy Institute*, January 6. Available at: http://www.epi.org/publication/charting-wage-stagnation/.
Mishel, L. and Shierholz, H. (2013) A Decade of Flat Wages, *Economic Policy Institute Briefing Papers* 365, August 21. Available at: http://www.epi.org/publication/a-decade-of-flat-wages-the-key-barrier-to-shared-prosperity-and-a-rising-middle-class/.
OECD *Average Annual Hours Worked*. Available at: http://stats.oecd.org/Index.aspx?DataSetCode=ANHRS.
Pala, G. (1999) Stati*sovra*stati. Riferimenti in margine a un convegno su marxismo e istituzioni. *la Contraddizione* 73: 59–71.
Piketty, T. (2014), Il *Capitale nel XXI secolo*. Milano: Bompiani.
Ruccio, D. (2014). The Wage-Productivity Gap in the G20. *Real World Economics Review Blog*. Available at: https://rwer.wordpress.com/2014/09/11/the-wage-productivity-gap-in-the-g20-2-graphs/.
Sanfey, Peter, Jakov Milatovic, Ana Kresic (2016) How the Western Balkans can catch up, *EBRD Working Paper* n. 186, January.
Schlitzer, G. (2015) L'economia italiana e il paradosso della produttività. *Luic Papers* 285. Available at: http://www.biblio.liuc.it/liucpap/pdf/285.pdf.
World Bank (2016) Part time employment, total. Available at: http://data.worldbank.org/indicator/SL.TLF.PART.ZS?end=2013&locations=US-GB-FR-IT-JP-DE&name_desc=true&start=1980&view=chart.

CHAPTER 7

Exploitation, Oppression, and Epistemology

Holly Lewis

Introduction

In the era between the end of the feudal age and the mid-to-late twentieth century, class antagonism and colonial expansion dominated both the collective political imaginary and real political struggle. By the mid-twentieth century, however, new social movements were forcefully interjecting contentions that had not yet been sufficiently analysed within the old problematic: in particular, the problem of how gender, race, and sexuality shaped and maintained the terms and conditions of class and anti-colonial struggles. But these social movements were not only concerned with investigating new topics, they were interested in developing new approaches to political problem solving altogether. Questions of epistemology, voice, and visibility within class and anti-colonial struggle was of special concern: how did the old movements stifle awareness of gender and racial oppression? How did movements ignore real material concerns of marginalised people within the working classes? Were labour, anti-colonial and anti-capitalist movements in fact replicating the problems they were attempting to solve?

In the United States, these new anti-oppression movements happened to emerge at the beginning of a now decades-long neoliberal employers' offensive. New attacks on unions and the privatisation of public space pushed political debates out of streets and workplaces into the universities where, by at the end of the twentieth century, the themes of the new social movements would undergo a conceptual 'neoliberalisation' of sorts, where problems of gender, race, and sexuality were debated in terms of individual experiences of suffering and interpersonal violence as opposed to inequalities produced by imperialism and exploitation. Class would become one oppressed identity category among many, and its political subjects would come to be understood as victims of *classism*, a phenomenon separate from though intertwined with other structural oppressions such as racism, sexism, and homophobia. By the twenty-first century, class was mostly discussed as a complication of other oppressions: not only did women, queer people, and people of colour suffer from sexism, homo/transphobia, and racism—they could also be 'classed', or made poor by these oppressions. In the new political imaginary, not only did exploitation no longer define political struggle, exploitation was epiphenomenal at best and, as a consequence, it was largely abandoned as a category of analysis.

But as the neoliberal offensive continued, the emergence of imperialist wars, the casualisation of work, the loss of public space, environmental catastrophe, and new crises of capitalism could not be theorised using models of interpersonal or even structural oppression alone. Capitalism itself, not just as an ideology, or as manifestation of greed, or as a system of overt violence, but as a system of exploitation, emerged as a category that urgently needed to, not only be interrogated, but in fact, needed to be politically challenged. However, in the global north, the industrial proletarian subjects of the nineteenth and twentieth century were no longer a clearly identifiable political force. Although identitarian movements are sometimes blamed for the current state of working class disorganisation, this hardly makes sense from a materialist perspective. Much of the industry in the global north has, of course, been relocated to the BRICS nations and the global south; and where manufacturing labour has not been relocated overseas, it has been moved out of city centres into gated suburban (or even rural) industrial campuses or has become unfree labour hidden behind prison walls. New post-Fordist management techniques and the precarious contracts have made it difficult for workers to sustain organising efforts.

If class struggle were to be organised in terms of identity, one of the first epistemological questions would be 'how do I know what class I am in?' After all, feminist standpoint epistemology has related to us the importance of one's subjective knowledge, of one's experience of one's place in the world. This can be understood in at least two ways: (1) through rooting oneself in popular working class culture, and (2) in relating experiences of one's labouring conditions. I would argue that the former has a complicated relation to class struggle in part because working class culture is always rooted in local language and histories, because culture can be marketed to and adopted by those outside the working class, and because cultural identities might be sexist, homophobic, racist, and/or nativist. Relating one's experiences of labouring conditions is, on the other hand, a direct contribution to the development of a broad picture of current exploitative practices and sheds light on what is necessary for working class resistance.

Objective analysis of social relations is another epistemological component of understanding capitalist exploitation. A politics based on class as an 'identity' is limited in a world where producers shift between various class positions: now existing as directly producing wage labourers, now participants in informal economies, now self-employed, or even precarious stints in the traditional middle-classes (professionals, waged recipients of redistributed surplus value, or even the petit bourgeoisie). Understanding not just where one's identity and immediate 'interests' lie, but also how the system of exploitation functions as a totality is critical to the development of broad anti-capitalist forces.

The re-centring of the problem of exploitation is not a dismissal of real crises of oppression under capitalism. It is critical that oppression not be understood as a mere matter of hurt feelings that somehow takes away from the concrete material questions of class exploitation. The oppression and marginalisation of identifiable groups is critical to the maintenance of capitalism. The dehumanisation and devaluation of groups facilitates downward pressure on wages; it undermines the struggles for state benefits that allow capitalism's 'surplus populations' to survive. Gender and racial ideologies lower the value and therefore the costs of reproductive labour, and they pressure women to donate services to the maintenance and development of capitalism's workforce. Oppression is always a material phenomenon.

However, oppression and exploitation are still distinct enough phenomenon to discuss them as two separate but mutually constituting processes within capitalism. Oppression is often intentionally palpable, even terroristic (i.e. physical brutality, imprisonment, geographic containment, psychological cruelty), where exploitation is *necessarily mystified* as the ratio between wages and surplus value. The mathematisation of exploitation makes it easy for capitalists to rationalise and even dismiss it through ideological obfuscation (i.e. hard work leads to wealth, you're paid according to the use values you produce).

This doesn't mean that oppression under capitalism is never subject to market abstraction and distancing effects. Pundits use neoclassical economic rationalisations to explain why the labour of women, people of colour, and the workers in the global south earn lower wages (i.e., because they have different values, cultures, and habits than working males and whites, etc.) to distract from the fact that industries use sexism, racism, and homophobia/transphobia to pay lower wages. However, exploitation, the extraction of surplus value from labourers, is not just disorienting, it is *necessarily* so. The reverse is also true, the mass *demystification* of wage-based exploitation would be an existential threat to the capitalist system.

How is Class Determined?

The Marxist conception of economic class is radically distinct from the dominant neoclassical economic framework in terms of its epistemological and ontological worldview and in its political ramifications. The definition of class informed by neoclassical economic theory holds sway in the popular imagination. The neoclassical model uses an income hierarchy to predict how much of the total commodity output an individual has the right to consume in a given society, while the Marxist model traces the exploitative relationship between the labouring and capitalist classes within the capitalist mode of production. In other words, the neoclassical model uses consumption to determine class, while the Marxist model emphasises the conditions of production.

Thorstein Veblen's concept of *conspicuous consumption*—how the ruling class cements their social status through the performative use of luxury commodities—is one non-Marxian method of how the capitalist class constructs itself. The Marxist model of class analysis doesn't deny that conspicuous consumption is a phenomenon; it simply doesn't regard individual consumption habits as foundational to class status. The Marxist explanation of class happens within the processes of production, which is also a site of consumption in that the production process consumes and transforms raw materials. In this model, the investment class owns the means of production and obtain seed money for future investments by squeezing profits from the masses who labour for their benefit. It is the relations between people *during* economic production (exploiter/exploited) and not the flamboyance of consumption after production that concretises class relations.

But Veblen's analysis does shed light on how the role of domination in the feudal mode of production is distinct from the role of capitalist exploitation. Under feudalism, a king had access to luxury items *because* he was royalty, *because* of the structural relations of domination. A serf would not be considered successful and hard-working if he wore royal garments. In fact, the serf would be considered confused, even mad if he wore the symbols of nobility. In reverse, it would have been equally strange for a queen to wear peasant garb as a fashion statement. By contrast, under the anarchy of capitalist production an individual becomes 'like' royalty through the performative consumption of luxury commodities. The luxury of royalty was substantiated by the divine right of kings, the idea that royals were ontologically distinct from their subjects. Within the capitalist mode of production, the right to consume luxury commodities becomes the marker of moral achievement through the Protestant work ethic: someone or someone in one's family (the assumption goes) either worked hard or risked capital or possessed a commodifiable talent that justified their access to not only luxury commodities, but to all commodities to the highest degree imaginable.

Whereas a serf in ermine robes was merely misunderstanding his place in the universe, under capitalism the commodified world is treated as a zero-sum game where the income scale is the marker of what one deserves. *Price is value.* Thus, the poor are denied luxuries on moral grounds. Any small comfort afforded to the poor is theft from the rich. This logic begins in the production process, where wages are begrudgingly bestowed upon the labourers who make and maintain the world of commodities. After production, which (with the exception of handicrafts) is always hidden from view, income is used to justify proportional rights to the total social product. The invisible hand of the market provides an ethical outcome. Everyone is where they choose to be and everyone has been given what they are worth because everyone is free to shift position within the market (free to invest the millions they received at birth, or free to starve because they have nothing but their labour power.) Because class position is moral and not ontological, any demands from the subjugated classes are assumed to be demands for 'more than one's share'. In the United States for example, politicians routinely argue that public aid recipients should not be permitted to purchase spices or sauces or even better quality potatoes and canned tuna. For the unemployed and low paid worker, anything beyond mere survival is considered theft—and sometimes even survival itself is considered such. Moreover, expansion of visual media and surveillance apparatuses have heightened awareness of conspicuous consumption thereby reinforcing and naturalising the inequality that begins in the (now largely hidden) production processes.

The Labour Process Obscured

The neoclassical model of economic class operates along an income spectrum. It is possible to turn this continuum into groupings—the upper-upper class, the upper-middle class, the lower-middle class, the lower class—but there is no real internal logic within this hierarchy that necessitates an analysis of class. The income spectrum is a graphic representation of millions of households. It might order segments of the hierarchy into classifications, but there is no necessary relation between them. The Occupy movement attempted to imagine a relationship between segments of the income scale by breaking the hierarchy into two groups: the 99% and the 1%. There are practical political applications for such a breakdown. For example, the vast majority of the population, including many small capitalists, don't benefit from trade deals. But neither is there any particular logic for the entirety of the 99% to solidarise with one another. Does the 98.9th percentile of income really share political interests with the bottom .001%? Are the differences between the political claims of the top .001% distinct from the rest of the top 1%? The numbers tell nothing about class composition, class formation, or the social relations between classes. Income-based assessments of class cannot answer questions about why income inequality exists to begin with. And if the reasons for income inequality aren't explained, then there is no location from which to launch a challenge to the status quo. The arguments that successful people work harder, that successful people come from cultures that teach success, that the rich deserve to possess the means of production are not refuted.

By comparison, the Marxist understanding of class is rooted in *qualitative* social relations. Class is not a sliding scale of wealth distribution between individuals and families, rather, class begins with wealth, with capital investment, with one class of people owning the means of production (factory, tools) and another class of people having no ownership of the means of production; in fact, having nothing to sell but their labour power in exchange for a wage. In other words, class is not a measurement of purchasing power or fortune, but a specific social relationship between those who exploit and those who are exploited. A petit bourgeois shopkeeper with two assistants could have a lower income than unionised factory workers who have negotiated higher wages for themselves. What delineates class is not individual wealth, but ownership of productive assets. Still, regardless of income, by definition, the labouring class as a whole produces more than it consumes because it creates surplus value for those who own the means of production, who then in turn, subsist off the remaining profits. The exploiting class survives off the labour of the exploited. There is a specific reason why they congregate at the top of the income scale. Thus, conspicuous consumption naturalises the income scale and masks the fundamental labour relations that make luxury commodities possible. While consumption is performative, production—and particularly *the relations of production*—is masked.

Labour is hidden in a number of ways. Manufacturing labour is hidden in back-of-house operations and in prisons; whereas once factories were at the centre of city life, factories are now pushed beyond the neoliberal city limits if not completely off-shored. Mining, manufacturing, and agricultural labour are written out of the script of visual culture. When mining finally becomes visible as mountaintop removal or when profit-seeking operations take tonnes of sand from beaches to sell to glass manufacturers, the (quite justifiable) public complaint tends to centre on the destruction of the landscape; and in this case labour, finally visible, is one of the culprits.

Service labour, on the other hand, is obscured in a different sense. Service workers are required to incessantly smile and nod as if work were pleasure. Workers are required to transform themselves into reflections of the corporate brand: they must not only work for the company, they must *believe* in it.

This is because their actual relationship with their employer is hidden behind terms such as 'partner', 'associate', and 'teammate'. Another obscuring tactic has been to hide union-busting behind a veil of self-determination by requiring that all workers take on a few supervisory tasks so that they can be redefined as management. The management theory of holarchy takes this redefinition of labourer as manager one step further. Holarchy, where workers in a particular company are not defined by particular jobs, where they 'self-manage' as a team to get the job done as quickly as possible and where compensation is horizontal, is yet another attempt to re-imagine labour relations without changing the social relations that ground them. The company can streamline production and prevent surplus value from being invested back into the firm by ridding itself of its non-producing managers and replacing them with a self-disciplined workforce that has so deeply internalised company policies and production goals that their job is not only to produce commodities, but to facilitate their own exploitation as their own self-managers. In this way, even if a CEO liberates his workforce by requiring that they function horizontally (or even democratically) the economic fact remains that his fortune grows through exploiting their labour power no matter how democratic the process *seems*.

Marx argued that the transition from feudalism to capitalism was fundamentally predicated on this latter instance of concealment: the obscuring of social relations through wages. Under feudalism, serfs were required to contribute to the estates of their lords by force. Capitalism, on the other hand, grows through the expropriation of the free labourer through a mathematical ratio between surplus value and socially necessary labour time. This rational element mystifies social relations. Put differently, the land-based, hierarchical feudal system operated through lords forcing serfs to work on the lord's land or hand over a certain amount of product. But because serfs had access to their own land, because the basic requirements of their survival were not subsumed into the market, lords could not control their labour except through overt domination. It was only through open force that they could be compelled to generate wealth for others. Their relation to the lord was not mysterious nor was the amount of energy expended on their lord's behalf. However, the widespread use of wages at the beginning of the industrial age mystified workers' ability to understand how much of the total social product they received as compared to their property-owning masters. How much the bourgeois class (i.e. those who now owned the new system of production) benefitted from their labour was unknown—almost unknowable.

Social relations under advanced capitalism have intensified this rational mystification, not only through explicit ideological pressures but through the effects brought about by the system's own logic. Not only do workers not know the ratio between how much they produce and how much shareholders profit from what they create, with global expansion, the capitalists themselves are often mystified into anonymous transnational bureaucracies, and the expansion of the financial sector has further obscured the mathematical connection between labour and profit.

It is no wonder that quantitative, income-based analyses have supplanted qualitative Marxian analyses that trace the actual dynamics of economic class formation. Income data are easily turned into pie charts and graphs. Finding ethical rationales for redistribution of wealth is easier to imagine than tackling the problem of exploitation. But analyses that ignore the dynamics of wealth creation cannot possibly address the injustices of wealth distribution because it is in the very process of production that the injustice of distribution occurs.

Oppression as Shock and Awe

It is common to attribute the decline of Marxist class politics in the developed world, both inside and outside of the academy, first to the rise of the new social movements in the mid-twentieth century that criticised Marx for not fully accounting for gender and racial oppression, and then to post-structuralist theory after that. But such an analysis is not particularly materialist. Even if one has no use for post-structuralism, bad ideas among the intelligentsia alone can't account for the decline in class struggle nor can bad ideas alone account for the predominance of consumption-based and income-based definitions of class. Neoliberal changes in the labour process, affective demands on service workers, the de-urbanisation of factory life in the global north, offshoring, and the prison-industrial complex have helped obscure exploitation even before the increasing complexity of financial capital is taken into account.

The embattled Left has shifted to combating more easily identifiable manifestations of social violence within the capitalist mode of production: imperialist wars for resources, racist policing, rape culture, the murder of queer and trans people, and hostility towards immigrants. While exploitation and the search for surplus value set the stage for such oppressions, analysis of oppression is often removed from capitalist economics and instead treated as products of entirely different systems, different 'power structures' outside capital: racism, ethnocentrism, ableism, nativism, sexism, heterosexism, cissexism. It's important to note that these are not just considered phenomena generated from material social relations but distinct structures with logics and material origins separate and separable from any given mode of production. Even when oppression is attributed to capitalist processes, those explanations often emphasise institutional power imbalances, consumerism, public passivity, and media representation of marginalised groups. At the lowest levels of contemplation, capitalism appears almost as a conscious malevolence, the antagonist in a morality play. But the protagonist of this morality play, the anti-capitalist, is largely untheorised and referred to with vague labels such as progressive forces, activists, the 99%, etc. In cases where capitalism is considered a separate or merely intersecting power relation, class relations may not appear at all or may masquerade as 'classism', the liberal, income-based version of class injustice where those at the top of the income scale are snobbish and insensitive towards those at the bottom.

Just as the social domination of serfs was clear because it was visible, the overt violence of imperialism, racism and gendered oppression is similarly visible. But oppression is not always overt. Violence can be surreptitiously written into law or delivered with a cold smile. However, eventually oppressive forces wage open campaigns of shock and awe. This can take the form of state-sanctioned violence (phalanxes of riot police, war, segregation, mass deportation) or generalised excuses for, minimisation of, and toleration of violence from below (gang rape, burning crosses, vigilante threats, racist murder, attacks on women nursing infants in public, gay-bashing, the killing of trans people).

Although dialectically related, oppression and exploitation are conceptually distinct and these subtle distinctions are, in part, rooted in knowledge processes. While exploitation is the consequence of rational economic processes, oppression, by contrast, is marked by irrational violence. Thus, there is a strong experiential component to oppression, while those who are highly exploited might not even be aware of how much surplus value has been expropriated from them—in fact, if past union activity has secured higher wages, segments of the working class may even consider themselves fortunate. A software coder may yield more surplus value for a capitalist than a warehouse worker. This is not to say that workers whose bosses happen to yield less surplus value suffer less than workers who yield more surplus value for their bosses, only that the misery of any given set of workers isn't a reliable measure of the rate of exploitation. Oppression, on the other hand, can be measured by the experience of suffering: there are micro-aggressions and there are macro-aggressions.

Exploited working populations tend to experience oppression when they rise up and make demands. (However, unlike feudal serfs, it is not the oppression that keeps them showing up for work but the demands of the market.) Oppression, particularly as it manifests in suppression and repression, is a mechanism that benefits exploitative capitalist social relations, keeping some groups hyper-exploited and establishing others as surplus populations, as the reserve army of the unemployed.

As capitalism has become more complex, class exploitation seems abstract compared to the visibility and concreteness of overt oppression. Therefore, one problem within contemporary class politics, particularly in the neoliberal landscape of the global north, is that the working class in-itself is not always readily known to itself.

But although exploitative social relations between capitalists and workers are not a matter of overt violence, this does not mean that the effects of neoliberalism don't leave working populations feeling stunned and terrified. Pitiful wages force workers to turn to informal, often criminalised, sectors such as selling drugs, survival sex, or vending loose cigarettes on street corners. Other workers must brave borders, border vigilantes, and detention centres. In less dramatic cases, many workers simply feel hopeless, trapped in precarious low-wage work, buried under student loan debt, unable to locate safe, stable housing. The destruction of unions has older workers fearing for their futures, anxious over the eradication of pensions and social safety nets, facing a lack of adequate elder care, and uncertain about the availability of medical care.

For those facing both oppression and exploitation, the shock and awe of state-sanctioned (and/or publicly-acceptable) violence and the fear of an uncertain future form a dreadful combination.

Social Ontology and Class *In-Itself*

Within neoclassical sociology, class is shorthand for income classifications that operate as research data sets. For Marxists, class is a relation between two qualitative groups, two distinct social forces: exploiter and exploited. These two forces are defined by who owns the productive elements (i.e. the means of production: the factories, land, equipment, etc.) in a given society and who has the power to control the labour process. As we see in the distinction between feudal serfs and the development of wage labour, ownership is not simply a matter of who owns the most property, it also requires either relations of direct force (feudalism) or a population that has nothing but its labour power to sell in exchange for survival (capitalism). In Chapter 33 of the first volume of *Capital*, Marx illustrates this phenomenon using the story of Thomas Peel who left England in an attempt to colonise Western Australia with the help of three-hundred servants. With plenty of land and resources to survive, his servants dispersed as soon as they arrived leaving Mr. Peel to care for himself. "Unhappy Mr. Peel who provided for everything except the export of English modes of production ..." (1979, 932–933) For capitalism to function, free labourers cannot own the land, resources, and tools required to sustain themselves.

In *The Poverty of Philosophy*, Marx notes a distinction between the existence of workers as a structured class (the class in-itself) and the organisation of that class operating in its own interests (the class for-itself). Marxist theorists since have been debating the dynamic between the formation of the class in-itself and how it comes to be a class for-itself. There are also debates about who and what constitutes the class in-itself. Those who produce surplus value for capitalists (direct producers) are the clearest members of the class whether they work on the line of an auto plant, pick tomatoes for agribusiness, assemble hamburgers, use repetitive gestures to accumulate coins inside video games for profitable 'gold-farming ventures',[1] or create online courses for for-profit companies. But many (even most) Marxists argue that there are others who fall within the category of the exploited class: the reserve army of labour who serves as downward pressure on wages (the unemployed), those who care for direct producers before and after their working day and working life thereby lowering the cost of labour power for capitalists (household labour, reproductive labour, family-based childcare and eldercare), public workers who assist the development of direct producers so that they are more useful to capitalists (public teachers, social workers) and those who maintain the capitalist state (i.e. non-subcontracted janitorial workers and food service workers in government offices). However, one of the most contentious debates has been over how to locate capitalism's ever expanding managerial layers.

In Marxist analysis, the middle-class is not quantitative, not the set of people whose incomes happen to fall between rich and poor. The middle class is the class whose position cannot be characterised as capitalist class or working class, but hovers between. The petit bourgeoisie (small-business owner) is the clearest example of the Marxist conception of a middle-class since the petit bourgeoisie exploit labour but are also at the mercy of larger industrial capitalists and in the vice-grip of finance capital. Another, less clear contender for middle-class is the expanding managerial layer who subsist off redistributed surplus value, although for the ultimate benefit for the capitalist. Some Marxists have emphasised that the managerial layer does not own the means of production, that managers sell their labour power, and are perhaps only a more complex and hidden form of wage labour. Though it has fallen out of

---

[1] "Virtual Gold Farming is basically the collective gathering of huge amounts of virtual coins at one time. This can be done individually, but is mostly practiced in groups of up to hundreds of workers/gamers at one time. It is a relatively new industry, but is growing fast." http://gblaze96.wix.com/virtual-gold-farming.

favour, this analysis might help make sense of lean production labour processes where workers are required to take turns managing one another. However, this does not solve questions about salaried, permanent managers. Others argue, along with Erik Olin Wright that instead of the 'middle' managerial layer being a mystified working class population, that middle management is a stratum with internal contradictions. Like the ruling class, management controls the labour process; however, managers are also in the position of the working class since they do not own the means of production and must sell their labour power on the market to survive. Another way of thinking about this problem is 'class fraction' theory, where exploiter and exploited constitute two warring classes that are themselves constituted by fractions. In this view, the capitalist class is not a monolith without internal contradictions, and neither is the working class. Other theorists find the above debate marred by essentialism. Influenced by Louis Althusser's antihumanism, Richard Wolff and Steven Resnick in *Knowledge and Class: A Marxian Critique of Political Economy* argue that Marx's economic theory does not refer to a clash between embodied essences let alone an ontological class whose essence determines history. Instead, using Capital Vol. 2 and 3, Wolff and Resnick focus on what they call *class processes*. By shifting the focus from subject to process, the analysis of class moves from identity to dynamic.

In addition to the possibility of a qualitatively distinct middle-class, others argue that the working class itself is not only fractional but split into different economic classes with different interests. One example is the concept of the precariat, which is argued to be a new class in a hostile relationship to workers who have secured ongoing employment (Standing 2014). However, there is good evidence that stable employment in North America and Europe under Fordism is more of a fluke within the history of capitalism than the norm (McNally 2011). Precarious employment was more common than not during the long nineteenth-century and it has always been a standard feature of labour relations in Latin America and on the African continent. The invention of a new class category has political consequences: if the precariat is a class in-itself oppressed by the rest of the working class then this goes beyond class fraction theory towards a post-Marxist or even anti-Marxist theory of economics where the working class itself is the exploiting class.

Another issue of class analysis is determining the effects of workers occupying multiple locations within the economy. Early twentieth-century labour relations in the United States were filled with pseudo-philosophical debates as to whether or not student workers were 'students' or 'workers' as if one position contradicted the other. A more pointed debate can be found in the economic analysis of slavery (since capitalism is predicated on free labour). The rise of prison labour has created an economic situation where convicts are both direct producers of goods and services and themselves commodities traded within the profit-based prison system. What's more, capitalist class positioning is relatively slippery when compared to feudal class structure. Someone who is born into the peasantry might go back and forth between peasant and proletarian labour processes. The working class might move into the middle class, into the capitalist class, or into the informal economy; capitalists, unlike the princes of the feudal age, are also in danger of sliding into the working class or even the reserve army of labour.

It is difficult to imagine how knowledge of what and where the class is (class formation) could be unrelated to what class forces can do or become (class struggle). Epistemological barriers within class formation—the mathematising of social relations through the wage, setting labour processes outside the general public's frame of vision, transnational production, the retitling of direct producers as management-lite (shift-supervisors, partners, associates, family, etc.)—have contributed to the decline in class struggle within the global north. However, while the working class has been debating its contours and contingencies, the capitalist class, as evidenced by decades of coordinated offensives and backroom trade deals, has had little problem defining itself or determining its interests.

Social Epistemology: The Class for-itself

The in-itself/for-itself dynamic is related to the problem of object/subject in Marxist thought. For intersubjective conditions to affect objective conditions it must be recognised that objective conditions affect intersubjective conditions. I use the term intersubjective because, as Lukacs points out, the subject/object dichotomy exists to enshrine the individual rational subject of bourgeois philosophy, the Kantian contemplator who, always at a distance, performs mental operations on the objective world. This separation of human existence from the world of objects creates an ontological split between man and nature as well as a split between labour and its product. It should be noted that Marx's dialectical understanding of human activity did not promote a subject/object split. Instead, Marx advances the idea of a *metabolic* relation between populations and their environments, one that is mutually transformative. This transformation is not dependent on human contemplation but on material processes.

In this spirit, I use the term 'intersubjective'. The subject is not only also an object, but subjectivity develops by interacting with one's environment, an environment that also includes other subjects. Subjects are not only in a metabolic relation with the objective world, but also in a metabolic relation with other subjects. This view is tenable whether the class is seen as beings located within processes, as class fractions, or as the distillation of human existence into two great classes.

Feminist thought complicates questions of subjectivity, as well as intersubjectivity and Althusserian critiques of subjectivity, by insisting that the subject is not just a spirit (even an interactive, relational one) but the localisation of experience through the fact of human embodiment. Our metabolic relations are filtered through the capacities and limitations of physical bodies. These bodies need not be individual. Political bodies experience strikes, massacres, as well as luxuries and freedom to move. Though it is to a much lesser extent (and indeed the term 'lesser' here marks a qualitative distinction) it is also possible to understand political bodies in a virtual sense—networked bodies sharing images and experiences affecting brain chemistry and neurological development. This reciprocal, interactive development of subjects (subjects as processes) does not mean, however, that the subject is a *tabula rasa*. Interactions don't occur in a series of disconnected moments. Subjects are not only dialogic, they exist in time. Intersubjectivity involves the relation between embodied agents within a historical process.

Culture, Recognition, and the Problem of Identity

Althusser and his followers have been widely criticised by E.P. Thompson and other labour historians, not only for their theoreticism, but also for their minimisation of the role of culture in class formation. (Labour historians tend to engage in localised research where the role of culture and identity in class formation has explanatory power.)

But what role does culture—defined here as collections of signs, stories, and processes created by groups to self-identify—and *habitus*—collective social dispositions developed by particular groups through mimicry—play in the intersubjective development of the working class as a totality? First, it is important to affirm that identification processes occur in response to life experiences grounded in economic realities. Resistance cultures develop among oppressed people. Art and narratives transcend national origin and connect exploited and oppressed people across territories. Shibboleths develop. This is particularly clear when the ruling class forms secret societies and fraternities that enforce strict social norms. However, there are two particular barriers for shared culture and identity having a profound impact on working class self-organising activity. First, working class status is transnational while culture largely develops in a local, national, and even subcultural context. Second, capitalist commodification of local cultures has estranged culture workers from themselves. Just as mass-produced woollen coats during the Industrial Revolution were eventually purchased by those who previously stitched coats by hand, contemporary objects rich in cultural significance are not immune to commodification. When such commodities are marketed globally, they become objects of fascination disconnected from their original context.

While the theme of the destructive power of white consumers' colonising cultural appropriation is centred in Western political discourse, this is itself a Euro-American construct that obscures the current cultural erasure imposed by capitalism in much of the global south. For example, in Durban, traditional ceremonial goods manufactured and sold in the informal economy between South Africans are increasingly being 'appropriated' by industrial capitalists in the Pacific Rim, whose mass-manufacture of traditional goods economically pressures African street vendors to sell mass-manufactured versions of the products they once created. This appropriation and destruction of culture happens without input from the Euro-American consumer. In fact, it is Western neoliberal ideology that places the emphasis and agency on consumer habits and desires rather than the compulsions of global capitalism.

Nonetheless, it makes sense that working people would turn to culture, and not economics, in order to understand class. Cultural markers help people secure a sense of belonging. But class is not reducible to culture, nor is it an identity. In fact, expropriated workers might have many competing identities. Workers hold various contradictory positions within economic operations. A working mother/caregiver is pulled between the cultural expectations of her role in productive and reproductive labour. All workers have multiple identities and may participate in cultures that are hostile towards other workers' cultures. Workers may live in multicultural working class neighborhoods, monocultural and nativist working class neighborhoods, or they may live in large cities where a mix of classes rent from the super-rich. Just as working people and poor people appropriate the motifs of ruling class culture (ex. drag culture's use of the notion of opulence, conspicuous consumption in rap music), the ruling class is free to participate in the traditional signs of working class culture (e.g. tattoos, sports fandom, trucker hats). Working class neighborhoods and cultures are not necessarily stable in the neoliberal cities of the global North. This is not to say that culture plays no role in working class struggle; however, it is to say that it currently plays an ambivalent role. The impact that working class cultures and identities will have on international class formation and international class struggle in twenty-first century capitalism is still largely unclear.

What is to be Done?

What can be done to renew interest in the Marxist theory of class in a highly visual, highly complex era? I have three possible suggestions given the above argument. First, a war of position must be waged on the terrain of economic education: how does exploitation work? Does the material world have value? Where does that value come from? Demystifying economics is essential for distinguishing between reactionary and progressive critiques of capital. If one way to think through exploitation is to say that the value of what workers consume is less than the value of what they produce, then the popular lament of the worker as 'mindless consumer' obscures exploitation. We do not live in a 'consumer society'. Capitalists do not produce use values for our benefit. They produce exchange values for the accumulation of profits. The second, internationalism, is dependent upon the first. An international understanding of how capitalism operates at a global level can facilitate solidarities between exploited people and between exploited people and all those who wish to end exploitation. This will not be achieved on the terrain of representation and cultural identity, but in a war of position that both uses the familiar motifs of identitarian experience while moving beyond identitarian loyalties. Finally, although it is important to acknowledge and stand against acts of oppression it is also critical to understand how oppression is produced, including the role that exploitation plays in the development of oppression. Much of this work must be done outside of the neoliberal academy (and when it is done within the academy it is critical that the work be conducted in universities with working-class student populations). In this way, the hidden operations of the capitalist mode of production can become known.

References

Lukács, G. (1972) *History and Class Consciousness: Studies in Marxist Dialectics.* Cambridge: MIT Press.
Marx, K. (1976) *Capital, Vol. 1.* New York: Penguin.
Marx, K. (1973) *The Poverty of Philosophy.* Moscow: Progress Publishers.
McNally, D. (2011) *Global Slump: The Economics and Politics of Crisis and Resistance.* Oakland: PM Press.

Mkhize, S., Dube, G., and Skinner, C. (2013) Street Vendors in Durban, South Africa Informal Economy Monitoring Study. http://wiego.org/sites/wiego.org/files/publications/files/IEMS-Durban-Street-Vendors-City-Report-English.pdf.

Olin Wright, E. (1997) *Classes*. London: Verso.

Standing, G. (2014) *The Precariat: The New Dangerous Class*. London: Bloomsbury.

Thompson, E.P. (1978) *Poverty of Theory and Other Essays*. London: Merlin.

Veblen, T. (2009) *Theory of the Leisure Class*. Oxford: Oxford University Press.

Wolff, R. and Resnick, S. (1987) *Knowledge and Class: A Marxian Critique of Political Economy*. Chicago: University of Chicago Press.

PART 2

Class and Culture

∴

CHAPTER 8

Peasants, Migrants and Self-Employed Workers: The Masks that Veil Class Affiliation in Latin America: The Argentine Case

Marina Kabat and Eduardo Sartelli

Introduction

The defeat of the revolutionary process that took place in the seventies in Latin America was not only political and material, but also ideological. This ideological setback was deepened with the restoration of liberal democracy. That is because democracy represents the moment when bourgeois hegemony is fully established, i.e. when bourgeois rule is stronger than ever because it does not rest only on material coercion, but also in the consensus of the exploited class. In this context, postmodernism promptly emerged in an academia which had already been purged of Marxist influence under military governments, when many Marxist intellectuals suffered forced 'disappearance'—i.e. were kidnapped and murdered- or were forced into exile. Other academics withdrew their advocacy of Marxism and became its fiercest contestants while most of those who resisted this ideological turn were cast out from universities and research centres.

The concept of class was deliberately attacked by Latin American postmodernist theorists and the working class was eliminated from their perspectives. This position was sustained by two lines of arguments. The first argument simply reproduces the Western postmodernist thesis that there are no levels of social reality that determines the other levels—given that they are all considered to have the same causal powers. Therefore, social subjects may be constituted in any sphere of society. From this perspective, social classes are considered just one of many possible subjects. The working class is denied any kind of primacy over other social groups (Laclau and Mouffe, 2001). But the second line of argument is built on alleged local characteristics of Latin American countries and claims that if the working class exists, it certainly does not in the highly mobile Latin American societies. Hence, the study of the Latin American social structure requires more flexible concepts such as that of "popular sectors". Theoretically, this current is rooted in the work of E.P. Thompson (Thompson 1991) or, better said, in a particular interpretation of his work.

In this chapter, we offer both a theoretical and empirical refutation of this thesis. On the one hand, we argue that gender, ethnicity, and other identity categories are secondary determinations that intersect with class. On the other hand, we assert that subjective identification based on these secondary determinations is deliberately promoted by the State in order to inhibit the emergence of wider class consciousness, thus maintaining and reinforcing class fragmentation.

We support this interpretation with evidence from Argentina's working class evolution in the last four decades, specially focusing on the proletarian fractions whose affiliation has been most debated—i.e. migrants, self-employed workers and peasants. We base this analysis on a long-time collective research developed in the CEICS—Centro de Estudios e Investigación en Ciencias Sociales—Center for Study and Research in Social Sciences, which includes our own studies and those under our direct supervision.

Thompson's Dual Heritage

In our view, the core points in 'Thompsonianism' -namely the work inspired by E.P. Thompson- are: 1. The importance of subjective elements in class constitution; 2. The role of "experience" in the constitution of those elements; 3. The subjects' self-construction through class struggle; 4. Resistance as a privileged course of action; 5. Popular cultural autonomy.

The first aspect to consider is Thompson's conviction that there is no social class without some form of consciousness. "A class cannot exist without some form of self-consciousness. Otherwise, it is not, or it is not yet a class..." (Thompson 1991b, 31 author's translation). This could be simply interpreted as the arrival point of a historical experience or, it could otherwise be understood as a constitutive role. In the first sense, the subjective element represents the culmination of the class formation process. In the second, the subjective element itself creates the class, which is not very far from Laclau's and Mouffe's view (Laclau and Mouffe 2001). The idealistic (discursive) drift is a danger already present—though in a latent form—in Thompson's work.

The second aspect (the role of experience) also has two possible readings based on the classic Marxist formulation, 'life determines *consciousness*'. As in the first point, the different emphasis on the existence of social hierarchies among social relations determines either a materialistic or an idealistic position. It can be understood that "life" refers to the contradictions within the social relations. Indeed, if we assume that relations of production are the basic social relations, and that the others line up behind and according to them, consciousness is, then, the expression of the experience of social exploitation. Thompson and Meiksins Wood have upheld this interpretation (Thompson 1978, 298 and Meiksins Wood 1995, 97). Conversely, if such a hierarchy is denied, any instance of social life has the same importance as the relations of production and therefore social subjects constitute themselves from other determinants or –more eclectically- from a mix of different determinations conceived as equally weighted. Thompson's notion of experience enables these two interpretations, as Anderson has rightly pointed out: The first one is pretty orthodox and presents no difference with Hobsbawn's line of thinking (Hobsbawm 2010a and 2010b, for instance). The second refers to any kind of experience, thus it blurs the primacy of structural determinants. The concept's ambiguity is reinforced because it means both the individual's consciousness of a personal situation as well as the situation itself (Anderson 1964 and 1980).

Despite the theoretical positions assumed by Thompson in response to some of his early critics, the effacement of the primacy of structural tendencies can be found in *The Making of the English Working Class*. In this masterpiece, the material process, i.e., the industrial revolution, is placed at the same level as the political factors (the anti-Jacobin repression) or the other subjective elements, such as cultural workers' traditions or the way exploitation is perceived by the workers. A similar analysis of Thompson's most classic work can be found in Anderson and Trimberger (Anderson 1964 and 1980; Trimberger 1984). The latter explains how the first part of *The Making of the English Working Class* elucidates the political culture inherited by the English workers; then, in Part 2, it analyses how groups of working people experienced the changes they were going through and the third part deals with workers' organisation. It is in Part 2 where the limits placed by the material relations of the capitalist- industrial revolution are expected to be found. But Thompson does not analyse the economic data he presents. "Rather, all the discussion is about experience and the degree to which this experience was *not* determined by economic circumstances" (Trimberger 1984: 222). Thompson disregarded the objective working conditions though he focused on how people felt about them. "In his zeal to correct the 'objectivist' biases of economic historians and more orthodox Marxists, Thompson fleshed out only one side of the dialectic of being and consciousness..." (Trimberger 1984, 224).

The idea that the working class makes itself during the struggle has two alternative interpretations. In a narrow sense, it means that by becoming aware of their condition, the working class transforms itself into a political subject and bearer of creative action. But, in a broader sense, it can be conceived as an autonomous, free and self-regulated subject. The notion of resistance may be employed to designate one specific course of action -the kind of action that a subaltern class is capable of in a moment of weakness or defeat, a defensive action. As *The Making of the English Working Class* shows, even in its worst political moments the subaltern class can find a gap through which to express its rejection of domination. Yet we need to distinguish between resistance and other types of action, for example ones that are more offensive. Without such a distinction, there is no point in addressing Latin American insurgency in the 1970's as Working class resistance actions (Berrotaran and Pozzi 1994). Many Postmodern authors misuse the concept of 'resistance' to devalue great events of class struggle by equating them with minor and individual actions such as joking with a foreman or producing graffiti (Palacio 1996).[1] Finally, we see that the belief in popular cultural autonomy can be sustained through two different lines of arguments. The first stresses that the subaltern class holds interests that are antagonistic to those of the class that exploits it; hence the subaltern class' interests can never match the ones of its ruling class. The second interpretation states that the subaltern class can in no way be assimilated to the bourgeois world and that it cannot even be known (Guha 1999).

These dissimilar lines of interpretation of Thompson's work lead to two different paths. The first one follows a recognisable Marxist trajectory, in no substantially way different from orthodox authors such as Eric Hobsbawn or Pierre Vilar. The second one, tends towards a variant of postmodernism.

Ellen Meiksins Wood has been the main defender of the orthodox interpretation of Thompson's work. She has attempted to refute most of Thompson's Marxist critics. However, as she herself recognises, in her defense of Thompson she has combined Thompson's and her own thinking (Meiksins Wood 1995, 77 and 93). While we largely agree with Meiksins Wood's class theory, we do not find it reflects Thompson's conception entirely accurately. In many aspects she tries to translate Thompson's concepts into more orthodox Marxist terms; for instance, she claims that "To say that exploitation is 'experienced in class ways and only thence give(s) rise to class formations' is to say precisely that the conditions of exploitation, the relations of production, are objectively *there* to be experienced." (Meiksins Wood 1995, 80) But as Caínzos López stresses, Thompson does not refer to "relations of production", but to the "living conditions". That is not a mere semantic difference because,

---

[1] In this point we find that Thompson himself does not make the same mistake that Thompsonian authors do. Thompson searched for little actions of class antagonism in a historical period where other authors were not capable of seeing any. He found, as it were, class struggle where others saw social peace. But in other historical contexts, and in the minds of less political committed authors, the term resistance is used to divert attention from major class actions.

while the more orthodox Marxist term, "relations of production" refers to the structural level, for Thompson "living conditions" means all aspects of social life. Thus, Thompson's notion of "living conditions" blends together objective and subjective elements, i.e. structural and super structural factors (Caínzos López 1989, 38) and therefore cannot simply be equated to "relations of production."

Caínzos López points out the confluence, despite their dissimilar departure points, between Thompson on the one hand, and Laclau and Mouffe, on the other (Caínzos López 1989, 61). A bit less categorically, we argue that Thompsonianism faces two different roads, one leads to the "history from below" (Genovese 1976, Meiksins Wood 1995, Reich, Gordon, Edwards, 1973, for example), and the other points to the 'subaltern group' (Guha, 1999). These two alternatives are present within Argentine historiography.

Argentine Thompsonianism

In Argentina, Thompson's work in the 1980s and 1990s served as a justification for two contrasting positions: on the one hand, the assertion of the working class as an endlessly creative force and, on the other hand, the denial of its existence. Both positions stemmed from the same idea: that class does not exist without class consciousness and that this consciousness arises from experience and expresses the working class' capacity—or impotence—to resist the attacks continuously unleashed on it. The first expression frames the following two in an idealistic perspective and can be interpreted in two divergent forms: if class does not exist without consciousness, as there is no class lacking any degree of consciousness, then any kind of consciousness is valuable and leads to—or may eventually lead to—socialism (Berrotarán and Pozzi 1994); or if class does not exist without consciousness and socialism is the working class' necessary consciousness, then the absence of a powerful socialist tendency is considered a proof of the inexistence of the working class (Romero 1990). The first reasoning corresponds to a populist political perspective. The second one was supported by social democratic historians.

With the overthrow of the military regime in the 1980s the social democratic current took control of academia. It was formed by a group of intellectuals who assumed the task of building a University at the service of the 'democratic transition'. This meant working steadily in the reconstruction of the consensus that the bourgeoisie needed in order to re-establish its tottering hegemony after the 1970s crisis. Those who had previously advocated for Marxist theories soon forgot about them because the defence of bourgeois democracy as the best and only possible political system required the elimination of class analysis. As Hilda Sábato states:

> We first questioned and then rejected a philosophy of history that gives a precise and progressive sense to the development of societies, as well as the assumption of the existence of subjects as bearers of historical change.
> SÁBATO 1993, 16

The working class had to be eliminated as a historical subject, and in its place these intellectuals set the concept of 'popular sectors'.

According to the historian Romero, the 'popular sectors' concept was much more useful to understand Argentine and Latin-American dynamics than the –in his opinion- archaic concept of class. In his view, the notion of the working class implied an automatic correlation between a social existence and its consciousness. In addition, he considers class to be a rigid notion that is incapable of accounting for the changes of social subjects and he questions the economic determinism he attributes to the concept. Finally, he stresses that whatever utility the concept could have had for other periods and regions, class was definitively not useful in Latin American countries with scarce industrial activity and high social mobility (Romero 1990).

It is quite clear that Romero only fights with the ghosts he created. No relevant Marxist author has ever exclusively associated the working class with industrial factory workers. In fact, Marx, Engels, Luxemburg, Lenin, have all analysed members of the proletariat who performed their work outside factories: rural proletarians, home-workers, peddlers, among others. For the Marxist tradition, the concept of 'the worker' makes reference to all persons who do not own the means of production and their livelihood of subsistence therefore depends on selling their labour force (or the collective labour force of relatives within a family). This engenders a wide variety of situations unified by exploitation. Where does Romero get the class definition that he endeavors to demolish? Nobody knows because he simply does not tell. He just invents a suitable foe that meets his criticisms.

Colloquially the term 'popular sectors' has often been employed as a synonym of people or even workers, but Romero was the first who attempted to give it a theoretical basis. However, he only achieves a mass of contradictions and a pitiful return to functionalism. Romero states that popular sectors constitute themselves in the cultural sphere, but on the same page he asserts that social subjects form themselves on both the material and the cultural ground

(Romero 1990, 29). As with Thompson, for Romero, both spheres are linked by the 'experiences' of the subject. These experiences unify and constitute the social subjects. What kind of experience may lead to the constitution of the popular sectors? Romero's answer is extremely vague: labour or housing conditions, the experience of being a foreigner in a xenophobic context, the participation in common struggles, political or other kinds of self-identification (Romero 1990, 36). Unifying and constituent elements may belong to any level of social reality, from labour to ideology or any fortuitous circumstance. Thus, the popular sector field may shrink or enlarge respectively by either including or excluding the lumpen-proletariat and the petit bourgeoisie in its upper and lower limits. Just like Thompson, Romero ends up giving to any kind of experience the same determining power. For example, a community soccer club or a popular library have the same influence in the determination of the characteristics of the "subject" as exploitation does. All these experiences equally forge identities, each one of which has the same value and significance.

Popular sectors theory is no less than a return to Functionalist theories of social stratification which deny inequality in the ownership of means of production to be determinant for the formation of social groups (for example, Parsons 1970). In fact, just as in Functionalism, society is divided into groups defined by their different access-capacity to certain key goods, such as income, education and status among others. These groups are regarded as totally unrelated to each other except for a mere gradation (more or less rich, educated, etc). In this way conflict disappears. When it emerges it is seen as something irrational. This is clearly depicted in, for example, responses to the 1919 January Red Week, a mass insurrectional strike. For instance, David Rock, who belongs to the same historiographic tendency as Romero and Sabato, denies any classist base to the Red Week of 1919, which he always refers to as a 'Tragic Week'. He finds people's actions emotional—as opposed to conscious or even rational (Rock and dos Santos 1971).

This conception did not only dominate academia but the school system as well. The same scholars in charge of higher education at universities designed school books, teaching programs and had a wide influence in the media. Some of the intellectuals that we have criticised here had permanent columns in the main newspapers from where they disseminated their point of view.

At this point, it is worth remembering an initial phrase of Thompson's classic work, usually forgotten by those who invoke his name to question Marxism:

> *Class*, rather than classes, for reasons which it is one purpose of this book to examine. There is, of course, a difference. 'Working classes' is

a descriptive term, which evades as much as it defines. It ties loosely together a bundle of discrete phenomena. There were tailors here and weavers there, and together they make up the working classes.

By class I understand a historical phenomenon, unifying a number of disparate and seemingly unconnected events, both in the raw material of experience and in consciousness....

THOMPSON 1991, 8

This quote clearly shows that Thompson does not intend to replace working class as a privileged social actor by a multiplicity of random groups as Romero and other social-democratic Argentine historians do. In this spirit, we are going to analyse some of the alleged new social actors, and show how they all belong to the same collective subject, i.e. the working class.

First Case: Migrants

Both in historical terms and in contemporary analyses serious attempts have been made to instil the notion 'migrant' as a concept with higher explanatory power than working class. This presupposes, first, that ethnic solidarity among migrants' communities is deeper than class solidarity among migrant workers and other workers and, second, that class conflicts within these migrant communities are weak. For instance, a historian, Devoto stated that ethnic solidarity was stronger than class solidarity at the beginning of the twentieth century because ethnic mutual aid societies had more affiliates than unions (Devoto 1984). Of course, Devoto forgets that unions were severely repressed by the State and that at that time there were many other proofs of class consciousness (general strikes, insurrectional actions such as the Red Week of 1919) that contradict his thesis (Sartelli 1996). Postmodern anthropologists also consider ethnic solidarity more important than class affiliation to comprehend migrants' experiences. The issue has been raised specially regarding Bolivian migrants working in the garment industry in Argentina. Many times, when labour conditions in this sector come to the fore, the media tends to portray garment workers as slaves. Some anthropologists reject this mischaracterisation as xenophobic, but at the other extreme they end defending intense exploitation (long working hours, low pay, and piecework system) as a particular cultural practice typical of this community. Summing up, migrant workers are portrayed either as slaves or as members of a hardworking and conflict-free community. Both characterisations are equally inaccurate because they neglect class analysis.

The term 'slave' is usually employed by the sensationalist press regardless of circumstances: if migrant workers are fighting against their dismissal newspapers immediately entitle it a 'slave protest'.[2] However, anyone can understand that there has never been a single slave who had to fight to keep his job. In this kind of media article, as in much scholarly research based upon them, economical and extra-economical coercion are blended together.[3] What distinguishes a capitalist worker from a slave or a serf is that he is not compelled to work by extra-economic coercion, but by economic constraint. This kind of coercion puts pressure on the proletariat's reproduction conditions, because his or her subsistence depends upon the actual sale of his or her labour power. Therefore, given certain conditions, high unemployment for instance, proletarians will compete among themselves for a job, which some could describe as slavery-like work due to its harsh conditions. That is the core of capitalism's production relations: the labour force is free, free to starve unless they get a job. Thus, under certain conditions, the proletariat will agree to taking the worst jobs for the lowest payment. That does not make a slave out of a person, it just means he/she is a proletarian and to put an end to this situation, it is necessary to transform the entire social system. Contrary to this, the Catholic Church prefers to talk about modern slavery because it allows for criticism of the harsh labour conditions in the capitalist society, without having to blame capitalism itself.[4]

At the other extreme, relativist approaches stress the role of hard work in the migrant communities. They argue that workers take jobs in the garment industry on their own will and work ten or twelve hours a day in order to transform themselves into workshops owners. In their defense of ethnic communities' practices they disregard child labour and working conditions that continuously put proletarians' life in danger. In fact much of these labour conditions

---

2 "Big brands' suppliers employ slave labour" *Info Blanco sobre Negro*, December 24, 2013. http://goo.gl/l7XRbQ Last accesed 25/8/2016.

3 An example is the work of Kevin Bales. We find that his 'modern slaves' are just old fashioned proletarians. But Bales fails to account for that because he simply dismisses class analysis. Further, he tries to establish that slavery is an institution that may affect anyone because it provides equal opportunities to be enslaved as modern slavery is democratic and affects all races, colors and ethnics group (Bales and Soodalter, 2009, 5–6). What he fails to see is that the common denominator of all the people that he labels as "modern slaves" is their belonging to the working class.

4 Papa Francisco dedica 48° Jornada Mundial de la Paz a lucha contra esclavitud" (Pope Francis dedicates the 48th World Day of Peace to fight against slavery). "ACIprensa, 21/8/14, https://www.aciprensa.com/noticias/papa-francisco-dedica-48-jornada-mundial-de-la-paz-a-lucha-contra-esclavitud-10308/.

came to light after some workshops were set on fire and many workers and their children who lived there died. They depict an image of a harmonious migrant community and are completely oblivious to class confrontation within this community.

Indeed there is no such a thing as a 'migrant'. There are worker migrants and bourgeois migrants. The ideology of the Bolivian migrant communities and compatriot solidarity is nothing else than the ideology of a long-established Bolivian bourgeoisie in Argentina. Most of these communities' media resources, such as radio stations or newspapers belong to this migrant bourgeoisie and it becomes useful to keep conflicts down. However, class conflict has arisen on many occasions. When workers turn to the unions or social organisations to enforce their labour rights, the main leaders of the community oppose such actions, even preventing the entrance of State Labour prosecutors to the workshops or by sending bullies to assault the workers who made the official complaint (Egan 2015).

Class conflict does not appear only in the workplace but also in other arenas. In December 2010, a homeless multitude occupied the Indoamericano Park with the intention of building their homes there. A government census of the occupants estimated them at over 13,000 persons. The occupants came from shantytowns near the park and many of them were migrants (mostly Bolivian and Paraguayans who work in garment sweatshops and in the construction industry). Before violent eviction of the occupants, which caused the death of three people, the city's mayor –Argentina's current president— Mauricio Macri gave a press conference together with leaders of the migrant communities. These leaders talked emphatically against the occupation and were severely criticised by the migrant workers that were occupying the park. It just happened that these community migrants' leaders were really the chiefs of business chambers. For instance, Alfredo Ayala—a migrant leader who spoke against the occupation—is a garment workshop owner and the president of the Bolivian Civil Association Federation (which is a trade association of Bolivian textile businessman based in Argentina). Naturally, the land occupation affected the interests of the Bolivian bourgeoisie. Migrant workers did not fail to notice that.

Second Case: Peasants

The concept of peasants hinders class analysis, just as the notion of migrant does when it is used without a class reference. Stricto sensu, the term peasant is only valid for pre-capitalist societies. Within a capitalist society, peasants may exist for a certain amount of time as a relic of the feudal period. No wonder authors who believe in the current existence of peasants in Latin-America also consider that capitalist relations are not fully developed in the region. In the feudal system, peasant communities were self-sufficient and were exploited by feudal lords by extra-economical coercion. Once capitalism develops, peasants are relieved of that coercion and consistent with the rules of accumulation they become either members of the bourgeoisie or the proletariat, passing through the transitional stage of petit bourgeoisie.

Argentine 'chacareros' (a kind of farmer), who are mostly plain members of the bourgeois class, tend to present themselves as peasants or poor farmers when it is suitable for them to claim special state benefits. The false equation between "chacareros" and peasants comes from the overestimation of the 'family work' performed on their land and the underestimation of the wage labour employed by them. The latter is commonly underrated because it is mostly seasonal work. However, when wage labour and family labour are measured in yearly hours and compared with each other, the results show a neat preponderance of wage labour. At present times, the alleged family labour is not actual work but managerial activities concerned with the control of the labour performed by wage labours (Sartelli dir. 2008 70–77). Thus Argentine 'chacareros' are just the rural bourgeoisie who live mainly from the exploitation of wage labour.

At the other extreme, most of the so-called peasants are truly rural workers. The provinces that supposedly have the poorest peasants are the main providers of rural seasonal workers for the entire country. This is for instance the case of Santiago del Estero Province. People in this district were initially employed in the tannin factories and related rural activities. When tannin production decreased and the tannin factories closed, they left a bunch of unemployed people who settled on the abandoned land previously used for tannin exploitation. Although some of these families engage in some production for their own consumption or for sale, their main incomes come from the wages as rural workers, and other proletarian incomes such as social assistance or pensions (Kabat et al., 2017). In Chaco province, the mechanisation of cotton harvest in the 1990s left a multitude of unemployed workers, some of whom, as means of subsistence turned to a very precarious agricultural production, for example sowing in tiny land surfaces at the roadside. They do not own their land or the means of production, as most of them use seeds provided by the state. Another part of the workers migrated to the provinces' city suburbs where they remain unemployed. That is why Chaco is one of the provinces that receive more social assistance per capita.

In Misiones province the advance of mechanisation in the forest industry also left thousands unemployed. Some of these unemployed families occupied the lands which had been deforested and abandoned by the Forest companies. Some of the occupants' main income is their wage labour (36% of domestic units) making them proletarians. Others (50% of domestic units) are hired by tobacco firms under the form of contract agriculture (UNAM 2004). Under this legal form, the alleged peasants are working on lands that do not belong to them, with the means of production owned by the tobacco firms, under their instruction and supervision. So, they do not possess any means of production and they do not control the productive process: contract agriculture clearly hides in this case the purchase of labour force. We find again workers whose only possession is their labour power: they are, then, proletarians too. Another 27% of all domestic units have a more extensive cultivated area and employ wage labour (Baranger-Schiavoni 2005). So, they belong to the petit bourgeoisie.

Many authors still defend the characterisation of peasants for this population based on subjective arguments, because they accept self-identification as the decisive criterion to establish class affiliation. They disregard that class identification is in itself an arena of class struggle as well. The bourgeoisie is continuously trying to prevent the emergence of a strong working class consciousness. To that end, it promotes alternative identifications such as nationalism, and attempts to fracture working class unity. Bourgeois ideology promotes the atomisation of the working class by dismembering it and fostering alternative identities.

This is clearly the case with peasant self-identification. As we have seen, many of the people characterised as peasants come from a previous proletarian occupation (tannin or forest industries or cotton harvesting). So, based on their own history, they do not have peasant roots. Most of them are landless and even live in cities such as Resistencia. However, institutions linked with the Catholic Church deliberately promoted peasant identification and the conformation of peasant organisations (Desalvo 2014). Some State organisms have pursued the same objective. With the advice of international organisms such as the World Bank and the International Monetary Fund they launched programs such as the rural development plan, whose goal was to reduce rural poverty. This initiative was not bottom-up, but rather top-down, from the upper echelons of the international bourgeoisie (Muñoz 2015; Manzanal and Schneider 2011). These international organisms promote these kinds of programmes because they rightly estimate that it is cheaper to maintain this rural population in a rural area than in urban cities. Thus, by promoting rural programmes and preventing these people migrating to the cities these organisms seek to reduce state social spending. In Argentina -where a strong unemployment movement was formed- keeping the relative surplus population in rural areas also forestalled the strengthening of that movement.

Self-Employed

As in the aforementioned cases, the self-employed sector hides a dual reality by merging together proletarian and petit bourgeois factions. In Argentina, 18 per cent of the people in a census who defined themselves as 'self-employed' lack any kind of tool, vehicle or shop (CEICS 2016). This means that they do not have any means of production and clearly belong to the proletariat. This 18% is a very conservative figure: cardboard collectors who possess a simple cart where they collect paper from the streets can be considered in official statistics as owners of a tool. The same happens with garment or shoe home workers who possess a simple sewing machine. In both cases these workers are usually accounted as self-employed workers when they can be better understood as output workers for the waste paper companies or the garment stores, respectively (Villanova 2012; Kabat 2014).

Research must focus on the production relations involved in a job regardless of their legal form. The latter expresses in a crystallised form the balance of power between the social classes. Thus, the same person doing the same job may be considered either an employee or an independent partner by different legislations. After the defeat of the working class' offensive in the 70's, the balance of power has favored the bourgeoisie. Correspondingly, labour laws have been modified at its request. Work relations have been redefined. According to the legislation, different workers are no longer considered as wage labour and are taken as independent partners instead, as happened, for example in Argentina with dairy workers (Kabat et al., 2014). The bourgeoisie always avoids recognising the labour nexus with their workers or tries to belittle the obligations that such a link implies. Thus, we need to differentiate the relations of production from the legal form in which they are portrayed by the legislation of the bourgeois class.

Conclusion

In the last decades we have heard a lot about alleged new collective subjects: new slaves that are not a possession or property of anyone; new peasants who are landless and live in big cities, new marginals that perform similar jobs to the ones described by Engels in his depiction of the nineteenth century Manchester working class. We cannot find any substantial difference between picking cardboard or picking dung in the streets (Engels 1993). All these subjects truly belong to one and only one class, the proletariat.

The bourgeoisie continuously works to weaken class consciousness and forge alternative identifications. Thus class consciousness does not arise spontaneously from mere experience. If left wing organisations accept self-identification as the main criterion to define class affiliation, they abandon a crucial battlefield. The way workers perceive themselves is conditioned by many factors, including their previous class status and bourgeois discourse and propaganda. It is not neutral that a worker considers himself as a part of the 'middle classes', a peasant or an indigenous and believes that he or she does not belong to the working class. Socialists should not compromise with populist and subjective views and should promote class consciousness among all proletarians. That is the first step towards solving the main challenge we face today: rebuilding working class unity out of its current fragmentation.

References

Anderson, P. (1964) Origins of the present crisis *New Left Review* 23: 26–53.

Anderson, P. (1980) *Arguments within English Marxism*. London: New Left Groups.

Bales, K. and Soodalter, R. (2010) *The slave next door: Human trafficking and slavery in America today*. Berkeley: University of California Press. Kindle Edition.

Baranger, D. and Schiavoni, G. (2005) Censo de ocupantes de tierras. *Estudios Regionales*, 13 (28): 80.

Berrotarán, P. y P. Pozzi, (eds.) (1994) *Estudios inconformistas sobre la clase obrera argentina, 1955–1989*. Buenos Aires: Letrabuena.

Caínzos López, M. (1989) Clase, acción y estructura: de EP Thompson al posmarxismo. *Zona Abierta*, 50: 1–70.

CEICS. (2016) *Informe estadístico*. Buenos Aires: CEICS.

Desalvo, M. (2014) El MOCASE: orígenes, consolidación y fractura del movimiento campesino de Santiago del Estero. *Astrolabio*, (12).

Devoto, F. (1984) Las sociedades italianas de ayuda mutua en Buenos Aires y Santa Fe. *Studi emigrazione* (75).

Egan, J. (2014) Entre paisanos y cooperativas. *El Aromo* (79). goo.gl/ByqYsV.

Engels, F. (1993) *The condition of the working class in England*. Oxford: Oxford University Press.

Genovese, E. (1976) *Roll, Jordan, Roll. The World the Slaves Made*. New York: Vintage Books.

Guha, R. (1999) *Elementary aspects of peasant insurgency in colonial India*. Durham: Duke University Press.

Hobsbawm, E. (2010a) *Age of Empire: 1875–1914*. London: Hachette.

Hobsbawm, E. (2010b) *Age of Capital: 1848–1875*. London: Hachette.

Kabat, M. (2014) From structural breakage to political reintegration of the working class: Relative surplus population layers in Argentina and their involvement in the piquetero movement. *Capital & Class* 38 (2): 365–384.

Kabat, M. et al. (2014) Avanços e retrocessos da flexibilização trabalhista na Argentina. Contribuições para uma comparação das trajetórias históricas de distintos ramos de atividade. *Mundos do Trabalho* 6 (12): 273–297.

Kabat, M. et al. (2017) The Tip of the Iceberg. Media Coverage of "Slave Labor" in Argentina. Latin America Perspectives. March http://journals.sagepub.com/doi/10.1177/0094582X17699909.

Laclau, E. and Mouffe, C. (2001) *Hegemony and socialist strategy: Towards a radical democratic politics*. London: Verso.

Lenin, V. (1958–1960) *Obras completas*. Buenos Aires: Cártago.

Manzanal, M. and Schneider (2011) Agricultura familiar y políticas de desarrollo rural en Argentina y Brasil (análisis comparativo, 1990–2010). *Revista Interdisciplinaria de Estudios Agrarios* 34: 35–71.

Meiksins Wood, E. (1995) *Democracy against capitalism. Renewing historical materialism*. Cambridge: Cambridge University Press.

Muñoz, R. (2015) La construcción estatal de la "Agricultura Familiar" en Argentina. Un análisis de los Programas de Desarrollo Rural. XV Jornadas Interescuelas/departamentos de historia.

Palacio, J.M. (1996) ¿Revolución en las pampas? *Desarrollo económico* 35 (140): 677–683.

Palmer, B. (1990) The Eclipse of Materialism: Marxism and the Writing of Social History in the 1980s. *Socialist Register* 26 (26): 111–146.

Parsons, T. (1970). Equality and inequality in modern society, or social stratification revisited. *Sociological Inquiry* 40 (2): 13–72.

Reich, M., Gordon, D.M., & Edwards, R.C. (1973). A theory of labour market segmentation. *The American Economic Review* 63 (2): 359–365.

Rock, D., & dos Santos, M.R. (1971). Lucha civil en la Argentina-la Semana Trágica de enero de 1919. *Desarrollo económico* 42–44 (11): 165–215.

Romero, L. (1990) Los sectores populares urbanos como sujeto histórico. *Sociedades Precapitalistas*, (3).

Sábato, H. (1993) Hobsbawn y nuestro pasado. *Punto de Vista* 46: 13–17.

Sartelli, E. (1996). Celeste, blanco y rojo. Democracia, nacionalismo y clase obrera en la crisis hegemónica (1912–22). *Razón y Revolución* 2: 48–78.

Sartelli, E. (dir.). (2008) *Patrones en la ruta. El conflicto agrario y los enfrentamientos en el seno de la burguesía*. Buenos Aires: CEICS.

Thompson, E.P.P. (1978). *Poverty of theory*. New York: NYU Press.
Thompson, E. (1991) *The making of the English Working Class*, London: Penguin.
Thompson, E.P. (1991b). Algunas observaciones sobre clase y "falsa conciencia". *Historia social* 10: 27–32.
Trimberger, E.K. (1984). EP Thompson: Understanding the process of History. In: Skocpol, T. (ed) *Vision and Method in Historical Sociology*. Cambridge: Cambridge University Press, 211–243.
UNAM (2004) Censo de Ocupantes de tierras privadas (2003–2004).
Villanova, N. (2012) ¿Excluidos o incluidos?: Recuperadores de materiales reciclables en Latinoamérica. *Revista mexicana de sociología*, 74 (2): 245–274.

CHAPTER 9

Capitalism, Class and Collective Identity: Social Movements and Public Services in South Africa

Adrian Murray

Introduction

In the context of the shifting nature of production and consumption under neoliberal globalisation, it has become fashionable to argue that unions—the classic 'old social movement' organisation and historically preferred agent of social transformation on the left—have been displaced by popular struggles in the form of the 'new social movements.' With this shift the locus of contention has supposedly moved away from the realm of production and towards the realm of consumption and from a focus on class politics to a focus on identity politics (Hardt and Negri 2000, 2004; see Harvey 2003 for a nuanced analysis and critique). This shift has coincided with a focus on individuals, identity and micro level analysis in both cultural and structural-rational approaches to social movements, and away from political economy and material determinations of social change, in particular, capitalism (Barker et al. 2013; Hetland and Goodwin 2013). Building on scholarship that seeks to push forward Marxist understandings of social movements, by contrast, this essay highlights the importance of capitalism and class for understanding the dynamics of social movements by providing an empirically grounded case study of anti-capitalist resistance based upon an analysis of the organising work of the Housing Assembly, an organisation struggling around access to public services in Cape Town, South Africa.

In this chapter, I enquire into the relationship between the de- and re-composition of the working class under neoliberal capitalism after apartheid, and the enduring salience of class as a model of understanding that can contribute to overcoming the fragmentation of the working class today. I argue that how class is understood and its relationship with forms of oppression such as gender and race, matter as much for theoretical conceptions of working

---

* Adrian Murray would like to thank Susan Spronk for her comments, the staff of Ilrig for discussions on earlier versions of this argument and the editors of this volume. This research was supported by the Social Sciences and Humanities Research Council of Canada.

class social movements, as it does for more practical processes of movement building based on the work that Housing Assembly organisers do on a daily basis. More specifically, drawing on the work of E.P. Thompson, I conceive of class as a constantly unfolding process, rather than as a static, formal category, highlighting the contingent and dialectical nature of organising and social change. The central argument of the chapter is that, within the context of the Housing Assembly, the translation and production of knowledge by organic, movement intellectuals and the molecular, catalytic work done by organisers in working class homes, workplaces and communities—in other words, their praxis—are at the core of a dynamic process of becoming at the heart of class formation.

The first part of the chapter discusses the theoretical elements of the disappearance of class from the study of movements and proposes a class struggle theory of social movements. This is followed by an elaboration of praxis as it relates to this recovered historical materialist understanding of social change. The next section sets the context with a brief overview of social movement struggles in post-apartheid South Africa and the debates surrounding them. The final section examines the theoretical and political relevance of recovering class for the study of social movements in relation to the case in and around Cape Town, South Africa.

Understanding Class and Revolutionary Praxis in 'New' Social Movements

In the past few decades, privatisation, liberalisation and de-regulation have increasingly exposed society to the vagaries of the market. As livelihoods have become increasingly precarious, trade unions, the classic 'old' social movement organisations, have found themselves in a weak bargaining position, unable to stem the onslaught of neoliberalism (Silver 2003). An increasingly diverse plethora of 'new' movements has emerged in this same era, shifting

> the terrain of political organisation away from traditional political parties and labour organising into what was bound to be in aggregate a less focused political dynamic of social action across the whole spectrum of civil society.
> HARVEY 2003, 168

With the expansion of struggles focusing on non-class forms of identity such as gender, race and orientation, many analysts have rejected the analytical tools associated with the supposed 'class fanaticism' of Marxism in favour of a post-class analysis centred on identity, discourse and autonomy (Laclau and Mouffe 1985; Melucci 1989; Touraine 1981; Escobar and Alvarez 1992; see Wood 1986, 1995 for a critique).

This move away from class was made largely in response to the, somewhat legitimate, perception that the Marxism of the day, dominated as it was by Althusserian structuralism, was not up to the task of understanding the emergence of new movements in the North in the post-1968 era, which was only compounded with the decline of actually existing socialism two decades later (Wood 1986). This shift towards 'radical pluralism' (Carroll and Ratner 1994) has had a profound impact on scholarly and activist writing and thinking about social struggle in the recent period. A chasm opened up between:

> old social movements (OSMs) … considered to advance working class-based, social democratic or socialist political projects, while new social movements (NSMs) are considered to advance non-class-based or cross-class-based political projects oriented toward identify formation or autonomy.
>
> HOLST 2011, 119

While a strength of the social movement literature in South Africa has been its attention to inequality, the state, and capitalism post-apartheid, some of which takes class quite seriously (e.g. Dwyer 2004; Alexander et al. 2013), it has not been immune to this current of post-class analysis. As Seddon and Zeilig (2005, 13) observe, the experience in Africa has been much the same, as "post-structuralism and postmodernism have swamped African studies with an emphasis on identity, indeterminacy, complexity and performance." Within such analyses, the tools of political economy and organisational forms associated with the 'old' social movements are rejected on the grounds that they are an imposition, the 'paradigm of the yoke,' and inapplicable to the unique nature of the continent (Bayart 1993). Rather, the complexity of social relations and formations becomes the object of inquiry informed by a diffuse theory of power (Mbembe 2002) and, in its most extreme forms, an aversion to the topic of struggle and liberation (Harrison 2002). Indeed, some South African scholars have suggested that as opposed to 'old' social movements, these 'new' movements reflect a genuine voice of the poor, and that they seek to assert local identities and carve out spaces relatively autonomous from the state, meanwhile downplaying the relevance of an organised working class (Pithouse 2008, 2009; Neocosmos 2009; Gibson 2011; see Sinwell

2011; Dawson and Sinwell 2012; Ngwane 2012; Dwyer and Zeilig 2012 for a critique).

There are at least two reasons to reject 'radical pluralism' in the context of analysing social movement protests in South Africa. First, as several authors have highlighted, the application of NSM theory, which emerged in post-industrial, capitalist democracies to the global South is highly problematic, where many analytical concepts fit awkwardly, if at all (Spronk and Terhorst 2012; Thompson and Tapscott 2010). In the African context, although the so-called NSMs make a heterogeneous set of claims and utilise diverse repertoires of contention, distributional issues remain at the forefront of their campaigns including those that foreground identity (Habib and Opoku-Mensah 2009). Indeed, with the dual transition of marketisation and (liberal) democratisation, social movement mobilisation has become a central, if not the dominant, form of civil society-state engagement in the global South and a vital conduit through which to claim and advance substantive citizenship rights, the bulk of which is directed at securing socio-economic rights (Thompson and Tapscott 2010).

Second, 'class fanaticism' need not be replaced with 'class rejectionism' for there are understandings of class and capitalism within the Marxist tradition that do not fall prey to the problems of 'structural Marxism', which are particularly relevant to understand struggles in the face of what appears to be a renewed era of austerity. Ironically, much was written in this tradition concurrent with the rise of NSM theory, that analysed the vibrant and complex interactions of race, class and gender in strikes and working class struggles in Europe at the time (Wood 1995). Spronk (2013) identifies British Marxist historian E.P. Thompson as providing us with one of the most salient critiques of the structuralist Marxism that spawned NSM theory, particularly his theorisation of class as both a 'process and relation' (Thompson 1991). Thompson (1978, 149) insisted that

> classes do not exist as separate entities, look around, find an enemy class, and then start to struggle. On the contrary, people find themselves in a society structured in determined ways (crucially, but not exclusively, in productive relations), they experience exploitation (or the need to maintain power over those whom they exploit), they identify points of antagonistic interest, they commence to struggle around these issues and in the process of struggling they discover themselves as classes, they come to know this discovery as class-consciousness. Class and class-consciousness are always the last, not the first, stage in the real historical process.

Although Thompson prioritises the lived experiences of working class people as they go about their daily lives both within and—I stress this—outside of the relations of production, he does so without constructing class as a purely subjective phenomenon as those who reject class entirely are wont to do. Rather, he "treats the process of class formation as a *historical* process shaped by the 'logic' of material determinations" (Wood 1995, 81 emphasis in original). It is through the lived experience of this historical process that people experience exploitation, organise and struggle against it, and come to 'behave in class ways'; it is in this sense that Thompson used the phrase 'class struggle without class', that is the latter (class) is the culmination of but not guaranteed by the former (class struggle). (Thompson 1978).[1]

Paula Allman's work is useful here to theorise the centrality of individual and collective working class agency that is at the centre of Thompson's conception of class and of the efforts of social movements to exercise it. Allman (2010, 39) understands capitalist social relations as:

> the structured relations of human beings into which they enter routinely in order to produce their material existence. Forms of organisation and physical structures, as well as the legal system that gives legitimacy to the structure, are created in order to 'cement' this structuring of human relations, but the real or material substance of the structure is the daily sensuous activity of human beings.

If we accept that "Marx's theory of consciousness was actually a theory of praxis, i.e., a theory of the inseparable unity of thought and practice rather than a sequential theory of praxis" (Allman 2007, 33–34) then:

> it is this practice, in both its individual and social expressions, that is the subject and object of the formation of critical or revolutionary

---

1 It is important to emphasize the interplay of structure and agency in Thompson's work, rather than the dominance of one or the other. As Spronk (2013, 78) elaborates:

in other words, class struggle does not always occur in a conscious way; much depends on the capacity of political agents and the forms of collective action taken by workers' [read: working class] movements. Furthermore, the construction of class identities is always an uneven process, replete with internal contradictions. In any given national context, the working class is divided into factions that display a host of views and attitudes. In short, while the division of society into social classes is a constant feature of capitalist society, class consciousness is something that emerges from time to time and unevenly when workers decide to act collectively to resist exploitation and domination by employers or the state.

See Wood (1995) for a brilliant exploration of Thompson's work on class and this and other debates around it.

consciousness, a consciousness that seeks a dialectical understanding of contradictions.

ALLMAN cited in CARPENTER, RITCHIE and MOJAB 2012, 7

Allman (2007, 34) identifies two different forms of praxis that emerge from engaging with social relations under capitalism: uncritical or reproductive praxis and critical or revolutionary praxis. The former refers to the reproduction of capitalist social relations, which may ensue due to the operation of ideological or material factors in the course of social movement mobilisation even if the intention is otherwise. The latter refers to a mode of praxis able to "see beyond the current appearance of global capital, and critically question the essence of the mode/relations of production and its associated forms of consciousness" (Carpenter, Ritchie and Mojab 2012, 9).

I would like to suggest that the patient organising work of the Housing Assembly in Cape Town, South Africa, in other words its praxis, based as it is on a critical, non-reductionist understanding of class and capitalist social relations is a potential basis for sparking critical working class consciousness, moving beyond the disabling narratives informed by post-class analysis and moving towards a revolutionary praxis. In so doing I hope to provide an experiential basis for my assertion that a recovery of class as a model for understanding social relations, like the one I have laid out above, can accomplish important theoretical and political work in the present.

Neoliberal Restructuring in South Africa

South Africa is no exception when it comes to the dynamics of neoliberal capitalism. After the fall of apartheid in 1994, expectations for a new South Africa and the possibility of 'a better life for all' were high. The new Constitution and the Reconstruction and Development Plan (RDP), passed shortly after the election of the African National Congress (ANC) in 1994, appeared to provide a progressive framework and policy program for building a more equitable society. Shortly thereafter, however, the ANC government initiated a policy shift in 1996 led by the plan for Growth Employment and Redistribution (Gear). Described as self-imposed structural adjustment (Bond 2000), Gear and subsequent legislation has restructured the economy in a number of key respects, which, pertinent to our case, have greatly impacted public service provision.

Under the watchful eye of international financial institutions, the legislative agenda introduced by Gear decentralised various public functions, downloading responsibilities for service provision onto local government while imposing fiscal austerity. This downloading without the transfer of needed resources led to a crisis of service delivery as local governments sought to corporatise and privatise services in an attempt to achieve financial efficiency (McDonald and Smith 2004). Large-scale protest erupted by the early 2000s in response to this crisis, exemplified by the nearly 1 million people per year who had their water and electricity disconnected from 1994–2001 (McDonald 2002). The state responded by moving from these unfunded mandates to what Gillian Hart (2014, 97) calls 'anxious interventionism.' Although free basic services (FBS) have been provided to 'indigent' households since 2001 as a part of this interventionism, side by side with a steady investment in the coercive arm of the state, provision levels remain well below international standards for basic subsistence (Marais 2012). By 2013, only 72.1% of dwellings were connected to piped water, 77.9% to improved sanitation, and 85.4% to electricity with only modest improvement over the previous decade (StatsSA 2013). While these statistics appear to be quite an achievement, the proliferation of pre-paid meters and other cost-recovery mechanisms, which play an important role in FBS initiatives, and the poor quality and reliability of services continue to limit the ability of South Africans to actually utilise and benefit from their connections to this expanded infrastructure (Dugard 2013).

The Social Movement Response

There has been consistent mobilisation since the late 1990s within and beyond the state in opposition to this political economic trajectory, particularly in relation to public services. Independently and in coalition, unions and community organisations have played an important role in these campaigns. Coalitions such as the Anti Privatisation Forum, the Anti-Eviction Campaign, and the Treatment Action Campaign drew on the experience of apartheid-era struggles and alliances, particularly those in the 1980s under the banner of the United Democratic Front (UDF) that provided an umbrella for the thousands of community organisations or 'civics', which, alongside labour unions, were the backbone of the resistance to apartheid, (Ballard, Habib and Valodia. 2006). The country's largest union of municipal workers, the South African Municipal Workers Union (Samwu) played a key role in many of these coalitions and successful anti-privatisation struggles (Pape 2001), and mobilised thousands in Cape Town and Johannesburg despite less favourable outcomes. Despite their successes, by 2003, these coalitions and organisations had either fallen apart or were in steep decline.

By the middle of the decade however, protest reignited with an average of 9,000 'crowd management' incidents recorded by police per year from 2004–05 to 2011–12 (Alexander 2012). In general, this new wave of protest has taken on a less focused and fragmented form relative to earlier mobilisations (Hart 2014). Samwu has been notable for its absence and the trajectory of the United Front, launched by the National Union of Metalworkers of South Africa (Numsa) to bring together labour and community struggles as the UDF did in the 1980s, remains questionable (Paret 2016). Though a number of more organised community formations in addition to the Housing Assembly have emerged, including the People's Movement, Abahlali baseMjondolo, they are few and far between, and have largely been unable to tap into the anger and discontent of popular protest (Hart 2014).

Speculating about the significance of these ongoing protests, Jane Duncan (2015) recently posed the following question in relation to the opposing perspectives on the issue: "Are they another means of pressuring the ruling African National Congress (ANC) into delivering better services, or do they represent a new form of anti-systemic politics that promises to change how society is organised, and for the better?" Following from Thompson (1978), I would argue that these protests are not merely just about service delivery (Booysen 2011; Fakir 2014), nor are they autonomous projects or privileged 'local' places in the 'space of flows' (Neocosmos 2009; Pithouse 2013). Rather, in line with Alexander's (2010, 2012) moniker 'rebellion of the poor,' Duncan (2015) muses that there is "little evidence of these demands being politicised, by being linked to broader failures of neoliberalised capitalism" but "just because protest organisers do not articulate their demands as being against neoliberalism and capitalism, does not mean that they are not reacting to their effects." In short, they are reflective of 'people acting in class ways' and merit Thompson's distinction of 'class struggle without class.'

The more interesting exploration for me then becomes the organising work that is involved in moving from "forms of consciousness that are shaped in various ways by class situations without yet finding expression in a self-aware and active class identity" to "the active awareness of class identity" (Wood 1995, 98–99). Alf Nilsen (2012a, 619) refers to these shifts as:

> learning processes that unfold as subaltern groups engage with and contest the hegemonic projects of dominant groups and the institutional complexes and discursive formations in which this hegemony is entrenched. Local rationalities are never *either* entirely autonomous of *or* totally encapsulated by dominant ideologies, but tend to be expressive of what Gramsci (1998, 333) called a 'contradictory consciousness.'

While the knowledge produced within and by movements is too often disregarded in the social movement literature (see Choudry 2015 and Barker et al. 2013 for a critique), not "all learning, evaluation, and analysis embedded in various forms of organising are rigorous or adequate. Indeed critical analysis of learning in 'progressive' movements necessitates looking critically at their claims in relation to actual practices" (Choudry 2015, 13) and the experience of marginalised participants. In this sense learning and organising that results in defensive struggles and/or adaptation can remain trapped in a reproductive praxis as Allman details above. Indeed, many of the initiatives which remain bounded in the local, or those that fail to engage with or situate their struggles in the broader relations of capitalism and the state, for example, demobilise after extracting concessions from local government (Sinwell 2011). Let me be clear: this is not to condemn such struggles, but rather to ask, as Choudry (2015, 34) puts it, how do social movement activists move from consciousness to action; and from learning to merely adapt to learning to resist?

Revolutionary Praxis in the Housing Assembly

The Housing Assembly (HA) is an umbrella of community organisations engaged in struggles for housing and services in and around the Cape Town. It formally emerged in 2012 from a group of activists and organisers that had been coming together for several years to learn and strategise in relation to ongoing struggles initially via popular education programs run by the International Labour Research and Information Group (Ilrig), a South Africa NGO founded in the late 1980s that continues to work closely with worker and community organisations. The HA has strong connections to and draws on the resources of local, regional and national social movement organisations, including unions, the now defunct Western Cape Anti Eviction Campaign and Abahlali baseMjondolo Western Cape, that have been at the centre of earlier waves of protest. It has developed extensive organisational structures and alliances, often with trade unions including Sawmu, Numsa, and the United Front, and has undertaken numerous campaigns and actions.

Despite these achievements, the HA remains limited in the extent to which it has been able to organise communities across Cape Town and beyond, which is its goal. However, strong pockets of organisation exist in communities in Cape Town and the surrounds, organised on a house-to-house, rank-and-file basis and are exemplary of its praxis and the potential therein. I would like to suggest that the organising of the HA is an alternative to the reproductive praxis above, and though limited and constantly under threat, is a concerted project with the aim of developing a critical, revolutionary praxis. In other words, the day to day organising work carried out by the HA seeks to rupture consciousness and politicise the social relations of capitalism which are so normalised in the experience of working class South Africans.

In the case of the HA, this praxis unfolds primarily within the context of struggles on the terrain of the local state around access to public services, including water, sanitation, electricity and housing. These struggles do not, however, remain mired in the immediacy of these problems with narrow demands for their amelioration by authorities, as the first of Duncan's assertions would suggest. Rather, through engaging the experience of poverty, the organising process turns to theorising experience and critically reflecting upon it, revealing the exploitation and oppression beneath (Choudry 2015).

Two slogans of the HA help to illustrate this praxis. The first of these, 'We don't want to live like this anymore'—'Ons will nie meer so bly nie.'—'Asifuni ukuhlala ngoluhlobo', reflects the starting point of the HA's organising: the issues that are experienced by working class people in working class communities and households.

> In terms of organising, which I think is a first step in a solution, talking about an alternative, and I think that it's been proven ... is working in our communities, going around and collecting peoples' demands, speaking to them about their issues, relating to their issues in their own comfortable space ... I introduce myself as a backyarder, I'm in the same situation and I'm relating with your issue and the importance of why we need to stick together, not as an organisation but as the working class.
>
> Housing Assembly Organiser, Interview B, 6 November 2015

An important part of taking the everyday seriously is the collective amelioration of living conditions, which engages with the everyday in the 'patient work' of organising in a way that goes beyond lip service. One such example is a HA breakfast program that does not just serve food, filling in for a state that has abdicated its responsibility for ensuring food security. Rather, akin to the Black Panther breakfast programs in the United States in the 1960s and 1970s (Bloom and Martin 2013), this space is used to encourage critical reflection by others, to have the often-difficult conversations with those other than just the already converted, while listening to experiences and collecting stories which can be used to challenge the state and its poor service delivery record.

In other words, your porridge comes with a side of political education that begins with your concrete social experience. This opportunity for reflection amidst the collective amelioration of basic needs, challenges

> the conditions of everyday life under neoliberalism [which] mean that few people have sustained, positive experiences of collective decision making, socialised resource allocation, or solidaristic, noncompetitive environments in which to work, learn, or play.
> SCHEIN 2014, 173

These molecular changes under neoliberalism, as David McNally (2011) refers to them, which have occurred at the most very basic levels of everyday life, can be significant obstacles to the organising process and are a part of the subjective working class experience that the HA attempts to acknowledge and prioritise.

As the final sentence in the quote above suggests, the HA's praxis then renders this experience of housing, service delivery and employment at the 'sensuous level of everyday life,' critical by situating it within a critique of the political economy of neoliberal capitalism in South Africa. A member of the organisation describes this as a learning process of "getting our humanity back" in the context of a hyper competitive, individualised fight for survival, in which the dominant discourse and method of service delivery places the responsibility for poverty squarely on the shoulders of the poor. This does not remain in the realm of the subjective, as is fairly clear I think, as the broader relations of capitalism in South Africa are linked by organisers with the materiality of working class life.

> In the short term we need to get organised, to collect and combine demands, because its basically one demand; the demand that capitalism must be gone. But people ... they don't have the words to say that. They make the connection when you're sitting there they say ya in Constantia [a rich suburb of Cape Town] ... there are two people living in a big house and here we are 15 people living on this property, three backyarders and we get 360L of water a day and then it comes up on TV 'please switch off your electricity' etc. People might not say capitalism, neoliberalism, but when they talk and what they say, they are saying that because of neoliberalism my electricity is going up and I can't afford to buy it.

> So as a first step we must connect people on their issues and then we need to talk about political education, you know ... Get everybody on the

same page, people must understand. Because I think for years there have been protests ... just as an example: if it was a backyarder protest around housing you'll get the backyarders all out and they're protesting about it but then they go back home and nothing happens because the only reason why they went out is because I'm a backyarder and I don't want to live like this anymore. But there's no political understanding of why you are a backyarder so I think we must get people to understand and be angry and ready enough to go out to the streets you know so everybody that's there on the street understands exactly what we are fighting for and we all come together to find solutions.
> Housing Assembly Organiser, Interview A, 6 Nov 2015

The critical and analytical nature of this learning process is clear. Nor is it an elite process of education or movement building, an experience quite prominent in South Africa (Marais 2012) whereby an intellectual in the traditional sense or some other singular leader or organisational elite gives guidance to the struggle or imparts the correct knowledge to working class people who, upon receiving it, become conscious and mobilised. Rather, it is a learning process that ensues in the course of working class political struggle facilitated by the work of organic intellectuals as Gramsci (1971) referred to them. The second HA slogan, '*Everyone An Organiser*,' speaks directly to this aspect of the learning process. Generally, "organisers and 'permanent persuaders' emerging from the grassroots/working class are not seen as intellectuals capable of creating knowledge" (Choudry 2015, 18). But this knowledge is an important part of any effective praxis as it plays a key role in connecting experience with broader social relations of exploitation and oppression and the maintenance of such relations. Recovering a collective memory of past struggles, as Benson (2015) notes in the case of South Africa, and challenging divisions in the working class, real and sown from above, on the basis of race, gender, orientation and employment status, are important examples of the generation of new knowledge, and are an important part of the HA's praxis as it challenges dominant and hegemonic discourses and practices in the present.

As another HA organiser put it, reflecting on an alliance between striking workers, unionised and seasonal, struggling around wages and conditions, and protesting communities, struggling around water cut offs and housing problems, in an organising context fraught with the politics of race and gender:

> In this generation we experience that workers and communities still find it difficult, even last year during the strike ... to see the link. It wasn't difficult for this group because we've come through the stage of being

conscientised, talking about the issues .... At the end of the day I'm from a community, I'm living in the community before I became a factory worker ... [the] community needs to support workers because that is our people in the community. They come home and their electricity has been cut, they are living in the backyards, so they also have waiting issues, and it's one big thing that needs to come together. And that's why we said one of the things we've learned out of the strike is that we need political education. Now is the time more than ever ... people need to understand that we need to bring the two together.

   Housing Assembly Organiser, Interview AA, 12 March 2016

In response, within the HA there has been an ongoing process of organising activities and direct actions, much like those described above. While a critique of political economy and the commercialisation of service delivery is emphasised, so are critiques, and strategies and tactics of organising and engaging the state and capital generated in the movement itself and in movements elsewhere in the process of struggle.

Conclusion: Crisis, Austerity and Revolutionary Praxis

In this essay I have argued that the production of knowledge in and by social movements, may play a key role in the formation of consciousness about the class nature of experience. As Ellen Wood argues "Class formations emerge and develop 'as men and women *live* their productive relations and *experience* their determinate situations, within "the *ensemble* of the social relations," with their inherited culture and expectations, and as they handle these experiences in cultural ways'" (Thompson in Wood 1995, 80 emphasis in original). It is through organising processes in the course of concrete struggles, like those discussed above, that this knowledge is both produced and used as a tool through which relations of exploitation and oppression under capitalism are laid bare within particular, historically-given contexts, cultural, national and otherwise.

 I have also argued that recovering class for social movement analysis and organising is a requisite for pushing forward our understandings of the 'new' working class in an era where precarity is increasingly the norm. A class struggle theory of social movements is also helpful in moving beyond the historical and theoretical pitfalls of NSM theory and its rejection of class. It is likewise an antidote to the structural variants of Marxism that other Marxists such as E.P. Thompson have reacted so strongly to.

 The organising praxis of the Housing Assembly appears to be a hopeful space in which experiences of exploitation and oppression at the sensuous level of the everyday, and their internal relations with the broader capitalist social whole, can be revealed and contested, but its organisers face many challenges. The South African state seems increasingly less averse to cracking down on oppositional formations (Paret 2015). Indeed, perhaps the starkest example, and what continues to frame the present period, is the Marikana massacre of August 2012, when police shot 34 striking miners. A wave of strikes has followed, including a five-month platinum belt strike in 2014, which was the longest and most expensive in South African history, and unprecedented action by farmworkers. This renewed wave of protest has been driven by both unions and informal workers' organisations, and in some cases, organisers have taken up the issues of working class communities, such as the crisis of service delivery. The departure of Numsa, the largest union in South Africa, from the ANC-led Tripartite alliance, the conflicts in the Alliance this provoked, and Numsa's creation of the United Front to bring together workplace and community struggles, are important fractures. The renewed wave of austerity announced in Finance Minister Pravin Gordhan's 2016 budget on the back of a significant decline in the value of the Rand, and unprecedented levels of protest suggests that the tension will only escalate in years to come.

While the renewed militancy of trade unions in South Africa in the past four years is likely to dampen the claims of NSM theorists that the 'old' social movements and the concept of 'class' can be relegated to the dustbin of history, as this essay has attempted to demonstrate, the politics of class and the challenges of building revolutionary praxis also remain ever present in working class communities, as reflected in the vital organising work of the Housing Assembly.

References

Alexander, P. (2010) Rebellion of the poor: South Africa's service delivery protests—a preliminary analysis. *Review of African Political Economy* 37 (123): 25–40.

Alexander, P. (2012) Protests and Police Statistics: Some Commentary. Research Chair in Social Change, University of Johannesburg. Available at: http://www.amandla.org.za/home-page/1121-protests-and-police-statistics-some-commentary-by-prof-peter-alexander.

Alexander, P., Ceruti, C., Motseke, K., Phadi, M., and Wale, K. (2013) *Class in Soweto*. Durban: UKZN Press.

Alexander, P., Ngwane, T., and Runciman, C. (2016) South Africa's rebellion of the poor. In: *III International Conference Strikes and Social Conflicts: combined historical approaches to conflict. Proceedings.* CEFID-UAB, 148–161.

Allman, P. (2007) *On Marx: An Introduction to the Revolutionary Intellect of Karl Marx*. Rotterdam: Sense.

Allman, P. (2010) *Critcal Education Against Global Capitalism: Karl Marx and Revolutionary Critical Education*. Rotterdam: Sense.

Ballard, R., Habib, A., and Valodia, I. (2006) Conclusion: Making Sense of Post-apartheid South Africa's Voices of Protest. In: Ballard, R., Habib, A., and Valodia, I. et al. (eds) *Voices of Protest*. Scottsville: University of KwaZulu Natal Press, 397–415.

Barker, C., Cox, L., Krinsky, J., and Nilsen, A.G. (2013) Marxism and Social Movements: An Introduction. In: Barker C., Cox L., Krinsky J., and Nilsen A.G., (eds) *Marxism and Social Movements*. Leiden: Brill, 1–37.

Bayart, J-F. (1993) *The state in Africa: the politics of the belly*. New York: Longman.

Benson, K. (2015) A 'Political War of Words and Bullets' Defining and Defying Sides of Struggle for Housing in Crossroads, South Africa. *Journal of Southern African Studies*, 41 (2): 367–387.

Bloom J. and Martin, W. (2013) *Black against Empire: The History and Politics of the Black Panther Party*. Berkeley: University of California Press.

Bond, P. (2000) *Cities of Gold, Townships of Coal*. Trenton: Africa World Press.

Carpenter, S., Ritchie, G. and Mojab, S. (2013) The Dialectics of Praxis. *Socialist Studies*, 9 (1): 1–17.

Choudry, A. (2015) *Learning Activism. The Intellectual Life of Contemporary Social Movements*. Toronto: U of T Press.

Dawson, M.C. and Sinwell, L. (eds). (2012) *Contesting Transformation: Popular Resistance in Twenty-first Century South Africa*. London: Pluto Press.

Duncan, J. (2015) The Political Significance of South Africa's Protests. *SACSIS*. 13 April. Available at: http://www.sacsis.org.za/site/article/2344.

Dwyer, P. (2004) *The Contentious Politics of the Concerned Citizens Forum*. Cape Town: AIDC.

Dwyer, P. and Zeilig, L. (2012) *African Struggles Today: Social Movements Since Independence*. Chicago: Haymarket.

Fakir, E. (2014) Protests are a cry for political recognition. *Mail and Guardian*, 29th August. Available at: http://mg.co.za/article/2014-08-29-protests-are-a-cry-for-political-recognition.

Gibson, N. (2011) *Fanonian Practices in South Africa: from Steve Biko to Abahlali base Mjondolo*. Durban: UKZN Press.

Gramsci, A. (1971) *Selections from the Prison Notebooks*. New York: International Publishers.

Habib, A. and Opokuh-Mensah, P. (2009) Speaking to the global debates through a national and continental lens: South African and African social movements in comparative perspective. In: Ellis, S. and van Kessel, I. (eds) *Movers and Shakers: Social Movements in Africa*. Boston: Brill, 44–62.

Hardt, M. and Negri, A. (2000) *Empire*. Cambridge, MA: Harvard University Press.

Hardt, M. and Negri, A. (2004) *Multitude: War and Democracy in the Age of Empire*. New York: Penguin.

Harrison, G. (2002) *Issues in the Contemporary Politics of Sub-Saharan Africa: The Dynamics of Struggle and Resistance*. New York: Palgrave.

Hart, G. (2014) *Rethinking the South African Crisis: Nationalism, Populism, Hegemony*. Pietermaritzburg South Africa: University of KwaZulu-Natal Press.

Harvey, D. (2003) *The New Imperialism*. Oxford: Oxford University Press.

Holst, J. (2011) Frameworks for understanding the politics of social movements, *Studies in the Education of Adults* 43 (2): 117–127.

Laclau, E. and Mouffe, C. (1985) *Hegemony and Socialist Strategy: Towards a Radical Democratic Politics*. London: Verso.

Marais, H. (2012) *South African Pushed to the Limit: The Political Economy of Change*. London: Zed Books.

Mbembe, A. (2001) *On the postcolony*, Berkeley: University of California Press.

McDonald, D.A. (2002) The bell tolls for thee: Cost recovery, cutoffs, and the affordability of municipal services in South Africa. In: McDonald, D.A. and Pape, J. *Cost Recovery and the crisis of service delivery in South Africa*. Pretoria: HSRC Press, 161–182.

McDonald D.A. and L. Smith (2004) Privatising Cape Town: From Apartheid to Neoliberalism in the Mother City. *Urban Studies* 41(8): 1461–1484.

McNally, D. (2011) *Global Slump: the Economic and Politics of Crisis and Resistance*. Oakland: PM Press.

McNally, D. (2015) The dialectics of unity and difference in the constitution of wage-labour: On internal relations and working class formation. *Capital and Class*, 39 (1): 131–146.

Melucci, A. (1989) *Nomads of the Present: Social Movement and identity needs in contemporary society*. Philadelphia: Temple University Press.

Neocosmos, M. (2009) Civil society, citizenship and the politics of the (im)possible: rethinking militancy in Africa today. *Interface*, 1 (2): 263–334.

Ngwane, T. (2012) Labour strikes and community protests: Is there a basis for unity in post-apartheid South Africa. In: Dawson, M.C. and L. Sinwell (eds) *Contesting Transformation: Popular Resistance in Twenty-first Century South Africa*. London: Pluto Press: 125–142.

Nilsen, A.G. (2012) Adivasi Mobilisation in Contemporary India: Democratising the Local State? *Critical Sociology* 39 (4): 615–633.

Paret, M. (2015) Violence and democracy in South Africa's community protests. *Review of African Political Economy*, 42(143): 107–123.

Pithouse, R. (2008) A Politics of the Poor: Shack Dwellers' Struggles in Durban. *Journal of Asian and African Studies* 43(1): 63–94.

Pithouse, R. (2009) The University of Abahlali baseMjondolo. *Occupied London. An Anarchist Journal of Action and Theory 1.* Available at: http://www.anarkismo.net/article/6979.

Pithouse, R. (2013) Conjuctural Remarks on the Significance of "The Local". *Thesis Eleven.* 115 (1): 95–111.

Schein, R. (2014) Hegemony Not Co-Optation: For a Usable History of Feminism. *Studies In Political Economy* 94 (Autumn): 169–176.

Seddon, D. and Zeilig, L. (2005) Class & protest in Africa: New waves. *Review of African Political Economy*, 32 (103): 9–27.

Silver, B. (2003) *Forces of Labour: Workers' Movements and Globalisation Since 1870.* Cambridge, UK: Cambridge University Press.

Sinwell, L. (2011) Is 'another world' really possible? Re-examining counterhegemonic forces in post-apartheid South Africa. *Review of African Political Economy* 38 (127): 61–76.

Spronk, S. (2013) Neoliberal Class Formation(s): The Informal Proletariat and "New" Workers' Organisations in Latin America. In: Webber, J. and Carr, B. (eds) *The New Latin American Left: Cracks in the* Empire. New York: Roman and Littlefield: 75–93.

Spronk, S. and Terhorst, P. (2012) Social Movement Struggles for Public Services. In: McDonald D.A. and Ruiters G. (eds) *Alternatives to privatisation: Public options for essential services in the global South.* New York: Routledge: 133–156.

StatsSA 2013. *General Household Survey.* Johannesburg: RSA.

Thompson, E.P. (1978) Eighteenth-Century English Society: Class Struggle Without Class? *Social History* 3(2): 133–165.

Thompson, E.P. (1991) (1963). *The Making of the English Working Class.* New York: Vintage.

Thompson, L. and Tapscott, C. (2010) *Citizens and Social Movements: Perspectives from the Global South.* London: Zed Books.

Touraine, A. (1981) *The Voice and the Eye: An Analysis of Social Movements.* New York: Cambridge University Press.

Wood, E.M. (1998) (1986). *The Retreat from Class: The New 'True' Socialism.* London: Verso.

Wood, E.M. (1995) *Democracy Against Capitalism: Renewing Historical Materialism.* Cambridge: Cambridge University Press.

CHAPTER 10

On Intellectuals

Deirdre O'Neill and Mike Wayne

Introduction

This essay explores the social and political role and significance of the intellectuals within capitalist society. It sets out to define the intellectual and the nature of what they produce (ideas) and their relationship to broader class relations. It shows how key Marxist thinkers provide the basis for a socio-economic understanding of the activities and products of the intellectual. At the heart of transforming the current role of the intellectual within the existing divisions of labour, lies the project to democratise the social role of the intellectuals. This requires expanding the social base of the intellectuals and connecting their activities to a self-reflexive project of social and political transformation. This is the basis and definition of truly *critical* thought. In this essay we discuss how Marx and Engels' began the task of establishing a theoretical framework for a historical and materialist account of the intellectuals in *The German Ideology*. We show how the Italian Marxist Antonio Gramsci further developed our understanding of the intellectual and we clarify and add to his key distinctions between the traditional and organic intellectual. Having set out the theoretical framework and broad philosophical and political implications of the intellectual, we then look at the role of the intellectual in the post-Second World War era, up to our contemporary moment. We discuss the relationship between the middle class and the hegemonic intellectual, the difficulties posed for the middle class intellectual to be genuinely counter-hegemonic and the need for the reconstitution of organic intellectuals from the working class. Finally we explore these issues in relation to the media and especially oppositional digital and social media practices.

Marx and Engels on the Intellectuals

The starting point for thinking about a Marxist conception of the role of intellectuals must be Marx and Engels' work *The German Ideology*. It is here that they begin to situate intellectuals in relation to the dominant class forces. "The class which has the means of material production at its disposal, has control at the same time over the means of mental production at its disposal" (Marx and Engels 1989, 64). This formulation would grow in relevance with the development of the mass media. At the same time, the very growth of what Ensenzberger later called the 'industrialisation of the mind' (Ensenzberger 1982) would require the development of a sophisticated account of intellectual production that could avoid the twin traps of reducing it to the economic class interests of the dominant class who formally own the media or believing that it transcended class relations and struggle. Marx and Engels noted that "mental production" was delegated to the "thinkers of the class (its active, conceptive ideologists)" (Marx and Engel 1989, 65). The beginnings of an account of intellectual production that could register how it may be affected by broader social, political and economic changes and conflicts is evident where they state that a "cleavage" between intellectuals and the dominant class "can develop into a certain opposition and hostility", although they are also (overly) quick to state this conflict "automatically comes to nothing" if the dominant class to which the intellectuals are attached, are "endangered" (Marx and Engels 1989,65). Their own political trajectory suggests that this is not necessarily the case.

Marx and Engels no doubt had in mind in this section of *The German Ideology* the German intellectuals and philosophers from whose ranks they emerged in the 1840s and from whom they wished to establish an epistemological and political break. *The German Ideology* opens with a satirical account of the post-Hegelian scene, in which Left and Right Hegelians fought over the legacy and meaning of the master philosopher Hegel, who had died in 1831. In the minds of said protagonists, these philosophical battles were momentous, a "revolution beside which the French Revolution was child's play" (Marx and Engels 1989, 39). Dissecting the moment, Marx and Engels lampoon the series of fashions and fads to which this intellectual production fell victim. In terms that seem strikingly relevant today, they pinpoint how commodification and competition erodes the authentic usefulness of ideas which suffer a gradual "deterioration in quality, adulteration of the raw materials, falsification of labels", the results of which "is now being extolled and interpreted to us as a revolution of world significance, the begetter of the most prodigious results and achievements" (Marx and Engels 1989, 39–40). With only a little less of a sweeping dismissal, these words do seem more than a little pertinent to some of our own intellectual 'revolutions' in recent years.

The problem for Marx and Engels was that the Left Hegelian 'revolutionary' philosophy "never quitted the realm of philosophy" (Marx and Engels 1989, 40). As a result, methodologically it remained flawed in its ability to ground idea-systems in their real conditions of existence. "It has not occurred to these philosophers" Marx and Engels noted, "to inquire into the connection of

German philosophy with German reality, the relation of their criticism to their own material surroundings" (Marx and Engels 1989, 41). It was this lack of self-reflexive interrogation that made German philosophy an ideology. Their own philosophy, historical materialism, would break with this lack of self-reflexivity and provide the basis for a socio-economic understanding of the activities of the intellectual. The intellectual and the most prestigious form of intellectual production, philosophy, could not, in their view, be seen as some free-floating, universal group transcending social conflicts. Ideas and the producers of those ideas had to be socially contextualised.

Along with this methodological break there was a political break to be made from the Left Hegelians. The intimations of change, the analysis of the need for change, the need to identify the forces of change and press them forward in a progressive direction, could not occur unless philosophy was integrated into those social forces and political action. As Marx famously put it in the Twelfth Thesis on Feuerbach: "The philosophers have only *interpreted* the world in various ways, the point is to *change* it" (Marx and Engels 1989, 123). In re-uniting philosophy with democratic social change Marx and Engels aim no less than to set in reverse the entire historical development of intellectual production and consciousness in class societies. This development has been marked by the division of labour between manual and intellectual labour and within the latter, the development of ever more specialised regions such as philosophy, ethics, theology, law, etc. (Marx and Engels 1989, 51–52).

The basis of a democratic conception of the intellectual is at least sketched out in this early work. Since consciousness for Marx and Engels develops out of our everyday practical productive life, satisfaction of needs and the production of new needs and the co-operation this requires, then an explicit and self-conscious reconnection of intellectual functions to the social production of life would seem both possible and desirable. Habermas argued that by

> turning the construction of the manifestation of consciousness into an encoded representation of the self-production of the species, Marx discloses the mechanism of progress in the experience of reflection....
> HABERMAS 1978, 43

Yet Habermas warned that this was vitiated by the fact that self-reflection was reduced to and made identical with labour. In so doing Marx "reduces the process of reflection to the level of instrumental action" (Habermas 1978, 44). If this were the case then Marx would be no more than a philosopher of the factory, as it were. But Marx neither saw labour in such instrumental terms (he saw it as intrinsically creative even if tasked with meeting certain historical needs) nor saw the intellectual and creative functions as having their highest manifestation necessarily within the material production of the species. Marx's philosophy is perfectly capable of sustaining the view that our intellectual activities find their highest culmination in culture, communication and aesthetics, where some distanciation from immediate needs have been established (Wayne 2016, 140–148). Historical materialism is not reductionist in relation to consciousness and its specialised manifestations, it merely poses the crucial question: what are the methodological and political-moral implications of the idea that intellectual activity has certain conditions of existence that involve the totality of society?

The question of the actual and desirable relationship between the intellectual and other forms of labour is significant primarily because it is capitalism that has the instrumental view of labour (which Habermas uncritically accepts in its impoverished form as inevitable). Furthermore, today it is capitalism that poses a clear and present danger in reducing intellectual activity to serving the needs of the labour process, subordinate as it is to capital, and thus eliminating the critical component of reflective thought. In order to realise that critical component Marx and Engels recommended articulating thought to those social agents struggling for progressive change. The internal conflicts within the 'conceptive ideologists' of the dominant class (the fight between the Right and Left Hegelians) were not insignificant. It helped expand the repertoire of discourses available and seed the ideas for change. However, for these seeds of change to be activated required intellectuals to break both methodologically and politically with the dominant class. This is what Marx and Engels did in fact do.

Gramsci on the Intellectuals

The Italian Marxist Antonio Gramsci (1891–1937) has widely and rightly been seen as making a significant contribution to the Marxist understanding of the role of intellectuals. Like Marx and Engels, he argued for a democratic conception of intellectual activity. Taking the most prestigious form of intellectual production, philosophy, as an example, he argued that "all men [sic] are 'philosophers'" insofar as everyone has a specific conception of the world, a "worldview" which they have forged out of their experience and circumstance. The task was to develop philosophy, both in its specialised form as scholarship and in its everyday form, into "critical awareness" (Gramsci 1967, 58). As we have seen, for Marx and Engels, the philosophy of the intellectuals would develop its critical potential the more it could interrogate its conditions of existence. With a slight nuancing, the same prescription was applied to the philosophy of everyday life. Gramsci argued that it needed to develop critical awareness by (a) not accepting ideas and value-systems passively from the dominant institutions in society and (b) overcoming its fragmented and disparate character and developing itself as a systematic and coherent worldview in the way traditional philosophers have had the time to do with their own more 'rarefied' systems. The ideal of developing a popular form of critical philosophy would have to overcome and address a number of problems concerning the actual historical development of intellectual production and its relationship to powerful socio-economic groups. It would have to overcome firstly the fact that "All men [sic] are intellectuals … but not all men have in society the function of intellectuals" (Gramsci 1998, 9). This is the division between intellectual and manual labour. Secondly, within the 'function of intellectuals' there are different types of intellectuals.

Gramsci identified two types of intellectuals. The first were what he called the traditional intellectuals, which he defined rather ambiguously in both historical terms and social-ideological terms. The historical definition of traditional intellectuals refers to the way intellectuals associated with one mode of production need to be assimilated by the intellectuals associated with a rising class and a new mode of production. So that for example, the intellectuals of the feudal mode of production (clerics, scholars, artists) had to be integrated and re-functioned according to the new practices and needs of the capitalist mode of production (Gramsci 1998, 10–11). Likewise, the intellectuals developed within capitalism would become the 'traditional' intellectuals vis-à-vis the development of a socialist mode of production, and again would need to be assimilated into new social priorities and needs. Gramsci also defined traditional intellectuals as those within the capitalist mode of production that remained remote and aloof from the economic and political needs of the capitalist class despite their assimilation. Again, clerics and philosophers and perhaps much of the arts and humanities within the academy might once have fallen within this type of intellectual function, where non-instrumental metaphysical values could be articulated. These intellectuals are 'traditional' when compared to Gramsci's other main category: organic intellectuals.

To understand the concept of organic intellectuals, we have to first relate this concept to two other concepts in Gramsci's work: the economic-corporative and hegemony. Gramsci argues that the political consciousness of a dominant class is one which must move beyond merely a defence of its own economic interests. It must move firstly to unite with other fractions of its own class, in the way that different kinds of capital, such as industrial, financial, commercial and landed capital have historically done. If a class stays at just this level of defending its economic interests, it stays at the level of the economic-corporative. Beyond establishing intra-class cohesion, a dominant class must move beyond their own collective interests and command the moral-political terrain across society, so as to convince all other classes that *their* interests can be met by aligning themselves with or accepting the rule of the dominant class. When a dominant class achieves this, it is not merely dominant but also hegemonic (Gramsci 1988, 205–206). By hegemonic, Gramsci means that this is a class that wins (at least to some degree) the consent of the exploited classes to their situation.

It is the role of the organic intellectuals to produce this consent and to do so they work primarily to change and influence culture, morality and political agendas. Classically, organic intellectuals would have been found in political parties, in the top most prestigious newspapers, in public relations and advertising and perhaps today also in think tanks. These intellectuals are tied organically to the economic and political needs of the dominant class. In recent times, these are the thinkers, commentators, editors, writers, broadcasters and so forth that try and persuade the general population that neo-liberalism means progressive reform.

However, Gramsci also refers to the practical organisers of production, the scientist and the engineer for example, and today also we would say managers, as intellectuals. We might think that the organic intellectual would automatically include these kinds of intellectuals organised at the heart of the production process. But this interpretation is at odds with Gramsci's analysis of the economic-corporate activity of the dominant classes and the need to go beyond their immediate economic needs and build political alliances and broader political-moral projects (such as neo-liberalism). A number of writers have suggested that with the expansion of corporate and state bureaucracies, the economic-corporate role of the intellectual, working within and primarily concerned with the needs of the state or the company, has expanded (Boggs 1993, and see Pratschke in this volume). This has led to the expansion and redefinition of intellectual functions that are neither 'traditional' because they are so obviously tied to the dynamic and moving terrain of occupations responding to economic forces, nor are they 'organic' in the sense that their agenda is more focused on the smooth functioning of an apparatus rather than the broader project of public persuasion and politics. We need then to supplement Gramsci's analysis with a new category, that of the *technocratic* intellectual. This is the 'expert' in science, engineering, law, economics, management, even the trade union leader and negotiator, etc. They embody specialised and instrumentalised forms of knowledge. They work within the framework of policy, which ultimately stems from the broader political struggle conducted on the terrain of the masses and the organic intellectuals. They administer but do not determine, they examine how things work but not why things work as they do, and within that framework they may produce new solutions, products and ideas. If they become great advocates of such new ideas and practices that re-shape how we look at the world more broadly, from Henry Ford to Steve Jobs, then they lift themselves out from the merely technocratic intellectual onto the terrain of the organic intellectual. The technocratic intellectual, long dominant in the natural and social sciences, has been in the last few decades, reshaping the humanities and arts as well as the critical social sciences. Edward Said argues that the greatest threat to independent intellectual thought comes from the dominance of this technocratic type of intellectual. For Said:

> The major choice faced by the intellectual is whether to be allied with the stability of the victors and rulers or—the more difficult path—to consider that stability as a state of emergency threatening the less fortunate.
> SAID 1996, 35

We can now tabulate the different types of intellectual functions we have discussed:

1. Traditional: either eclipsed by the new rising class and/or the economically and politically marginalised intellectuals within capitalism.
2. Technocratic: numerically the biggest class of contemporary intellectual activity, working within economic-corporative horizons.
3. Organic Intellectuals. They are defined not by their occupation but by the scope and compass of the change they seek to initiate.

This last category can be subdivided between:

(i) Hegemonic organic intellectuals who work on behalf of the capitalist class and whose main business is in helping to shape the broader political-moral, social and cultural agenda.
(ii) Counter-Hegemonic organic intellectuals. They work to call the dominant frames of reference, the dominant assumptions, and the dominant policy trends that favour capitalism, into question. They are organically tied to the classes and groups for whom stability is 'a state of emergency'. This group can in turn be sub-divided between:
   (a) those that, like Marx and Engels, come from the middle classes but who have distanced themselves from the hegemonic group politically, psychologically and ideally, in terms of their practices (but

often they fall short of this crucial need to democratise their practices, retaining instead the stamp of elitism);
(b) those intellectuals that develop from *within* the working classes and other subaltern groups (but who must resist assimilation and neutralisation within the established institutions).

Organic Intellectuals Today

In his 1967 essay on the role of the intellectual in Western democracies Chomsky considered the intellectual in relation to the concepts of responsibility, power and truth seeking. He argued that their relative power bestows upon them a responsibility to interrogate, critique and expose the disastrous effects of right wing ideologies.

> Intellectuals are in a position to expose the lies of governments, to analyse actions according to their causes and motives and often hidden intentions. In the Western world, at least, they have the power that comes from political liberty, from access to information and freedom of expression. For a privileged minority, Western democracy provides the leisure, the facilities, and the training to seek the truth lying hidden behind the veil of distortion and misrepresentation, ideology and class interest, through which the events of current history are presented to us
> CHOMSKY 1967, 60

There are two significant contextual points to be made here. Firstly, Chomsky was writing in relation to the Vietnam War over fifty years ago. It was a challenge to the intellectuals of the time to expose the lies that were disseminated in order to justify a war that killed over a million people in total. Secondly, he is referring here to a particular kind of intellectual, that is the *counter hegemonic intellectual*. As we have pointed out in the discussion of Gramsci, we can consider the role of intellectuals in two ways as hegemonic or as counter hegemonic. While the type of intellectual Chomsky refers to is one that works to expose the facade of the powerful there are intellectuals who can just as easily play a role in reinforcing the status quo. The Vietnam War as with the Iraq War in 2003 had its intellectual cheerleaders, giving power the gloss of higher ideals (the 2003 war was we were told about defending and extending freedom, democracy, etc.).

Conventionally those who are considered to be intellectuals—or we could call them professional thinkers—have hailed from the upper and middle classes. This is not because these groups possess an inherent intelligence consistently absent from the working class. Rather it is because those from the middle and upper class designated as intellectuals—or as Gramsci would have it fulfilling the function of the intellectual—are in possession of the social, cultural and economic capital that makes such a designation possible and ensures they are recognised and acknowledged as such by other members of their class. This means it is possible to understand the hegemonic intellectual not in relation to a superior 'intellect' (whatever that might mean) but in terms of their significant role in the reproduction of the socio-economic relations of capital.

It remains true today that the majority of contemporary hegemonic organic intellectuals in the UK are drawn from the middle and upper classes. The decision-making professions within which many institutional intellectuals operate are dominated by privately educated Oxbridge graduates who possess a shared culture, value system and set of attitudes which when taken together coalesce into a world view which they hold in common. The link between education and the production of intellectuals has meant that formal education has been a crucial filter by which to reproduce an intellectual class dedicated to reproducing the class system (Reay 2010, 400). It is within the private education system and the universities of Oxford and Cambridge that the middle and upper class intellectuals learn about the way in which the world works. Here they are prepared to run that world as if opposition to their view of the world is a deviance from the norm.

What this means in effect is that as members of a middle-class elite whose perspective is universalised, intellectual engagement with the condition of society and the way in which it is organised and regulated is filtered through the sensibilities of those for whom the prevailing structural arrangements do not appear to be alienating and exploitative. Whilst there is no suggestion that the hegemonic intellectual is unable to engage critically with the world—indeed they even, at times, are able to appear radical—the depth of their analysis and level of critical engagement is typically limited because the position they inhabit is a privileged one. Consequently, their radicalism only appears as such when presented to other hegemonic intellectuals. Significantly their intellectual endeavour evaluates the immediate situation and typically accepts the given parameters in place to make sense of that situation while a more critical intellect "evaluates evaluations" (Hofstadter 1966, 25). As Schwartz has pointed out, many university students are aware of the reason that corporate boardrooms should promote diversity "but few question the concept of corporate rule itself" (2013, 184).

If the role of the critical intellectual as Chomsky claims is to make public what the powerful would rather keep hidden, we need to recognise the significance of this in relation to a contemporary society consistently divided along class lines and to realise any intellectual endeavour wishing to 'evaluate the evaluation' must eventually engage with the question of class and the unequal distribution of economic and cultural resources which class divisions rest upon. It is the approach to this question we would argue that separates the hegemonic and counter-hegemonic intellectual. As Marx made clear it is only by engaging with the question of class, the ways in which class is structured and reconfigured over time, that we can begin to understand the nature of capitalism and come to terms with his claim: "the history of all hitherto existing society is the history of class struggles" (Marx 1985, 79).

The crucial point here is that for the hegemonic middle class intellectual, class is not an overtly exploitative or antagonistic relationship. Their experiential horizons are confined by lives of privilege where the politics of identity takes a primary position. The last thirty years of neoliberalism has witnessed class as a source of intellectual analysis take second place to the politics of race, sexuality and gender, concepts that affect the middle class the most. In the meantime, economic inequality has increased to historically high levels, the working class have been incrementally excluded from the public sphere and immigrants forced to live and work in the most appalling conditions. Yet those in positions of intellectual power have normalised and universalised this inequality. While their own class world becomes normalised questions of class, which are essential to any transformative process, are secondary. This has allowed for an on-going abdication of any responsibility towards the working class and no demand for a critical self-interrogation necessary to consider the role class plays in the social relations of exploitation. As Marx has made clear, it is not the consciousness of men that determines their existence, but their social being that determines consciousness (Marx 1977, 181). While it is possible, through social change and political events (e.g. war, political revolutions, etc.) for consciousness to be reconfigured and established dominant patterns of social conditioning that has formerly shaped a life to be questioned, the tendency is for social being to produce the consciousness that is most conducive for the reproduction (within a range) of the social relationships in which social being is formed.

The problem then becomes one of praxis; of intellectual work that is able to inquire into and evaluate the connection between ideas and their material affects and translate them into new ways of being as Marx and Engels called for in *The German Ideology*. The process of re-evaluating ideas about the world can bring about the potential to transform the world. Thus, conservatives and liberals are certainly not averse to acknowledging that inequality exists, but they never come up with policy ideas that could remotely change this situation.

When they are confronted with policy ideas that could have a positive impact on inequality, they attack those ideas as 'extreme' because they encroach, necessarily on the prerogatives of private property. Gramsci linked the economic rule of the elites to the complex practices of everyday existence where to a great extent there is an unquestioned conformity to the rules and conventions of a given social order. This intellectual acceptance of hegemonic boundaries, this refusal to surmount the imposed limitations of the institutions, politics and ideological framework of neoliberalism, illuminates the distinction to be made between the hegemonic and counter-hegemonic intellectual.

Non-conformity to these rules, a refusal to live by their precepts, engenders in the counter-hegemonic intellectual the condition of potential isolation and marginalisation and indicates an acknowledgement that analysis is informed by and dependent upon action—and vice versa. At present the hegemonic power of the dominating groups is such that the critical analysis required for strategic explorations of the consequences of objective material structures exists in isolation from the action required to transform society.

This is no more apparent than in the claim associated with the Occupy movement that began in the US: 'we are the 99%'. This slogan functioned to differentiate the majority from the obscenely rich capitalist class minority right at the top of society. We would argue that this contradictory model of inclusivity is problematic and functions to exclude the working class by smoothing out the differences in lives that are significantly different *within* the majority. On the one hand the slogan draws attention to a powerful global elite at the top of society who exist in a shadowy world of financial deals and political agreements. At the same time, it eradicates the peculiarities, oppressions and exploitative relationships of many members of the working class and the very real class differences and conflicts that exist between groups within the 99%. This collapsing of the working classes and the more privileged lives of the comfortable middle class into one homogenous mass inevitably functions to exclude the working class from the struggle for change and leads to a weakening of the potential to build intellectual and political arguments and crucially, anti-capitalist alliances that acknowledge the material realities of working class life. As a 'unifying' slogan it is unable to engage with the complexities of a classed stratified, multi ethnic globalised world. What is envisaged, as a tool against neoliberalism becomes in effect a method of annihilation—a theoretical and essentialising meme which both conceptually and practically results in the destruction of the working class as a category. Similarly, orthodox Marxist conceptions which equate 'the working class' with wage-labour are problematic, since they disavow the different types and levels of cultural, social and economic advantage the middle-class wage-labourer has, as well as their position of administrative, managerial or intellectual dominance over other strata within the category of 'working class'.

This returns us to the concept of praxis and its relationship to working class intellectuals. What it demonstrates is the need for the middle class intellectual to adequately address their relationship to existing structures and patterns of inequality in which they are implicated and their increasing control of the means of communication, their domination of the media, academia and other decision making professions, all of which are conduits for the transmission of power and the construction of ideology (Wayne and O'Neill 2013). The truly counter-hegemonic middle class intellectual who seeks an organic relation to the working class must remember that, as Marx wrote in 'The Theses on Feuerbach', "it is essential to educate the educator" (Marx and Engels 1989, 121). A dialectical relationship of mutual learning means that organic intellectuals must also emerge from *within* the working class.

The counter-hegemonic working class intellectual traditionally was dependent on organisations and institutions such as trade unions, adult education institutions and socialist parties (Rose 2001) to provide the means to develop as counter-hegemonic thinkers. Yet neoliberalism has progressively destroyed or neutralised these organisations. It is a political truism to claim neoliberalism is responsible for the rolling back of the welfare state and the destruction of the public services that function within it. One of the consequences of this is a shrinking of the public sphere and the access to it that is essential to making subaltern voices heard (Wacquant 2008).

Neoliberalism has destroyed the fabric of the communities in which the working class found material and ideological strength and in the process strategically depoliticised the working class. The left intelligentsia has receded into a kind of "ideological policing" (Hall 2012, 9) obsessed with theories of differences and transgression that has resulted in its increasing insignificance and the erosion of the concept (and practice) of social solidarity. Schwartz reinforces this point in his discussion of radical theory:

> As the right's growing hegemony from the 1980s onwards eroded majoritarian support for progressive taxation and universal public goods, radical theory, through its dominant concerns for difference and transgression, abandoned any intellectual defence of the core democratic value of social democracy
> SCHWARTZ 2013, 395

The destruction of the civil society in which the working class had established some organisational and institutional bases, has also eroded the links between the working class and the middle class. Middle class intellectuals could once be rooted in working class struggles such as trade union movements, social movements (such as Lesbians and Gays Support the Miners) or in the colleges and working-men's institutes, civil rights protests, and so forth. As all of these have become weakened, so the role of the counter-hegemonic radical intellectual has declined. Our reading of this situation leads us to suggest that the middle-class counter-hegemonic intellectual requires movements and working class intellectuals to work alongside and to learn form. A symbolic moment when the working class counter-hegemonic intellectual and the institutional production of middle class intellectuals converged, was Jimmy Reid's 1972 inaugural address as Rector of Glasgow University. Reid was a leading figure in the 1971 work-in to save the Upper Clyde Shipbuilders from bankruptcy. In Britain now it is virtually unthinkable for a University to appoint a radical trade union leader to such a position and to acknowledge that the 'educators need educating'. Ours is not the era to give such a platform, such a vindication and such an acknowledgement, to a radical organic intellectual of the working class. In his famous address, Reid made a direct appeal to the students as intellectuals in the making:

> A rat race is for rats. We're not rats. We're human beings. Reject the insidious pressures in society that would blunt your critical faculties to all that is happening around you, that would caution silence in the face of injustice lest you jeopardise your chances of promotion and self-advancement. This is how it starts, and before you know where you are, you're a fully paid-up member of the rat-pack.
> REID 2010

Yet if the old established platforms (the universities, the press) have become integrated into the neoliberal order and hostile to participation of the working class as critical thinkers, new spaces have opened up around the digital media.

Counter-Hegemonic Spaces and the Digital Media

In our multi-media saturated society, the significance of the media as a site of hegemonic and counter-hegemonic struggle takes on a dynamic role in framing our social and historical experiences and the ways in which they are interpreted, evaluated and made sense of. Within the dominant media environment, the processes of public debate, policy-making and political power are asymmetrically skewed towards both the middle classes and large capital interests. The dominant media are run by middle class intellectuals who largely operate within the spectrum of liberal and conservative thought and opinion in the current period. In the UK, the leading editorial thinkers on the premier liberal paper *The Guardian* have overwhelmingly been privately educated and went through Oxford or Cambridge. They police the boundaries of the acceptable and at their more 'radical' end of the spectrum they present as counter-hegemonic intellectuals and 'left-wing firebrands'. The ideological effect of incorporating 'radical' politics inside such dominant organs is that anything outside those boundaries can be labelled and dismissed as 'extremist'.

One example of the policing of who gets to speak, where and on what issues is Russell Brand. Brand crossed boundaries that unsettled the established hierarchies and divisions of labour. Here was an 'entertainer' who became politicised and began commenting critically on political matters. But he was also from a working class background that was outside the golden Oxbridge circle and this seemed for many liberals to disqualify him to speak on political issues and be a political actor (See Fisher 2013, El-Gingihy 2014 and for an example of the established political commentators' collective noses being firmly put out of joint, O'Hagan 2014).[1] In particular, his critique of the current state of representative democracy in the UK and its inability to bring about progressive change (through voting) enraged many in the political and media class who are invested in the status quo. Brand disrupted the middle-class norms of style in the way he talked (the accent and content), the way he dressed, his very tactile interactions with interviewers, etc., all spoke to an informal unpredictability that was seen as a symbolic attack on 'serious discourse'. Brand launched his Trews news channel on You Tube which has more than one million subscribers and which regularly makes the media itself and their questionable shaping of the public agenda, his topic.[2] The development and popularisation of such media literacy is an important component of the oppositional digital and social media world, which defines its identity precisely in terms of its difference from the dominant media. The dominant media in turn fear this growing media literacy and meta-commentary on its practices since it calls them to account and deconstructs the naturalisation of the dominant media's perspectives. The success of Brand's Trews channel demonstrates that the digital and

---

1   Brand was accused of sexism by some high-profile commentators. The delight with which they leapt onto his remarks about his 'love of a good women' curing him of sexism suggested a certain keenness to find something to attack him on and deflect away from the other unequal power relations he was drawing attention to. In fact, Brand showed a good deal more reflexivity about his own sexism than his critics did of their own class privilege.
2   Brand has shifted to a less overtly political position now but See https://www.youtube.com/user/russellbrand.

social media also threaten the dominant media in terms of audience reach and not just ideological critique.

Social media and digital media may also be seen as a counter-hegemonic model of labour or intellectual production. In contrast to those that have a corporate contract, bloggers, micro-bloggers, commentators, memes, online papers, You Tube political rappers such as bin-man Sean Donnelly (NXTGen) and so on, produce material in their spare time and in most cases for free.[3] The demographic backgrounds of the politicised social media are far more diverse than the narrow private school/Oxbridge nexus that filters and shapes the formation of British intellectuals. Although social media is often criticised for encouraging a privatised and individualistic politics (the so-called 'keyboard activist'), we would argue that it can be a perfect example of praxis. Social media can offer clear and succinct explanations of what is happening and why it is happening; it provides the 'theory' in a idiom that is accessible to non-academics, and that can seed political action.

The digital and social media help produce horizontal communication that is very important in helping people overcome the sense of isolation and marginalisation that one feels when they have political views and opinions that find little or no place in the dominant media. In such a situation of tacit censorship it is easy to believe that few people share those beliefs and opinions, and this can lead to a demoralising atomisation of the left. Since many of the public spaces where working class people used to congregate have been decimated, virtual networks in the social media have provided one forum to reconstitute such opportunities for conversation and knowledge exchange. As with any other form of media, the social and digital media can be used for a variety of purposes, including highly reactionary ones. But the left has often shown itself to be suspicious of social and digital media as a mode of political engagement and this has meant underestimating its potentialities, or concentrating exclusively (in a reaction to the techno-determinists and techno-utopians) on the way the political economy of the internet for example is dominated by corporations (Dean 2009).

---

3   We do not agree with the argument that voluntary cultural labour for online digital dissemination constitutes 'exploitation' in the Marxist sense. Such labour produces no value directly (no ratio between investment and surplus extraction). Even when advertising makes use of this content, this is a re-distribution of value produced elsewhere by the workers who produce the goods which advertisers sell on behalf of their clients. Labour that chooses to produce what it wants, when it wants and without any direct economic compulsion, can in no way be described as 'value producing'. If it was, there could be no Marxist theory of capitalist crisis rooted in the tendency for the rate of profit to fall. See Williamson elsewhere in this volume for more on this question.

Gramsci's argument that everyone is an intellectual but that only some people have the social function of being intellectuals is relevant here. We are arguing that the digital and social media enormously expands the range of people who can assume the social function of being an intellectual. The genre of citizen journalism has been enriched by an influx of counter-hegemonic intellectuals who do not respect the narrow norms and rules of political discourse. To take one random example, Rachel Swindon has been micro-blogging on her Twitter account exposing Conservative MPs who voted to cut benefits while spending thousands of pounds of public money on their expenses claims. Interestingly this was a story in the dominant media back in 2009. But what Swindon has done is firstly pursue the story consistently over time, demonstrating that little has changed, whereas the dominant media tend to move on and have largely left the issue behind. Secondly, she has linked the on-going issue of MP's expenses to the brutal cuts in benefits under austerity politics. By contrast the dominant news media keep such issues separate, thus failing to make the connections that reveal the class dynamics of the social totality. On the back of this successful campaign (she has more than forty-four thousand Twitter followers at the time of writing) Swindon has launched a blog declaring that the British media are failing to hold the Conservative government to account. Subscription models from readers/supporters often provide some financial support for this kind of citizen journalism.

Conclusion

Praxis is the integration of theoretical activities that have been cut off from the widest possible social base and restricted to elite demographics and narrow circles of action and knowledge. This is why Marx, Engels and Gramsci called for philosophy, the most elite but also most highly developed system of thought, to be brought back into contact with not 'reality' (since philosophy is hardly unreal) but the reality of the lives of the majority. Education—in the broadest sense and not just in formal institutions—is therefore a crucial part of developing praxis. Praxis means not only linking theory and practice, as it is typically defined, but *democratising* who gets to have access to those frameworks, perspectives and intellectual resources that provide the basis of critical thought and critical action.

The system-integrated intellectuals take different forms: the traditional intellectuals, remote from the immediate political or economic needs of capitalism, have always been on hand to provide spiritual, artistic, philosophical or other ideals that have provided important resources for the bourgeoisie in the ideological struggle. The organic intellectuals—those elites within the intellectual elite—who link the economic interests of the capitalist class with the broader strategic political and cultural goals of the class, fight the ideological struggle in the more immediate, day-to-day battle over the direction of social life. The massed ranks of the technocratic intellectuals follow their lead in the myriad institutions of modern society. It is from this dense bloc of integration that the middle class counter-hegemonic intellectual must emerge. Radical social change will need the critical leverage and resources within existing public opinion formation which intellectuals from the middle class already have. The contradiction between their access to the most sophisticated intellectual culture and the absurdity and irrationality of capitalism has often thrown them into conflict with it. But counter-posing rationality against the evident waste and crisis tendencies of capitalism does not break down the privileged superiority of the intellectuals.

Intellectuals from the middle class can only play a truly counter-hegemonic role if they are sufficiently and critically self-reflexive about the class divisions and competitive culture from which they have emerged. Their educational privilege "creates a bond of solidarity which attaches him [sic] to his class, and still more attaches his class to him" (Benjamin 1998, 102). Even the 'proletarianisation' of the intellectual (real or imagined) does not alter this instinctive "bond of solidarity". Benjamin's call for intellectuals to change the production relations within which they work, to find ways of democratising the apparatus, to create collaborators and co-producers from their audience, must fight against the constant tendency of the broader social relations to shore up privilege and expertise (through cultural capital for example). The paradoxical task of the middle-class counter-hegemonic intellectual is that they must aim to abolish their own conditions of existence, that is the class privilege from which they have emerged. Like withering the state, this has proved difficult to do, although there have been inspiring examples that provide pointers in the right direction.

The democratisation of the function of intellectuality requires then the development of organic counter-hegemonic intellectuals from the working class itself, without which the middle-class intellectual cannot forge an organic relationship to any class but their own. The danger for organic intellectuals of the working class is that they become assimilated within the status quo leaving behind their own class and taking on the hegemonic precepts of the class in which they find themselves but in which they are heavily outnumbered. The institutions, organisations and workplaces which once would have fostered and nurtured working class organic intellectuals no longer exist or have been neutralised. This means that the possibility of organising around the demands of working class life—one of the functions of the counter hegemonic intellectual—is severely limited. As the neoliberal state privatises what once were accepted as public rights, the spaces for the counter hegemonic intellectual become severely restricted, particularly for those who wish to challenge the universalisation of middle class competitive individualism. The choices for the working class counter hegemonic intellectual appear in our contemporary moment to be stark: incorporation into the traditional hegemonic institutions that reinforce the status quo—or an enforced, politically convenient marginalisation in which all conversations around class that actually include the working class are ignored. We have discussed how the digital media potentially and also in practice, have played a role in re-opening up civic-political spaces that have been closed down elsewhere. Of course, it is not enough. Of course, digital media openings for organic intellectuals in general must be linked with real political action, which must in turn be linked to re-enfranchising politically, socially and culturally, the working class. The social order does not want the evaluation to be evaluated from the interests and perspectives of the working class. Which is why democratising the function of the intellectual is so hard and so necessary.

References

Benjamin, W. (1998) *Understanding Brecht*. Trans. A. Bostock. London: Verso.
Boggs, C. (1993) *Intellectuals and the Crisis of Modernity*. New York: State University of New York Press.
Chomsky, N. (1967) A Special Supplement: The Responsibility of Intellectuals. *New York Review of Books*. February 23. http://www.nybooks.com/articles/1967/02/23/a-special-supplement-the-responsibility-of-intelle/.
Dean, J. (2009) *Democracy and other neoliberal fantasies, communicative capitalism and left politics*. Durham NC: Duke University Press.
El-Gingihy, Y. (2014) 'Russell Brand vs the bloody liberal majority', *New Internationalist*, https://newint.org/blog/2014/10/28/russell-brand-liberal-majority/#comments.
Enzensberger, H.M. (1982) *Critical Essays*. New York: Continuum.
Fisher, M. (2013) Exiting the Vampire Castle. *The North Star*. Available at: http://www.thenorthstar.info/?p=11299.
Gramsci, A. (1967) *The Modern Prince and other writings*. London: Lawrence and Wishart.
Gramsci, A. (1988) *A Gramsci Reader*. Forgacs D. (ed) London: Lawrence and Wishart.
Gramsci, A. (1998) *Selections from the Prison Notebooks*. Hoare Q. and Nowell-Smith G. (eds) London: Lawrence and Wishart.

Habermas, J. (1978) *Knowledge and Human Interests*. London: Heinemann.

Hall, S. (2012) *Theorising Crime and Deviance: A New Perspective*. London: Sage.

Hofstadter, R. (1966) *Anti-Intellectualism in American Life*. New York: Alfred A. Knopf.

Marx, K. (1977) 'Preface To A Contribution To The Critique of Political Economy'. *Karl Marx and Frederick Engels, Selected Works*, Vol.1. London: Lawrence and Wishart.

Marx, K. and Engels, F. (1989) *The German Ideology*. London: Lawrence Wishart.

Marx, K. and Engels, F. (1985) *The Communist Manifesto*, Harmondsworth: Penguin Books.

O'Hagan, E. (2014) 'Russell Brand's "love of a good woman" is not what feminism needs', *The Guardian*, January 17. https://www.theguardian.com/commentisfree/2014/jan/17/russell-brand-no-more-page-3-feminism?CMP=fb_gu.

Reay, D. (2010) Sociology, social class and education. In: Apple M., Ball S. and Gandin L. *The Routledge International Handbook of the Sociology of Education*. London: Routledge.

Reid, J. (2010) 'Still irresistible, a working class hero's finest speech', *The Independent*, August 12. http://www.independent.co.uk/news/uk/politics/still-irresistible-a-workingclass-heros-finest-speech-2051285.html.

Rose, J. (2001) *The Intellectual Life of the British Working Classes*. New Haven: Yale University Press.

Said, E. (1996) *Representations of the Intellectual*. London: Vintage.

Schwartz, J. (2013) A Peculiar Blind Spot: Why did Radical Political Theory Ignore the Rampant Rise in Inequality Over the Past Thirty Years? *New Political Science* 35 (3): 389–402.

Wacquant, L. (2008) Relocating Gentrification: The Working Class, Science and the State in Recent Urban Research. *International Journal of Urban and Regional Research* 32 (1): 198–205.

Wayne, M. (2016) *Red Kant, Aesthetics, Marxism and the Third Critique*. London: Bloomsbury.

Wayne, M. and O'Neill, D (2013) The Gentrification of the Left. *New Left Project*. Available at: http://www.newleftproject.org/index.php/site/article_comments/the_gentification_of_the_left.

CHAPTER 11

The British Working Class Post-Blair Consensus: We Do Not Exist

Lisa Mckenzie

Introduction

Whether politicians, the media commentariat, or the Urban liberal middle class like it or not, there is a growing and distinct group of people in the United Kingdom that are faring badly in this period of advanced capitalism. As inequality rises and the gap between the top and the bottom of society widens their lives are becoming more precarious and the void that community and family and class struggle once filled is now filled with hopelessness, fear and anger (Mckenzie 2015; Savage 2015).

The people that are in this constant struggle are working class people but unlike previous generations they have little in the way of self or state organised stability, from trade unions, political parties or from identities connected to their employment. It is this group of people at the bottom of society who have been harmed the most by capitalist economics and have traditionally relied upon 'the social', whether in their employment, or in their communities, to thrive. We cannot ignore the connections between widening inequality, de-valuing of our social goods, and the rising anger coming from populations all over Europe and the USA with established politics, and what I argue is a de-stabilising of democracy. For some time there have been debates around the 'hollowing out' of democracy (Mair 2013) that describes the process of an apathetic electorate. I argue that we have surpassed this hollowing out phase, and democracy is now unstable. Who could have imagined even a year ago that Donald Trump would be the President of the United States, and the United Kingdom would have voted to leave the European Union? None of these outcomes can be attributed to a left or right swing in the political spectrum, they are the consequences of a political system that is no longer working in the interests of the greater good.

The post-war consensus in 1945 put social goods at its centre: education, social housing, state pensions, child benefit, and the National Health Service. These social goods have always been important to working class people, however over the last thirty years there has been a marked retreat from the post-war consensus and a definite policy of 'rolling back' publicly owned and publicly run social services. Simultaneously there has been an over-professionalisation of politicians who see their purpose as managing economies rather than representing people.

Thirty years of de-industrialisation resulting in the loss of manufacturing industries, and the privatisation of those industries that were once publicly owned have devastated working class communities, economically but also culturally, socially and symbolically. Housing policy has shifted over the last 30 years towards the home owning democracy and away from a large social renting culture. Consequently, changing the way that the population view housing from 'home' to 'asset' has serious implications for how communities organise and operate (Hodkinson, Watt and Mooney 2013). At the same time removing state support for further education for all adults over the age of 25 and introducing and raising fees within higher education have ensured that even the myth of social mobility is now unbelievable (Holmwood 2014, Bathmaker, Ingram and Waller 2013). As a result, the debate in the United Kingdom has moved away from how we use and maintain social goods in tackling poverty and inequality to the usefulness of an individual, their productivity, their behaviour, their culture and their values (Skeggs 2004, 2014; Welshman 2006). This is not an entirely new phenomenon. There have been institutional and moral judgments regarding the poorest for as long as there has been a 'poor law' naming them (Welshman 2006). Consequently, naming and identifying the poor has been used to divide them into two distinct groups: the deserving poor, those deemed 'respectable', doing their best and perhaps becoming 'unlucky'; and in opposition to them, the undeserving, the deviant, dangerous, and criminal.

This chapter focuses upon those people who have become the most precarious, the people who have historically used many forms of collectivism within their employment but also within their social lives, in order to get by, a group that once were called 'the working class'. This group now appears to be struggling in an ever-competitive jobs market, rapidly changing faster than they can accumulate the skills they require. Added to this is the rolling back of many state social programs as Governments follow the ideology of a neo-liberal market driven economy for both its public and private services. Public services have been hollowed out yet there has been little in the way of empathy towards those working class communities and the struggles they face. Instead they have been demonised, stigmatised and ridiculed for their apparent failure. Subsequent Government policy for almost 40 years has compounded this with rhetoric that has shifted the focus from the market to the individual by looking specifically at the culture and the practices of the poorest.

Policy and rhetoric from the full spectrum of British politics have followed the undeserving/deserving mantra from the Conservative Government's theories of the underclass during the 1980's (Levitas 2005) to New Labour's social exclusion agenda and back to the current Conservative Government's concept of 'Broken Britain' (Mckenzie 2015, 7). By naming the poorest through negative narratives there has been a removal of class struggles, class politics and class inequality from the public consciousness to the point where the British Labour Party has eliminated 'class' from its vocabulary, preferring the hollow terms 'working people' and even worse 'hard working people' which suggests there are another group of people who are not hardworking. Removing the language of class, and removing the struggles of class from our politics is to de-politicise inequality, removing the critique of the system and instead placing that critique onto the individual through a narrow understanding of failure or success.

Market Value

The debate around value during this period of advanced capitalist ideology is central. When the 'market has become God' (Frank 2001) and dominated by the logic that capital is only there to make capital by any means necessary, the concept of value only has an economic meaning. Who we value, and why we value them has to some extent replaced the debate around class struggle. Rather than understanding inequality as structural with collective beneficiaries at the expense of collective losers we attribute value to an individual (Sayer 2015). The debate is often subtle, and can be addressed in many ways, for example 'the hardworking families' rhetoric that is used in Westminster political language. This is effective in removing the concept of class but also removing the critique of social structure, by making distinctions between 'hard working' people and others that we must assume are not hard working. Bev Skeggs' (2014, 2) recent research on 'value' argues that this forceful logic opens out, and "commodifies every aspect of our lives, making everything, every person and every interaction subject to a value that can be bought, sold or exchanged". Consequently, over the last forty years this intense neoliberal project means there has been a naturalising and normalising of capitalism that has reduced the ideas of social interaction into rational action and a self-interested calculation. This is apparent in the current 'crisis' for homes in London, but also in specific 'hotspots' across the United Kingdom where people and communities have been reduced to their wealth value, and the cost of the land they live on. Recent research undertaken by the estate agent Savilles (2016) has calculated that London is now the most expensive city to live and work in the world. Savilles is an estate agent that is also at the forefront of several regeneration projects across the UK that aims to turn unproductive land into productive land. According to Savilles and to the many local councils around the UK unproductive land is known as 'brownfield'. However, many brownfield sites are actually council estates with a resident population. Productive land on the other hand is where private development can be enabled; consequently, land and property can be valued appropriately to market value. The terms used for this process by private developers is 'place making' (Emmett 2016) where they specifically look for high value land that is close to improving infrastructure so they can 'value uplift', meaning pushing up prices. The estate agent also noted in their report in January 2016 that the cost of space an individual needs for accommodation, and work in London totals a figure of £80,700 a year per person. This reduces people to a 'market value' figure of their earning power, as Skeggs says, only seeing value "from within the blinkers of capital's logic" and removing all recognition of "the values that live beyond value" (Skeggs 2014, 2). The consequences of this 'place making' by private developers is that poorer residents have been socially cleansed out of their communities where there might be good or improving social infrastructure, to places further out of the city where the infrastructure that they need is lacking.

This logic has had severe consequences for working class people through stigmatisation and re-branding them as of a lesser value, and in some cases valueless. This connection between an individual's market value and their moral value have been central in producing new ways of exploitation through the fields of culture and media, strengthening established forms of class differentiation but also inventing new forms of class prejudice. This process of differentiation can be subtle and unseen but has terrible consequences for those whose social value is being undermined, a process that Pierre Bourdieu (1986) would term symbolic violence. This refers to an act of violence that is symbolic (cultural, representational) and often difficult to detect through the normalisation process of everyday practice. These are practices that appear 'normal' and are inflicted upon a less powerful group by a more powerful group. These 'normal' or 'common sense' practices can be demonstrated in the way that social cleansing is being used by cities to ensure that land and property have 'value uplift'. Social cleansing is an act of violence, families being moved out of their communities are actual acts of violence. However, reducing people to their market value alone and distinguishing them as deserving and undeserving, valuable and valueless are also forms of symbolic violence.

The Symbolic Violence and Class Acts

A way we can demonstrate the difficulties in recognising and naming acts of symbolic violence is to show how working class and middle-class cultural capitals are not seen as equal but different. The difference which working class people display is 'made into inequality' through a de-valuing process. We can see this in the ways that working class people are regularly ridiculed and despised within popular culture.

Defining working class people as valueless has taken on new forms in recent years, in often very negative ways. This has manifested itself into a growing genre of popular television programmes that 'watch the poor' in pseudo-documentary formats, a phenomenon known as 'Poverty Porn'. This trend of 'watching the poor' is evident in programmes such as Channel 4's *Benefits Street* and *Dogs on the Dole*. Even the BBC have cashed in with *We Pay Your Benefits*, and a whole host of the genre on Channel 5 that are shown nightly at prime time. This genre of television has become an outlet for those 'hard working families' that Westminster politicians have helpfully differentiated for us against 'Benefits Britain' to vent their anger, and have given them someone to blame for the rising inequalities in Britain and the continued precarity that millions of families are experiencing. These are based on familiar narratives, the benefit claiming young single mother taking too much from the state, or the lazy benefit family with no intention of ever working. These are myths and stories, rather than coherent narratives but are still extremely damaging and hurtful to these communities and individuals. Symbolic violence hurts families and has severe consequences on communities because the removal of social goods either through 'brownfield' regeneration, or through austerity measures can be justified because the poor can be blamed for their poverty.

However recent and rigorous research by Shildrick, Macdonald et al (2012) shows clearly that poverty in the UK is caused by an insecure employment market where people move from no-pay to low-pay, to zero hour contracts, to welfare benefits. In addition, the crisis for homes which has been purposefully orchestrated by successive government policy on housing has meant that there has been an inflated property market, and a lack of genuine affordable rented accommodation and a rise in 'buy to let' private landlords (Dorling 2014). Consequently, social goods that the poorest in society have needed and relied upon are being removed and justified through the narrative of value: who is of value and who is not.

Drawing upon my own ethnographic research in Nottingham in the East Midlands and in Bethnal Green in London's East-end, I will argue that despite the naturalising of the market, and the normalising of all 'value' being linked to an exchange value within the market, working class people in both locations resist this neoliberal model of society through placing their own understanding of value firmly located within and amongst their families, friends and local communities.

Narratives from the Bottom

It is July 2014 and I am sitting in the back yard of a local pub in Bethnal Green with a group of people who have lived within staggering distance to this establishment for either all or most of their lives, as have their families and friends. We are talking about the local neighbourhood, the gossip, the news and of course as always the fears of the residents by the rapidly changing nature of the community. Today's talk consists of a new film being made about the Kray Twins, the notorious East-end gangsters which is being filmed in the Café two doors down from the pub, the rise in popularity of 'loom bands' amongst their children, and the Elvis Presley tribute act that is on Saturday night. Peppered amongst this conversation are the personal worries and the public state of the severity of inequality in Britain today. This seems remarkable. Most of the people who drink in this pub in the East-end did not vote in the 2015 general election, and would be known as the 'politically disinterested'.

Although conversations change daily the constant is the talk about how difficult it is to make ends meet in London; this conversation never changes, and never ends. The people who I am sat with in this pub are finding themselves in increasingly precarious positions regarding their work, the men are on very precarious contracts within the building trade, sometimes a day at a time and the women mostly work cleaning the offices and homes of the more affluent and they are unlikely to earn the London living wage. They are also worried about their ability to stay in this community, rents are rising, and they tell me that the local council are putting more and more pressure upon local people to move out of this part of London and move further east into Essex, or even North as far away as Birmingham and Manchester.

The talk in this pub is what will happen to them: will they be allowed to stay in this neighbourhood, and if not what will happen to their relatives particularly the elderly who have more secure social housing and are more difficult to move. One woman in her 80's 'Mary' told me she was stranded 'amongst the yuppies'. Her daughter had been moved out when the private landlord raised the rent well beyond her minimum wage job. New pressures had been placed on this family by Mary's grandson moving in with her in order to get work and stay close to the building sites in central London. Their positions are unstable, they are precarious, not knowing whether they will be in work, not knowing where they might be living in a year's time. Constantly changing cuts in welfare keep them precarious. They never know what new cuts will be implemented and how it will affect them. This is particularly salient in relation to housing benefit capping and the cost of renting privately, the benefit just doesn't fit the rent. The result is that whole communities that have been stable for generations are forced to move further out of London. The value of 'the social' and of family and community is becoming increasingly diminished and over-ridden by the needs of a capitalist system extracting as much market value as possible out of each and every relationship, interaction and person. This method of de-valuing low income working class people is not subtle, it is extremely blunt. If you live in Bethnal Green, and within walking distance to the City of London and the financial district and you are not worth the £80,700 that Saville's the estate agent has calculated the cost of the space you are taking up, you need to leave, no value can be extracted from you. This type of blunt and simplistic logic is having a severe effect on working class families within London and wider within the South East as rents rise and house prices sky-rocket. The bottom line to whether you are allowed to stay in a neighbourhood where you have perhaps lived most or all of your lives, where you have a job, a family and a connection is based upon—are you worth it? In this case the social is sacrificed mercilessly. As 'Mary' told me, "you aint worth it mate".

Sharon's Story

The East Midlands is a part of the United Kingdom that has been hit for over 30 years with total de-industrialisation by the closure of the mining industry, the large engineering industries, and the textile industry. The de-valuing process here has been economically and culturally pitched because of the closure of local industry, leading to unemployment and extremely low paid work. However there has been a cultural de-valuing of these communities. Through their lack of 'social mobility' there is a perception that these people are unwilling or unable to 'join in' and become market driven. I was undertaking research during the mid-2000s with a group of women in the local community centre where after 8 years of ethnographic research it was very clear that the de-valuing process was strategic and purposeful and focused upon what the women did, and also who they are.

Out of the 8 years of ethnographic research in this neighbourhood I spent almost every day for two years in a community centre that was in the centre of the St Anns council estate in Nottingham. This community had suffered high unemployment, low wages, and increasing amounts of class prejudice for generations (Mckenzie 2015). It was home to almost 15,000 people and predominantly social housing was still controlled by the local council. The estate itself had no real aesthetic value for gentrifiers or property developers; being built in the 1970's using grey concrete pre-moulded or pre-casted sections of square and uniformed small terraced houses. The neighbourhood had the local reputation as the dangerous place in the City, the place where you should never go. It was the place where there were drug dealers, single mothers, gangsters, and the poor. The estate throughout Nottingham was known as a pretty lawless place, but also ugly with nothing worth going to within the neighbourhood. Consequently, both place and people have been de-valued and stigmatised over several generations. I lived on this estate for more than twenty years and spending a lot of time with local women highlighted to me how stigmatised the neighbourhood was but also the effects of stigmatisation on the community. I visited the community centre most days, and sat around talking, drinking tea and coffee with the local women; there was always a lot of gossip and a lot of laughing. The women used this community space as a meeting point usually after dropping their kids off at school during term time. At 9.30 every morning it was very busy usually 10 or 12 mums would turn up and sit for a few hours with toddlers and pushchairs, laughing and talking. At lunch time the space was used by elderly people, the community centre had a kitchen run by a local 'social enterprise' and it provided very cheap hot meals every day, two courses for £2.50, and a tea was only 50p.

The community centre was busy and vibrant, often very noisy, and was well used. There was one woman 'Sharon' who volunteered in the kitchen every day. She would arrive at 9.15 am after dropping her own children off at school, and make all the drinks, clean up the tables and do some washing up. Her constant presence at the community centre was comforting; she knew everyone by name and made everyone feel welcome. Feeling welcome, is important in a community: it allows a sense of belonging, and a sense that you are not entirely on your own, just having someone knowing your name, and asking after you, is important in a local community. Sharon knew everyone's names, but she also knew about their families, and their illnesses. The doctor's surgery and the chemist was next door and people would often call in for a cup of tea and a chat afterwards. She also had a knack of bringing other people into a conversation; she was a lightning rod for local social capital. Sharon had been central within my own research, introducing me to people and vouching for me, and including me within the conversations, the gossip, and the laughing. Her contribution to the community was enormous, although her contribution to wider society was de-valued. Sharon claimed full state benefits to live, she received income support for her two children and herself that amounted to £110 per week. She lived in a 3 bedroom council house on the estate and received the full rental amount in housing benefit of £52.50 a week. Consequently, she was costing the tax payer approximately £8,500 a year in living and subsistence costs. Sharon worked in the community centre approximately 16 hours a week but received no pay. I remember asking her whether she wanted a paid job;

> yes I want to work in the community ... something like a youth worker ... working with the youth on the estate ... although I kind of do that already. That's the kind of job I want ... as long as it pays enough ... enough for the rent and that ... it would be nice to have a car and perhaps a holiday ... but mostly I want to stay in the community.

I then went on to ask her about qualifications and what she thought she might need in training:

> Well I haven't got any official qualifications; I weren't very good at school ... since being here errr 3 years now since (son's name) went to nursery I've done a health and hygiene course in catering ... I kind of enjoyed that ... yeh more stuff like that I would like although being here you get loads of experience (laughing).

Sharon's voluntary position at the community centre is really important for the community and the centre advertises volunteering positions as ways to 'build up your CV'. She has had the very minimum in support from the community centre, although this doesn't stop her being hopeful and optimistic for the future that she might find her way into a paid job within the community. I conducted this interview early in 2008, two years later I met with Sharon again. Things had really changed for her personally and the global financial and political events had affected her life and sledgehammered into this small community centre on a council estate in Nottingham. In 2008 a few months after I had interviewed Sharon, the then Chancellor of the Exchequer for the Labour Government Alistair Darling agreed to a bank rescue package totalling £500 billion in response to the instability of the British banking sector. This measure according to all politicians within the British parliament was crucial in safeguarding the stability of our economic future following a global banking crisis that was born out of reckless banking industry borrowing and trading on the debts of others. Subsequently, similar measures were introduced by the United States and the European Union in response to the financial crisis. The developed world went into recession and most governments in Europe and the United States applied austerity measures to their finances, warning their citizens there would be significant cuts in public spending.

During the spring of May 2010 the UK government had held a general election and a coalition government was formed as no political party had secured an outright win. The coalition between the Conservative Party and the Liberal Democratic Party immediately began new and much harsher austerity measures with an estimated loss of 500,000 public sector jobs mainly from front line services. In addition, tougher welfare measures in the forms of entitlement, and capping of benefits were also introduced. Job centres and Benefit Agencies throughout the UK were instructed to carry out more frequent work capability assessments in order to ensure that benefits were only given to 'the right people'. Simultaneously Government language and rhetoric regarding unemployment and worklessness became harsh and punitive. The new Chancellor of the Exchequer made much political capital in the old trope that lazy people receiving benefits were living the good life on the backs of the hard-working families. In September 2010, he announced £4 billion worth of welfare cuts with this rhetoric. "People who think it is a lifestyle to sit on out-of-work benefits ... that lifestyle choice is going to come to an end. The money will not be there for that lifestyle choice" (Quoted in Wintour 2010).

The reasons why people claim welfare benefits are complex as the research undertaken by Shildrick and McDonald (2012) shows, and people are not living well as my own research in Nottingham shows (2015). The chancellor's statement shows clearly that by reducing the message to one of morality, a person is good or bad, hard working or work shy. You do not need to explain fully why spending cuts fall onto one group of people over another. It is simply a matter of value, who is valuable and who is not.

About this time, I met with Sharon again and she told me she had received a letter telling her go to an appointment at the local Benefits Agency. During the interview, she had been questioned about her availability to work and she told them she was working albeit without pay in the community centre. The advisor asked her whether she thought it was about time she stopped taking from society and gave something back, in the form of paid work. Sharon wanted to work in the local community but Nottingham City council had just sent out thousands of 'under threat' redundancy letters to current public sector workers, put a freeze on recruitment and announced that there needed to be £28 million in public sector cuts. Despite this reality of what was happening to the global, national and local labour market, the benefit agency pushed on with Sharon's case that she needed to get a paid job and contribute to society. Sharon was eventually sanctioned, her benefits were cut from £110 per week to £30. Needless to say she didn't manage well, and admitted defeat taking the offer of 'help' that the Job centre extended to her in putting her forward for a job in a cheese packing factory 6 miles away. This meant that Sharon could no longer volunteer at the community centre and had to leave her two children then aged 7 and 12 alone from 6.30 am in the morning to get ready for school themselves. Sharon earned £177 before taxes for a 30 hour week in the cheese packing factory, and with the changes in her housing benefit and council tax benefit she was £9 a week better off financially, although her health very quickly deteriorated through working in a freezing cold environment, and the constant stress of leaving her children alone. After 3 months Sharon had to quit the job through ill health and depression. 'Sharon' didn't have the right type of 'aspiration'. She had aspired to stay within her community, and wanting a friendly and safe place for herself and her family. 'Sharon' didn't want to earn money for the sake of it, she wanted to make sure her children had a safe home, a good school, and that they were all healthy and happy. Social Mobility for Sharon did not make any sense, she wanted to stay, and not be mobile, she didn't aspire to 'better' or different but safer, healthier, and happier.

Sharon's story is not unique; if you look you can find thousands of these stories in many of the mainstream press. They may be told in many different ways depending upon the politics of the editor and the readership. In the *Daily Mirror* and the *Guardian* the stories might be more sympathetic, in the *Daily Mail*, the *Sun* and the *Express* the focus would be on lazy and undeserving, morally bankrupt families taking too much from the state. Mary O' Hara in 2015 collected stories from around the UK for her book *Austerity Bites* that criticises the austerity measures and policies in the UK as cruel, and actually irrational. John Hills' (2014) research shows that the austerity measures had actually transferred funds from the poorest to the pockets of the better-off, with single parent families being hardest hit. The very richest in the top of the 1% most wealthy lost some of their wealth but as John Hills notes clearly the austerity measures that saw cuts to the poorest in society saved very little from the public purse. Therefore, the economic argument for cutting social services and public goods was made on the political ideology of shrinking the state rather than balancing the books. Following the resignations of the then Prime Minister and Chancellor of the Exchequer in July 2016 following the European Union referendum result, the 'all in it together' rhetoric has disappeared.

The Conservative Prime Minister Theresa May appeared to acknowledge that deep divisions lay behind the referendum result, but rhetoric aside, the realities for those that rely on our public services has not changed.

Conclusion

Critiquing the economic arguments against cutting social goods is important but simultaneously we must also critique the way that culture is used to prop up the economic argument. Television programmes like *Benefits Street*, and *Skint*, which I discussed earlier within this chapter develop the already stigmatised view of the poor for a new era and does the work of austerity. These tropes that are peddled through the media perpetuate and strengthen the neoliberal rationale that value can only equate to a person's wealth, and their monetary value. This work is done subtly by linking moral worth to monetary worth. As Sharon found out, her position in the community as a volunteer in the community centre was valueless and instead in order for her to become 'useful' and a recognised part of society a paid job in the private sector was her only way of redemption. The people who live in East London know that they are not worth the land that they live on and are waiting one by one to be cleansed out. Being part of the community, being a mother, being a volunteer, or a low paid worker is not good enough now. If you are in a position of economic deficit you are also morally deficit, your connection and care to your family, community, or fellow human is valueless.

The working class in the United Kingdom over several generations, have been reduced by de-valuing them, misrepresenting them, and since Tony Blair's New Labour project in the mid-1990s, denying their existence. All politicians since then have taken the lead in removing social goods, demolishing working class politics, demonising working class culture and pushing a fake agenda of social mobility and aspiration. I end with an argument: I want no social mobility, no cherry picking, no aspiring to become middle class, or the coded version: 'better versions of ourselves'. We rise together.

References

Bathmaker, A., Ingram N. and Waller R. 2013. Higher education, social class and the mobilisation of capitals: recognising and playing the game. *British Journal of Sociology of Education*. 34 (5–6): 723–743.

Bourdieu, P. (1986) *Distinction: A critique of the social judgement of taste.* London: Routledge.

Dorling, D. (2014) *All That Is Solid: How the Great Housing Disaster Defines Our Times, and What We Can Do About It.* London: Allen Lane.

Emmett, S. (2016) Making Better Use Of Land 4 May 2016, by Susan Emmett http://pdf.euro.savills.co.uk/uk/residential---other/spotlight-london-mixed-use-development-2016.pdf.

Frank, T. (2001) *One Market Under God: Extreme Capitalism, Market Populism, and the End of Economic Development.* New York: Doubleday.

Hills, J. (2014) *Good Times, Bad Times: The Welfare Myth of Them and Us.* Bristol: Policy Press.

Hodkinson, S., Watt, P., and Mooney, G. Introduction: 2013 Neoliberal housing policy: time for a critical re-appraisal. *Critical Social Policy* 33 (1): 3–16.

Holmwood, J. (2014) Beyond capital? The challenge for sociology in Britain. *The British Journal of Sociology*, 65: 607–618.

Levitas, R. (2005 2nd edition) *The inclusive society.* London: Macmillan.

Mair, P. (2013) *Ruling The Void: The Hollowing of Western Democracy.* London: Verso.

Mckenzie, L. (2015) *Getting By: Estates Class and Culture.* Bristol: Policy Press.

O'Hara, M. (2015) *Austerity Bites.* Bristol: Policy Press.

Savage, M. (2015) *Social Class in the 21st Century.* London: Penguin.

Sayer, A. (2015) *Why We Can't Afford the Rich.* Bristol: Policy Press.

Shildrick, T., MacDonald, R., Webster, C., Garthwaite, K. (2012) *Poverty and Insecurity: Life in low-pay, No-pay Britain.* Bristol: Policy Press.

Skeggs, B. (2004) *Class self and culture.* London: Routledge.

Skeggs, B. (2014) Values beyond value? Is anything beyond the logic of capital? *British Journal of Sociology* 65 (1): 1–20.

Welshman, J. (2006) *Underclass: A History of the Excluded, 1880–2000.* London: Continuum International Publishing.

Wintour, P. (2010) George Osborne to cut £4bn more from benefits. https://www.theguardian.com/politics/2010/sep/09/george-osborne-cut-4bn-benefits-welfare.

CHAPTER 12

From Class Solidarity to Cultural Solidarity: Immigration, Crises, and the Populist Right

Ferruh Yılmaz

A spectre is haunting Europe—the spectre of Islam and Muslim immigrants. All the Powers of old Europe have entered into a holy alliance to exorcise this spectre: Social Democrats, Liberal Democrats, Conservatives, Socialists, right-wing Populists, Feminists, all types of progressives and radicals, social workers and the [previous] Pope. Where is the opposition party that has not been decried as "soft on immigration" by its rivals in power? Where is the Opposition that has not hurled back the branding reproach of "misunderstood tolerance," against the more advanced opposition parties, as well as against its reactionary adversaries?

Paraphrased from MARX & ENGELS, *The Communist Manifesto*, 1848

Introduction

"The history of all hitherto existing society is the history of class struggles," Karl Marx and Fredrick Engels wrote in *The Communist Manifesto* (1948, 9). Although class is not an originally and exclusively Marxist term, its contemporary use has its origins in Marxism. Working class denotes those who share common economic interests vis-à-vis the capitalist class that exploits the workers. In Marxist theory, people's class positions are determined by their positions in the relations of production: those who own the means of production belong to the capitalist class; and those who sell their labour to the capitalists form the working class. Then there is the petty bourgeoisie which owns or rents small-scale businesses with a few or no employees. Marxists have been grappling with the difficult task of placing people who do not fit within the class structure of capitalism.

According to Marx and Engels, the development of the manufacturing system and opening up new markets produced the modern capitalist society on the ruins of feudal society but the new society has not done away with class antagonisms: on the contrary, it has brought into existence the modern working class which has the historical task of doing away with the antagonism.

Marxist theory teaches us that the common interests of the working class are determined by their exploited position within the capitalist relations of production and they can only be free when they take over the means of production and collectively own them. This will get rid of the capitalist class and the end point will be a classless society.

On the other hand, we know that many working class members support political parties that represent the interests of the capitalist system. Especially during the last few decades in Europe, the 'working class' abandoned the social democratic parties and shifted their allegiance to the populist far right parties that have become the 'real' working class parties of the new millennium. Trump, too, received a substantial support from the American 'working class' people even though he is a representative of the antagonistic class and his economic policies clearly clash with 'working class' interests (e.g. tax breaks for the wealthy or further deregulation of the corporations and environmental protections).

Can we merely explain it as 'false consciousness'?[1] This chapter offers an alternative view of belonging that may explain why so many 'working class' people support the populist far-right parties in Europe, Trump in the US, Islamist populists in Turkey and Malaysia, or populist Hindu nationalists in India, although they all have an economic agenda that is supposed to conflict with their own interests. The main argument is that how people conceive their interests and thus sense of belonging in a particular historical conjuncture is not necessarily determined by their economic position (i.e. class position) but by whom they come to see as the main adversary. The nature of the antagonism between a social group and the adversary will also determine how the common interests of the group are imagined. The antagonistic force may be seen as a threat

---

1 'False consciousness' is a term that attempts to explain why the working class does not revolt against the conditions of oppression. It means that members of a subordinate class do not realise what their real class interests are as the ideologies produced by the dominant class that owns the means of cultural production conceal and obscure the realities of oppression and exploitation. Marx himself did not use the phrase but his writings, especially in *The German Ideology* (1970), lay the ground for the concept of false consciousness. According to Marx, one's ideology is dependent on the material conditions under which a person lives. Since a person's social class is determined by his or her position within the system of production relations, it must be a false consciousness that prevents the working class from seeing their real interests and overthrowing the system of their oppression.

to the freedoms or moral values which will create collectivities/solidarities around those freedoms or values. In other words, who the adversary is and which interests it is threatening are a question of political articulation; they do not emerge prior to the political articulation.

This chapter focuses primarily on Europe and argues that right-wing populists in Europe have been able to push the ground for social-political struggle from the economic to the cultural realm. The impact of this shift has been the articulation of the 'common interests' as cultural in essence rather than class (economic).

Here is the thing with culture: any political articulation that takes culture as the terrain on which solidarities are established would define themselves as opposed to the adversaries characterised by their place in the cultural structure of society, or what I call the cultural ontology. Ontology refers to the way the fundamental differences between social groups are established.[2] My argument in this chapter is that the ontology of society is increasingly structured by cultural differences rather than class and this has a fundamental impact on how social and political solidarities (and alliances) are forged.[3]

I would like to illustrate this change with my personal history that is part of the larger story of how Europe has moved from left to right by moving the focus from class to culture. Along the way, I will explain the main theoretical concepts that I use to explore this transformation and conclude the chapter with a brief discussion of how this transformation has implications for our understanding of class in the contemporary juncture.

---

[2] Ontology refers to the way one thinks of the nature of being; or the basic categories of being. Ontological categories are considered to be mutually exclusive; i.e. dogs are dogs, cats are cats and there is an unbridgeable gap between these categories. If the ontology of the social is race, then you are either white, black (or mixed). You cannot be both white and black. The same goes for culture if it becomes the basis for the ontological distinctions. There is a difference between an ontological category and ontic content. Ontic content refers to the actual person; the ontological category does not gain its meaning from its ontic content. The same person can be imagined to be member of a particular class, gender, race, etc. However, these ontological categories of the social are not essential units of being; they are the result of political articulations. Hence, I am not talking about intersectionality as people being crisscrossed by these categories.

[3] This transformation is examined in detail in my book, *How the Workers Became Muslims: immigration culture and hegemonic transformation in Europe* (2016). In this chapter, I focus on what this transformation means for our understanding of class which is not the analytical focus of the book.

From Class to Culture

I am an eternal immigrant who has lived in four different countries.[4] My first migration was to Denmark, a Scandinavian country famous for its social democratic culture. I was a nineteen years old, progressive activist. One of the first things that struck me was the way Danish culture often was associated with working class culture: workers spent time in their kolonihaver (allotment gardens often with a shack); people were proud of belonging to the working class; the prime minister who came from labour movement biked to his job. A couple of months after I moved there, I started to work in a small book binding business; the other workers did not oppose an immigrant who could not speak the language but would only accept me if I were willing to join the labour union. By joining the union, I became part of the Danish working class.

Many labour unions had a direct relationship with the Social Democratic Party which was considered as the political representative of working class interests. I had many different jobs in the following years: I cleaned hospitals, schools, department stores, carried furniture, taught in a preschool, and finally worked as a journalist for many years. In almost all of these jobs, I was a member of the labour union of the line of business I was in. I was told to include the cleaning jobs in my CV even if I were applying for a white-collar job; it would demonstrate my knowledge and experience of working class conditions. This was the Danish national culture I immigrated into.

Two decades later, I migrated away from a different national culture. I was no longer being hailed as a worker. I had become a 'Muslim' despite the fact that religion never played a role in my life; on the contrary, I thought of religion as the opium of people. I was still an active member of my union but by the time I left Denmark, class was no longer the prominent framework within which immigrants were understood. The focus had moved away from class that brought immigrants and native Danes together around common class interests despite cultural differences, to culture that brought cultural (religious, ethnic, racial) differences to the forefront. In other words, class brought immigrants and Danes together, whereas culture divided them, because a perspective that foregrounds culture (or race as it were) as the defining feature of people sees cultural difference as the essential part of the relationship. But there is more to it: cultural differences were already there a part of the conversation about immigrants; differences can be part of the social fabric without becoming antagonistic; they do not necessarily mean insurmountable gaps between social groups. Antagonism, in turn, means that society is divided into two hostile

---

4 A shorter version of this story is told in the Introduction to my book. See the note above.

camps one of which prevents the other from achieving its aspirations, and the tension can only be resolved by removing the oppressive force, as Marx and Engels explained in *The Communist Manifesto.*

My 'conversion' from an immigrant worker to a Muslim immigrant had clearly nothing to do with my own religious conversion but with the central place immigration took in the public debate since the mid-1980s. The incessant stories about the bad behaviour of the immigrants said to be rooted in their fundamentally different cultures increasingly organised public and private talk around immigration and their culture. The more the media focused on controversial stories about immigrant criminality, misuse of the welfare system, honour killings, female circumcision, their disrespect for freedom of speech, of women, of gays, or of Danish culture in general—all of which were explained with reference to 'their' cultural and religious background—the more we were forced to talk about the negative impact of immigration. The media love controversy as scholars of media would testify but the often-intentional provocation of controversies around Muslim immigrants usually by not only the populist right but also by social democratic mayors often created moral panics about Muslim immigrants (Yılmaz 2016). Krinsky (2013, 1) defines a moral panic "as an episode, often triggered by alarming media stories and reinforced by reactive laws and public policy, of exaggerated or misdirected public concern, anxiety, fear, or anger over a perceived threat to social order". With the cycles after cycles of moral panics, it was difficult not to feel that Muslim 'folk devils' were a threat to the peaceful cohesion of society.[5]

The chains of moral panics and the constant debate on Muslim immigrants progressively forced the labour unions, feminists, gays, and other progressives to position themselves vis-à-vis these 'cultural' practices that clearly were not in line with the political values of these organisations or movements. The intense focus on immigrants' culture slowly turned immigrants into a challenge to 'the' Danish way of life (i.e. culture). Ironically, Danish culture came to be redefined in this process to be whatever the Muslims were threatening: gender equality, gay friendliness, freedom of speech and peaceful coexistence. These issues, although unwittingly, brought left and right together around some purported common values—none of which had been considered to be common or cultural in essence—in the face of the threat by the culturally alien Muslim immigrants.

Neither mine nor my friends' political views or values changed much during the two decades I lived in Denmark, but the intense talk about immigration changed the dynamics between us. The cycles of moral panics and controversies

---

5   Stanley Cohen's *Folk Devils and Moral Panic* is considered to be the first fully developed definition of the term (1972).

around Muslim immigrants' cultural values and practices would constantly force us to discuss these issues. By the mid-1990s, our political conversations would generally focus on immigration, racism, and culture although we also talked about the neoliberal dismantling of the welfare system and disempowerment of the labour unions. But these issues came up less and less as they also disappeared from the public agenda. The ongoing conversations tagged me as an immigrant with Muslim background regardless of my views or beliefs. Outside my social and political circles, I was always an immigrant but in the early days, I was hailed with an ethnonational label that was not necessarily cultural in essence.

The process that turned me into a Muslim in the public eye also increasingly made my social circles think about their society in terms of values such as gender equality or freedom of speech that had primarily been thought of as rights won through hard-fought struggles by the progressive movements. But the immense focus on the 'Muslim threat' slowly turned them into cultural values that became 'Danish' in their opposition to the perceived threat. At the end, there was little place for thinking about belonging in other ways; the identity templates that were readily available were culturally designated.

My story illustrates the general transformation of society in Denmark and many other countries in Europe. When I arrived in Denmark, immigrant associations were organised around nationality or ethnicity (e.g. Union of Workers from Turkey) and generally affiliated with the Danish left. As Saunders (2012) notes, Islam was just the background of their lives but was not the way they thought of themselves. They would find more affinity with non-Muslims from their birthplace than they did with Muslims from other countries. They faced discrimination as Turks, Arabs or 'Pakis' in their struggle to find work and housing. Their associations provided networks of support and liaisons to the host society via the labour unions and political organisations.

By the time I left Denmark, these associations were replaced by crossnational Muslim associations focused on defending the religious rights of the immigrants and their dialog was with the official Denmark rather than social and political organisations of the country. The more the focus moved on to culture—often used as synonymous with religious values—as a way of characterising the immigrant populations, the more European governments felt the need to tame Islam by integrating it into the system which meant establishing official channels of communication with Muslim immigrants and that in turn could only happen if there were representative bodies (associations) to communicate with (Yurdakul 2009).

The transformation of the immigrants into Muslims is especially striking with the younger generations. As political parties, journalists, and activists started to call them 'Muslims', young people—usually called second or third generation immigrants—started to embrace Islam as a "a way to hold their heads up in a country that had belittled and humiliated them" (Saunders 2012, 140). They began to call themselves as Danish, German, British Muslims, not Turks, Arabs or Pakistanis, which means, as Fernando (2014) notes, that the Muslim hailed by the majorities in Europe is not the same Muslim that 'Muslims' inhabit.

The transformation of immigrants from 'guest workers' to 'Muslims' corresponded to the transformation of Denmark from a society that used to understand itself in class terms to a society that aspires to social cohesion based on cultural unity. This story needs to be told against a larger historical context. During 1980s and 1990s the right-wing governments in much of Europe were trying to impose neoliberal economic policies, which were aimed at the dismantling of the welfare systems: deregulating the economy, cutting taxes on the corporations, and decreasing social security benefits and rights. These policies could only be implemented by weakening working class organisations that were the source of the strongest resistance. The Thatcher government's crushing of the British miners' strike is just one example of this strategy.

But weakening of labour unions does not necessarily change the workers' consciousness about their class position. One of the important developments was the evolution of the European social democratic parties that traditionally were considered working class parties into 'centre parties' to the detriment of the workers (Laclau and Mouffe 2001). They claimed that the left-right division had become obsolete with globalisation and the advance of the information society which necessitated 'flexibility' in a globalising world—a position known as the 'third-way' championed by Bill Clinton and Tony Blair the then leader of the British Labour Party. Flexibility meant tight government spending and fewer taxes on the companies that could otherwise easily take their business somewhere else in a globalised economy. The social democratic parties' uncritical acceptance of this neoliberal dogma created a political void in which the working class 'interests' and their discontent with the capitalist system were no longer represented within the mainstream political system.

Hegemony and Crisis of Representation

Gramsci (1971) calls this a 'crisis of representation' or 'hegemonic crisis'. These terms are central if we want to understand the global populist upsurge, the abandonment of class politics and the 'loss of class consciousness'. According to Gramsci, hegemony is about a political force gaining

> ... the upper hand, to propagate itself over the whole social area—
> bringing about not only a unison of economic and political aims, but
> also intellectual and moral unity, posing all the questions around which
> the struggle rages not on a corporate but on a 'universal' plan, and thus
> creating the hegemony of a fundamental social group over a series of sub-
> ordinate groups.
>
> GRAMSCI 1971, 181–182

So, hegemony is a way of ruling society mainly by the consent rather than coercion of subordinate classes. The dominant group aligns its own interests with the interests of the subordinate groups thereby forming what he calls "a certain compromise equilibrium" between the dominant and subordinate groups. Gramsci calls this formation a 'historical bloc'.

The Western European party systems were until the 1980s mainly characterised by the conflict between labour and capital (i.e. class struggle) (Andersen 2004; Betz and Meret 2013). The 'compromise equilibrium' was created by bringing the interests of the working class and the other social groups in sync with the interests of the capitalist class through social democratic redistributive policies (i.e. welfare society) paid for by high taxes (especially on the wealthy). This was the social democratic consensus, which meant that even the mainstream right-wing governments continued redistributive policies and expanding the welfare system (Rydgren 2004).

It was this equilibrium that was broken by the right-wing governments' neoliberal policies and social democratic submission to the philosophy behind it. Gramsci argues that a crisis occurs when the situation of well-being in a society is threatened and the normality of the situation can no longer be sustained by hegemonic forces. During these crises, social groups become detached from their traditional political parties that are incapable of adapting themselves to new tasks. This is evident in the working class' massive abandonment of the social democratic parties in favor of the populist far-right.

Where I differ from Gramsci is that we should not think of this process as a shift in the "previously existing disposition of social forces" (Gramsci 1971, 178). Although I use Gramsci's concept of hegemony as the constitution of a historical bloc between the ruling class and the subordinate groups though the alignment of interests, I do not understand hegemonic transformation as a simple realignment of the previously existing groups and their interests. Rather, it is a process of redefining the collective interests which transforms the collectivity itself. In other words, what has been transformed is the very ontological fundament on which political parties are based and this has caused a deep identity crisis for the European political parties on the left with traditionally working class bases.

Hegemonic Intervention: Redefining Collective Interests

As I explained in the introductory sections of this chapter, common interests are generally determined by the nature of the antagonistic force that is thought to be subverting these interests. The right-wing populists have so far been very successful in articulating the antagonism as one between the rigged system that allows immigrants and ethnic and racial minorities to destroy the nation (and the national welfare system) built by the hard-working [native] people.

Populism is characterised by a political style that divides society into two antagonistic camps: the 'corrupt' elites on the one side and the 'pure' people who, if given the power, would correct the wrong-doings of the elite. The nature of the antagonism between the elite and the people is not, however, given a priori: while right-wing populists antagonise the corrupt, cosmopolitan political and cultural elite who do not care about their 'own' people, understood as the backbone of the nation, left-wing populism targets the political elites in the pockets of the economic elites (capitalists) that destroy living conditions for the working class as well as minorities and immigrants. In the latter case, the struggle of the working class is articulated as part of the same larger struggle for justice, equality and welfare for all (these slogans change in particular instances and historical conjunctures).

The interesting question that is not paid much attention to in the abstract treatises of populism is this: how do the fringe voices such as the populist far-right gain almost unlimited access to public discourse and gain so much influence?

My careful answer is that controversies and crises (e.g. moral panics) about the subversive groups open the channels of discourse for fringe voices even if they are portrayed negatively in the media. Indeed, the negative portrayal is turned around and used by populists as the evidence for the elite contempt for anyone who speaks up on behalf of 'silenced' people whose concerns are disdained as racist and ignorant. Does it ring a bell from Trump's campaign?

A few studies support this thesis. Bail (2015), for example, demonstrates that the anti-Muslim narrative of the political fringe has captured large segments of the American media and influenced public opinion through public controversies around Muslims and Islam. Moffitt (2016) also argues that the populists actively participate the "spectacularisation of failure" that underlies crisis, allowing them to pit 'the people' against a dangerous other, radically simplifying the terms and terrain of political debate.

Stuart Hall and his collaborators' seminal work, *Policing the Crisis* (1978) examines one such moral panic around the 'black mugger' in the early 1970s that started a chain of events eventually creating a crisis of representation, breaking down the social democratic consensus and mobilising "widespread but unfocussed anxiety about social change, engineering populist calls from 'below' to the state 'above' to save the country by imposing social order" (Hall 2011, 712). Hall subsequently called attention to the cultural component of Thatcherism that played a new game of identity, ethnicity and race through which the New Right gained the consent of the British working class, even though the new system worked against the working class' economic interests.

Today's Muslim immigrant functions in the same manner as yesterday's 'black mugger' in Europe. In the Danish case, a moral panic around Muslim refugees in the mid-1980s created the conditions for reframing immigration as a cultural issue rather than a labour (guest/immigrant workers) and humanitarian (refugees) issue in a period of deep social anxiety over the erosion of welfare benefits and rights. The populist far-right forces were central to this reframing. Shortly after the consensual passage of a humanitarian law in 1983 granting the immigrants extensive rights, the number of refugees began to rise as the result of wars in the Middle East, Africa and East Asia. Government officials from the mainstream right blamed the new law for causing the refugee crisis and fed the media with a stream of stories about the 'refugee influx'. The intense stream of stories resulted in a media frenzy that produced a moral panic around the number of refugees seeking asylum in Denmark. The populist far-right quickly capitalised on the moral panic and destabilised the political system by intervening at the right moment with the right appeal. In September 1986, Søren Krarup, a priest known for his extremist views that chastised women, feminists, and anything progressive created a huge controversy by calling for a boycott of an iconic humanitarian fundraising campaign for refugees abroad. His bold rhetorical strategy turned the brewing moral panic around asylum seekers into a hegemonic crisis by articulating discontent with Denmark's immigration policy as discontent with the political system (i.e. the political and cultural elite). The media's penchant for controversies and crisis paradoxically contributed to the success of Krarup's arguments. The journalists covered Krarup's intervention with furious attacks on his persona (calling him a racist, a hateful evil) while also criticising him for factual errors. In the heated debate following his call for a boycott, Krarup's basic argumentative premises that the future of the nation was the primary concern of the Danish people, that alien Muslims posed a threat to the Danish nation, and that the political order no longer represented the Danish people went unquestioned. On the contrary, he used the furious attacks by the media and the cultural and political elites to accuse them for brutally oppressing any dissent against their corrupt system. Racism was the main tool in the elite's silencing of the people.

My analyses of newspaper reports show that Krarup's opponents were gradually forced to acknowledge 'the concerns of the Danish people' about the future of the nation and conceded that 'we have to listen to people'. They also tacitly accepted his claim that there was an unbridgeable cultural difference between Muslims and Danes.

In the following period, the focus quickly moved on to the immigrants who were already there as the mainstream political actors, including social democrats, capitalised on the anti-immigrant sentiment. The shift in focus from refugees to immigrants meant a simultaneous shift from humanitarian considerations (for or against refugees) to cultural issues (positive or negative about immigrants) and contributed immensely to the culturalisation of the immigration debate. By the end of 1987, the Danish debate about immigration was largely made up of arguments about the significance of cultural differences.

The success of the far-right populists depends on the existence of an external threat to the well-being of 'the people' and a continuous sense of threat can only be upheld by a constant focus on their threatening actions. Otherwise, the sense of threat will fade away as people will start talking about other issues. A continuous series of public controversies and moral panics are necessary for producing the experience of an ongoing crisis. The far-right actors are often—though not always—the initiators of these crises.

Crisis and Collective Interests Today

One of the contemporary examples of these crises is the reaction to the attacks on the French satirical magazine, Charlie Hebdo. There was a broad consensus on describing the horrific murders as an attack on freedom of speech and democracy. 'Freedom of speech' was presented as a universal value under attack by Muslims who do not share these values rather than a right instituted through struggles against the state power and may mean different things to different people. And inversely, the reactions to the attacks created a sense that despite 'our internal differences' we in the 'West' share some core values such as freedom of speech and democracy. In other words, crisis such as this around Muslims and 'their' culturally motivated actions are used to rally people from different political and social background around some 'core values' that 'unite us'.

Controversies and moral panics around the so-called Muslims practices such as polygamy, female circumcision, homophobia, criminality and disrespect for human rights create new bedfellows across the political spectrum around women's rights, gay rights, or animal rights as 'common core values' none of which virtually had been considered universal or common before their juxtaposition against Islam. Consequently, the feminist, gay, environmentalist, and human rights movements are gradually being disarticulated from the progressive politics with which they had traditionally been aligned. They were once born as strategic demands by conjunctural political articulations but are now being elevated to the level of universal values that characterise national (or 'Western') culture.

These crises around Muslims do not only keep the populist far right actors relevant by making them one of the main protagonists of the debate; the ongoing focus on the Muslim threat connects the popular anxieties about the neoliberal dismantling of the welfare state and the erasure of national sovereignty in a globalised world (generally expressed in anti-European Union rhetoric) to the impact of alien Muslims on society. In the long run, they shift the new ontological imagination (i.e. how the structure of society is imagined) in which social harmony is no longer destroyed by class oppressors but by Muslim immigrants. This is evident in the characteristic populist claim to restore the country/nation/society back to its greatness.

It is, however, only possible to imagine a better past by retrospectively re-imagining the past through the contemporary social structure. The past is claimed to be great when immigrants, Mexicans, Blacks or Muslims were either not present or were not given the power to destroy society by the corrupt elite. The re-imagining the past in today's social horizon means also that the welfare system is now understood to be the result of social harmony and solidarity based on a cultural sameness that existed before. The claim about a golden past is, therefore, one of the central elements of populist far right strategy.

To summarise, the political void that is created by the left's abandonment of class politics has been filled by populist far-right forces that managed to turn the popular discontent into a crisis of the representational system. They claimed that the system is rigged against hard working people who built the nation and that they would restore the country back to its cultural harmony. They also convinced the mainstream parties that the main concern of the 'people' was about the future of the nation with the result that the focus on cultural struggle and common cultural values has been adopted by the mainstream political parties.

This is not only a Danish phenomenon. Mondon (2013) describes the same transformation in France and Austria where the populist far-right forces successfully articulated people's discontent with the neoliberal policies in terms of a new antagonism

> which has shifted the understanding of politics in the minds of the *classes populaires* from a class struggle, in the Marxist sense of the term, to a struggle of race and 'civilisation' (159).

I have been arguing that a new historical bloc is formed around 'common interests' now understood as shared values that secure social harmony (and subsequently the welfare system). However, it does not mean that this is merely predicated on culture; it means that the welfare system (or democracy) is now presented as anchored in a 'cultural sameness' whose continuity becomes the political goal. Erased is the traditional notion that the welfare system and democracy are the result of the social democratic reforms based on class politics.

The Trump Phenomenon

The populist strategy that I describe above fits well with Trump's populist rhetoric in the US as well as the media's (predominantly negative) reaction that paradoxically seems to have empowered his position. There are, however, some fundamental differences when it comes to the transformation of the social identity categories from class to culture in the US. As Lipsitz (1998) reminds us, race has always been central to the American imagination of the social space as a divider. The weak class consciousness in the US may indeed be attributed to the prominence of race. Portello (1991), for example, explores the defeat of the miners' struggle to unionise in the 1930s in Harlan County and explains the defeat with conflicting use of religious and national symbols and the White workers' uneasy relationship with Black workers who had joined the union. Despite the dividing force of racism, Roosevelt's New Deal and Johnson's Great Society policies built up some welfare institutions through a set of social programs such as Medicare, environmental legislation, educational funding and civil rights laws.

It was not long before right-wing populists such as Barry Goldwater, George Wallace, and Richard Nixon mobilised the ingrained racism of the White working class to turn the White working class against the welfare reforms which they portrayed as 'hand-outs' to the undeserving Blacks. Wallace's populist presidential campaign, although nowhere near winning the presidency, had a lasting effect by articulating the discontent with the federal government as a radical right-wing position that has later become a Republican trademark. As Kazin explains:

> By the end of the 1960s, whether one earned a wage or owned a little business, carried a union card or chafed at the restrictions imposed by labour was often less important than a shared dislike of a governing and cultural elite and its perceived friends in the ghettos and on campus (1998, 250).

Trump's populism is not, in this sense, unique or new but continues the radical right-wing's use of race as a destabilising tool that has foregrounded racial identities rather than class which traditionally allied the White workers—especially in the South—with the Democratic Party. Republican candidates do not hesitate to name Washington elites in the same sentence as 'hand-outs'. This is how a Republican Party of big business, whose candidates split over whether to shrink the Environmental Protection Agency or abolish it outright, appeal to the victims of what one can only call environmental injustice (Hochschild 2016). (See also Heather Cox Richardson (2014) for a detailed account of how the Republican Party changed).

Conclusion: How to Understand Class Consciousness

The global success of the populist far right seems to have paralysed the progressive left forced to choose between two options: insistence on identity politics or going back to class struggle. The story I have told can be interpreted in support of both positions: since class does not exist anymore, and since the populists succeed through racism and Islamophobia, we need to focus on creating solidarities among people who suffer from racist, Islamophobic, sexist or homophobic oppression. Or conversely, it could be understood as if I am arguing that since identity politics brought us here, we should go back to class struggle. I believe both positions share the same universalist premise. Let me start with 'back to class struggle'.

The story I have told demonstrates that the right-wing hegemony is premised upon the populist right's identity politics that has shifted the focus from class to cultural identity. Consequently, to undo the right-wing hegemony, one may argue that we need to define ourselves in class terms again. Such an interpretation would be premised upon the notion that 'class consciousness' (i.e. class identity) and 'class interests' are two separate entities the latter of which determines the first—a separation that corresponds to Marx's famous base-superstructure distinction. Class struggle in its traditional sense presupposes that the working class is the privileged political agent of change and this privilege comes from its position in the relations of production. A class consciousness that goes against its own interests would be considered 'false consciousness'. The task for the left is, then, to raise consciousness and bring the working class in sync with its 'real' interests so that they can fulfil their historical task of changing the system.

This premise is, in turn, based on the presumption that the left intellectuals have a direct, ideologically undistorted access to reality. In my theoretical universe, class is not a neutral sign that has a stable connection to its referent that has its own objective existence independent of the sign. On the contrary, language is constitutive of what it refers to. This should not be understood as if I am reducing reality to its symbolic expressions. I do not make a distinction between class interests and the articulation of these interests as class interests. They come together. In this sense, there is no superstructure that can be disconnected from its base leading to false consciousness of a class that "presupposes an enlightened elite whose possession of the truth makes possible to determine what the 'true interests' of a class are" (Laclau 2006, 670). There is no necessary relationship between an ontological category such as 'working class' and its ontic content that is 'workers'. In the US, for example, many people who can be labeled as workers identify as 'middle class'. Likewise, 'working class interests' have been articulated in different ways through history while the category of 'working class' was kept intact. What kept it intact was not a consistent ontic content but the experienced gap between its members and its adversaries.

This framework has radical implications for how we understand class or the displacement of class structure. If people no longer identify as members of the working class, we are not talking about a disjuncture between a class and its members' consciousness but a real ontological transformation where society is structured by different type of antagonism(s).

Once the new ontological structure of the social becomes well-established, articulating alternative politics that could be realised within that structure becomes extremely difficult (Yılmaz 2012, 2016). 'Back to class politics' will, therefore not necessarily have the desired appeal as there is no longer a 'class base' in the traditional sense unless it is rearticulated with reference to the relations of production. But then, who are the antagonists of global finance capitalism?

The same perspective can be applied to identity politics that is often offered as an alternative to class politics, more so in the US for historical reasons than in Europe and elsewhere. Identity politics moves the ground for political mobilisation from class to racial, ethnic, sexual or religious identities and consequently, one's identity is equated to one's background in these categories (even in its variants that emphasise intersectionality). I can testify to the commonsensical use of these identity categories with numerous stories. I have often been invited to talks as a person who can talk 'of' and/ or 'for' the Muslim view/experience rather than a scholar who studies these phenomena. The 'expert' position is reserved for people who do not need to identify themselves in terms of an 'oppressed' identity category. The proponents of identity politics point to the fact that class politics often ignores the oppression that some people suffer because of their identities and that focusing on class politics often contributes to 'white privilege'. However, in identity politics, the focus often is on recognition and representation. The question is: recognition and representation of what? Do racial, ethnic or sexual relations provide common values around which socio-political collectivities can be formed and represented?

As my story illustrates, the populist focus on identity politics has led to the replacement of the immigrant workers unions with cross-national Muslim associations. The former organised on a national basis and fought for making anti-racism part of the general struggle for equality while the latter focuses on defending the religious rights of the immigrants. Admittedly, the populist focus on Islam turned me into a 'Muslim' in public discourse. Where does that leave me? A collectivity based on defending religious rights of Muslims is not where I imagine being part of. Many Muslims—like any other religious group—tend to be conservative and do not necessarily care about democracy and equality. The same can be said about the traditionally 'progressive women or gay movements'. They are increasingly aligned with the populist right against the 'corrosive impact' of the Muslim immigrants on 'our common cultural achievements'. Judith Butler's refusal to receive Berlin Gay Pride's courage award with reference to their racism against Muslims is a clear indication that gay identity politics is not inherently progressive. Jasbir Puar uses the term, 'homonationalism' to explain how gay identity politics can be mobilised for reactionary ends (Puar 2007). Similar criticisms are leveled against feminist movements.

I understand both class politics and identity politics to be strategic interventions at particular historical conjunctures in the fight against oppression and for equality rather than politics based on identity categories objectively identifiable in the relations of production or oppression. As such, these are shaped by historically specific conditions; they should not be elevated as timeless, universal truths that one can easily access if one has the right perspective, as the established narratives of linear progress would promote.

The problem with insistence on the dichotomic framework as the only framework within which the progressive politics can be understood is that they both take the political out of politics. It carries the risk of reducing the political work into raising consciousness about people's 'real' interests and fighting for the policy implementation of their inherent rights (recognition and representation). A related risk is that the binary classification of people on the right or wrong side of the history around value-based dichotomies places the left into the category of 'politically correct' experts (i.e. part of the elite); something that has been exploited by the populist right successfully.

Once a new hegemonic formation is in place, it can be difficult for counter-hegemonic perspectives to be articulated. However Podemos in Spain and Sanders' presidential election campaign in the US gives us some indications for how a new progressive agenda can get traction with a new structural critique, shifting the ground for how identities are formed and antagonizing a different and inclusive notion of the 'people' against the neo-liberal order. After all, the same white working class voters who re-elected Obama voted for Trump merely four years later. They may have racial advantages but they also suffer from the neoliberal restructuring of the world. The task is to develop a political program that re-connects the lived experience of precarity by the white working class to the discrimination and oppression experienced by racial, ethnic and sexual minorities.

I want to conclude with Laclau and Mouffe's preface to their seminal work, *Hegemony and Socialist Strategy* (2001, xix):

> Without a vision about what could be a different way of organising social relations, one which restores the centrality of politics over the tyranny of market forces, those movements will remain of a defensive nature. ...If one is to build a chain of equivalences among democratic struggles, one needs to establish a frontier and define an [different] adversary, but this is not enough. One also needs to know for what one is fighting, what kind of society one wants to establish. This requires from the Left an adequate grasp of the nature of power relations, and the dynamics of politics. What is at stake is the building of a new hegemony. So our motto is: 'Back to the hegemonic struggle'.

References

Andersen, J.G. (2004) The Danish People's Party and New Cleavages in Danish Politics. Working paper at the Centre for Comparative Welfare Studies, Aalborg University, DK.

Bail, C. (2015) *Terrified: How Anti-Muslim Fringe Organisations Became Mainstream.* Princeton, NJ: Princeton University Press.

Betz, H-G., and Meret, S. (2013) Right-Wing Populist Parties and the Working class Vote: What Have You Done for Us Lately? In: Rydgren J. (ed.) *Class Politics and the Radical Right.* London: Routledge, 107–121.

Cohen, S (1972) *Folk Devils and Moral Panics.* London: Routledge, 1972.

Fernando, M.L. (2014) *The Republic Unsettled: Muslim French and the Contradictions of Secularism.* Durham, NC: Duke University Press.

Gramsci, A. (1971) *Selections from Prison Notebooks* (edited by Hoare Q. and Smith G.N.). London: Lawrence and Whishart.

Hall, S. (2011) The neo-liberal revolution. *Cultural Studies* 25 (6): 705–728.

Hall, S, et al. (1978) *Policing the Crisis: Mugging, the State, and Law and Order.* London: Macmillan.

Hochschild, A.R. (2016) *Strangers in their own land: Anger and mourning on the American right.* New York: The New Press.

Kazin, M. (1998) *The populist persuasion: An American history.* Ithaca: Cornell University Press.

Krinsky, C. (2013) Introduction: The Moral Panic Concept. In: Krinsky C. (ed.) *The Ashgate Research Companion to Moral Panics.* London: Ashgate, 1–14.

Laclau, E. (2006) Why constructing a people is the main task of radical politics. *Critical Inquiry* 32 (4): 646–680.

Laclau, E. and Mouffe, C. (2001) *Hegemony and Socialist Strategy: Towards a Radical Democratic Politics.* 2nd ed., New York: Verso.

Lipsitz, G. (1998) *The possessive investment in whiteness: how white people profit from identity politics.* Philadelphia: Temple University Press.

Marx, K and Engels, F. (1948) *The Communist Manifesto.* New York: International Publishers.

Moffitt, B. (2016) *The Global Rise of Populism. Performance, Political Style and Representation.* Stanford, CA: Stanford University Press.

Mondon, A. (2013) *The Mainstreaming of the Extreme Right in France and Australia: A Populist Hegemony?* London: Ashgate.

Portello, A. (1991). No Neutrals There: The Cultural Class Struggle in the Harlan Miners' Strike of 1931–32. In: *The Death of Luigi Strastulli and Other Stories: The Form and Meaning in Oral History.* Albany, NY: State University of New York Press, 216–238.

Puar, J. (2007). *Terrorist Assemblages: Homonationalism in Queer Times.* Durham, NC: Duke University Press.

Richardson, H.C. (2014). *To Make Men Free: A History of the Republican Party.* New York: Basic Books.

Rydgren, J. (2004) Explaining the Emergence of Radical Right-Wing Populist Parties: The Case of Denmark. *West European Politics* 27 (3): 474–502.

Saunders, D. (2012) *The Myth of the Muslim Tide: Do Immigrants Threaten the West?* New York: Vintage.

Yılmaz, F. (2012) Right-wing hegemony and immigration: How the populist far-right achieved hegemony through the immigration debate in Europe. *Current Sociology* 60 (3): 368–381.

Yılmaz, F. (2016) *How the Workers Became Muslims: Immigration, Culture, and Hegemonic Transformation in Europe*. Ann Harbor: The University of Michigan Press.

Yurdakul, G. (2009) *From Guest Workers into Muslims: The Transformation of Turkish Immigrant Associations in Germany*. Newcastle, England: Cambridge Scholars.

CHAPTER 13

Recovering the Australian Working Class

Tony Moore, Mark Gibson and Catharine Lumby

Introduction

In the latter half of the twentieth century, there was in Australia a lively, distinct and shared culture best described as working class. This culture activated a sense of possibility and agency for people in communities with high concentrations of manual workers, early school leavers and low-income families, not only in neighbourhoods, workplaces and through leisure activities, but also at a wider political level. It was an agency that found expression in traditional organisational forms such as unions, sporting and service clubs and the Australian Labor Party,[1] but also in extra-curricular cultural activities in state schools, adult education and do-it-yourself popular cultural forms such as sport, rock music and comedy. Iconic figures who emerged from working class backgrounds to contribute aspects of this way of life to the broader Australian culture included early school leaver and Labor Prime Minister Paul Keating, ex Sydney Harbour Bridge rigger turned television comedian and *Crocodile Dundee* creator Paul Hogan, sporting heroes Dawn Fraser and Lionel Rose and rock 'n' roll music legends the Easybeats, Cold Chisel and AC/DC.

Much of this cultural potential has been obscured, however, following the economic and social changes that have transformed Australia—as other Western nations—since the 1980s. The concept of class has greatly receded, especially in policy discourse and academic research. Rather than facilitating the civic potency and cultural richness of a distinct working class way of life, governments and well-meaning NGOs have conceptualised low-income communities as 'disadvantaged' and sought to remediate, manage or compensate. Despite the good intentions of such programs, their low expectations have often become self-fulfilling prophecies. The loss of the concept of class has meant that differences in low-income communities from the wider society can

---

1 In 1912 the ALP adopted the American spelling 'Labor' that is the official and only spelling allowed for Australia's oldest political party, clarifying a confusing use of both spellings for the party up to that date, and has since served to distinguish the political wing from the wider 'labour movement' that uses the British spelling.

appear only as inadequacy or failure against what are implicitly middle class norms.

This chapter introduces a project being developed by the authors, examining the potential for rearticulating the concept of class in Australian scholarship and public policy. We argue for the value of recovering an understanding of class as *culture*, rather than as simply socio-economic categories or abstracted relations to production. The first part of the chapter examines a retreat from the concept of class in three major areas in Australia over the last thirty years: firstly, in policy discourse, which has seen the ascendancy of 'stratification' approaches over those of class; secondly, in politics, where the Australian Labor Party has embraced an abstracted notion of 'disadvantage' in preference to an older historic investment in working class potency; and thirdly, in academic scholarship, most notably in Cultural Studies, where there has been a retreat from class as a critical analytical concept in preference to other modes of identity. We then consider the prospects for a return to the concept of class, drawing on the recent 'class culturalist' turn in the UK and also reaching back to the cultural materialist perspective of early British cultural studies and Australian sociological studies of the 1970s and 1980s. Finally, we briefly discuss the value of a class culturalist approach to researching working class media practices in so-called 'disadvantaged' communities today.

Policy without Class

Many of the conditions would appear right today for a return to questions of class. Internationally, the global financial crisis of 2007–8, brought a sharpened attention to differences of income and wealth, with responses ranging from the Occupy movement of 2011 and the rise in Europe of political parties such as Syriza and Podemos to the publishing sensation around Thomas Piketty's (2014) *Capital in the Twenty-First Century*. The recent OECD (2015) report *In It Together* confirms that the problem is being taken seriously at the highest policy level, pointing out that apart from the human impact on those at the bottom, increasing inequality is damaging to social cohesion and reduces the prospects of long term economic growth.

Although Australia avoided a recession following the Global Financial Crisis, its levels of inequality are above the OECD average and have increased significantly over the past twenty years (ACOSS 2015, 8). The issue has become a key theme across a number of recent policy debates. Work on housing affordability and the structure of the job market has pointed to widening gaps between the life prospects of different social groups (Hulse & Pinnegar 2015; Coelli &

Borland 2015). The Gonski Review of school funding has brought to light major differences in opportunity through education, finding that students from low socioeconomic backgrounds "are disproportionately represented in Australia's 'underperforming tail'" (DEEWR 2011, 114). The National Preventative Health Taskforce has identified significant inequalities in health outcomes according to income, urging a reversal of the "inverse care law", whereby "those with more get more, and those with less get less" (NPHT 2009, ix).

Despite this, however, the concept of class still appears remarkably absent. A survey by the authors suggests that the concept of class is almost entirely missing in the Australian policy literature. There has been no shortage of policy-oriented work on disadvantage and inequality over the past decade, with a steady stream of studies, reports and recommendations from academic researchers, government agencies, religious organisations and consultancies on their various aspects—from poverty and social exclusion (Phillips *et al.* 2013; McLachlan *et al.* 2013; Scutella *et al.* 2009), to health (Turrell *et al.* 2006; ABS 2010); education (Rorris *et al.* 2011) and housing (Cheshire *et al.* 2014). Yet in none of this work does the concept of class appear.

Social inequality is, of course, identified in other ways—as 'disadvantage', 'low socioeconomic status' or 'social exclusion'. These more abstract terms are derived from a stratification model of inequality, developed by American sociologists from the 1950s onwards. Stratification maps the location and movement of people against economic, occupational, educational or other social criteria with a statistical and mathematical precision. Stratification theory and method was championed in Australia in the 1960s and 70s by social scientists such as Broom et. al (1968, 212–238) and Encel (1971), as a technocratic and supposedly non-ideological alternative to neo-Marxist approaches to class being debated and refined by researchers influenced by Gramsci, Althusser and the Frankfurt School. It found favour within a public service and academic policy constituency increasingly focussed on inequality in the early 1970s influencing social reform initiatives being developed by the Whitlam Labor opposition as part of its program for government.

While the abstract terms of stratification theory have a certain value in extending beyond inequalities of wealth to cover those of gender, language, ethnicity and indigeneity, they also have major shortcomings. As veteran Australian sociologist R.W. Connell pointed out at the time, a major weakness of the stratification model in comparison to class is that it is descriptive rather than analytical. It can identify a disadvantaged or an elite category, but not what they are *doing* in society (Connell 1983, 88). Unlike class, the stratification model is a-historical, failing to account for the transformation of societies and the reproduction of inequality over time and generations, via families, education, occupations or patterns of recreation. The model views a category of people in isolation, as opposed to the relationships between different classes in workplaces, public space, institutions like schools, hospitals, courts or in media. There is an assumption that problems of inequality will be solved by mobility of individuals into a higher stratum by changing their educational credentials, occupations, and incomes, without reflection on the structural causes of this inequality.

The focus of stratification theory on instrumental economic criteria—as reflected in categories such as 'low Socio Economic Status' or 'disadvantaged'—provide little sense of the lived culture of those so labelled, and how that culture helps them make sense of the material conditions in which they find themselves. Most significantly, these measures of inequality presume a deficit model: the communities identified as 'disadvantaged' are represented only in terms of what they *lack*, closing off consideration of the positive resources they may be able to call upon and entrenching assumptions of dependency rather than cultural agency. While it has become an established principle in framing policy in Australia for Indigenous or migrant communities that recognition must be given to cultural capacities in addressing inequalities, no such principle is applied in the case of low SES or disadvantaged communities.

Labor without Class

In the political arena, the main bearer of the concept of class in Australia has been the Australian Labor Party (ALP). The conservative Liberal Party has, since its founding in 1944, de-emphasised class in favour of a pitch to business, individualism, and a middle class characterised as the 'forgotten people', supposedly neglected because they fell outside twentieth century class struggle. In contrast, the social democratic ALP has had a historical commitment to improving conditions for a working class base seen as an agent of progress and 'the fair go'. This commitment remains institutionalised in union control of the committees, conferences and votes that count within the party, a legacy of the creation of the party by the union movement in the 1890s to represent workers' interests in parliaments.

The disappearance of the concept of class in politics is a story, therefore, of a shift in the ALP to a more technocratic, managerial and neoliberal economic and social framework, in which class is substituted by the concept of 'disadvantage'. It began to gain traction as a problem to be compensated in progressive funding initiatives of the Whitlam Labor Government (1972–75) such as the Disadvantaged Schools Program. While most of Whitlam's redistributive and public infrastructure programs benefitted the party's working class base, the government defended these as good for all citizens, and the ALP was rewarded with new middle class votes and a significant influx of middle class professionals and tertiary educated young people into the party's ranks.

By the 1977 National Inquiry in to Labor's Future, Labor reformers had ceased using the term 'working class', preferring 'low income and less educated sectors of society' (ALP 1979, 3). Concerned at the party's loss of working class consciousness, Methodist lay preacher and future Deputy Prime Minister Brian Howe, criticised this shift as patronising, replacing the sense of mission of the working class to modernise and improve society with a middle class charitable impulse to help and improve the poor. Howe warned that the workers would be the losers of Labor's increasingly "vicarious representation of the manual working class" (1984, 168).

The notion of disadvantage became further entrenched in the Hawke government of the 1980s, particularly through the introduction of socio-economic metrics designed to better direct income support and other welfare measures via means tests. This policy approach assumed a universalisation of upper middle class values, taking little or no account of working class cultural dispositions and customs unrelated to rates of pay. For example, means tests excluded the children of better paid skilled manual workers from tertiary education allowances, despite the resistance of many parents in this category to further study and traditional beliefs that school leavers should earn to contribute to the family income (Moore, Developmental Youth Services Association 1988).

The Hawke and Keating Labor Governments are strongly associated in social policy with attempts to address ethnic and cultural diversity. The embrace of a burgeoning social and identity rights movements led to a multiplication of disadvantaged or marginalised categories not based on income, to be assisted by much needed participation and equity programs designed to ensure full exercise of citizenship. Often mirroring conventions of the United Nations, new anti-discrimination, equal opportunity and funding policies and programs were rolled out for women, Indigenous Australians, people with disabilities, non-English speaking background migrants and their children, regional and isolated families, and the homeless. Governments made sense of increasing social and identity pluralism through genuine policy consultation with various community-based or special interest peak lobby groups, usually facilitated by special offices within Federal public services, often duplicated at the state level.

While this diversity strategy was a just response to long endured discrimination and exclusion, Labor's traditional working class heartland was not specifically addressed as workers. The only exception was the Hawke Government's corporatist 'Accord' with the Union movement, but this required wage restraint from ordinary workers in exchange for the expansion of a more nebulous 'social wage'. This shift signalled a move away from a class-based understanding of social structure to one in which different groups were addressed on the basis of their 'identity'. By the late 1980s, however, the imposition of means tests that arbitrarily excluded many 'blue collar' Australians from a range of income support benefits and programs created downward envy, even resentment, of 'special interests'. By the recession of 1990, deep divisions were opening in working class communities themselves, between those under stress in work and those dispossessed of a place in an increasingly post-Fordist Australia, with income support and programs targeted to those most in need: long term unemployed, young early school leavers unable to start in downsizing industries, the homeless, Indigenous Australians and recently arrived migrants and refugees (Moore 2003, 124–126).

The government was alerted to the impact of its economic policies on working class communities in a report to its own Commission for the Future by Richard Eckersley (1988) entitled *Casualties of Change*, in a paper by the Australian Council for Trade Unions *Australia Reconstructed* (ACTU 1987) exploring the Nordic alternative, and in the major ABC television documentary *Nobody's Children*, researched and written by Moore (Goldie and Moore 1989). This last investigated the unravelling of traditional career pathways in working class communities such as Wollongong and Shepparton as industry declined, and the growth of a new youth underclass of long term unemployed in traditional Labor electorates.

The Hawke and Keating governments never quite grasped that an 'economic rationalist' agenda comprising industrial restructuring and automation, privatisation of public assets, outsourcing and reduction in tariffs would have a long term impact on Labor's voter base. Some among that base enjoyed unprecedented material mobility thanks to transferable skills, flexible, easy credit and long booms in property and mining, while others endured insecure, casualised work in growing but poorly regulated service occupations or a treadmill of unemployment, welfare dependence and warehousing in victim-blaming remediation programs that have now become intergenerational (Moore 1999, 2003). Following stratification theory's focus on individual deficit, these programs took an individualist, rather than a community or political economy approach to unemployment, compelling retrenched industrial workers to learn job seeking skills, as if this would summon back occupations that had been automated or moved offshore (Moore 1999, 229). As well as a policy failure, Labor had unintentionally broken its heartland and set in train the dissolution and disillusionment of its traditional base.

In the absence of a more sophisticated appreciation of social class, Labor's pluralism, means-tests, and positive discrimination missed out on helping many of the losers from economic reform, and fuelled the politics of envy. In the final years of the successor Keating Government, Liberal leader and social conservative John Howard successfully portrayed Labor's favoured social and identity movements as 'elites' and their causes as special interest pleading antipathetic to the interests of ordinary Australians. Campaigning under the slogan 'For all of us', the Liberal-National Coalition won the 1996 election, picking up significant numbers of working class and lower middle class voters, who became dubbed 'the Howard battlers'.

In opposition, a backlash against the identity rights agenda developed among a cross-factional group of senior Labor ex-ministers (including Martin Ferguson and Peter Walsh) and MPs who worried that the Keating Government had sacrificed working class people for a politically correct 'box-ticking' of cultural causes beloved of a university-educated inner city left. Their paradoxical agenda of freer markets and suburban working class materialism, exemplified in the polemic *Labor Without Class* (Thompson 1999), had the effect of discrediting class rhetoric within the ALP Socialist Left faction, which increasingly embraced identity rights as the progressive alternative.

A more imaginative antidote to the 'disadvantage' orthodoxy was promoted by a new generation of ALP activists in the late 1990s, who sought to unite the winners and losers of economic liberalisation through a simultaneous appeal to the increasingly affluent self-employed skilled manual workers of the outer suburbs, dubbed 'aspirationals' and the growing 'under class' living cheek by jowl in neighbouring housing estates, that could be lifted out of welfare dependency not by a bureaucratic paternalist state, but through the actions of 'social entrepreneurs' from within their ranks. This latter approach, influenced by Amartya Sen (1992), and UK Labour's 'Third Way', sought to marry a concept of working class agency with the neoliberal ascendancy and had its strongest advocates in firebrand western Sydney MP (and later Leader of the Opposition) Mark Latham, Queensland Aboriginal activist Noel Pearson and academic Peter Botsman (2001), and took aim at conservative and left of centre statists. Notwithstanding the pro-market inflection of this minority push within the ALP policy debates, it retained a sense of a public investment, though the state was to be an 'enabler' rather than manager of the less well-off. The controversial Latham, who grew up in public housing, had a strong sense of the salience of class for sound policy and politics, advising, in colourful Australian vernacular, that the Labor Party should 'stick to the working class like shit to a blanket'— a far cry from Tony Blair's paternalistic 'creepy communitarianism' (quoted in McGregor 1997 79; Rundle 2006). Labor's disastrous result in the 2004 Federal election under Latham's leadership effectively killed off this community empowerment impulse and invocation of agency from below within the party.

When Labor finally regained government in 2007, the Rudd and Gillard Governments sought to recognise, assist and manage marginalised groups, notably Indigenous Australians and people with disabilities, but paid little direct attention to class. A centrepiece of Labor's so-called 'Education Revolution' was the Gonski scheme to align school funding more closely with needs and redirect the disproportionate flow of federal funding to private schools to assist state government comprehensive schools. David Gonski's (2011) report, and the modified scheme legislated by the Gillard Government demonstrated that children from low socio-economic backgrounds performed worse at 'basic skills' at key age stages, making up the bulk of early school leavers and achieving lower academic results in final matriculation examinations. Notwithstanding this evidence, at the time of writing it remains to be seen whether the Gonski scheme's emphasis on low SES will be eclipsed by other, more visible measures of disadvantage in the schooling Resource Standard Formula, notably 'disability', especially for schools in materially better off communities vying for a share of funds.

Cultural Studies without Class

The absence of class analysis in policy and political discourse was paralleled by a decisive turn away from class in academic scholarship from the second half of the 1980s. In the 1970s and early 1980s, there had been a sophisticated Australian scholarly interest in class, represented, for example, in the work of sociologists R.W. Connell (1983), Ann Game and Rosemary Pringle (1984), educationalists Dean Ashenden and Gary Dowsett (Connell et al 1982), and historians Terry Irving (Connell and Irving 1980) and Ann Curthoys (1975, 1987). While varying in many ways, all these studies would agree that social inequalities are transmitted and learned in institutions such as schools, workplaces, public spaces of recreation, and welfare, policing and correctional services, in ways that the stratification model measures does not explain. They shared more broadly in a project of countering the individualism and sociological positivism of other intellectual influences of the time.

The turn away from class in Australian scholarly work broadly parallels the pattern seen in the UK, Europe and the United States. It was initiated by a recognition of a need to address other areas of inequality and discrimination—particularly gender, sexuality, ethnicity, indigeneity and disability. It coincided with the rise of identity politics, structurally supported though increasingly professional extra-party social movements, and by new work informed by poststructuralist, postcolonial and feminist theories that refocused cultural studies, sociology and history around the condition, rights and cultural agency of other marginalised groups. At the same time, the turn from class was perhaps particularly marked in Australia because of the urgency of political questions around multiculturalism, indigeneity and postcolonialism, and because of the way in which new intellectual formations of the 1970s and 1980s came to be associated with a distinctive 'Australian' style of work.

This style was exemplified above all in cultural studies, which attained the status for a period in the 1980s and 1990s of a preeminent field in the humanities and social sciences, giving it a centrality and prominence in Australia that was greater perhaps even than in the UK. Australian writers were very early to engage with European structuralist and post-structuralist theory (e.g. Morris and Patton, 1979), which was used in part to assert an independence from the Anglophile literary culture that had dominated intellectual life in universities up until the 1970s (Gibson 2007, 163–165). This theory meshed most closely with the politics of the new social movements—feminism, multiculturalism and, somewhat more problematically, Indigenous rights. Australian cultural studies never had a 'class moment' of the kind that was seen in Britain around the work of Richard Hoggart, Raymond Williams, E.P. Thompson and the early Birmingham School. While the British work was read in Australia, and the leading figures were sensitive to questions of class, it was rarely a central focus in their own writing.

The quality of the leading work in Australian cultural studies is undeniable (see e.g. Frow and Morris 1993) and it acquired an international reputation significantly above the earlier 'classical' period of class analysis in sociology, education and history. What was sometimes lost, however, was an attention to how gendered, ethnic and other identities worked in with, and were reinforced by, class inequalities. The best of the earlier period had grappled with the questions of the relationship of class and gendered bodies, and the class aspects of the Aboriginal and migrant experience, not just within the economy, but as reinforcing cultural responses to intertwined systems of capitalism, patriarchy and racism. Socialist feminist scholars such as Ann Curthoys (1975) examined the specificity of patriarchy and women's exploitation under capitalism, and how this impacted on working class and bourgeois women, in employment, family life and politics. Ann Game and Rosemary Pringle's study *Gender at Work* (1984) sought to complicate working class solidarity, demonstrating how men and women had different relations to work places, technology, authority and freedom, evident within factories and offices. In *Making the Difference*, Connell *et al* (1982) argued that gender and class were elegantly synthesised in embodied identities, and expressed in particular types of masculinity and femininity that made sense within their families, schools, communities and workplaces.

Work on the experience of Aboriginal and Torres Strait Islander people as victims of colonisation and racism was married with a sense of their struggle as the most marginalised of workers against capitalist exploitation, especially in rural industries. Indigenous activists and scholars such as Marcia Langton (1983) located a source of strength and hope in the success of collective action, such as indigenous participation in the Communist Party from the 1930s or the Gurindgi cattlemen's strike for wages against British company Vestey, that morphed into a struggle for land rights. Studies of postwar migration and settlement such as the work of Andrew Jacubowicz (1984), Stephen Castles, Mary Kalantzis *et al* (1988), joined in the 1990s by Ghassan Hage (1998), engaged with the growing ethnic diversity of the Australian working class through postwar immigration, and of the participation of migrants in work and unions as a site not just of exploitation, but as a gateway to citizenship and a means of acquiring national cultural capital.

It is important, of course, to note that there was not a simple rupture in academic research into culture and society that pitted class-focused research against cultural studies research. It is, however, true to say that, in the 1990s, the preponderance of cultural studies research focused on other kinds of identity formation. While this shift in emphasis was important in addressing questions of gender, ethnicity and other dimensions of social difference, the disappearance of cultural class analysis in much academic discourse meant that social science research on the impact of economic restructuring on 'low SES' groups has lacked attention to continuities with older working class cultures and to the creativity and agency through which these cultures might be in the process of being remade.

Recovering Class as Culture

Against this background, there are two main challenges in attempting to recover the concept of class in Australia today. The first is to address some of the reasons why the concept has been abandoned. Primary among these is a belief that to foreground class is to commit to an oppositional standpoint that is impractical in policy, a dead end politically and discredited intellectually. This is perhaps clearest in the political arena, where any mention of class is immediately pounced upon as attempt to provoke 'class war', which led the Rudd government to substitute the banal, if inclusive, 'working families'. The Labor party knows that this is an argument it cannot win. The old industrial working class—never as large in Australia as it was in Europe or the United States—is now far too small a proportion of the population on which to base an electoral strategy. Some groups who might be considered working class, notably tradespeople, have benefited materially from many of the economic changes of the last thirty years and have little interest in anti-business rhetoric. And there are other interests—women, non-Anglo populations, the LGBTI community—who must also be appealed to. Similarly, in the intellectual and scholarly arena, attempts to return to class are often seen as suggesting a return to Marxism, with all its known problems of economic reductionism and political simplification—not to mention the record of regimes that have acted in its name.

The second challenge is to recognise the social, economic and political changes that have occurred since earlier historical moments in which the concept of class has taken form. Notwithstanding that in a recent Essential Research poll 31 per cent of Australians identified themselves as working class, if the concept of class is to continue to serve in thinking about social policy today, it clearly needs re-grounding (Essential 2016, 6). The last two decades have seen enormous changes to the ways of life that have given meaning in the past to the term 'working class': the decline of the industrial sector relative to services; the rise of part-time, casual and contract employment; the increase in school retention rates to Year 12; easy access to credit; and the increasing feminisation and multiculturalism of the workforce—to name but a few. Older forms of working class political organisation have been widely challenged for privileging the white male worker, excluding women, ethnic minorities, Aboriginal people and other groups heavily represented in disadvantaged populations. Online and social media have also restructured the whole terrain on which social relations are formed. Just as they have disrupted and reformed social relations around friendship, commerce, sex and romance, they provide a very different matrix for relations of class by giving unparalleled agency to speak to groups who were often marginalised by the opinion-leading mainstream media. The rise of reality television shows and talk shows in the 90s gave voice—however structured and edited—to the views and lives of those who did not conform to white liberal and educated notions of discourse (Lumby 1999). The rise of online and social media has accelerated this phenomenon, flattening the hierarchy of discourse which largely privileged the educated, the wealthy and the politically powerful.

The response by the authors to these problems has been to adopt a 'class as culture' perspective. This draws in part on 'class culturalist' work that has emerged in the United Kingdom over the last twenty years in the work of authors such as Mike Savage (2000, 2010), Beverley Skeggs (1997, 2004) and Fiona

Devine (1998, 2004). This work has freed the concept of class from earlier associations with a white, male perspective, aligning it with feminist scholarship and critical work over the last thirty years on race and ethnicity. Skeggs' (1997) *Formations of Class and Gender* is exemplary here, demonstrating the ways in which class identities can be grounded in experiences such as caring, associated with women's work and very different from traditional masculinist images of blue collar labour. This kind of work has taken a little longer to develop in Australia, but has recently begun to emerge in the work of scholars such as Barbara Pini and Josephine Previte (2013), Kate Huppatz (2012) and Ramon Spaaij (2011).

Our approach to renewing an engagement with the concept of class is inspired by our work in media and cultural studies—disciplines that are grounded in an interest in what people are conjuring with in culture—not simply how they are represented, but how they speak back to those representations. Some of the most valuable insights here are to be found in media and popular culture. Television comedy has been particularly perceptive, offering sharply observed sketches of new class cultures against the backdrop of the shifting contexts in which they are taking form (cf. Campbell 2014). Jane Turner and Gina Riley (*Kath and Kim*) and Robyn Butler and Wayne Hope (*Upper Middle Bogan*) draw attention, for example, to the cutting edge commodification of outer suburban life, while Paul Fenech (*Pizza, Housos*) and Chris Lilley (*Summer Heights High, Angry Boys*) reflect the ethnic diversity of disadvantaged communities as well as the *lumpen*, often feral culture into which the children of Anglo blue collar workers can fall, especially in the outer suburbs and regions. Significantly, the characters in all these comedies share a sense of agency, even defiance, and a capacity to thrive in their particular domains, whether they be schools, the domestic sphere, recreation or even juvenile detention.

A major influence running through most of the recent class culturalist turn has been the sociological theory of Pierre Bourdieu (1994). While the Bourdieusian tradition has much to offer, particularly its attention to the intersection between class and culture, it has limitations in understanding the transformation of working class ways of life, notably a frequent tendency towards a kind of functionalism in which culture is reduced to an instrument of power.

In avoiding such a reduction of culture to power and working class people to victims of domination, we argue for reconnecting with an earlier moment in cultural studies in which class cultures were considered more in terms of their internal structures of sense and meaning than their function in reproducing social hierarchies. As Gibson (2007) has pointed out, power was not a key term in the work on class of some of the founding figures of British cultural studies, such as Richard Hoggart and Raymond Williams. Hoggart (1957, 16) was critical, for example, of the 'middle class Marxist' who, in their determination to see the working class always in terms of its subordination, "succeeds in part-pitying and part-patronising working class people beyond any semblance of reality". Similarly, Williams (1989, 7) rejected the idea that the working class was 'excluded from English culture'.

The relative absence of the concept of power in Hoggart and the earlier work of Williams has generally been seen since as problematic. The *locus classicus* of the critical case against it was E.P. Thompson's (1961) vigorous critique in *New Left Review* of Williams' *The Long Revolution*. It is certainly important that questions of power in relation to class can be raised at some level. However, the structural models of power that developed from the 1970s and which came, increasingly, to be seen as defining of class (and then later of other dimensions of social difference) obscured much of the value that can be found in the understanding of class as culture. This value still remains to be retrieved (Gibson 2007, 53–68).

We are now in the early stages of a project entitled *Recovering Class*, using a cultural understanding of class to examine contemporary media practices within so-called disadvantaged communities that have traditionally been considered working class. Media and communication are centrally implicated in questions of social division and the transformation of cultures, yet there has been little policy or academic attention in Australia to lower SES or disadvantaged people's media consumption patterns and more importantly their media making. This is surprising, as inequalities in relation to media have significant 'spillover' effects, affecting inequalities in many other areas, including health, government services, civic engagement, education and economic development (Mossberger *et al.* 2012, 2493). The potential of a cultural concept of class in addressing new social divides in and through media is demonstrated by earlier historical moments in which progress in the area has been achieved via a vibrant working class media sphere that emerged in Australia in the late nineteenth century and jostled and overlapped with bourgeois and mass commercial variants for most of the twentieth century (Lumby 1999; Moore 2012). Since 2016, the election of Donald Trump in the United States, the Brexit referendum in the United Kingdom, and advances by Pauline Hanson's One Nation in Australia have forced a recognition of significant class-based differences and antagonisms, including the use of social media by working-class-identified communities to communicate their discontent outside the mainstream media.

If the concept of class is to continue to serve in thinking about how media practices today can enable cultural self-determination and be a force for equality and civic participation, the impact and potential of digital communications must be considered. However, little is known about how working class communities have responded to the huge transformation of media, both heritage and digital, in Australia over the past twenty years. Access to high-speed broadband has increasingly come to be seen as comparable to education and literacy as a key to promoting democracy and economic growth (DiMaggio & Bonikowski 2008; Mossberger *et al.* 2008). The relation between media and citizen participation in addressing inequality has therefore become a critical area of research, with most scholars now agreeing that divergences in the adoption of digital media are one of the major reasons for widening inequalities of income in many areas over recent years (Hargittai 2008; DiMaggio & Bonikowski 2008). Recent international work on the social dimension of inequalities relating to digital media has shifted focus from the 'digital divide' to 'differentiated use' (DiMaggio *et al.* 2004), giving increasing attention to sociological distinctions, including to those of class (Hargittai 2008; Robinson 2009; Wessells 2013).

Revivifying E.P. Thompson's methodological focus on 'the making' of class, we argue that there needs to be a renewed consideration of how class is produced through traditional, online and social media practice—consuming, value-adding, interacting, creating, distributing, organising socially—as a way of investigating the *positive potential* of the class-based cultures of disadvantaged communities.

Conclusion

This chapter has made the case for Australian scholars of society and culture to reconsider the value of the concept of class for understanding and responding to inequality and other intractable social problems. In doing we advocate a class culturalist approach, drawing on recent work applying Bourdieu, but also an early period of British cultural studies and Australian work, that emphasised the agency within working class communities and ways of life. We argue for new empirical research engaging with the transformation of working class cultures, and to that end introduce a project exploring contemporary media practices in low socio-economic communities, to determine whether a working class media sphere is being remade.

We are interested in knitting together the threads of the best research in the sociological class analysis and media and cultural studies to explore how class and culture work in the contemporary online and social media environment. We are interested in understanding how people, once designated as working class, are conjuring with culture—not simply how they are represented, but how they speak back to those representations.

Popular media, fictional and journalistic representations are important in reminding us of the specifically *cultural* dimension to class, providing a corrective to the widespread reduction of social difference to a set of colourless statistics and demographic profiles. They are also valuable in offering sketches of contemporary class cultures—sharply observed *hypotheses* as to the ways in which older working class ways of life have changed. However, the absence of a formal research base limits their circulation beyond the level of casual observation, restricting the purchase of a class cultural perspective in more formally regulated domains. We contend that documenting new cultural formations among transformed low income communities in Australia can provide policy-makers and public institutions with a better understanding of these communities, improving their capacity to relate to them realistically and appropriately.

References

ABS (Australian Bureau of Statistics) (2010), Health and Socio Economic Disadvantage, http://www.ausstats.abs.gov.au/Ausstats/subscriber.nsf/0/5703A93771AE2E4ECA25 76E70016C8D3/$File/41020_%20healthandseifa.pdf.

ACOSS (2015) *Inequality in Australia—A Nation Divided*. Strawberry Hills, NSW: Australian Council of Social Services. Available at: http://www.acoss.org.au/wp-content/uploads/2015/06/Inequality_in_Australia_FINAL.pdf.

ACTU (Australian Council of Trade Unions) (1987) *Australia Reconstructed: ACTU/TDC mission to Western Europe: a report,* Canberra : Australian Govt. Pub. Service.

ALP (Australian Labor Party) (1979) *National Committee of Inquiry: ALP Discussion Papers,* Bedford Park: APSA.

Bourdieu, P. (1994) *The Field of Cultural Production: Essays on Art and Literature.* Cambridge: Polity Press.

Broom, L., Lancaster Jones, F., and Zubryzcki, J. (1968) Social Stratification in Australia. In: Jackson J.A., (ed) *Social Stratification*. New York: Cambridge University Press.

Campbell, M. (2014) Opposite Ends of the Freeway: Upper Middle Bogan and the Mobility of Class Distinction. *Metro Magazine* 181: 36–40.

Castles, S., Kalantzis, M. *et al.* (1988), *Mistaken identity: multiculturalism and the demise of nationalism in Australia.* Annandale: Pluto Press.

Cheshire, L., Pawson, H. *et al.* (2014) *Living with place disadvantage: community, practice and policy.* AHURI Final Report No.228. Melbourne: Australian Housing and Urban Research Institute. http://www.ahuri.edu.au/publications/projects/myrp704.

Coelli, M. and Borland, J. (2015) Job Polarisation and Earnings Inequality in Australia. *Economic Record*. Early View, DOI: 10.1111/1475-4932.12225.

Connell, R.W. (1983) *Which Way is Up?: Essays on Sex, Class and Culture*. Sydney: Allen & Unwin.

Connell, R.W. and Irving, T. (1980) *Class Structure in Australian History*. Melbourne: Longman Cheshire.

Connell, R.W., Ashenden, D.J., Kessler, S., and Dowsett G.W. (1982) *Making the Difference—Schools, Families and Social Division*. Sydney: Allen & Unwin.

Curthoys, A. (1987) *Women and Work*. Commonwealth Schools Commission.

Curthoys, A., et al. (eds) (1975) *Women at Work*. Canberra: Australian Society for the Study of Labour History.

DEEWR (2011) *Review of Funding for Schooling—Final Report*. Canberra: Department of Education, Employment and Workplace Relations, https://docs.education.gov.au/system/files/doc/other/review-of-funding-for-schooling-final-report-dec-2011.pdf.

Devine, F. (1998) Social Identities, Class Identity and Political Perspectives. *Sociological Review*, 40 (2): 229–252.

Devine, F. (2004) *Class Practices—How Parents Help Children Get Good Jobs*. Cambridge: Cambridge University Press.

DiMaggio, P. and Bonikowski, B. (2008) Make Money Surfing the Web? The Impact of Internet Use on the Earnings of U.S. Workers. *American Sociological Review* 73 (2): 227–250.

DiMaggio, P., et al. (2004) Digital inequality: From unequal access to differentiated use—A Literature Review and Agenda for Research on Digital Inequality. In: Neckerman, K. (ed.) *Social Inequality*. New York: Russell Sage Foundation, 355–400.

Eckersley, R. (1988) *Casualties of change: the predicament of youth in Australia*, Canberra: Australian Govt. Pub. Service.

Encel, S. (1971) *Equality and Authority: A Study of Class, Status and Power in Australia*. New York: Barnes & Noble.

Essential (2016), *The Essential Report 29 November 2016*, Sydney: Essential Media Communication, http://www.essentialvision.com.au/wp-content/uploads/2016/11/Essential-Report_161129.pdf.

Frow, J. and Morris, M. (eds.) (1993) *Australian Cultural Studies—A Reader*. Illinois: University of Illinois Press.

Game, A. and Pringle, R. (1984) *Gender at Work*. London: Pluto Press.

Gibson, M. (2007) *Culture and Power—A History of Cultural Studies*. Oxford: Berg.

Goldie, D., and Moore, T., (1989) *Nobody's Children*. ABC Television Documentaries.

Gonski, D. (2011) *Review of Funding for Schooling: Final Report*. Canberra: Australian Dept of Education, Employment and Workplace Relations.

Hage, G. (1998) *White Nation: fantasies of white supremacy in a multicultural society*. London: Pluto Press.

Hargittai, E. (2008) The Digital Reproduction of Inequality in D.B. Grusky, *Social Stratification—Class, Race and Gender in Sociological Perspective*. 3rd Edition, Boulder: Westview Press.

Hoggart, R. (1957) *The Uses of Literacy*. London: Chatto & Windus.

Howe, B. and Rorty, R. (1984) Class, Politics and the ALP. In: Eastwood, J., *Labor Essays 1984*. Drummond Publishing.

Hulse, K. and Pinnegar, S. (2015) *Housing markets and socio-spatial disadvantage: an Australian perspective*. AHURI (Australian Housing and Urban Research Institute), http://www.ahuri.edu.au/publications/download/ahuri_myrp704_rp6.

Huppatz, K.E. (2012) *Gender capital at work: intersections of femininity, masculinity, class and occupation*. Palgrave: Hampshire.

Jakubowicz, A. (1984) *Ethnicity, Class and Social Policy in Australia*. Social Welfare Research Centre, University of New South Wales.

Langton, M. and Peterson, N., (1983) *Aborigines, land and land rights*. AIAS Series, Canberra: Australian Institute of Aboriginal Studies.

Latham, M. and Botsman, P. (2001) *The Enabling State: People before bureaucracy*. Annandale: Pluto Press.

Lumby, C. (1999) *Gotcha: Life in a Tabloid World*. Sydney: Allen and Unwin.

McGregor, C. (1997) *Class in Australia*. Ringwood: Penguin.

McLachlan, R., et al. (2013) *Deep and Persistent Disadvantage in Australia*. Productivity Commission, Commonwealth of Australia, http://www.pc.gov.au/__data/assets/pdf_file/0007/124549/deep-persistent-disadvantage.pdf.

Moore, T. (1988) *Counting the Costs: Youth Income Transfers*. Developmental Youth Services.

Moore, T. (1999) To Praise Youth or to Bury It. In: Patmore G. and Glover D. (eds) *New Voices for Social Democracy*. Annandale: Pluto Press: 216–232.

Moore, T. (2003) Hawke's Big Tent: Elite Pluralism and the Politics of Inclusion. In: Ryan S. and Bramston T. (eds) *The Hawke Government: a Critical Retrospective*. North Melbourne: Pluto Press: 112–127.

Moore, T. (2012) *Dancing with Empty Pockets—Australia's Bohemians*. Millers Pt, NSW: Allen & Unwin.

Morris, M. and Patton, P (1979) *Michel Foucault: power, truth, strategy*. Sydney: Feral Publications.

Mossberger, K., et al. (2012) Measuring Digital Citizenship: Mobile Access and Broadband. *International Journal of Communication* 6: 2492–2528.

Mossberger, K., et al. (2008) *Digital citizenship: The Internet, society, and participation*. Cambridge, MA: MIT Press.

NPHT (2009) *Australia: the Healthiest Country by 2020—A discussion paper by the National Preventative Health Taskforce*. Canberra: Commonwealth of Australia.

OECD (2015) *In It Together: Why Less Inequality Benefits All*. OECD Publishing, Paris.

Phillips, B., et al. (2013) *Poverty, Social Exclusion and Disadvantage in Australia*. National Centre for Social and Economic Modelling, University of Canberra, http://www.natsem.canberra.edu.au/storage/Poverty-Social-Exclusion-and-Disadvantage.pdf.

Piketty, T. (2014) *Capital in the Twenty-First Century*. Cambridge, MA: Belknap Press.

Pini, B. and Previte, J. (2013) Gender, Class and Sexuality in Contemporary Australia: Representations of the Boganette. *Australian Feminist Studies* 28 (78): 348–363.

Robinson, L. (2009) A Taste for the Necessary—A Bourdieuian approach to digital inequality. *Information, Communication & Society* 12 (4): 488–507.

Rorris, A.P. et al. (2011) *Assessment of current process for targeting of schools funding to disadvantaged students*—A report prepared for The Review of Funding for Schooling Panel, http://research.acer.edu.au/policy_analysis_misc/10/.

Rundle, G. (2006) 'Grotesque: After the Grand- Recent British Comedy', *The Monthly*. Available at: https://www.themonthly.com.au/issue/2006/october/1166764584/guy-rundle/grotesque-after-grand.

Savage, M. (2000) *Class Analysis and Social Transformation*. Milton Keynes: Open University Press.

Savage, M. (2010) *Identities and Social Change in Britain Since 1940*. Oxford: Oxford University Press.

Scutella, R., Wilkins, R and Horn, M (2009) *Measuring Poverty and Social Exclusion in Australia: A Proposed Multidimensional Framework for Identifying Socio-Economic Disadvantage*. Melbourne Institute Working Paper No. 4/09, http://melbourneinstitute.com/downloads/working_paper_series/wp2009n04.pdf.

Sen, A. (1992) *Inequality Re-examined*. Oxford: Oxford University Press.

Skeggs, B. (1997) *Formations of Class and Gender: Becoming Respectable*. Sage.

Skeggs, B. (2004) *Class, Self, Culture*. London: Routledge.

Spaaij, R. (2011) *Sport and Social Mobility: Crossing Boundaries*. New York: Routledge.

Thompson, E.P. (1961) The Long Revolution. *New Left Review* 9 and 10: 24–33 and 34–39.

Thompson, M. (1999) *Labor Without Class: the Gentrification of the ALP*. Annandale: Pluto Press.

Turrell, G., et al. (2006) Health Inequalities in Australia: Morbidity, health behaviours, risk factors and health service use. *Health Inequalities Monitoring Series*, No. 2. AIHW Cat. No. PHE 72. Canberra: Queensland University of Technology and the Australian Institute of Health and Welfare.

Wessells, B. (2013) The reproduction and reconfiguration of inequality: Differentiation of class status and power in the dynamics of digital divides. In: Ragnedda M. and Muschert G.W. (eds.) *The Digital Divide—The Internet and Social Equality in International Perspective*. Abingdon: Routledge, 17–28.

Williams, R. (1989) *Resources of Hope*. New York: Verso.

PART 3

Class and the Media

∴

CHAPTER 14

'Everything Changes. Everything Stays the Same': Documenting Continuity and Change in Working Class Lives

Anita Biressi

Introduction

Central to this essay is a critical engagement with the representation of working class experience as both a theoretical problem and as a political practice. I ask how documentary can represent and articulate working class lives and working class experiences of continuity and change in the current moment. While the opening theoretical discussion will be broad, my analysis specifically foregrounds the value of theorising the articulation of working class experience through well-chosen exemplars and under local conditions. To do this my analysis focuses in on an examination of the British documentary film *The Condition of the Working Class* directed by Mike Wayne and Deirdre O'Neill (2012, henceforth TCWC). The film was inspired by Friedrich Engels' now famous 1844 chronicle of the exploitation of the poor in the industrial North of England and offers us an ideal platform to think through the tensions between repetition, continuity and change which characterise the current experience of working class subjectivity and its representation.

The chapter begins by tackling the characterisation of the working class as the archetypal class in the representation of British class-capital relations and the challenges this throws up for 21st century documentarians. I then move on to explore how this challenge is further complicated by the argument that a defining characteristic of our current neoliberal age has been the so-called "dissolution of the working class" (see Savage 2000, 148ff), the globalisation of labour and the emergence of more individualised, fragmented and precarious post-class identities. I conclude by engaging with Wayne and O'Neill's film; exploring how it negotiates working class archetypes and arguably re-inflects them with urgency and currency. My overall purpose is to argue the ongoing importance and social value of documentary film-making in representing the (un)changing patterns of class injury, vulnerability and resistance in the context of long-term social change.

Farewell to the Archetypal Working Class?

There is a tide of critical approaches which quite understandably warn against forming generalisations about the working class, about shared working class experience and about its representation in the early years of the 21st century. The following discussion is attuned sympathetically to this scepticism and the doubtful applicability of grand narratives about class relations and the working class to current neoliberal times. Nevertheless, for practical and political reasons, it is important not to exclude, *a priori*, the possibility of thinking more abstractly about the tricky business of mediating past and present working class lives because we have so much evidence that classed subjects continue to experience both symbolic injury and social injustice.

The working class has been widely characterised as the archetypal class in the discursive practices of philosophers, sociologists, historians and the media. All of these knowledge regimes have ascribed what we might call past-ness to the archetypal working class, some of them stigmatising it as redundant or irrelevant. Pronounced to be either a dead or dying social formation, its apparent demise triggers powerful emotions in those who have 'moved on', including feelings of triumph, relief, regret, anger and nostalgia. An archetype can be understood variously as either a typical character, an idealised model or as a universally recognised symbol (more on these below) and we can see that the working class as a personification and as an abstraction has borne the historical burden and sometime promise inherent in all three of these definitions. These three definitions of the archetypal and their political implications often overlap or intersect. For the sake of clarity I shall outline and illustrate each of them in turn in order to reflect on how the working class becomes constructed as an object of judgement and then becomes consigned to the oubliette of history. Later I will return to this tripartite model in order to offer a reading of Wayne and O'Neill's documentary.

Our first definition is that of the *typical character* of the working class and it is easily conveyed by the British media in a short-hand lexicon that most people will recognise even if it is at variance with their own personal experience. Recognition is possible because social class has become embedded as a common sense set of markers of social difference in Britain and, despite arguments by scholars that the nomenclature of class is increasingly inadequate, it is still popularly deployed as a 'folk sociology' (Sayer 2005, 4). One clear example, is the typical character of the industrial worker and specifically the figure of the trade union activist which has been heavily stereotyped in some quarters. Media depictions of labour are diverse and change over time (Marin-Lamellet 2016). For example, the heroic image of labour which was promulgated during the 1930s and 1940s was superseded by an increasing diversity of labouring figures. These included the alienated de-skilled worker, the redundant worker and the flexible worker adapting to newly imposed temporary, casual or even self-employed status (Beynon 2001, 25–40). We also know that, in reality, British industries and later the service sector have always been sustained by *diverse* workforces in terms of gender, ethnicity and region. Moreover, in recent years Britain has seen industrial action mobilised *by various social classes* e.g. by junior doctors, British Airways cabin crews, teachers and Virgin train drivers. Yet, despite this complex history of labour and its representation across the piece, the union activist continues to be stereotyped in the mainstream news media, according to well-established conventions. For example, in the politically partisan press the activist is figured as the personification of white working class belligerence and as a knee-jerk proponent of disruption at any cost. In addition, the union leader himself (rarely herself) has also been styled as an anachronistic throwback to an earlier era; someone who is, more often than not, self-aggrandising, self-serving and overpaid (Biressi and Nunn 2013, 177). Coverage in the national press, such as the *Daily Mail*, sustains this mythology of working class agitation as corrupt and backwards-looking with headlines such as "Union barons in strike plot to topple the Tories" (Salmon 2016) and "Up the shirkers! Union boss 'Red' Len McCluskey parties the night away" (Walters and Owen 2016). These and newer working class character stereotypes, such as the Essex Girl and the Chav, heavily populate the British political imaginary and arguably contribute to the felt injuries of classed subject-hood. And we will see in my discussion of Wayne and O'Neill's film below that people continue to struggle to resist and to rise above them. As Beverley Skeggs (1997,6) sums up so neatly:

> ...the long and continual process of representing the working class did not have its history in the re-presentation of an original, or a real; yet the continual re-presentation of representations ... does have real effects in the responses that people make to them.

A second working class type is the *model* or idealised archetype which comprises a range of publicly approved characters such as the barmaid with a heart of gold, the nurse who goes the extra mile to comfort a patient (both of these are stalwarts of British TV drama) or the soldier fighting for British values (as eulogised in the tabloid press). Prominent among these is the chirpy, hard-working 'respectable working class' woman who, whether buffeted by misfortune or blessed with success, retains her classed values of family, local ties, decency and resilient good humour. As the historian Carolyn Steedman (2013, 67) notes, working class respectability was originally a nineteenth century conceptualisation of a "set of qualities and behaviours required of or imposed on plebeian people by the better sort"; a condition which later became opposed to and contrasted with the "unrespectable poor" by social visionaries and reformists. In the twenty-first century, respectability for women has transmuted more fully into properly-directed aspiration and social mobility (McRobbie 2009).

These historically embedded images and stories of working class respectability and aspiration persist and continue to connect with audiences and publics despite political assertions that we are all middle class now or that we live in a post-class society. For instance, following the death of the popular British TV star and singer Cilla Black on the 1st August 2015 commentators attributed her career longevity to the fact that she never forgot her working class roots and that she had retained the 'common touch' even while she rose to stardom. She was praised for her properly expressed ambition to succeed while caring for her family; a stance which is often important in approved working class femininity. For instance, during the TV tribute show *Our Cilla* (2015) she was eulogised and endorsed as someone who "always wanted to do better and never gave up". The left-of-centre *Guardian* newspaper lamented the passing of an "archetypal working class pop star" noting:

> Cilla's passing reminds us that we are finally leaving the 20th century. Or, at least, losing the 20th century—losing the certainties of a particularly British kind of pop culture, a working class culture, that have slowly been erased since the 1980s.
> STANLEY 2015

In this and in many other examples, working class narratives and their attached iconography occupy a doubled temporal space because they position the archetypal working class subject as still present only as a remnant of a dying culture (Biressi and Nunn 2010 and 2013, 106–107). The lost certainties referred to in *the Guardian* relate to what critics, in cultural studies, have called a 'common culture' in which the lived experiences of working class life are knit together through a 'structure of feeling' arising from close affiliations across the social, cultural and political realms (Williams 1961). As indicated by Wayne and O'Neill's own film, the 1980s are often regarded as pivotal years of social change in Britain as Thatcherism, City trading, deregulation and globalisation together catalysed the creative and destructive forces which would finally cut the weakening bonds of class consciousness. Class difference had not disappeared, of course, but it had been reconfigured and its archetypes, of which the trade union agitator and the working class 'Liverpool Lass' were but two, were mainly recognisable as (often nostalgic) signifiers of how far society had changed and mostly (but not entirely) for the better.

Our third conceptualisation of the working class archetype is that of the universal symbol by which I mean the *idea* of the working class as the embodiment of a *collective* force. Thinking theoretically, and at a high level of abstraction across the history of ideas about class relations, we can see how the working class has been characterised as either a force for change or as an obstacle to progress. For example, Engels (1999, 317) observes that while Communism exists to free all classes:

> So long as the wealthy classes not only do not feel the want of any emancipation, but strenuously oppose the self-emancipation of the working class, so long the social revolution will have to be prepared and fought out by the working class alone.

Viewed positively, the Marxist notion of the working class as an historical actor carries with it ideas of agency, self-determination and an investment in the future. As such it depicts the working class as moving forwards temporally and progressively. In contrast, those sceptical or critical of the capacity of collectives to resist capitalist imperatives and its social implications have viewed the working class as either woefully ill-equipped to keep up with the productive forces of social evolution and economic development or even as wilfully obstructive. Its collective power to resist, refuse and to protest through public gatherings or strike action, for example, becomes characterised in the mainstream media as always threatening to flare into the incontinent behaviour of the mob. In Britain, this is evidenced in the media coverage of the 1984–5 miners' strikes and associated events such as the infamous Battle of Orgreave (Williams 2014, Hart 2016). From this perspective the working class, *en masse*, has become figured as an evolutionary throwback rather than as a potential agent of revolution. The result is that the working class as a collective (as well as its individual members) is condemned or mocked for its backwardness in both senses of the word: as both regressive and stupid. This problematic representation and re-representation of classed social subjects continues to have real social effects and its injurious consequences are revealed in interviews with sociologists and the testimony gathered by documentarians. In sum the notion of the working class as static and easily characterised is not simply damaging to its members, it is also shot through with political problems for progressive political projects. It implies that its members are *de facto* resistant to change, it draws boundaries around its constitution (i.e. potentially excluding those who could be counted amongst its number such as migrant workers) and it helps to undermine notions of collective agency *going forwards*.

Having indicated some of the ways in which the British working class has become fixed in the popular and political imagination and thereby figured as historically outmoded or irrelevant we might ask then how this unhelpful reification has been countered. Again, a schematic approach is revealing here as it allows us to explore these questions with both a wide-angled and later a more closely focused documentary lens. The innovative work of socialist historians and thinkers opens up a route into understanding the emergence and development of the working class as a *dynamic* phenomenon engaged in historical processes rather than as an already formed, uniform and unchanging social group. Engels' (1999, xiv) own journalistic and ethnographic work helped to forge this path by stressing that the working class encompasses the great majority of British subjects across a spectrum of changing social conditions:

> ...the working class of the great cities offers a graduated scale of conditions in life, in the best cases a temporarily endurable existence for hard work and good wages, good and endurable, that is, from the worker's standpoint; in the worst cases, bitter want, reaching even homelessness and death by starvation.

So too Engels, and of course Marx, proposed an explanatory social model which is predicated on the shifting structural *relations* formed among and between social subjects which set the proletariat on its 'historic mission' (Marx 1963, 238). This formulation is nicely encapsulated by E.P. Thompson (2013, 9) who states that rather than seeing class as a category "it is something which happens (and which can be shown to have happened) in human relationships". The pioneering approach undertaken in cultural studies scholarship therefore has been to further unfix these sediment categories through an examination of classed relations *in situ* and this has been done through studies foregrounding working class *experience*, through ethnography, auto-ethnography and, more schematically, by employing a more nuanced understanding of historical change as fluid and relational (Hall 1990, 12).

The enduring notion of a homogenous and unchanging working class now also sits awkwardly alongside new and emergent historical subjects which are considered to better reflect the challenges of surviving and thriving in a world of free market economics and neoliberal values. The turbulent context of a post-industrial western setting has arguably produced 'new' or newly inflected disenfranchised or disadvantaged groups including the "ageing traditional working class" (Savage et al 2013), the white working class (Sveinsson 2009), the unproductive 'underclass' (Welshman 2006), the non-class subject (Gorz 1997), the precariat (Standing 2011) and the working poor (Andreß and Lohmann 2008). This diversity of figures is arguably more useful in conveying the fluidity of the contemporary experience of material inequality and social exclusion. The speed with which the labels for new classed social figures are coined also suggests that commentators are striving to keep up with the making and the re-making of working class identities. But the political challenge which accompanies this proliferation of labels, variously coined by philosophers, sociologists and media pundits, is that they may work to further fracture social relations across generational, ethnic and other fault-lines at the precise economic pinch-points where mutual bonds of solidarity might form. In my final section I will consider how these tensions between past and present, continuity and change, stasis and flux, division and solidarity take shape and are articulated in Wayne and O'Neill's documentary.

Documenting the Working Class in England: From Archetype to Experience

TCWC is set in Salford and its near-neighbour Manchester. This film interleaves the past and the present, resurrecting Engels' 1844 reportage and refracting it through the reflections and memories of a present-day theatre group comprising mostly non-professional performers across the generations. The participants devised and performed a play based on their own experiences and Engels' book. The filmmakers followed the process from first rehearsal to first night performance over eight weeks; engaging with its development through various strategies including cast interviews, vox pops, readings from Engels' work and through academic commentary. The film was made in the wake of the global financial downturn which began in 2007–8 and revealed the vulnerability and resilience of people who had been enduring the difficult years of economic austerity in Britain. It also provided a platform, in addition to the play itself, for people to participate creatively in the politics of their own representation and to consider the ways in which their own voices and aspirations had been silenced, ignored or over-ruled. My aim in this concluding section is to reveal how this documentary practice engaged with and challenged the archetypes described above through the privileging of working class voices and working class experience and how it set these in the context of a larger political project about continuity and change.

Manchester is an obvious setting for a creative practice around class politics and Engels' text is the logical stepping off-point. The city was, in fact, the crucible of the world's industrial proletariat and hence it has become the locus of a number of post-Engels artistic, avant-garde and mainstream explorations of the status and vitality of 'traditional' working class cultures and the impact of social change. Wayne and O'Neill's film follows, most notably, in the honourable footsteps of the theatrical innovator Joan Littlewood who devised and wrote *The Classic Soil*, a radio documentary broadcast to the Northern Region in 1939. This radical programme cut contemporary voices together with extracts from Engels' text to highlight issues of continuity and change (Holdsworth 2011, 6, see also Chignell et al 2015, 83). In the words of the Radio Times magazine it contrasted "the life of the Manchester working man and his wife today with the life lived by their ancestors" (in Murphy 2016, 140). Since then creative projects and working class studies have continued to attach symbolic importance to Manchester and its environs. There has been a diversity of creative outputs yoking Engels' text to contemporary concerns since the global financial downturn; all testifying to the pertinence of his work for new times. In 2009 the BBC Radio 4 series *Whatever Happened to the Working Class* launched with 'From Engels to Oasis [the music band]', arriving at the conclusion that a return to class politics was on the cards, or at least, for white Mancunians. Rainer Ganahl's 2011 (Austria/USA) short film *The Condition of The Working Class In England—Little Ireland 1842/2011*, exposed the degraded environment of the contemporary urban city. More recently, 2014 saw the broadcast of *Manchester: Alchemical City* (BBC Radio 4) in which sounds of Manchester, past and present, are woven into a reflection by the writer Jeannette Winterson as well as the launch of The Poor Theatres Project. The latter "documented five local projects working at points on Engels' map of Manchester and its towns. The idea here was to explore how theatre projects navigate a culture of austerity … to revise Engels' account of deprivation by documenting the ways in which artists and communities draw on theatre activity to critique and celebrate their localities" Hughes (2016). These examples demonstrate how creative projects and working class studies continue to attach symbolic importance to Manchester and its environs.

The tag-line for TCWC, "Everything changes. Everything stays the same", economically sign-posts the entanglements of capturing past and present, continuity and change. The challenges involved are explicitly addressed in the filmmakers' 2013 essay on the documentary which begins by reviewing the applicability of class labels during a period of seismic change. They note that while the category of class has fallen, in some contexts, into disuse, that nonetheless, what "was striking to us when we read Engels' book … was the shocking relevance its analysis still had for the twenty-first century" (Wayne and O'Neill 2013, 490). In interview, they also ask:

> What's changed? Some things have. When Engels wrote his book, working class political consciousness was very high and there was a thriving and independent working class culture. Today working people and their organisations in the UK, and especially England, have been broken up by years of attacks by neoliberal policies. We wanted to bring back a little flavour of that revolutionary spirit that was in Engels' book....
> in NWONKA 2013

Throughout the film the play's cast, alongside others, ably articulate and describe their own formation as working class subjects, the ways in which class has been inscribed upon them and also how they have negotiated the stigmatisation and injury of social inequalities. They generously share their individual stories of ambition, exploitation and disappointment. Consequently, there are many revealing occasions where working class archetypes of labour and social respectability (and their cultural and ideological associations) are grappled with by the film's subjects as they recall their own encounters with work, the education system, with welfare and with politics. I argue that the film overall actively tackles and even dismantles archetypes, such as those described above, by integrating these stories into its wider interrogation of the relevance of Engels' work for today's working class subjects.

De-stabilising Archetypes Through the Individual and the Collective

Stories of labour, industry, work and lack of work permeate the film and arguably complicate the media stereotype of the militant worker as a luddite trouble-maker. A number of the film's subjects made it clear how labour (and/ or lack of well-paid work) and the power structures which underpin labour both historically and currently inform working class consciousness. For example, at the beginning of the film, the recruits reflect on their social class positioning and they signal how labour was, and is, a key determinant of their social identity (my ellipses throughout):

> "I describe myself as working class because I've got to sell my labour, either I sell my labour or I starve or ... survive on 67 pounds a week on the dole."

"…there used to be a wonderful pride … I was proud that my dad went to work in the pit … there can't be any pride … when they are considered lower class … when there aren't any damn jobs."

"I live with five other people … working class … lasses and lads … every single one of them … has a decent degree and they are all working in jobs in either like Sainsbury's or Wagamama's … and doing really awful hours for the work they put in."

[the perception is] "the working class are these people on the benefits…".

The past relations of power played out in work settings are conveyed by Ray (Figure 14.1) [this figure, and the three that follow, are stills from the 2012 film, *The Condition of the Working Class* by Mike Wayne and Deirdre O'Neill, reproduced by permission] who recalls his factory days; a time in which workers benefitted from excellent working conditions driven forward by a powerful union. He recalls that following the 1979 General Election in which the Conservatives triumphed: "we went into work in the morning and the managers were waiting for us … to stand there and say it's our turn now… '[be]cause [Margaret] Thatcher had won … within months … they were sacking people.'" Interviewee Kate, among others, conveys the perceived consequences of this regime change: "I'm one of Thatcher's children … the first generation … who didn't expect to get work when they left school and … every time I get a job … I've been made redundant and had to start all over again." And Garry is one of a number of interviewees who tracks a historical arc from past pride to present-day

FIGURE 14.1 *Ray provides a historical perspective in the film.*

DOCUMENTING CONTINUITY AND CHANGE IN WORKING CLASS LIVES   247

poverty forged by Thatcherism and its aftermath: "she's taken away the working class man's dignity; at the same time brought in institutions like banks and Cash Generator [national pawn broker] ... to fleece the poor even more."

Voices such as these establish the historical relations of labour within which class inequalities have taken shape and in which pride and also shame come to be produced. Many of the stories told are difficult to hear and some highlight the dangers of exploitation in the precarious present. For example, JD, one of the youngest cast members, shares her story of sexual exploitation by the manager of the bar where she worked [edited here for brevity]:

> the fact that I had no money was the only reason I stuck around in that job, it was hell, I hated it. It was one of the most degrading things I think I've ever made myself do ... I only did because if I didn't I wouldn't have had any food ... just none ... I was ashamed as well ... if it hadn't been because of the position I was in, because of the class I was in, I would never have had to stick my job ... it was really hard trying to stay there with the abuse ... but knowing I had to keep going and I kept going for nine months.

These personal stories are exemplary of the many ways that the film conveys "the gradual effacement of a way of life based around a coherent sense of the dignity of others and of a place in the world" (Charlesworth 2000, 2). It also enriches and complicates viewers' understanding of the environment in which people struggle or thrive by highlighting, through editing and location

FIGURE 14.2   *Interviewees reflect on the past outside the Royal Bank of Scotland which was rescued by taxpayers following the 2007–2008 crash.*

shooting, the turbulence of the current employment marketplace where finance and the service sectors predominate. This is nicely captured in a street interview discussing the fall of traditional industries filmed outside the Royal Bank of Scotland (Figure 14.2) which was financially saved by the British Government. Taken together these examples de-stabilise the established stereotype of the politicised worker as a self-serving and mulish agitator by disclosing personal histories and present damaging relations of power around work and unemployment, austerity and wealth.

The film also tackles and complicates the more positive, publicly-approved archetype of the working class woman whose driving aspiration, determination and hard work both guarantees and explains her successful social mobility and her family's future security. As with the story of Cilla Black above, the film depicts women "who always wanted to do better and never gave up". But these stories sharply articulate the real conditions which inhibit ambition, block progress and undermine any serious investment in futurity. As such they act as a refutation of the celebrity narratives of social mobility articulated in media discourse and the underlying meritocratic model which supports them. For example, Lorraine as one of the older cast members shares a lifetime of experiences, of past plans and present disappointments. Her testimony, emerging piecemeal throughout the film, unpacks the impediments to social mobility which hindered her progress and her personal development across a lifetime. She recalls first the psychic injury caused by the mockery of her working class accent when she arrived at a 'posh' school and how damaging this was to her self-esteem. Nonetheless, she thrived academically and planned to qualify as a doctor; an aim stymied by her step-father who insisted that she left school at sixteen to earn a living. Lorraine explains "…they wanted my income … because I wouldn't leave school and … give him my earnings they threw me out. I was thrown out at fourteen and a half". The film's editing adroitly juxtaposes Engels' observations with those of interviewees to further reflect on the implications of life ambitions curtailed. In one sequence a reading from Engels' book about working class ambition "to secure for themselves a better, more human position" is juxtaposed with Lorraine's recollections of taking a degree in later life despite health problems and her joy in subsequently securing an ideal short-term job at a university. The fact that she had to decline because employment put her Incapacity Benefit in jeopardy again encapsulated the systemic faults in the welfare system which both brands her as under-productive and insists on her dependency.

In another poignant scene, independent shoe-shop owner Angie (Figure 14.3), who should by all accounts be the heroine of the neoliberal project of enterprising individualism, presents instead as embattled and out-manoeuvred.

FIGURE 14.3   *Angie fears for her children's future.*

She becomes increasingly distressed as she conveys the hazards of running her small business and her faltering hopes for her children's future. These "big business are just taking away things from the working class who are trying to make a living; it's difficult". ..."everybody is struggling down here..." She confides: "I pray for a future for my kids ... that my life will be an example for them ... I want them to continue where I left off ... if I die that they will still have this premises. If they want to they will be able to carry it on or expand it ... and not have it taken away from you." Angie's disclosures, alongside many others, powerfully expose the precariousness of even modest success i.e. the ability to make a living and to ensure that the next generation thrives. Her legacy is in doubt and her labour is no guarantee of long-term success. The life-stories of these individuals substantiate the answer to the question as framed by Imogen Tyler (2015, 496): "what is the problem that 'class' describes? The answer is a surprisingly simple one, the problem that 'class' describes is inequality".

What then of our final archetype, of the working class as a universal symbol and a collective force? The film, as a political project pays keen attention, not only to individual voices as above, but also to the aggregated notion of the working class as a political agent and its historical status as the embodiment of a *collective* force. The film opens with the introductory scenes of Paul Rotha's 1946 documentary film *A City Speaks*; its voiceover calling for a "city of justice ... of plenty ... of brotherhood". Rotha's utopian vision of post-war development plans for Manchester, made on behalf of the City council, jars tellingly against Wayne and O'Neill's subsequent account of fractured social relations and presentation of down-at-heel urban spaces. While both films quote from

FIGURE 14.4   *Collective cast curtain call.*

Engels it is the former which situates his reportage as past record rather than present commentary as its trajectory moves towards a promising investment in the future underwritten by the conviction that "it's always in the heart of man to search for the better" and that 'our people' control the power of modern technology and industry. The re-deployment of Rotha's introduction casts a poignant shadow across the ensuing action but it also arguably sign-posts the optimism which underpins the theatrical project and the assembly of citizens who will become The Ragged Collective (Figure 14.4).

Tellingly, the subsequent scenes and editing, together, highlight a shift on the part of the actors from positions of individual anger or disappointment to collective action, passion and energy. Actors' observations can be latched together by an engaged viewer to tell a progressive story: "I'm here [be]cause I'm angry", "the working class essentially serve the upper class", "the group is bonding", "the ethos is the group". Artistic Director Jimmy Fairhurst confirms this: "things aren't perfect, so how do we change them, how do we make them better? I think theatre is a wonderful way". Later he remarks: "at the end of the day people talk about politics … for me politics are people, politics are the way we live together … people can be better at working together". Collaborator Sergio Amigo tells the cast: "we rehearse for life, we rehearse for changes and we rehearse for the revolution". An important point to take away from the film perhaps then is also how the performers' engagement with the theatre project becomes a project of the self and of the collective which ties together pleasure, educational empowerment and the reinvigoration of the peoples' theatre as a political enterprise. In this was it builds on and intersects with theatre/documentary projects past and present in the line of both Joan Littlewood and more recently Penny Woolcock's *Shakespeare on the Estate* (1994) and *Macbeth on the Estate* (1997).

The hazy golden nostalgia attached to so many working class archetypes and embedded in memoirs of lost class affiliations is conspicuously absent in Wayne and O'Neill's production. Despite the recorded recollections of early political passions, working men's pride, the importance of industry and the power of the unions, the films' participants (and the film itself) are remarkably clear-eyed in their articulation of their experiences of continuity and change. As Tim Strangleman (2014, 1235) notes in his review of working class studies:

> If there is nostalgia present in accounts ... given by working class respondents ..., it is more complex, nuanced and reflective than is often given credit. The voices recorded ... possess a complex relationship with the past. The positive aspects of the past are always grounded in realities ... these voices are quite rightly asking critical questions of the present and the past in comparison.

I argue that the message that emerges across the documentary piece is that individual experiences of political disenchantment, reawakening, bonding and political activism are complicated and unique but that taken together these produce a single story of disenfranchisement, disadvantage and defiance. In another scene, in which Unite Union officer Geoff Southern reflects on Engels' relevance, he suggests: "I actually think ... it's probably exactly the same now ... if you are rich and you've got a lot why would you change anything? It's only people that don't have anything that want change, that make progress."

So how are we finally to understand the film's depiction of continuity and change and its relationship to archetypal notions of the working class in the context of politics and documentary making? My suggestion is to draw on the innovative work of Silke Panse (2008, 66) who analyses the GDR film series *Children of Golzow* (1961–2007) and compares it with the British television series *7-Up* (1964-). Her astute essay on documentary interview practices in socialist versus capitalist societies highlights the ways that change, memory and time is represented in particular ideological contexts. Panse (2008, 70) argues that the socialist film shows how everyday 'mundane' changes in interviewees' lives reflect larger historical changes in "material ways" and that these changes, great and small, can be more ably represented as a collective as well as individual experience. Like that of the *Children of Golzow*, the narrative in TCWC arguably "grows out of a situation" rather than being heavily directed, formatted and thereby 'overcoded.' Also, and ostensibly paradoxically, "by letting us see how the protagonists cope with a 'lack of change'" the film allows "change to become evident, not only historical change ... but material change in the everyday" (Panse 2008, 71). Following Panse's schema, I suggest that TCWC has more in common with films made under collective social conditions than with western public service documentary tradition because it is evident too that "the filmmakers were always on the same side as their subjects" (Panse 2008, 66). As such the socialist documentary "not only witnesses but allows and acknowledges change" (Panse 2008, 71) and de facto refutes the accusation that a politics of class is outmoded and historically redundant.

References

Andreß, H.-J. and Lohmann, H. (eds) (2008) *The Working Poor in Europe: Employment, Poverty and Globalisation*, Cheltenham: Edward Elgar Publishing.

Beynon, H. (2001) Images of Labour; Images of Class. In: S. Rowbotham and H. Beynon (eds) *Looking at Class: Film, Television and the Working Class in Britain*. London: Rivers Oram Press: 25–40

Biressi, A. and Nunn, H. (2010) Shameless?: Picturing the 'underclass' after Thatcherism. In: Hadley L. and Ho E. (eds) *Thatcher and After: Margaret Thatcher and her Afterlife in Contemporary Culture*. Basingstoke: Palgrave Macmillan, 137–157.

Biressi, A. and Nunn, H. (2013) *Class and Contemporary British Culture*. Basingstoke: Palgrave Macmillan.

Charlesworth, S. (2000) *A Phenomenology of Working class Experience*. Cambridge: CUP.

Chignell, H., Franklin, I. and Skoog, K. (eds) (2015) *Regional Aesthetics: Mapping UK Media Cultures*. Basingstoke: Palgrave Macmillan.

Engels, F. (1999 [1844]). *The Condition of the Working Class in England in 1844*. Oxford: Oxford World's Classics.

Gorz, A. (1997). *Farewell to the working class: an essay on post-industrial socialism*. London: Pluto Press.

Hall, S. (1990) The Emergence of Cultural Studies and the Crisis of the Humanities. In *October*, 53: 11–23.

Hart, C. (2016) Metaphor and intertextuality in media framings of the (1984–85) British Miners' Strike: a multimodal analysis. *Discourse and Communication*. (In Press) http://eprints.lancs.ac.uk/79412/.

Holdsworth, N. (2011) *Joan Littlewood's Theatre*, Cambridge: Cambridge University Press.

Hughes, J. (2016) Art, devolution and economic justice at http://blog.poortheatres.manchester.ac.uk/art-devolution-economicjustice/.

Marin-Lamellet, A-L. (2016) The representation of strike in British cinema since 1956: from class to gender and ethnicity. In: Cloarec N, Haigron D and Letort D (eds) *Social Class on British and American Screens*. North Carolina: McFarland and Co, 134–152.

Marx, K. (1963/1845) The Dynamics of Revolution. In: Bottomore T and Rubel M (eds) *Karl Marx: Selected Writings in Sociology and Social Philosophy*. Harmondsworth: Pelican Books, 236–238.

McRobbie, A. (2009) *The Aftermath of Feminism: Gender, Culture and Social Change*. London: Sage.

Murphy, K. (2016) *Behind the Wireless: A History of Early Women at the BBC*. Basingstoke: Palgrave Macmillan.

Nwonka, C.J. (2013) The Condition of the Working Class: what's changed? At http://www.redpepper.org.uk/the-condition-of-the-workingclass-whats-changed/.

Panse, S. (2008) Collective subjectivity in the Children of Golzow vs. alienation in 'Western' Interview documentary. In: Austin T and de Jong W (eds) *Rethinking Documentary: New Perspectives, New Practices*. Maidenhead: Open University Press, 67–81.

Salmon, J. (2016) Union barons in strike plot to topple the Tories: Junior doctors, rail guards and teachers co-ordinate walkouts to increase chaos, *Daily Mail*, 21 August http://www.dailymail.co.uk/news/article-3752116/Union-barons-strike-plot-topple-Tories-Junior-doctors-rail-guards-teachers-ordinate-walkouts-increase-chaos.html.

Savage, M. (2000). *Class Analysis and Social Transformation*. Buckingham: Open University Press.

Savage, M., et al. (2013) A New Model of Social Class? Findings from the BBC's Great British Class Survey Experiment. *Sociology* April 47 (2): 219–250.

Sayer, A. (2005) *The Moral Significance of Class*. Cambridge: Cambridge University Press.

Skeggs, B. (1997) *Formations of Class and Gender: Becoming Respectable*. London: Sage.

Standing, G. (2011) *The Precariat: The New Dangerous Class*. London: Bloomsbury Academic.

Stanley, B. (2015) Cilla Black was the archetypal British working-class pop star, *The Guardian*, https://www.theguardian.com/music/musicblog/2015/aug/03/cilla-black-archetypal-british-working class-pop-star.

Steedman, C. (2013) *An Everyday Life of the English Working Class: Work, Self and Sociability in the Early Nineteenth Century*. Cambridge: CUP.

Strangleman, T. (2014) Remembering Working class Life: History, Sociology and Working class Studies. *Sociology* December 48 (6): 1232–1237.

Sveinsson, P. (2009) Who Cares about the White Working Class? Runnymeade Trust, http://www.runnymedetrust.org/uploads/publications/pdfs/WhoCaresAboutTheWhiteWorkingClass-2009.pdf.

Thompson, E.P. (2013 [1963]) *The Making of the English Working Class*. Harmondsworth: Penguin Classics.

Tyler, I. (2015) Classificatory struggles: class, culture and inequality in neoliberal times. *The Sociological Review*, 63: 493–511.

Walters, S. and Owen, G. (2016) Up the shirkers! Union boss 'Red' Len McCluskey parties the night away at £1,200-a-night Monte Carlo hotel, Daily Mail, 13 August http://www.dailymail.co.uk/news/article-3739380/Up-shirkers-Union-boss-Red-Len-McCluskey-parties-night-away-1-200-night-Monte-Carlo-hotel.html.

Wayne, M. and O'Neill, D. (2013) The Condition of the Working Class: Representation and Praxis. *Working USA: The Journal of Labor and Society* 1089–7011 (16) December: 487–503.

Welshman, J. (2006) *Underclass: a history of the excluded, 1880-2000*, London: Hambledon Continuum.

Williams, G. (ed.) (2014) Settling *Scores: The Media, The Police & The Miners' Strike*. London: Campaign for Press and Broadcasting Freedom.

Williams, R. (1961) *The Long Revolution*. London: Chatto and Windus.

CHAPTER 15

Ghettos and Gated Communities in the Social Landscape of Television: Representations of Class in 1982 and 2015

Fredrik Stiernstedt and Peter Jakobsson

Introduction

This chapter presents an analysis of to what extent different social classes are represented on Swedish television and how the different classes are portrayed in the programmes. The study has a comparative ambition as it replicates a study of class on television from the 1980s and uses the same methods for sampling and principles for analysis as the previous study. This opens up the possibility for systematic comparisons over time. Such comparisons are of interest since the political, social, cultural and televisual landscapes have been transformed in the neoliberal era. The main question we ask in this chapter is whether and how, these social, technical and cultural changes are registered in television's representations of class. From our study, we conclude that the fact that the number of media outlets, channels, genres, business models, etc. have multiplied and that the televisual landscape now offers an abundance of choices and diversity, has not meant an increased diversity in the representation of social class. Our analysis show however a higher degree of 'fragmentation' and 'polarisation' between the social classes in 2015. Different social groups are now visible in different parts of the output, in what can be described as the creation of ghettos and gated communities in the television landscape. For example, the working class has been more or less eradicated from news and factual programming.

The research method used for this chapter is content analysis—what we have elsewhere referred to as distant viewing (Stiernstedt & Jakobsson, 2016)—through which we have found answers to the questions: To what extent are different social classes represented on television? To what extent are different occupations and positions on the labour market represented on television? What differences are there between different genres in relation to the representation of social class? How are the different social classes portrayed and what roles do they get to play on television? The method in itself does not provide clues to how these representations relate to anything outside of themselves, for example if they are reflections of, or even, agents of social change. Television can sometimes be a driver of social change, but often television is responding to society-wide social changes rather than the other way around.

To say that television responds to social change does however not put an end to the story. Television might sometimes try to represent someone's—a producer, a writer, a journalist—perception of reality, but only as seen from a certain perspective, filtered through the dominant ideologies and articulated with the help of the available discursive frameworks (Fairclough 1995; Hall 1977). Furthermore, the televisual image is filtered through professional practices and ideologies and through the institutional knowledge and know-how of the people working in the television industry (Altheide 1976; Schlesinger 1978). It gets even more complicated when the purpose from the beginning is not to represent reality but to tell a story, to entertain, or even to change reality. Consequently, we argue, that it is not possible to make any claims beforehand on causal links and changes in the televisual text, due to societal changes. It is however reasonable to expect that wide-ranging social change will have some implications for the kind of stories told and the kinds of images shown on television. If we are to arrive at any conclusions, however tentative, about the way that the social is mediated through the cultural text we need to take into account both ideological and discursive effects, as well as institutional and medium-specific norms and rules. At the end of this chapter we discuss how the ghettoisation of television relates to both changes within the institution of television and to changes in the social structure and ideology.

The outline of the chapter is as follows: Following the introduction is a section that provides context for the following analysis; here we give a brief picture of, what we believe to be the most pertinent social, cultural and technological changes between 1982 and 2015. Naturally, this section will be unsatisfactory in many ways, since the relevant context is much larger and more complex than what we have space to even begin to sketch out here. The next section gives the reader an overview of the empirical study and a discussion of some of the methodological issues. Then we move on to a presentation of the results that regards the representation of social class on television. In the final section, we discuss the results of our study in light of the contextual changes sketched out in the introduction and suggest some avenues for future work.

Class and Television in the Neoliberal Era

The context and background for the empirical analyses are two distinct systemic transformations that have taken place in Europe as well as in other parts of the world during the last 30 years. These systemic transformations relate to the system of television and the class system. The changes in these systems is in many ways overlapping with and dependent on what we label the 'neoliberal era' (McBride & Teeple 2011). Neoliberalism is, drawing on Michel Foucault's work in *The Birth of Biopolitics* (2008), the transformation of liberal governmentality that "does not ask the state what freedom it will leave to the economy, but asks the economy how its freedom can have a state-creating function" (Foucault 2008, 95). It is safe to say that the consequences of a neoliberal regime of governing—phenomena such as privatisation, new public management and financialisation—has had marked effects on both television (and the media in general) and the class system.

Class

Since the 1980s, there has been a lively discussion within the social sciences and in wider public debate about the relevance of the class-concept. There are two main strands among those who try to proclaim the concept of class as outdated. The first strand argues that the structure of society has changed so that the individual's objective relation to the means of production no longer presents good explanations for (or predictions about) human action (Esping-Andersen 1996, Lash & Urry 1987, Offe 1985). The second strand points to the fact that class has a diminishing relevance as an identity marker and that empirical studies have shown that class consciousness is weak and falling (Beck 2007, Giddens 1991). The first strand has not found any support in the empirical data, the second, however has been at least partly confirmed as data shows that there is an increasing insecurity about the meaning of the concept of class (Crompton 2008) and that there is a significant amount of confusion about what class-position one holds, especially among working class people (Oskarson, Bengtsson & Berglund 2010).

In general, however, the discussions about 'the end of class' are mainly a reflection of contemporary political and economic tendencies. A combination of forces, such as a weakening of the traditional labour movements and parties, a dominating ideology of neo-liberalism that suppresses class-identification, wishful thinking about increasing equality and changes in what concrete forms of work people do (e.g. the move from industrial, to post-industrial societies) has spurred narratives about the irrelevance of the concept of class. David Morley (2009) has even gone as far as suggesting that the concept of class has been 'deleted' (487) from media and cultural studies.

Sociological analyses have, however, repeatedly shown that class still matters (Crompton, 2008; Svallfors, 2006; Wright, 1997), but also that the composition of the different social classes, as well as their relative size and importance have been transformed during the last 30 years. During the 20th century, the most dramatic change in class composition was how the group of landowners (i.e. farmers) became much smaller. Correspondingly, the group often referred to as the 'middle class' holding the contested position between workers and owners of the means of production has grown during the same time-period. The working class on the other hand has been quite static in size—somewhere between 40% and 60% of the population most of the Western world—during the whole of the 20th century (Ahrne, Roman & Franzén, 2000).[1]

A major shift is obviously the changing nature of (especially) working class jobs. Manufacturing and transportation were for a long time the dominant sectors for the working class, and in the 1960s, they made up as much as 40% of the population (Ahrne, Roman & Franzén, 2000). Beginning in the 1970s and accelerating during the 80s and 90s there was an industrial and economic shift in most of the Western world that meant an increasing focus on service work and knowledge work (see for example Florida 2014). This means that the nature of the working class in Western democracies has changed since the 1980s and that service work is now the largest sector within the working class. Some commentators have taken this development, in combination with cheap loans and the spread of higher education to new groups, as a pretext for proclamations about the end of class society as such, and for infamous statements such as 'we are all middle class now'. In reality, however, the working class has been quite static in size. In Sweden, the statistical evidence shows that the working class in 1980 was 51% of the population and in 2010 48% (Ahrne et al., 2000; Oskarson et al., 2010). Nevertheless, developments within the composition of the working class (from industry to service and communication) is an important change. So also is the gender-composition within the working class. Women are more highly represented within the working class than they used to be, and are now in a clear majority among the workers. There have also been tendencies of what Göran Therborn (1981) calls the 'proletarianisation' of the middle class and especially the lower tier of white-collar workers. Even though higher education is more widespread and university diplomas are increasingly demanded in the labour market, the actual tasks of clerks and professionals has, at least to some extent become more precarious, de-professionalised and de-skilled (see Stiernstedt, 2015 for an example from the media industries).

---

1   The data is Swedish but the tendency is similar in the whole Western world.

Television

The television landscape has also undergone changes during the same period. Following John Ellis (2000) it is possible to summarise the changes in the television system as a transformation from an era of 'scarcity' to an era of 'plenty'. Privatisation, commercialisation and technological developments (satellite, internet) have resulted in a television landscape that is fragmented and where a multitude of channels are competing over different, increasingly well-defined and narrow, niche-audiences (Turner & Tay 2009). As stated above there are multiple driving forces behind this development, but the neoliberal era, with its focus on so-called de-regulation and privatisation is one of them (Harcourt 2003, Van Cuilenburg & McQuail 2003). But economic interests on behalf of the advertisers also pushed a development from 'mass' to 'niche'-marketing and helped pave the way for cable television (Turow 2007) as well as a move of televisual content to an online environment.

To take one example, the data from 1982 that we use in this article was collected from two (public service) television channels. They were at the time the only two channels broadcasting in Sweden. The data from 2015 comes from the five largest television stations in a television landscape where there are no less than 63 television channels operating in the terrestrial television network (and thousands available via cable and digital distribution). This has had consequences for audience behavior. Even if the reach of television as a medium is the same as it was in the early 1980s (about 70–80% of the population watches television on a daily basis) the audience has become increasingly segmented and fragmented. The degree of change should not be overstated however; research shows that the large brands and channels still gathers large shares of the audience (Bjur & Bolin 2014) and that patterns of audience behavior is much more habitual and consistent than is often imagined (Gentikow 2010).

Between the 1980s and the 2010s there have also been important changes in the genre system and the output of television. For one thing, the importance of formatted shows and programme imports have increased, not least since the many new channels need material to fill the increasing amount of broadcasting-hours. The reality tv genre, and programmes containing 'ordinary people', have for example become an important and in some segments a dominant form of broadcasting (Bonner 2003, Hill 2005; Keane & Moran 2008). The importance of reality television in relation to representations of social class has been widely discussed in previous research and the often degrading representations and visualisation of the working class in this genre has been analysed and criticised (Tyler & Bennett, 2010).

The Study

We explore and analyse class on television as expressed in a specific television landscape (Sweden) at two specific moments in time (1982 and 2015). Only half of the material analysed are, however, Swedish productions, and the rest consist of imported materials. The public service channels in Sweden broadcasts circa 70% Swedish productions but the amount of Swedish productions in the commercial channels varies between 5–60% (Wändahl 2015). These numbers do not reflect however the increasing prevalence of adaptations of international formats, which are produced locally and thus counts as domestic productions, but follow the guidelines of an internationally distributed original.[2] A general trend is that American formats, and format imports, are dominant in many parts of the world, alongside the already high ratio of direct imports of US programmes. In this study, 28% of the programmes are produced in the US and even more are, as discussed, adaptations of US formats. The results presented here are thus, at least partly, transferable and valid for television more generally, in countries residing within the televisual cultural sphere dominated by US programming.[3]

The study is a content analysis with the ambition to create a database that is representative of Swedish mainstream television in 2015. This means that we have only included channels with a daily reach above 10% (MMS, 2015). The study includes about 1000 hours of television material from 2015, in comparison with 336 hours in the study from 1982. The study from 2015 includes the two public service broadcasters in Sweden (SVT1 and SVT2) and three commercial broadcasters (TV3, TV4 and Channel 5). The commercial channels in the sample did not exist in 1982 and this material thus only consists of the public service broadcasters (SVT1 and SVT2).

Advertising dominates the output in 2015 (21%), followed by reality television (16%) and drama (15%).

The analytical units in this study are the persons who appear on television and the sampling unit is time. Sample images were created by pausing the recording at 10-min intervals. The benefit of this method is that it cuts across all genres and types of output and gives a representative picture of what kind of

---

2 Aslama and Pantti (Aslama & Pantti, 2007) has studied national adaptations of international formats and shown that there are some variations in these adaptations due to the changing national context.

3 See for example Banerjee (2002) and Straubhaar (2015) for case-studies of the limits of the US domination of television and the emergence of alternative cultural spheres to the dominant English-speaking sphere.

individuals are most frequently portrayed in the material as a whole. In addition to the persons appearing in each image, each sampling unit was also classified according to more general attributes, such as genre. In total, we have collected circa 5500 sampling units and 10 000 analytical units (since some of the sampling units contained several persons).

We coded the analytical units (i.e. each person appearing in a sample image) in relation to variables such as age, gender, occupation and class, as well as in relation to how they are partaking and how they are portrayed within the programme. All coding has been done with the programme as context, for example when deciding what importance the person has or what occupation s/he holds. The most important variables in the analysis are:

- Class;
- Occupation;
- Gender;
- Nationality; and
- Genre.

We use a definition of the term 'class' that acknowledges that a person's formal position in relation to the mode of production is of primary importance in determining class position but also include a person's status, power and influence over his/her own as well as others living conditions (Wright 1997). Hence we operate with three possible class positions: (1) working class people who sustain themselves by selling their labour, including people who are self-employed (2) upper-class people who live off capital and/or off the labour of others, but also including for example high-ranking politicians, and (3) middle-class people who cover the broad range of functionaries who deal with capital (administrators and clerks, middle managers, etc.) and who also include professionals such as academics, doctors, lawyers and journalists. Although the latter group must also sell their labour power in order to sustain themselves, they have a relative degree of autonomy in relation to production. In comparison to the working class that means that the middle class have more power to affect their working conditions as well as their living conditions in general. The coding scheme defines the upper class in a deliberately narrow way, as "persons who due to their economic position, their place in the social hierarchy or position in their work life, can exert a large social influence". This definition excludes owners of small and medium businesses, even if they live off the labour of others. In the television programmes the upper class is composed of for example successful entrepreneurs, wealthy business-owners, rentiers, top-tier venture capitalists, large-scale employers and the like.

Both of these ways of measuring class rely on determining the occupation of the persons appearing on television, and in general, there is no difficulty in doing so. Occupational information is often given directly and if not, is generally revealed in other ways, for example through activities undertaken by the person, clothing (e.g., uniforms) or from the general context of the programme. The occupations of 65% of the persons in the sample were identified. It is, however, sometimes possible to code class based on factors other than occupation (e.g., explicit references to capital and resources, or representations of certain kinds of lifestyles). Thus, 77% of all persons in the material were coded according to class position.

Intercoder agreement is crucial for content analysis. During the research process, several measures were taken to ensure agreement, such as coder training, test coding, joint coding and daily coder meetings with the coder group (made up of five people) to discuss difficult aspects and interesting cases. Several tests for intercoder agreement were also conducted and analysed according to Fleiss' Kappa, Cohen's' Kappa and Krippendorff's Alpha. Only one of the variables had to be excluded due to weak reliability, while the others gained sufficient reliability according to all three of the measures mentioned above. The average intercoder agreement for all of the variables—according to Krippendorff's Alpha—was 0.770 (H: 939, L: 687).[4]

Class on Television

The changes in Western societies, the media landscape, and television in particular, that are described in the previous section raises the expectation that television's representation of the social landscape in 2015 should be different from in 1982. It is not only a question of how the world has changed economically, socially, demographically etc., but also how these changes are understood and discussed. An increasingly hegemonic neoliberalism and the emergence of new discursive formations during the last 30 years, as discussed above, mean that the position of enunciation for the televisual text has been fundamentally altered. The commercialisation of television that in many European countries started in the 1970's and 80's was sold to the public as reforms aiming for increasing diversity and pluralism (the result, however, was different, as well as the motives behind the commercialisation). The number of new channels, new formats, and at least one new genre (reality television), together with the

---

4   The methodological description of the project has been published previously, see Stiernstedt & Jakobsson (2016).

continued pressure on the commercial media to cater to its audiences tastes, also means that it would be highly surprising to find that the social world of television hasn't changed in any significant way since the beginning of the 1980's. Knowing that, we also know however, from both media, literary and visual studies, that genres and traditions of storytelling are in some respects remarkably stable. Some visual motifs, certain dramatic characters and story formats have a very long history. Any one-sided hypotheses such as 'the song remains the same' or 'everything has changed' should thus be rejected from the start.

Nevertheless, it is a somewhat surprising finding that the representation of working class people on television is remarkably stable. Within the total amount of people that was present on television (visually, audible or both) in 2015 11% belongs to the working class, 70% belongs to the middle class and 19% to the upper class. The corresponding figures from 1982 was 12%, 66% and 22% (see Table 15.1). Previous studies have shown that television from its very inception in the 1950s has presented a social world that in some respects differs strongly from the surrounding society. The gallery of social types that appear on television typically consists of middle class persons, often from the upper middle class. Upper class persons have traditionally always been more common than working class persons in television and the upper class is also heavily overrepresented in comparison with its size in the actual population (Butsch 2003; Butsch & Glennon 1983; Nowak & Ross, 1989).

The lack of change is interesting and opens a range of questions, about genre and narrative, as well as of production and audience composition. Even though such questions mainly fall outside of the range of this study, some remarks can be made. The dominance of the middle-class on television can for example be specified as a dominance of a 'media class'. Even when we exclude journalists and people employed by the broadcasters themselves (studio hosts etc.) it is clear that people in media related professions are the most dominant group on television, that is people working within the media or related

TABLE 15.1 *The social classes as represented on television in 1982 and 2015.*

	1982	2015
Working class %	12	11 (−1)
Middle class %	66	70 (+4)
Upper class %	22	19 (−3)
Total %	100	100

industries such as singers, performers, designers, authors, actors, artists, etc. In addition, fictional content—TV-drama and films—are overpopulated with people with middle class professions. One reason for this might be that these professions offer environments that are more exciting and offer more dramatic opportunities than working class jobs. But previous research has shown that social status and the class-background among producers and writers also has a role in this (Ross 2008, 54). The many popular films and TV-series with a focus on working class environment also show that this is a matter of choice from the side of the producers rather than due to the rules of the creation of televisual drama.[5]

Our study also provides information on what kind of jobs and professions that people on television have (see Table 15.2). With this information, the makeup of the social classes on television becomes clearer. We can for example see that a large part of the upper class persons on television consists of high-ranking politicians, i.e. members of parliament, ministers, and presidents.

It also becomes clear that a large part of the middle class people represented belong to the upper middle class, with professions that require education at an advanced level. As noted above these people often have artistic and creative jobs within the cultural sector. The working class people that are visible on television are to a large extent people working in the service sector with only a few having the kinds of jobs that were more representative of the working class in 1982, i.e. jobs in construction, manufacturing and transportation.

TABLE 15.2 *Occupations among persons on television in 2015.*

Politicians, high ranking %	9
Management, high ranking %	3
Professions requiring Masters degree %	14
Cultural work, requiring Masters degree %	22
Professions requiring Bachelors degree %	6
Cultural work, requiring Bachelors degree %	30
Service and sales %	9
Construction, manufacturing, transportation %	2
Other occupations %	5
Total %	100

---

5 A notable example of this is the British soap-opera focusing on everyday life and on working class people, with examples such as EastEnders, Cathy Come Home and Brookside (Ross, 2008, 52).

TABLE 15.3 *Gender among different social classes in the television output in 1982 and 2015.*

	1982		Total %	2015		Total %
	Men	Women		Men	Women	
Working class	66	34	100	54 (−12)	46 (+12)	100
Middle class	77	23	100	61 (−16)	39 (+16)	100
Upper class	77	23	100	45 (−32)	55 (+32)	100
All classes	75	25	100	57 (−12)	43 (+12)	100

This is not surprising and probably a reflection of changes in the actual social world. As we have shown elsewhere it might also partly be explained by the fact that most working class people in reality television—the genre with the largest population of working class people—are people with the kind social skills that are required both within sales and services and for participating in a reality television show (Stiernstedt & Jakobsson 2016).

A more careful analysis however also finds some significant changes in how class is represented on television in 2015 compared to in 1982. One such change is how the social classes on television are gendered (see Table 15.3).

The representation of the working class has changed from an overrepresentation of men to a more equal gender balance in 2015 (54% men and 46% women). Just as the number of service workers on television has increased this also reflects changes in the actual world, where 'feminisation' of the working class means that there are more women than men occupying working class jobs today. This could however also be an indication of the fact that women's role in society in general has changed since 1982, along with the relative success of the feminist movement. The latter interpretation is also supported by the fact that the upper class on television consists of more women than men (45% men and 55% women) in 2015. This is not consistent with the results from 1982 where women were equally represented in the middle and upper class (23%).

Another difference between our results and the results from the previous study is that the social classes are not represented in the same way regarding their nationality (Table 15.4). In 1982, it was mostly Swedish working class people that were represented on television and this is no longer the case. Instead, it is twice as common that a working class person originates from another European country or from the US.

TABLE 15.4 *Nationality among different social classes in 1982 and 2015.*

	Sweden		Europe (except Sweden)		USA		Other	
	1982	2015	1982	2015	1982	2015	1982	2015
Working class %	6	5 (−1)	5	9 (+4)	6	9 (+3)	11	7 (−4)
Middle class %	68	70 (+2)	64	56 (−8)	73	53 (−20)	62	50 (−12)
Upper class %	8	10 (+2)	19	9 (−10)	7	18 (+11)	9	7 (−2)
Unable to code for social class	18	15	12	26	14	20	18	36

This is likely also a reflection of changes in the actual world, where many working class jobs have moved abroad, within both manufacturing and the service industry. It also tells of the increase of migrant workers that Sweden's entry into the EU has brought with it. Even if the number of migrant workers are relatively few it could still be argued that the image of the worker has changed and it is this changed image that is being reflected in the symbolic world of television. The upper class also typically has another nationality than Swedish in our material and is most often a US-citizen. That the upper class is non-Swedish is in agreement with the results from 1982 even though it has changed nationality from primarily European to US. This is probably due to the fact that there are more US imports in 2015 and that the 'most powerful country in the world' also is portrayed from the perspective from its most powerful citizens, whether it is the president or Hollywood celebrities.

The most significant change in how class is represented on television between 1982 and 2015 has to do with in what genre and what type of television output the different social classes are most frequent (Table 15.5). In this respect, the biggest change is that working class people have become almost invisible in news and factual programming compared to the data from the 1980s. In 2015, it is only one third of the relative number of working class people in these genres compared to with how many it was in 1982. Only four percent of the people appearing in news and factual programming in 2015 belong to the working class, whereas 69% belong to the middle class and 27% to the upper class.

This result indicates that news and factual programming has undergone radical changes since 1982 concerning what is considered newsworthy and relevant to depict as well as in its priorities of who should be given voice.

TABLE 15.5 *Social classes in different types of television output 1982 and 2015.*

	News 1982	News 2015	Drama 1982	Drama 2015	Entertainment 1982	Entertainment 2015
Workers %	11	4 (−7)	10	14 (+4)	10	6 (−4)
Middle class %	69	69 (−)	65	73 (+8)	84	85 (+1)
Upper class %	20	27 (+7)	25	13 (−12)	6	9 (+3)
Total %	100	100	100	100	100	100

TABLE 15.6 *The class composition of reality television in 2015.*

Working class %	17
Middle class %	53
Upper class %	30
Total %	100

Workers were already underrepresented in news and factual programming in 1982 but 30 years on they have more or less been eradicated from these programmes.

It is however interesting to note that the relative invisibility of working class people within the news does not mean that working class people are equally invisible in all genres on television. In the same way that the relative number of working class people has gone down in the news, they have gone up in feature films and television drama. Reality television—the only genuinely new televisual genre since 1982 (Table 15.6)—also stand out in this respect and features more working class people than any other genre on television.

As a genre, reality television is complex and multifaceted and incorporates many different sub-genres and styles. In the context of this chapter it is tentatively defined as television programmes and formats that claim to represent reality and to be (at least partially) unscripted and to present real people (Hill 2005). During coding of the material, the coder group also used the industrial classification when coding for genre, accessed through the help of the database IMDb or the homepages of the television channels broadcasting the programme. The results show that there are twice as many working class people in reality television as in television in general. Even if the general pattern still holds that the middle class are dominating the output and that the upper class is heavily overrepresented it is still obvious that reality television has brought with it something new to television in general.

Others have described reality television as being part of a broader pattern, the 'demotic turn', in which ordinary people are allowed into the media (Turner 2010). It is interesting to note here, as pointed out by Helene Wood and Beverly Skeggs (2011) that the term 'ordinary people' in relation to reality TV is nothing more than a euphemism for working class people. We have argued elsewhere that this is only partly true in the case of reality television, since one of the most striking finds from our study is the large proportion of upper class people that are being put on display through the genre (Stiernstedt & Jakobsson, 2016). Now, when the figures from reality television are put next to the figures from the other genres, it is however also possible to put the so-called demotic turn within a larger context. It seems to us that what we can witness in the figures from 2015 is a ghettoisation of television, or the creation of 'gated communities', in which the social classes are compartmentalised into different channels, different genres and different programmes. The upper and middle classes have erected high walls around the news and factual programming and the working class is instead invited into the ghetto-like world of reality television.

Discussion

The results from this 'distant viewing' of contemporary television shows that the development of television as a medium at least to some extent is analogous with developments in society, the static class composition on television for example resembles a relative stasis in the class structure in the real world. Other tendencies, such as the feminisation and 'internationalisation' of the working class also reveals themselves in the television programmes we analysed. The most interesting, and perhaps worrying, find in the present study—what we have referred to as the ghettoisation of television—needs however to be discussed in a more nuanced manner than seeing it as a mere reflection of processes in society. Even if it is true that a similar development has affected western societies during the last 30 or 40 years, with widening gaps and deepening social inequalities (Piketty 2014), representations are never merely reflections, but are both mediators of- and are mediated by numerous interests, perspectives, assumptions, relations, processes, etc. One important aspect in trying to understand the gated community of contemporary news and factual programming, and the ghetto of reality television, is the neoliberal ideology that has been triumphant during the past decades (Hall, Massey & Rustin 2013).

The social landscape of television has been constructed according to the worldview of the neoliberal ideology and its perspective on society's winners and losers. We have already described how one of the most important changes for the working class between 1982 and 2015 lies in its decreased power and loss of influence in society. Socialist parties, organised labour and workers in general have been in retreat ever since the beginning of the 1980's. This is also a factor in trying to understand why there are less workers on the news in 2015 than in 1982. The commercialisation of television is yet another reason for its ghettoisation since commercial actors are less likely to allow critical voices on television. It could also be argued that the results presented here speaks to a more general tendency within the media that is connected to an increased diversification: the tendency that more channels and more niche programming facilitates a situation in which audiences become fragmented and programming increasingly personalised (Bjur & Bolin 2014; Gentikow 2010). The most likely explanation for our results is however a combination of all of the above.

As important as understanding the causes is however to understand the effects of the transformation of television into an instrument for the separation of the social classes. Nick Couldry (2010), among others, has discussed the importance of 'voice' and the need that the media, in democratic societies, to be organised in such a way that it gives voice not only to the powerful and to social elites (Couldry 2010). The ghettoisation of television is however a step in the other direction and it might have destructive effects on the public sphere and for democratic society as such. Television has of course always been an elite medium in the sense that the upper-class and middle-class has been strongly over-represented in the television output, and there are other more democratic media channels today, that didn't exist in 1982, but television is still an important medium that plays a major role in many people's lives.

The ghettoisation of television can also be seen as in itself an obstacle towards achieving social justice. The tendency described here is not only an effect of a weaker working class and a decreasing identification among people as belonging to the working class, but it can also be an obstacle in creating the social organisation required to reverse these social trends. Television can even be understood as partaking in a 'class warfare' directed towards the working class, where practices such as symbolic annihilation, shaming and ridiculing are some of the weapons for this symbolic violence (see for example Biressi & Nunn 2008). Television is then understood as a way of creating norms and reproducing cultural patterns, as well as forming ideas about different social classes. As shown by for example Imogen Tyler (2015) specific television programmes have been used directly as a pretext for certain political decisions.

The fact that some television programmes have showed the working class as having 'low morals' or being lazy has for example motivated paternalistic and controlling political interventions.

What is missing from the picture provided here however is knowledge about the presence or absence of the working class in other media than television. There is clearly more research needed that maps the access that people from different classes have to different media.

References

Ahrne, G., Roman, C. and Franzén, M. (2000) *Det Sociala Landskapet: En Sociologisk Beskrivning Av Sverige Från 50-Tal till 90-Tal*. Göteborg: Korpen.

Altheide, D.L. (1976) *Creating Reality: How TV News Distorts Events*. Beverly Hills: Sage.

Aslama, M. and Pantti, M. (2007) Flagging Finnishness: Reproducing National Identity in Reality Television. *Television & New Media* 8 (1): 49–67.

Banerjee, I. (2002) The Locals Strike Back? Media Globalisation and Localisation in the New Asian Television Landscape. *International Communication Gazette* 64 (6): 517–35.

Beck, U. (2007) Beyond Class and Nation: Reframing Social Inequalities in a Globalising World. *The British Journal of Sociology* 58 (4): 679–705.

Biressi, A. and Nunn, H. (2008) Bad Citizens: The Class Politics of Lifestyle Television. In: Palmer, G. (ed) *Exposing Lifestyle Television: The Big Reveal*. Aldershot: Ashgate, 15–24.

Bjur, J. and Bolin, G. (2014) Massa, Individualiserad, Nätverkad: En historisk återblick på Framtiden För Radio Och TV. In: Carlsson, U. and Facht, U. (eds) *MedieSverige 2014: Statistik Och Analys*. Göteborg: Nordicom.

Bonner, F. (2003) *Ordinary Television: Analysing Popular TV*. Thousand Oaks, Calif.: Sage.

Butsch, R. (2003) A Half Century of Class and Gender in American TV Domestic Sitcoms. *Cercles* 8: 16–34.

Butsch, R. and Glennon, L.M. (1983) Social Class: Frequency Trends in Domestic Situation Comedy, 1946–1978. *Journal of Broadcasting* 27 (1): 77–81.

Couldry, N. (2010). Why voice matters: culture and politics after neoliberalism. London: Sage.

Crompton, R. (2008) *Class and Stratification*. Cambridge: Polity.

Ellis, J. (2000) *Seeing Things : Television in the Age of Uncertainty*. London: I.B. Tauris.

Esping-Andersen, G. (1996) *Welfare States in Transition: National Adaptations in Global Economies*. London: Sage.

Fairclough, N. (1995) *Media Discourse*. London: Edward Arnold.

Florida, R. (2014) *The Rise of the Creative Class–Revisited: Revised and Expanded*. New York: Basic books.

Foucault, M. (2008) *The Birth of Biopolitics: Lectures at the Collège de France, 1978–1979*. Basingstoke: Palgrave Macmillan.

Gentikow, B. (2010) Television in New Media Environments. In: Gripsrud, J. (ed) *Relocating Television: Television in the Digital Context*. London: Routledge, 141–55.

Giddens, A. (1991) *Modernity and Self-Identity: Self and Society in the Late Modern Age*. Cambridge: Polity Press.

Hall, S. (1977). Culture, the Media and the 'Ideological Effect'. In: Curran J., Gurevitch M. and Woollacott J. (eds). *Mass Communication and Society*. London: Edward Arnold.

Hall, S., Massey, D. and Rustin, M. (2013) After Neoliberalism: Analysing the Present. *Soundings* 53: 8–22.

Harcourt, A. (2003) The Regulation of Media Markets in Selected EU Accession States in Central and Eastern Europe. *European Law Journal* 9 (3): 316–40.

Hill, A. (2005) *Reality TV: Audiences and Popular Factual Television*. London: Routledge.

Keane, M, and Moran, A (2008) Television's New Engines. *Television & New Media* 9 (2): 155–69.

Lash, S. and Urry, J. (1987) *The End of Organised Capitalism*. Cambridge: Polity.

McBride, S. and Teeple, G. (2011) *Relations of Global Power: Neoliberal Order and Disorder*. Toronto: University of Toronto Press.

MMS. 2015. MMS Årsrapport 2015. http://mms.se/wp-content/uploads/_dokument/rapporter/tv-tittande/ar/Årsrapporter/Årsrapport%202015.pdf.

Morley, D. (2009) Mediated Class-ifications: Representations of Class and Culture in Contemporary British Television. *European Journal of Cultural Studies* 12 (4): 487–508.

Nowak, K. and Ross, S. (1989) Samhällsklasserna I TV. In: Nowak, K (ed) *Folket i TV: Demografi och Social Struktur i Televisionens Innehåll*. Stockholm: Centrum för masskommunikationsforskning vid Stockholms Universitet, 59–78.

Offe, C. (1985) *Disorganised Capitalism: Contemporary Transformations of Work and Politics*. Cambridge: Polity.

Oskarson, M., Bengtsson, M. and Berglund, T. (2010) *En Fråga Om Klass: Levnadsförhållanden, Livsstil, Politik*. Malmö: Liber.

Piketty, T. (2014) *Capital in the Twenty-First Century*. Cambridge, Mass.; Belknap Press of Harvard University Press.

Ross, S. (2008) Klasstolkningar. En receptionsanalys av hur klassaspekter uppfattas i Tre kärlekar, Falcon Crest och TV-nyheter. Stockholm: JMK.

Schlesinger, P. (1978) *Putting "Reality" Together: BBC News*. London: Constable.

Stiernstedt, F. 2015. The Automatic DJ?: Control, Automation and Creativity in Commercial Music Radio. In: Bonini, T. an Belen, M. (eds) *Radio Audiences and Participation in the Age of Network Society*. London: Routledge, 137–154.

Stiernstedt, F. and Jakobsson, P. (2016) Watching Reality from a Distance: Class, Genre and Reality Television. *Media, Culture & Society, Online first*, August 2016.

Straubhaar, J. (2015) Global, Regional, Transnational, Translocal. *Media Industries* 1 (3). http://www.mediaindustriesjournal.org/index.php/mij/article/view/105.

Svallfors, S. (2006) *The Moral Economy of Class: Class and Attitudes in Comparative Perspective*. Stanford, Calif.: Stanford University Press.

Therborn, G. (1981) *Klasstrukturen I Sverige 1930–1980: Arbete, Kapital, Stat Och Patriarkat*. Lund: Zenit.

Turner, G. (2010) *Ordinary People and the Media: The Demotic Turn*. London: Sage.

Turner, G and Tay, J. (2009) *Television Studies after TV: Understanding Television in the Post-Broadcast Era*. New York: Routledge.

Turow, J. (2007) *Breaking up America: Advertisers and the New Media World*. Chicago: University of Chicago Press.

Tyler, I. (2015) Classificatory Struggles: Class, Culture and Inequality in Neoliberal Times. *The Sociological Review* 63 (2): 493–511.

Tyler, I. and Bennett, B. (2010) 'Celebrity Chav': Fame, Femininity and Social Class. *European Journal of Cultural Studies* 13 (3): 375–93.

Van Cuilenburg, J. and McQuail, D. (2003). Media Policy Paradigm Shifts towards a New Communications Policy Paradigm. *European Journal of Communication* 18 (2): 181–207.

Wändahl, M. 2015. Svenskt Medieutbud 2015. Myndigheten för press, radion och tv. http://www.radioochtv.se/Documents/Publikationer/Svenskt_medieutbud_2015.pdf.

Wood, H. & Skeggs, B. (ed.) (2011). *Reality television and class*. London: BFI.

Wright, E.O. (1997) *Class Counts: Comparative Studies in Class Analysis*. Cambridge: Cambridge University Press.

CHAPTER 16

Class, Culture and Exploitation: The Case of Reality TV

Milly Williamson

Introduction

There has been much important work on the appeal of 'ordinary celebrity' on reality TV, its circulation in the wider media, and its symbolic and representational importance in the public arena. Television culture and the 'ordinary celebrity' that it has produced, have played a significant role in providing working class audiences with popular images of meritocracy—fuelled as it has been historically by the myth that anyone can 'make it' and the sham that fame and fortune are open to all and are desirable (Dyer 1979). Contemporary television culture has advanced that myth, as more and more ordinary people seem to 'make it' on reality TV, even while they are often denigrated and exploited (Skeggs 2009; Skeggs and Wood 2012; Williamson 2010).

However, there has been less examination of the political economy of ordinary celebrity in the television industry, in particular the exploitation of 'ordinary' working class people on reality TV, and its increasingly important role in the profitability of television in a changing technological and commercial environment. This chapter will examine the role of ordinary celebrity in the television industry from the 1990s on and will suggest that the producers of reality television came to rely on formats built around 'ordinary' celebrity in order to undermine the power of unions representing workers in the US and UK television industries and increase the rate of exploitation of workers in the industry—including the temporarily celebrified ordinary contestants of reality TV.

The Growth of Reality TV: History and Context

The growth and profitability of 'ordinary celebrity' has been driven by reality TV. Television has, from its inception, produced a type of fame that is based on 'the personality' (Langer 1981). Television personalities have always been distinguished by their 'will to ordinariness', and have been 'experienced as *familiar*' (Langer 1981, 355). Television has recently put this longstanding personality-celebrity to work in ways that have been extremely profitable, where the performances of ordinary celebrified[1] participants on reality TV have been exploited to great effect for the television industry, but not for those caught up in its maws.

Reality TV developed rapidly at the end of the 20th century because of the way that it was able to respond to challenges and changes facing the international commercial television industry (Deery 2014, Magder 2004, Raphael 2004). While there are particular national contexts involved in understanding this process, there are also several interlinked broad trends whose reach have been global: a policy environment which promoted deregulation, increased competition and commercialisation; the introduction of new technology, channel proliferation and media convergence in this highly marketised moment. The result was rising broadcasting costs and a simultaneous loss of revenue which lead to a series of cost-cutting exercises.

The combination of technological innovation and the ideologically driven shift in policy approaches were crucial for shaping the television industry in the 1990s and into the 21st century. The development of new technology (firstly VCR and cable, followed by satellite and digital technology) created multi-channel TV at a time when governments across the globe carried out deregulation, facilitated privatisation, and generally favoured competition and markets. In the UK, Margaret Thatcher's Conservative government pushed through a contentious Broadcasting Act (1990) that encouraged market competition and mergers and that abolished the existing regulator (Independent Broadcasting Authority), placing broadcasting regulation in the hands of the television companies themselves through the light touch Independent Television Commission from 1991 and later OFCOM. The Act also allowed for the introduction of new regulation-lite terrestrial and satellite channels and forced the publically funded BBC to source 25% of its output from independent companies. A series of mergers ensued that used public money to finance the private sector and this enabled the creation of large media conglomerates who now dominate the field.

In the US, the 1996 Telecommunications Act lifted caps on cross-media ownership, deregulated the converging broadcasting and telecommunications markets and opened up markets to competition by removing further regulation on distribution caps. The result was staggering media concentration. The development of digital technology and the end of spectrum scarcity (which enabled channel proliferation) had a huge democratic potential—the

---

[1] A term Olivier Driessens uses to distinguish between long term cultural trends of 'celebritisation' and the 'celebrification' of individuals and social groups (2013: 643).

possibility of opening up access to television to a wider range of voices from working class and ethnic minority backgrounds and other groups marginalised on the basis of gender, sexuality or disability. Instead, it occurred in a policy environment that pushed deregulation, amped up competition and encouraged mergers and acquisitions. And this has, as Murdoch and Golding argue, "exacerbated ...[media] concentration and centralisation" (2002,125) rather than encouraging horizontal access and control.

Yet, despite the growing power of huge media conglomerates, this policy environment did not secure the broadcasting industry from its own illogical economic logic. For there were two interconnected consequences of the proliferation of channels in this context which commercial television cannot solve in the long-term: the first was the fragmentation of audiences and the second was a resulting drop in advertising revenue, upon which commercial television depends. From the late 1980s in the US and the 1990s in the UK, broadcasters found it increasingly difficult to win mass audiences to 'peak' or 'primetime' television programming because, as the number of channels grew, so the size of audiences for any one channel dropped. Large sections of the audience were tuning in to niche and specialist channels and audiences for the large terrestrial broadcasters fell as a result.

The television industry responded in several ways to the crisis, including commercialising programmes as fully as possible (Deery 2014) and embarking on a series of cost-cutting exercises. As in any industry, one of the main ways that broadcasters sought to cut costs was by attacking the condition of the workers who produce the programmes (Sparks 2007). In the case of television, significant above and below-the-line staff cutbacks in broadcasting systems resulted in the US, Britain and Europe, and working conditions deteriorated significantly for those left in the industry, with short term contracts replacing full-time jobs, lower pay, and greater job insecurity (Sparks 2007).

Even so, broadcasters were under pressure to search for new ways of reaching both large audiences to attract advertising revenue—particularly those segments of the audience that advertisers are keen to reach—young adults with disposable incomes. Reality TV seemed to offer a solution to the problem of falling advertising revenue by attracting relatively young audiences in large numbers. For example, in the US, the reality TV show *Survivor* (2000—) enabled CBS to compete with NBC for primetime audiences. Thursday evening primetime is the most lucrative for networks in the US because it is the most expensive advertising slot; advertisers are willing to pay a premium to reach audiences on that evening in order to boost weekend sales. By the end of the 1990s NBC had this slot cornered with a range of sitcoms and dramas such as *ER, Friends* and *Will and Grace*. A thirty second advert slot during these shows cost between $465,000 to $620,000 (Madger 2004, 138). In 2001 CBS decided to air *Survivor* in direct competition with NBC at 8:00pm on a Thursday evening, a seemingly bold move because channels usually avoided direct competition with NBC and instead programmed around it. It paid off—by the end of the 2001 season of *Survivor*, CBS had doubled its Thursday evening audience from 10 to 20.5 million viewers and substantially increased its ratings among young adults (Magder 2004, 139).

But this was less of a risk than at first it might have appeared. From the perspective of network executives, one of the advantages of reality TV formats is the reduction of risk associated with new production. Broadcasters can buy in internationally traded, already successful, pre-packaged shows. Format TV, such as programmes like *Survivor*, are easily adaptable to different national cultures and television environments, cost nothing in development expenditure to broadcasters, and come with a successful track record abroad. Format television in general has the ability to inexhaustibly generate new content for familiar formats (Turner 2010, 19) and this fits the needs of advertisers who want predictability for their investment. *Survivor*, having already aired in Europe under a different title and proven popular with young audiences, reduced the risk to CBS, who also saved on the development costs that would have had to go into original production.

But more important than either of these considerations was the fact that the co-executive producer of the programme, Mark Burnett, presold 30 second advertising spots and in-show sponsorship to eight advertisers who each paid $4 million for the ad time, product placement in the show and a website link (Magder 2004, 140). It was this guarantee of advertising revenue that ensured that *Survivor* was aired on Thursday evening primetime television. The success of *Survivor* was based on persuading advertisers to invest in the programme in advance of airing—it was successfully sold, not to audiences in the US, but to the advertising wings of General Motors, Visa, Reebok and others. If Burnett had not generated advertising prior to airing the show, (creating guaranteed profits for CBS), it is unlikely that the broadcaster would have aired it on primetime at all.

However, in the following decade the price of ad slots began falling and continued to decline so that by 2013, the highest paid slot had dropped significantly to $264, 575 per 30 second slot (and this for the highly successful sitcom *The Big Bang Theory*, 2007—, CBS) while *Survivor* took tenth place in the pricing for 30 second ad slots dropping to just over $110,000.[2] While this

---

2 Mahapatra, L. (2013) The Economics of Prime Time: How Much Does It Cost To Place A 30 Second Ad In A Prime Time Weeknight TV Show? Oct 14, http://www.ibtimes.com/economics-prime-time-how-much-does-it-cost-place-30-second-ad-prime-time-weeknight-tv-1424544/ accessed July 28 2016.

still generates over $2 million per episode, the pressure of declining advertising revenue continues to put pressure on the commercial television industry to cut costs.

Another significant area of pressure for broadcasters is the cyclical tendency towards rising costs and debts associated with above-the-line costs. Reality TV enables production companies and broadcasters to side-step some of these costs by avoiding salaries to established talent. For instance, *The Big Bang Theory* may be the highest earning show on American television, but is also one of the most expensive to make, and it still does not pull in the ad revenue of primetime shows ten years ago. Much of this cost increase is due to the 'talent' or the stars of the show. The three principle actors had an initial annual contract of $350,000 per episode, but this grew to $1 million per episode as the popularity of the show grew, contributing significantly to its soaring production costs. Their co-stars earn between £100,00–£750,000 per episode each[3] (the two female actors taking the smallest salaries) meaning that the total cost of the star talent per episode is nearly $6 million. This makes a significant dent in the advertising revenue that the show generates per episode.

Reality TV seems to offer a solution to this problem by doing away with expensive actors altogether and bypassing expensive celebrity talent (at least temporarily) because it is based on the unscripted performances of ordinary people who are paid next to nothing, or nothing at all, for their performances. In short, ordinary people have been used by the producers and broadcasters of reality TV as a cost cutting exercise. The celebrification of some ordinary participants on reality TV enabled programme makers and networks to cash in on the draw of a celebrified performer without having the outlay of a celebrity salary, as we shall see below.

But reality TV also enabled producers to avoid other expensive costs such as script writing and directing—neither of which are central labour costs for reality TV. There is no need to pay scriptwriters, often no rights clearances for music, or rehearsals to cost, etc. These production conditions also enabled the producers of reality TV to bypass union labour and control labour unrest.

According to Chad Raphael, the 1988 writer's strike in the US 'proved crucial' to the rise of reality TV because these shows were largely unaffected by a strike which delayed the opening of the autumn season for scripted shows. The delay of the season "gave producers and programmers the impetus to develop future shows that did not depend on writing talent" (Rafael 2004, 125). Bypassing unions meant lower wages for workers and worse employment contracts. In

---

3 Regalado, M. (2016) 'The Big Bang Theory': How Much Money Does the Cast Really Make? Aug 09, http://www.cheatsheet.com/entertainment/the-big-bang-theory-cast-how-much-money-make.html/?a=viewall, accessed Aug 09 2016.

addition, to further cut costs, broadcasters outsourced programme production to independent production companies who, in order to cut their own costs, employ personnel on zero hour or part time contracts or relied on the unpaid labour of interns (this outsourcing was enshrined in law in the UK after the 1990 Broadcasting Act, as part of the attack on public service broadcasting). These cost-cutting activities resulted in much smaller production budgets than those needed for other types of programming, sometimes over 50 percent cheaper than the cost of drama (Raphael 2004, 127). Perhaps it is no surprise then, that 14 of the top 25 highest earning shows in the US in 2013 were reality TV shows.

Of course, the cycle of rising costs associated with commercial television has eventually been reproduced in reality TV; born out of the logic of competition, the format does not escape it. The global marketability of reality TV has led to competition and to the reintroduction of expensive celebrity talent in order to entice audiences to shows with popular celebrity presenters, such as duo-act Ant and Dec (Anthony McPartlin and Declan Donnelly), who earn an estimated £6 million per year each for hosting three of the ITVs most popular peak viewing shows, *Britain's Got Talent, I'm a Celebrity Get Me Out of Here,* and *Saturday Night Takeaway*.[4]

It seems that ordinary celebrity and reality TV, which are now a major feature of our cultural landscape, did not permanently solve the problems of rising costs as was anticipated. It also seems that the inequalities of wealth that mark late neoliberal capitalism are to be found in the so-called 'democratainment' that some attribute to reality TV (Hartley 1999, 2008). A few grossly overpaid celebrity hosts parade over the humiliation and degradation of ordinary contestants, who are hardly remunerated for their trouble, if at all, but who are lured instead by the promise of fame and escape from the grind of 'ordinary' life in late neoliberal capitalism.

Exploitation, Reality TV and Ordinary Celebrity

Some theorists of television culture, such as John Hartley, consider reality TV to be a form of plebiscitary 'democratainment'. Hartley coined this neologism to refer to 'plebiscitary formats'—television shows which invite audiences to vote for contestants—which he sees as a sign of democratic progress (Hartley 2008). However, the unions that protect people working in the television do not agree. In 2011, the trade union for professional performers and creative

---

[4] 'Ant and Dec Double their Earnings in One Year To Reach A Combined Income of £12 million,' The Huffington Post, 21 October, 2013. Accessed 10 May, 2016. http://www.huffingtonpost.co.uk/2013/10/21/ant-and-dec-earn-12-million_n_4136200.html.

practitioners in the UK (Equity) produced an official *"Response to the Low Pay Commission General Consultation on the National Minimum Wage"* which identified unpaid labour as a major cause for concern. The report identifies an "increase in the level of unpaid and low paid work" (3) to be a main cause of this form of exploitation and points to reality TV as one of the main culprits. The report states:

> Talent search programmes and reality TV formats continue to attract large audiences and are favoured by many of the large broadcasters. Contestants in programmes such as *Britain's Got Talent* are compelled to enter into restrictive contracts and because of a loophole in the National Minimum Wage Act for competitions they generally do not get paid (3).

Equity challenged ITV for refusing to pay any of the 24 finalists of the show and objected to the company's insistence that contestants sign away rights to performances or protection under working time laws. But the case was lost, giving commercial production companies and broadcasters the green light to refuse to pay the participants of reality TV, and often, to lock them into atrocious contracts. For example, it was revealed in 2015 that the contestants of one of the most lucrative shows on UK TV, *The X Factor*, are not paid, but instead are given an allowance of less than £50 per week. In addition, the money earned from selling contestants' songs to ITunes goes directly to the production company rather than the performer, who takes no percentage of the earnings.[5]

The false promises of ordinary celebrity come at a time of increased marginalisation of working class people from public culture, the decline in the numbers of working class actors, the replacement of thoughtful narratives of working class experiences with crass documentaries about benefits[6] Britain and derogatory representations of working class people across the media. In fact, the exclusion of working class people from participation in the creative arts has been commented upon recently by a number of actors and artists from working class backgrounds in the UK. In January 2014, the actors Julie Walters, David Morrisey and Stephen McGann all spoke out about lack of opportunities for aspiring working class actors and commented that the British art, pop and acting scene is now dominated by the privately educated and privileged (O'Hagan 2014). More recently, Christopher Eccleston objected to the fact that

---

5 Harvey, C (2015) 'Lauren Murray reveals how much X Factor contestants actually earn on the show,' Cosmopolitan, Dec 8. http://www.cosmopolitan.co.uk/entertainment/news/a40089/lauren-murray-x-factor-contestants-earnings/ accessed August 15, 2016.

6 'Benefits' is the term in the UK to refer to those who receive welfare and social security payments.

working class actors are finding it harder than ever to make it in the industry, and he argues that British culture has become anodyne because of the dominance of those from privileged backgrounds (*Guardian* 2015). This speaks directly against the logic of 'democratainment'—while certain types of (circumscribed) representation of ordinary people are on the increase, the actual participation of members of working class people in the media is in decline.

The picture is little better in the US. Reality TV has not only radically restructured the television business; it has also undermined the unions who offer protection to workers. Both the American Federation of Television and Radio Artists (AFTRA) and the Screen Actors Guild (SAG) have reported large numbers of job losses with the rise of 'unscripted' reality formats, such as the docusoap, gamedoc and talent show, over which they have no jurisdiction. This is part of the casualisation of cultural work, in which 'precarity' for much of the workforce has become a central feature. These formats rely on ordinary contestants, all searching for fame, who provide an endless supply of unskilled labour or 'raw talent' (ordinary celebrity), helping to cut the costs and risks associated with TV production, through reduced salary costs and the continual adaptation of successful formats. Sue Collins argues that "the field for ordinary, untalented people vying for potential fame is virtually inexhaustible, and the production of short-term, non-skilled, non-union celebrity generates novelty with minimal financial risk and greater control" (Collins 2008, 97).

Collins also points out that many contestants on American TV are trapped in iniquitous contracts. CBS, for instance, controls the contestants on the American version of *Survivor*, by a contract which

> stipulates that contestants are subject to authorisation by CBS for any media contact or appearance for three years after the show airs, including paid celebrity work not sanctioned by CBS and a 'life story rights' section that effectively binds the signatory into 'relinquishing control over his or her life story and public image' 'in perpetuity and across the universe'.
> COLLINS 2008, 98

In addition, a confidentiality proviso protects 'trade secrets' and any breech of this contract entitles CBS to sue the contestant for damages of up to $5 million. As Collins points out, "this contractual arrangement underscores the enormous differential in power relations between producer and cultural worker" (2008, 98).

It is clearly the case that production companies are engaged in the commercial exploitation of the 'performance of ordinariness'; this performance is *labour* carried out by individuals who create such performances. Their labour in front of the camera is as much a part of the generation of value as the technical, administrative and other creative personnel involved in the production. Furthermore, it is exploited labour because it generates value over and above the wages paid to perform the task, which, in any case, tend to be non-existent or tiny. But the exploitation of performances of ordinary contestants on reality TV is hidden under a blanket of unfulfilled promises and ideological constructs. Graeme Turner interviewed several contestants of *Big Brother Australia* and New Zealand's *Popstars*, who explained to him that they were "grossly misled about their career prospects before the show was produced, caricatured while the show was on air, and offered only those opportunities which would promote the franchise or the networks after the show was complete" (Turner 2010, 36). For Turner, "[t]he commodification of these contestants is relentless [...] the continuing success of the format depends on their expendability; it is important that they are easily replaced by the next series' crop of contenders" (2010, 36).

Rather than a question of 'democratainment' (Hartley 1999, 2008), or the spread of 'participatory culture' (Jenkins 1992, 2008) the spread of ordinary celebrity is connected to a deepening mistreatment of ordinary people in the media both in front of the camera and behind the scenes. One of the most consistent critics of the iniquitous treatment of reality TV contestants is Marc Andrejevic. Andrejevic suggests that contestants on reality TV perform the 'work of being watched' (2003). He draws on a tradition of critical thinking known as 'autonomous Marxism', to argue that contemporary forms of exploitation have moved beyond the traditional confines of the workplace to extend out into 'the social factory'—"the realm of leisure, domesticity, and consumption" (2011, 18). According to Andrejevic, both reality TV and the online economy rely on a form of 'voluntary' work, which he likens to the exploitation of women's voluntary domestic labour: "the capture of value generated in non-waged forms of value-generating activity" (2011, 26). Drawing on Anotella Corsani, he argues that just as 'voluntary' domestic labour produces value based on aptitudes and services connected to affectivity and language skills, reality TV and social media produce the practices of 'monitoring' that transform everyday leisure and domestic activities "into directly profitable activities" (2011, 24). This is accomplished by the activity of participants creating content that makes the show or site desirable to advertisers and who then "generate value in the form of information commodities that can be bought or sold" (2011, 24). In the case of reality TV, the camera captures the activity of ordinary people, which is then sold as an entertainment commodity in which audiences are invited to monitor the behaviour on display. In the case of social media, the labour of "building, maintaining and extending social relationships online", enables the owners of the sites to monitor and capture personal information, to be sold as data about the online activities of participants, which is the "economic machine driving the customised targeted, and 'accountable' model of interactive online advertising" (2011, 25).

Andrejevic is rightly tackling those who make claims about the "'democratisation' of access to the means of media production" (2011, 27) that is seen to reside in both reality TV and the internet and it seems unquestionably the case that both rely in some ways directly on the exploitation of unwaged or poorly paid labour, as we shall see below. However, there are a number of questions to be raised in Andrejevic's account of exploitation. Firstly, the logic of his argument rests on drawing a parallel between the activities of participants on reality TV shows and the 'consumer labor' of those using social media and in this he draws an equivalence between quite different practices. The unpaid labour of *Big Brother* housemates is not the same as the unpaid labour of a Facebook user who unintentionally makes available personal data for sale to third parties. They are different activities, even if both are subject to commodification. And although both generate value, only one can be considered to be the exploitation of labour.

Marxist thought provides a specific analysis of exploitation which importantly differentiates between the everyday sense of the concept, when one group takes advantage of another though domination and/or oppression, and a theory of exploitation which identifies one of the fundamental economic relationships of capitalist society. In the Marxist sense, exploitation is not only a question of capturing value, but crucially it is a question of the socioeconomic relations that govern the creation of value—the relations of production. The Marxist account of labour exploitation is based on the labour theory of value, which explains how surplus value is created and its relationship to profit. In the Marxist sense of the term, labour 'exploitation' (such as the work of being watched on reality TV) differs from the practice of being monitored by corporations who track and collect consumer/participant activity to be packaged as a commodity and sold on to advertisers. Engaging in unpaid/lowpaid labour and having one's online information mined as data are both instances of being taking advantage of, but they *are* different and the value generated from the activity of each has a distinctive and different relationship to the relations of production.

Autonomous Marxists identify all free/voluntary or 'immaterial' labour as homogenous in the sense that it is a structural part of labour in late capitalism (Negri and Hardt 2000; Negri and Hardt 2004). But these activities are greatly varied and we must determine whether or not they are a form of labour exploitation or some other form of economic manipulation and domination and/or one group taking unfair advantage over another, or some other practice altogether. I will argue that the participant in one activity is having her labour exploited, while the activity in the other is a form of active consumption through which companies generate revenue on the basis of exploited labour elsewhere.

Gholam Khiabany (2015) has recently pointed out that Marx draws a distinction between different forms of labour under capitalism. A key distinction is between 'productive labour' and 'unproductive labour' (Khiabany 2015, 264). For Marx, these are not moral or judgmental categories; instead they are terms used to describe the different relationship that different forms of labour have to the social relations of production and the accumulation of capital. For Marx, productive labour is "wage-labour which, exchanged against the variable part of capital (the part of capital that is spent on wages), reproduces not only this part of the capital (or the value of its own labour-power), but in addition produces surplus-value for the capitalist" (Marx 1963, 152). Productive labour is exploited labour because it produces enough value to replenish the portion of capital spent on its wages and produces a surplus—a profit for the owner. A worker exchanges her labour for a wage from capital, but that labour produces more value than she is paid, and is hence the source of the capitalist's profit.

Let's take an example from reality TV. An episode of *Britain's Got Talent* is estimated to cost £1 million pounds to produce, including salaries to the production team and hosts, studio and location fees, equipment etc. But the show earns the two production companies (Syco TV and Freemantle) and the broadcaster (ITV) an estimated £9 million per show.[7] Even if we assume that most of that £1 million pounds goes in salaries to the production team (rather than in celebrity salaries and infrastructure costs) the combined wages of the numerous producers, editors, music production personnel, vision mixers, make-up artists, post production staff, graphics and art production staff, publicists, legal affairs staff, runners, floor managers etc., is *nine time less* than the show earns. If we split that labour into a nine-hour day (although cultural workers often work even longer hours than this) it means that each worker earns her salary (the value of her work) during the first hour at work, and for the subsequent 8 hours, her labour produces surplus value which is profit for Syco, Freemantle and ITV. This is 'productive' labour because it produces a surplus above its cost—it is exploited by capital.

We can contrast an actor employed by a capitalist firm (and who is paid less than the value she creates for her work in a film, television programme—ie productive labour) to an actor who is paid, for example, to go to the house of a rich capitalist to provide the entertainment for a party. She is not exchanging

---

7   http://www.campaignlive.co.uk/news/1131211/.

her labour for a portion of capital and then producing surplus value above it; she is not producing profit for the capitalist, instead she is exchanging her labour for revenue (i.e. paid out of the capitalist's own private disposable income). Khiabany reminds us that for Marx, "The former's labour is exchanged with capital, the latter's with revenue. The former's labour produces a surplus-value; in the latter's, revenue is consumed" (Marx 1963, 157). Similarly, the labour of creating content online might *seem* to be the same as the labour on reality TV, but they are not the same and this is because of "the social relations of production, within which the labour is realised" (Marx 1963, 157). One is labour that directly creates surplus value, while the activities of the other only produce surplus once it is acquired and packaged by the exploited labour of others.

Conclusion

Andrejevic (and others who share this view such as Fuchs and Sevignani 2013) are right to argue that value in commercial television and the internet is generated through advertising and users *do* create content which makes the site attractive to advertisers. But it is only attractive because it can be captured and used to direct advertising back to the user. Unlike the television performer whose labour directly contributes to the television commodity, the labour of the social media user indirectly contributes to the production of the commodity—which is actually personal data. This data is monitored and captured by the burgeoning online companies, such as Digilant, who produce the information for online advertisers. It is the workers in this industry whose labour is exploited because their total wages are considerably smaller than the advertising revenue they generate for their companies through their labour. Of course, it is the case that these sites are only able to attract advertising because of the number of users who can potentially be reached. All profit in any industry is ultimately realised in the act of selling, (or exchange), whether it be advertising space or a fast food hamburger, but in both cases profit is generated in the act of labour rather than the act of consumption. The activities of social media users are forms of active consumption, rather than 'productive' in the sense discussed above. These activities would take place without any advertising revenue being generated at all were it not for the exploitation of another pool of labour that in various ways monitors and processes this information, which is then sold back to the internet giants whose platforms provide the basis of content creation.

Andrejevic is also right to point out that audiences of reality TV and users of the internet are being economically manipulated by large corporations who use their activities as a means of creating commodities for advertising revenue. However, the logical conclusion of the extension of the concept of exploitation to all activities in 'the social factory', (ie society as a whole) is that everything we do in society is part of the process of exploitation. In this definition, the 'multitude' replaces the working class, regardless of their position in relations of production and is thus overly optimistic about how power is confronted and overly pessimistic about the organised, collective power of the working class. But exploitation as a concept provides an understanding not just of domination, but of the potential for resistance. Exploitation is, as has been argued, the extraction of surplus value and the basis of profit. But it is also a dynamic concept, for it raises the conflict at the heart of the relations of production and the means of struggling against exploitation though collective action. Capital is driven by the need to increase surplus value by cheapening the cost of labour. This is as much the case for the cultural industries as any other. As we saw in the first section of this chapter, the television industry dealt with the rising costs which are an endemic part of its business models, by attacking the conditions of those who work in the industry (including unpaid or poorly paid contestants and performers). This directly clashes with workers' need to minimise the rate at which surplus is extracted from their labour, (that is, the rate of their exploitation) in order to have a decent life, or at least to be able to sustain themselves. But those companies who exploit workers also directly rely on the surplus value they create, and this gives the collective workforces in the television industry and the digital economy the capacity and the potential power to resist, and in the process, potentially at least, to call for new forms of television reality, both in form and in meaning.

References

Andrejevic, M. (2003) *Reality TV: The Work of Being Watch*. London: Rowman and Littlefield.

Andrejevic, M. (2011) Real-ising exploitation. In: Kraidy M., Marwan M., & Sender K., (eds) *The Politics of Reality Television: Global Perspectives*. London: Routledge, 18–31.

Collins, S. (2008) Making the Most out of 15 Minutes: Reality TV's Dispensable Celebrity. *Television and New Media*, 9 (2): 87–110.

Deery, J. (2014) Mapping Commercialisation in Reality Television. In: Ouellette L., (ed) *A Companion to Reality Television*. Chichester: Wiley Blackwell, 11–28.

Driessens, O. (2013) The Celebritisation of Society and Culture: Understanding the Structural Dynamics of Celebrity Culture. *International Journal of Cultural Studies* 16 (6): 641–657.

Dyer, R. (1979) *Stars*. London: BFI.

Equity (2011) *Response to the Low Pay Commission General Consultation on the National Minimum Wage*.

Fuchs, C. and S. Sevignani (2013) What is Digital Labour? What is Digital Work? What's Their Difference? And Why do these Questions Matter for Understanding Social Media. *TripleC*, 11 (2): 237–293.

Guardian (2015) Christopher Eccleston hits out at inequality in acting. *The Guardian*. Available at: https://www.theguardian.com/media/2015/apr/14/ex-doctor-who-christopher-ecclestone-hits-out-at-inequality-in-acting.

Hartley, J. (1999) *Uses of Television*. London: Routledge.

Hartley, J. (2008) *Television Truths*. Oxford: Blackwell.

Jenkins, H. (1992) *Textual Poachers: television and participatory culture*. London: Routledge.

Jenkins, H. (2008) *Convergence Culture: where old and new media collide*. New York: NYU Press.

Khiabany, G. (2015) Uneven and Combined Independence of Social Media in the Middle East: Technology, Symbolic Production and Unproductive Labor. In: Bennett J,. and Strange, N., (eds) *Media Independence: Working with Freedom or Working For Free*. New York: Routledge, 261–280.

Langer, J. (1981) Television's 'personality system'. *Media Culture and Society* 3(4): 351–365.

Magder, T. (2004) The End of TV101: Reality Programs, Formats, and the New Business of Television. In: Murray S. and Oullette L., (eds.) *Reality TV: Remaking Television Culture*. New York: New York University Press, 141–164.

Marx, K. (1963) *Theories of Surplus Value: Part I*. London: Lawrence and Wishart.

Murdoch, G., & Golding, P. (2002) Digital Possibilities, Market Realties: The Contradictions of Communications Convergence. *Socialist Register* 38: 111–128.

Negri, A., & Hardt, M. (2000) *Empire*. Cambridge, MA: Harvard University Press.

Negri, A., & Hardt, M. (2004) *Multitude: war and democracy in the age of empire*. London: Penguin.

O'Hagan, S. (2014) A working class is something to be ... but not in Britain's posh culture. *The Guardian*. Available at: https://www.theguardian.com/culture/2014/jan/26/workingclass-hero-posh-britain-public-school.

Raphael, C. (2004) The Political Economic Origins of Reali-TV. In: Murray, S. and Oullette, L. (eds.) *Reality TV: Remaking Television Culture*. New York: New York University Press, 119–134.

Skeggs, B. (2009) Haunted by the Spectre of Judgement: Respectability, Value and Affect in Class Relations. In: Sveinsson K.P. (ed.) *Who Cares About the White Working Class*. London: Runnymede, 36–45.

Skeggs B. & Wood, H. (2012) *Reacting to Reality Television: Performance, Audience and Value*. Abingdon, UK: Routledge.

Sparks, C. (2007) Reality TV: The Big Brother phenomenon. *International Socialism Journal*, 114. Available at: http//isj.org.uk.reality-tv-the-big-brother-phenomenon/.

Turner, G. (2010) *Ordinary People and the Media*. London: Sage.

Williamson, M. (2010) Female Celebrities and the Media: The Gendered Denigration of the "ordinary Celebrity". *Celebrity Studies*, 1(1): 118–121.

CHAPTER 17

Class Warfare, the Neoliberal Man and the Political Economy of Methamphetamine in *Breaking Bad*

Michael Seltzer

Introduction

During the course of a cozy Christmas interview with the *New York Times*, Barack Obama confessed that *Breaking Bad* was his favourite television entertainment. One journalist commented that it was unlikely that the president had much time to watch TV so he most probably asks "one of his rich, fancy friends, 'What should I watch?' Rich fancy friend says, '*Breaking Bad*' because that's the kind of thing rich, fancy people watch"(Fallon, 2013). Given Obama's own expensive private schooling and education at elite universities, this is not surprising since the cable network AMC specifically aimed this series at 'upscale audiences' (Smith 2013, 159). It was nonetheless disconcerting to learn that a series chronicling the career of a methamphetamine producer was the favourite of the leader of a nation where the drug had already ruined the lives of millions of working class families while costing more than 23 billion dollars each year in health, criminal justice and social services expenditures (Steinberg 2009). These factors, however, represent but a fraction of the class-related facets of this highly popular and much discussed program. In following the career of a middle class professional whose brilliance and ingenuity in producing and marketing a highly addictive drug brought him immense riches, the series celebrated entrepreneurship, avarice, disdain for government controls and related neoliberal values. Yet, as we shall see, this storyline was peripheral to the main ideological work of *Breaking Bad*, namely the production of images and ideas rationalising the fate and justifying the treatment of those on the losing side of a vicious class war raging in the US since the 1980s.

This chapter begins by briefly attending to the popularity of this series among middle class professionals before discussing its celebration during five seasons of a cluster of key neoliberal values. The focus then shifts to an exploration of the images and themes central to *Breaking Bad*'s treatment of the working class, methamphetamine and addiction. Significantly, nearly all the poor and working class men and women foregrounded in the series are portrayed as depraved and dangerous persons unworthy of respect, concern and sympathy. In so doing, *Breaking Bad* becomes a media project like *Benefits Street* and *Shameless* contributing to the demonisation of working people, while ignoring the brutal forces of neoliberal capitalism and austerity regimes destroying their lives (Jones 2016). In shrinking the field of view for audiences and decontextualising the cruel realities of working class life, the series provides ideational ammunition justifying the fates of those no longer of value for capital.

If You're So Smart, Why Aren't You Rich

First of all, some attention needs directing to that class fraction providing some of the most ardent fans of the cliff-hanging plots, highly innovative camera angles and brilliant acting of this series. Contrary to claims made by devotees about its originality, the core values presented by *Breaking Bad* deviate little from longstanding quintessential myths of American television celebrating the sacredness of the nuclear family, praising individualistic competitiveness, and applauding triumphs of the individual over governmental interference (Himmelstein 1984). Similarly, the protagonist's use of his knowledge of chemistry and laboratory skills to solve problems in episode after episode reproduces nearly exactly the storyline of *MacGyver*, a US television series from the 1980s focused on a non-violent protagonist using his expertise in physics and chemistry to solve in each episode a diversity of problems (Turley 2013). Perhaps the only feature of *Breaking Bad* setting it apart from comparable series like *The Sopranos* and *Mad Men* involves the contrast between its largely sympathetic portrayal of a core cast of middle class professionals and its negative treatment of working people and others from the lower strata of American society.

By creating a protagonist like Walter White having a post-graduate education and experience as a laboratory scientist, the series clearly appealed to what Barbara and John Ehrenreich early identified as the 'professional managerial class' or PMC comprised of 'mental workers' positioned between the working class and the capitalist class (1977). Reinforcing this appeal throughout the series were law enforcement bureaucrats, physicians, teachers and others qualifying for PMC membership owing to their positions as salaried workers broadly engaged in "the reproduction of capitalist culture and capitalist social relations" (Ehrenreich and Ehrenreich 1977,7). Not surprisingly, this societal positioning was shared by many of those producing a substantial literature about the series focusing on such issues as the protagonist's masculinity (Cowlishaw 2015; Gercke 2013; Lotz 2014), his role as an anti-hero (Martin 2012; Vaage 2016) and his position as a symbol of contemporary morality and ethics

(Koepsell and Arp 2012; Meek 2013). The rags to riches storyline of the series, too, resonated well among those well-educated persons working like Walter White, the protagonist, as underpaid and underappreciated teachers and other mental workers accustomed to hearing the taunt: "If you're so smart, why aren't you rich?"

More significant than commentators from this class fraction identifying with one of their own was the timing of his transformation into the ruthless head of a vast drug empire serving as the main story line of the series. *Breaking Bad* opened in 2008, the year of the financial meltdown devastating and trapping many Americans in the ruins of collapsed housing and labour markets. Perhaps one thing making this breakdown especially traumatic for PMC members stemmed from their own educational backgrounds. They had done all the right things by obeying school authorities, working hard and exercising self-discipline in gaining their educations and planning their careers only to discover after the crash that they were "no more indispensable, as a group to the American capitalist enterprise, than those who had honed their skills on assembly lines or in warehouses" (Ehrenreich and Ehrenreich 2013, 11). Walter, too, did the right thing by never smoking, only to discover inoperable lung cancer threatening his own life but more crucially, the future of his unemployed and pregnant wife and a handicapped son.

The Birth of the Neoliberal Man: From Mister Chips to Scarface

Given the attention received by *Breaking Bad* from so many talented commentators, it is surprising that few have noted that the chain of events triggered by this diagnosis mirrors in key respects what Foucault (2008, 226) described as neoliberalism's "replacement of homo economicus as a partner in exchange with a homo economicus as entrepreneur of himself". The development of this 'entrepreneurial self' skilled in making choices among various options begins precisely when Walter 'chooses' to reject offers of charity from others and decides instead to use his knowledge of chemistry to pay for treatment and to support his family by producing and selling methamphetamine. In the course of carrying out the strategic choices incumbent upon the entrepreneur as the hero of the neoliberal project, he sheds his previously weak and ineffectual persona and becomes a ruthless, mighty and fabulously wealthy drug lord. Throughout all but the last of the 62 episodes of the series, Walter constantly echoes Margaret Thatcher in defining all his actions as those of an individual man for his family while coldly calculating all other social relationships solely in terms of profits and losses. It is only in the last episode when he finally confesses to his wife that he did not build his empire for her and the children. True to his 'entrepreneurial self' as the neoliberal man writ large, Walter emotionally declares, "I did it because I was good at it, I liked it and it made me feel really alive" (*Breaking Bad* 2013).

According to the late Doreen Massey and Michael Rustin, neoliberalism's ideological nucleus is one revolving "around the supposed naturalness of 'the market', the primacy of the competitive individual, the superiority of the private over the public" (2013, 9). In practice, the success of the neoliberal project depends in great part on triumphing over meddlesome governmental laws and *Breaking Bad* illustrates this in episode after episode chronicling what its creator described as the transformation of Mr. Chips into Scarface (MacInnes 2012). Throughout the series, Walter employs an arsenal of different strategies to outmanoeuvre attempts by law enforcement agencies to close down his empire-building project. In claiming and protecting his territorial rights, he uses an equally creative assortment of tricks and schemes to destroy or to dominate competitors. Early in the series, his wife displays her entrepreneurial self in marketing and profiting from small eBay sales before joining him in skillfully running a massive money laundering operation at a car wash they acquire through trickery. Like Walter and her sister who tells of having 'managerial ambitions', she becomes what Wendy Brown describes as the "model neoliberal citizen who strategises for her or himself among various social, political and economic options, not one who strives with others to alter or organise these options" (2005, 43).

Creating Deserving Candidates for Disposal

Gustavo Fring, Walter's main competitor for control of the drug market, shows similar entrepreneurial strategising in first founding and expanding a legitimate chain of fast food restaurants before achieving similar success in establishing and expanding his drug empire. However, his PMC habitus sets him miles apart from other Latino drug empire builders in the series. With his conservative dress, soft, measured and refined speaking style and even his decidedly solid but drab Volvo, he could easily be mistaken for a mid-level bureaucrat or university lecturer. Nevertheless, as perceptively noted by a recent commentator, Gustavo shares the fate of the members of the Latino working class portrayed in the series who end up destroyed or dominated by Walter (Marez 2013).

For the most part, *Breaking Bad* continues American television's longstanding practice of portraying working people as nameless and faceless elements comprising a distanced backdrop for actions performed by foregrounded characters from higher social strata (Parenti 1992). One of the earliest studies of prime-time US television showed that audiences viewed a world nearly devoid of working people (Johnson, 1981). Another study conducted by a trade union found that less than 10 percent of the characters on popular evening programming in the US were working people (IAM 1980). Even today, when prime time American television allows a few working class men to enter the limelight, often as fathers in traditional families, they appear like Homer Simpson and Al Bundy as crude and simple-minded buffoons (Butsch 2003). It is significant that this near-invisibility of workers on American television screens occurred during a period when the working class as defined by different measures was reckoned to constitute somewhere between 60 to 70 per cent of the US labor force (Zweig 2011).

Breaking with this tradition, the series foregrounds a tiny group of characters having membership in or close association with the working class. There is, however, little about these men and few women capable of evoking any degree of sympathy and concern among viewers. On the contrary, the actions of this collection of drug dealers, murderers, white supremacists, torturers, gang members and other unsavoury characters deviate markedly from the norms of respectable society. If *Breaking Bad* can be understood as a tale celebrating the values of neoliberal capitalism in showing the transformation of its protagonist into a ruthless, successful and wealthy entrepreneur, it also can be understood in its treatment of the class most victimised by the same economic order as an example of what Brad Evans and Henry Giroux have perceptively characterised as 'spectacles of violence' rendering "some lives meaningful while dismissing others as disposable" (2015, 32).

Central among those having disposable lives are the men, women and young persons addicted to the commodity providing Walter and his competitors with great wealth. Even though growing stores of cash serving as a common thread throughout *Breaking Bad* testify to the existence of massive numbers of methamphetamine users, only two persons addicted to this drug appear as foregrounded characters and the series portrays them as thoroughly repulsive persons. One is Wendy, a prostitute with the scabby skin and bad teeth of the long-term meth addict, ready to do anything to feed her addiction, while the other is Spooge, a demented thief and father of a starving and severely maltreated child.

There is considerable significance in the use of this disgusting pair to personify addiction to what had become the drug of choice for the white working class in late 20th and early 21st century America. By wrapping in invisibility millions of workers suffering from the effects of methamphetamine while representing them with two disgusting characters, the series promotes in class warfare an ideological project paralleling what in conventional warfare has been called 'the architecture of indifference' (Tirman 2013). After documenting for *The Lancet* the scale of suffering and losses of lives in Iraq caused by UN sanctions and two invasions, its principal investigator, John Tirman, tried to explain the widespread indifference of his fellow Americans to the fate of these victims. Using architectonic terminology, he described a long existing ideological system converting the victims of American wars into lesser beings not entitled to compassion and empathy. He found that indifference to the fate of others in the US depended in great part on their invisibility. If, however, a few of these 'others' became visible, they invariably are portrayed as barbaric beings unworthy of sympathy.

The creator of *Breaking Bad* makes no ideological claims for a series he describes as "a story of transformation in which a previously good man, through sheer force of will, decides to become a bad man" (MacInnes 2012). Despite this claim, the series clearly produces ideas and images reinforcing indifference among its viewers to the fates of working people in the US victimised during the past 35 years by the triumphant forces of neoliberal capitalism. Comprehending how this works demands an exploration of two overlapping processes. One involves the series' decontextualised picture of methamphetamine use and users, while the other involves its reinforcement of recent media representations of American workers as persons responsible for their own poverty and suffering.

Reversing the Panoptical Process and Expanding the Synoptic Focus

One way of exploring these processes comes from a simple but extremely insightful suggestion inspired by Michael Foucault's classic account of the evolution of penal systems (1979). Two decades ago, Thomas Mathiesen pointed out that the growth in the modern world of panoptic processes enabling the few to see and to assess the many brilliantly described by Foucault was matched by the growth in the mass media of synoptic processes enabling the many to see and to judge the few (1997). Mathiesen emphasised that these synoptic processes in television produced in viewing audiences a consciousness of the world dominated by "the deviant, the shuddering, the titillating" (1997, 229). In several ways, this aptly describes the tiny company of nasty characters chosen by *Breaking Bad* to represent the working class. In narrowly focusing on the many horrendous deeds of these persons, the series makes them less than human in ways similar to those employed by perpetrators of human rights violations in defining their victims as lower forms of beings "with less right to compassion with others, less ability to feel and less entitlement to compassion or empathy" (Cohen 1995, 79). Like *Benefits Streets* and *Shameless* also employing synoptic processes to spotlight the moral shortcomings of a select few chosen to represent the working class, *Breaking Bad* provides its targeted upscale viewing audiences with rationales justifying the treatment of society's weakest and most vulnerable members by its most powerful and privileged members. The rationalisations provided to these viewers, as Ben Dabney pithily observed, are little more than "the bullshit stories we tell ourselves to neutralise our consciences by tricking them into thinking we're good people when we're not" (2015, 10–11).

If, however, this tightly confined field of view of the despicable and dangerous provided by television's synoptic processes can be greatly expanded, a rather different picture emerges. Occupying a central place in this formerly excluded context are the tens of millions of American workers who have been experiencing during the past three decades the disappearance of jobs and stability from their lives. The launching of *Breaking Bad* in 2008 came at the end of a decade marked by the closure of 40,000 factories (McCormack 2009). These closures, often triggered by moving production overseas, together with workforce reductions at still operative factories resulted in job losses for more than 5.7 million workers representing one-third of the manufacturing sector of the American work force (Baily and Bosworth 2014, 4). Closely related to these and other massive layoffs was the deteriorating power of organised labour in the United States. Paradoxically, this occurred at a time when a majority of Americans shared a favourable view of unions and 90 percent of all US workers were calling for a greater collective say at their workplaces (Freeman and Rogers 2006). Nonetheless, in contrast to the 1960s when unions organised 33 percent of the American workforce, only 10 percent of workers in 2008 were union members (Sweets and Meiksins 2008, 33).

Much of this decline is owed to the highly effective weapon of overseas outsourcing used by employers to counter demands by workers for higher wages and improved benefits (McNall 2016). Such threats were not empty ones as evidenced by one study showing that giant brand-name US companies employing one-fifth of American workers had slashed their domestic workforces by 2.9 million jobs from 2000 to 2010 while increasing overseas workforces with more than 2.4 million employees (Wessel 2011). The neoliberal agenda pursued by Republican and Democratic administrations since the 1980s promoting pro-business policies, union busting tactics and domestic outsourcing to low-wage subcontractors reinforced an already precarious existence for those workers managing to stay employed (Weil 2014). Their situation was by no means coincidental; it was the result of deliberate policies pursued by successive economic planners in Washington aimed at increasing job insecurity, keeping wages low and otherwise disciplining American workers (Mason 2016).

The 8 million people defined by the US Labour Department as the working poor provide one illustration of this kind of insecurity. In 2008, this group, representing one fifth of 41 million Americans existing at or below the federally defined poverty level, led working lives marked by low wages, periods of unemployment and involuntary part-time employment (US Department of Labour 2008, 3). For other workers at that time even these low paid jobs were unavailable. In 2008, 64 percent of working age Americans reported finding it difficult to get jobs where they lived (Pew Research Center 2008). Five years later, one-sixth of all Americans aged 25 to 54 years were unemployed or out of the workforce altogether (Desilver 2014).

The Political Economy of Methamphetamine: A Powerful Drug for Powerless People

Those workers managing to stay employed during these massive waves of plant closings and work force downsising found little comfort and security in their wage packets. Using adjustments for inflation, one study showed that despite increasing productivity by 60 percent, an average American male worker earning 48,000 dollars in 1978 was in 2012 earning 33,000 dollars (Lewis 2014). In attempting to regain some of this lost financial ground, American workers more than doubled their overtime from 1990 to 1997 and soon "put in 20 percent more hours in 2000 than they did in the 1970s" (Hermann 2014, 185). It was during this period that law enforcement officials, medical personnel and social workers began reporting with arrest sheets, hospital admission forms and child welfare placements the destruction wrought by a tsunami of methamphetamine abuse sweeping through working class communities (Gonzales, Mooney and Ranking 2010). In 1990, the drug was unknown to prison officials in North Dakota, but 15 years later a special facility for female meth-using offenders had been constructed (Robinson 2006, 1432). In 2009, the number of people sentenced to prison in Minnesota for meth-related offenses had quadrupled since 2001 and these prisoners totalled more than all those convicted of offenses related to other drugs (Mannix 2015). In 2007, health officials in Idaho reported that the drug was involved in 80 percent of placements of children in care and that 75 percent of all prison inmates identified methamphetamine as their drug of choice (Central District Health Department 2007). At the same time, the governor of Illinois announced the building of two prisons confining only inmates identified as methamphetamine users (Illinois Government News Network 2006).

Investigations of these and related statistics need to make note of the fact that the cheap household and automotive products needed to manufacture this drug had been easily and legally obtainable at US department stores and grocers since the 1950s. Many of these retailers together with pharmacies in nearly every American state sell cold remedies containing the pseudoephedrine essential for the making of methamphetamine. These medicines annually generate profits of more than 600 million dollars for the pharmaceutical industry whose lobbyists have successfully resisted almost all governmental attempts to require prescriptions for purchasing these remedies (Engle 2013, 29). The availability of cheap ingredients for making the drug and the relatively low incidence of its abuse throughout most of the 20th century raises a question about the timing of the devastation this drug first brought to working class communities in the late 1990s.

One possible answer lies in findings from studies of earlier upsurges in the use of amphetamine. This drug, nearly identical to methamphetamine in chemical composition, similarly acts on the central nervous system in combating fatigue and increasing alertness and feelings of power and wellbeing. Amphetamine, unlike methamphetamine, is difficult to make in home laboratories and its purchase requires a physician's prescription. Despite these restrictions, the drug has been for sale on the black market – especially in the years between 1950 and 1970 when it was widely used by workers in the US trucking industry. Two investigations of amphetamine use among drivers during that period found that industry deregulation and increased competition for profits forced many to lengthen their time on the road and that this, more than any other factor, accounted for their increased use of this drug (Frydl 2013; Riley 2014).

These findings strongly suggest that radically changed working conditions in the 1990s and later years played similar roles in the upsurge in the use of a drug whose inexpensive ingredients long had been easily available but had remained unused during earlier decades. Lending support to this is a 3-year investigation of a methamphetamine epidemic in a small one-industry American town (Redding 2009). This drug first appeared there shortly after the corporate takeover of the town's meatpacking plant. After destroying the union, the new owners reduced hourly wages from 24 to 8 dollars. This led many to work double shifts and long hours of overtime. In the beginning, meatpackers needing extra energy and endurance to carry out this demanding and dangerous work purchased methamphetamine from drug dealers. After a time, however, many workers found they could cut their expenses by producing the drug themselves. Using internet recipes and mixing cold medicines with other chemicals, they began cooking meth at home – often with disastrous consequences resulting in explosions, fires and deaths.

A host of studies showed that workers in the 1990s and later years began using this drug while working long hours and at multiple jobs – especially in manufacturing, trucking, constructions work and other workplaces demanding energy for 'getting things done' and endurance to work many hours over long stretches (Lende et al. 2007). Unlike such expensive *recreational* drugs like powdered cocaine favored by members of the PMC and their betters, methamphetamine as a *vocational* drug gives its users feelings of great power and boundless energy. Once addicted, however, they begin to pay for this stimulation in constantly experiencing paranoid delusions, hallucinations, long periods of sleeplessness and often-suicidal depressions. Typically, their skin begins to rot away owing to relentlessly scratching to remove imagined bugs under the surface and their teeth decay and fall out owing to ceaseless grinding. They lose much weight and acquire rapid and/or stymied speech, high blood pressure, and elevated pulse rates. Worst of all, their chances for recovery from addiction are abysmally low as evidenced by relapse rates of 92 to 95 percent (Bartos 2005; McKetin 2012). Perhaps most tragic are the costs in human lives stemming from the use of this and other drugs. Researchers recently were shocked to discover that while life expectancy for women and men in industrial societies had increased on average 11 years during the past 4 decades, it had decreased dramatically from 1999 to 2013 among white working class Americans having 12 years of schooling or less. The three main causes of a 22 percent increase in the death rate of this group aged 45 to 54 were suicide, alcohol-related liver disease, and poisoning involving overdoses and toxic interactions of methamphetamine, opiates, and alcohol (Case and Deaton 2015). These figures, however, say almost nothing about why these poisoning victims sought to treat their feelings of helplessness and hurt with substances acting, however briefly, to deaden their pain and to make them feel powerful and good about themselves. In critically commenting on these mortality statistics, two researchers, a physician and a sociologist, had this to say:

> The sequence leading up to the death is shrouded in mystery, no deeper understanding of the socio-cultural and economic factors are sought. Instead, the victim or his/her culture is blamed for the end-result of a complex chain of elite capitalist economic decisions and political maneuverings in which a worker's premature death is a mere collateral event.
> PETRAS and EASTMAN-ABAYA 2016

A Final Note on Demonisation and Demonisation Light

As I have tried to show in this chapter, the synoptic focus of *Breaking Bad* effectively excludes these factors and other aspects of the tough and precarious working conditions, joblessness, poverty and hopelessness experienced by growing numbers of women and men. By excising work-related and other structural causes of substance abuse, addiction among working class Americans fits into victim-blaming schemes linking drug use to individual agency or 'lifestyle choices' as ex-British Prime Minister David Cameron liked to put it. Nonetheless, the kinds of images promoted by the series represent only a milder variant of recent victim-blaming framings of those defined by the neoliberal economic order as having no value. Writing about working class communities in economically depressed parts of the US, one journalist for a conservative periodical newly delivered this contemptuous pronouncement:

> Nothing happened to them. There wasn't some awful disaster. There wasn't a war or a famine or a plague or a foreign occupation. Even the economic changes of the past few decades do very little to explain the dysfunction and negligence—and the incomprehensible malice—of poor white America ... The truth about these dysfunctional, downscale communities is that they deserve to die. Economically, they are negative assets. Morally, they are indefensible.
> WILLIAMSON 2016

Shortly thereafter, one columnist writing for the same periodical, called for the destruction of working class communities owing to the immorality of their members:

> I ... have seen the challenges of the white working class first-hand. Simply put, Americans are killing themselves and destroying their families at an alarming rate. No one is making them do it. The economy isn't putting a bottle in their hand. Immigrants aren't making them cheat on their wives or snort OxyContin.
> FRENCH 2016

The future will doubtless witness the growth of even more virulent demonising and victim-blaming proclamations by ruling class ideologues as neoliberal regimes increasingly funnel members of the working class into what Zygmunt Bauman and Henry Giroux have perceptively described as the 'Zero

Generation' – an assemblage of those having zero jobs, zero possibilities, and zero hopes (Bauman 2011; Giroux 2011). Just as surely as the growth of this group in the coming years will be the proliferation of media productions providing milder and more subtle spectacles demonising those defined by capital as useless and hence disposable. Doubtless, too, these productions, especially television dramas and series, will feature like *Breaking Bad* and *Shameless* casts of accomplished actors and captivating storylines. Like their precursors, these future synoptic productions with their constricted fields of view can be expected to attribute the suffering of the powerless to their own depravity while shoving out of sight the brutal economic forces impacting violently and lethally on their lives. Doubtless, too, these finely crafted spectacles will help create and reinforce indifference to the fates of these disposable women and men – especially among viewing audiences comprised of rich, fancy presidential friends and other class fractions enjoying the ever-so-small privileges temporarily granted them by the same oppressive regimes.

References

Baily, M. and Bosworth, B. (2014) US Manufacturing: Understanding Its Past and Its Potential Future. *Journal of Economic Perspectives* 28 (1): 3–26.

Bartos, L. (2005) Devastating Effects of Methamphetamine. *NEB Newsletter*, July.

Bauman, Z. (2011) On the Outcast Generation. *Social Europe Journal*, 17 January: 1.

Breaking Bad. Episode 62. Directed by Vince Gilligan. Written by Vince Gilligan. AMC, September 29, 2013.

Brown, W. (2005) *Edgework: Critical Essays on Knowledge and Politics*. Princeton, NJ: Princeton University Press.

Butsch, R. (2003) A Half Century of Class and Gender in American TV Domestic Sitcoms. *Cercles* 8: 16–34.

Case, A. and Deaton, A. (2015) Rising morbidity and mortality in midlife white non-Hispanic Americans in the 21st century. *Proceedings of National Academy of Sciences* 112 (49): 15078–15083.

Central District Health Department (2007) *Idaho Meth Project*. Available at: http://www.cdhd.idaho.gov/CHEC/Etc/meth.htm.

Cohen, S. (1995) *Denial and Acknowledgement: the Impact of Information about Human Rights Violations*. Jerusalem: Hebrew University Center for Human Rights.

Cowlishaw, B. (2015) *Masculinity in Breaking Bad: Critical Perspectives*. Jefferson, NC: McFarland and Company.

Dabney, B. (2015) The Political Economy of Scapegoating: The Oldest Trick in the Book. *Counterpunch* 22 (8): 10–14.

Desilver, D. (2014) More and more Americans are outside the labor force entirely. Who are they? *Pew Research Fact-Tank.* Available at: http://www.pewresearch.org/fact-tank/2014/11/14/more-and-more-americans-are-outside-the-labor-force-entirely-who-are-they/.

Ehrenreich, B. and Ehrenreich, J. (2013) *Death of a Yuppie Dream: The Rise and Fall of the Professional-Managerial Class.* New York: Rosa Luxemburg Stiftung.

Ehrenreich, B. and Ehrenreich, J. (1977) The New Left and the Professional-Managerial Class. *Radical America* 11 (3): 7–22.

Engle, J. (2013) Merchants of Meth. *Mother Jones* 38 (4): 28–39.

Evans, B. and Giroux, H. (2015) *Disposable Futures: The Seductions of Violence in the Age of the Spectacle.* San Francisco: City Lights Open Media.

Fallon, K. (2013) Obama Loves Breaking Bad Because Of Course He Does. *The Daily Beast,* 30 December. Available at: http://www.thedailybeast.com/articles/2013/12/30/obama-loves-breaking-bad-because-of-course-he-does.html.

Foucault, M. (2008) *The Birth of Bio-Politics: Lectures at the College de France 1978–1979.* Basingstoke: Palgrave Macmillan.

Foucault, M. (1979) *Discipline and Punish: The Birth of the Prison.* New York: Vintage.

Freeman, R. and Rogers, J. (2006) *What Workers Want.* Ithaca, NY: ILR Press.

French, D. (2016) The Great White Working class Debate: Just Because I'm 'Nasty' Doesn't Mean I'm Wrong. *National Review,* 21 March. Available at: http://www.nationalreview.com/corner/433060/white-working class-debate-facts-can-be-nasty.

Frydl, K. (2013) *The Drug Wars in America, 1940–1973.* New York: Cambridge University Press.

Gercke, M. (2013) Masculinity Breaking Bad: Walter White and the Fallouts from Complicit Masculinity. *The Society Pages Org/Sociology Lens.* Available at: http://thesocietypages.org/sociologylens/2013/10/10/masculinity-breaking-bad-walter-white-and-the-fallouts-from-complicit-masculinity/.

Giroux, H. (2011) *Zombie Politics and Culture in the Age of Casino Capitalism.* Bern: Peter Lang.

Gonzales, R., Mooney, L. and Rawson, R. (2010) The Methamphetamine Problem in the United States. *Annual Review of Public Health* 31: 385–398.

Hermann, C. (2014) *Capitalism and the Political Economy of Work Time.* Abingdon: Routledge.

Himmelstein, H. (1984) *Television Myth and the American Mind.* New York: Praeger.

IAM – International Association of Machinists (1980) *Television Entertainment Report Part II.* Upper Marlboro, MD: International Association of Machinists and Aerospace Workers.

Illinois Government News Network (2006) Governor proclaims today 'Meth Prevention Day in Illinois'. Available at: http://www3.illinois.gov/PressReleases/ShowPressRelease.cfm?SubjectID=2&RecNum=5559.

Johnson, R. (1981) World Without Workers: Prime Time's Presentation of Labour. *Labor Studies Journal* 5 (Winter): 199–206.

Jones, Owen (2016) *Chavs: The Demonisation of the Working Class.* London: Verso.

Koepsell, D. and Arp, R. (eds) (2012) *Breaking Bad and Philosophy: Badder Living Through Chemistry.* Chicago and La Salle: Open Court.

Lende, D., Leonard, T., Sterk, C. and Elifson, K. (2007) Functional Methamphetamine Use: The Insider's Perspective. *Addiction Research and Theory* 15 (5): 465–477.

Lewis, H. (2014) Culture Watch: Jump Into the Mini Cooper for a Journey Across the American Economic Landscape With 'Inequality for All'. *Firesteel.* Available at: http://firesteelwa.org/2014/03/culture-watch-jump-into-the-mini-cooper-for-a-journey-across-the-american-economic-landscape-with-i.

Lotz, A. (2014) *Cable Guys: Television and Masculinities in the Twenty-First Century.* New York: New York University Press.

MacInnes, P. (2012) Breaking Bad Creator Vince Gilligan: the man who turned Walter White from to Scarface. *The Guardian.* Available at: https://www.theguardian.com/tv-and-radio/2012/may/19/vince-gilligan-breaking-bad.

Mannix, A. (2015) As of 2014, meth-related crimes accounted for more beds in state prisons than all other drugs combined. *Minnpost.* Available at: https://www.minnpost.com/politics-policy/2015/11/even-meth-offenders-fuel-boom-minnesotas-prison-population-treatment-resource.

Marez, C. (2013) From Mr. Chips to Scarface, or Racial Capitalism in Breaking Bad. *In the Moment: Critical Inquiry.* Available at: https://critinq.wordpress.com/2013/09/25/breaking-bad/.

Martin, B. (2012) *Difficult Men: Behind the Scenes of a Creative Revolution: From The Sopranos and The Wire to Mad Men and Breaking Bad.* New York: The Penguin Press.

Mason, J. (2016) The Fed Doesn't Work For You. *Jacobin Online.* Available at: https://www.jacobinmag.com/2016/01/federal-reserve-interest-rate-increase-janet-yellen-inflation-unemployment/.

Mathiesen, T. (1997) The Viewer Society: Michel Foucault's 'Panopticon' Revisited. *Theoretical Criminology: An International Journal* 1 (2): 215–232.

McCormack, R. (2009) The Plight of American Manufacturing. *The American Prospect Online.* Available at: http://prospect.org/article/plight-american-manufacturing.

McKetin, R. (2012) Methamphetamines rehab and recovery. *Of Substance* November: 19–21.

McNall, S. (2016) *The Problem of Social Inequality: Why It Destroys Democracy, Threatens the Planet and What We Can Do About It.* New York: Routledge.

Meek, J. (2013) It's the Moral Thing to Do. *London Review of Books* 35 (1): 7–9.

Parenti, M. (1992) *Make-Believe Media: The Politics of Entertainment.* Belmont, CA: Wadsworth.

Petras, J. and Eastman-Abaya, R. (2016) 'Genocide by Prescription': Drug Induced Death in America. *Global Research* 12 July. Available at: http://www.globalresearch.ca/genocide-by-prescription-drug-induced-death-in-america/5535449.

Pew Research Center (2008) *Tough Job Market*. Available (consulted 10 August 2016) at: http://www.pewresearch.org/daily-number/tough-job-market/.

Redding, N. (2009) *Methland: The Death and Life of an American Small Town*. New York: Bloomsbury.

Riley, K. (2014) Driving on Speed: Long-Haul Truck Drivers and Amphetamines in the Postwar Period. *Labor: Studies in Working class History of the Americas* 11 (4): 63–90.

Robinson, L. (2006) Meth in North Dakota. *North Dakota Law Review* 83: 1431–1433.

Smith, A. (2013) Putting the Premium into Basic: Slow-Burn Narratives and the Loss-Leader Function of AMC's Original Drama Series, *Television New Media* 14 (2): 150–166.

Steinberg, P. (2009) The Costs of Methamphetamine: A National Estimate. *Rand Corporation Research Brief* 9438.

Sweet, S. and Meiksins, P. (2008) *Changing Contours of Work: Jobs and Opportunities in the New Economy*. London: Sage.

Tirman, J. (2013) *The Deaths of Others: The Fate of Civilians in America's Wars*. New York: Oxford University Press.

Turley, J. (2013) The Ten McGyver Moments on 'Breaking Bad'. *Salon*. Available at: http://www.salon.com/2013/07/30/the_top_10_mcgyver_moments_on_breaking_bad/.

United States Department of Labor (2008) A Profile of the Working Poor, 2008. Available at: http://www.bls.gov/opub/reports/working-poor/archive/workingpoor_2008.pdf.

Vaage, M. (2016) *The Anti-Hero in American Television*. Abingdon: Routledge.

Weil, D. (2014) *The Fissured Workplace: Why Work Became So Bad for So Many and What Can Be Done to Improve It*. Cambridge, MA: Harvard University Press.

Wesssel, D. (2011) Big US Firms Shift Hiring Abroad. *Wall Street Journal*, 19 April. Available at: http://www.wsj.com/articles/SB10001424052748704821704576270783611823972.

Williamson, K. (2016) Father Führer. *National Review*, March 28. Available at: http://www.nationalreview.com/article/432876/donald-trump-white-working class-dysfunction-real-opportunity-needed-not-trump.

Zweig, M. (2011) *The Working Class Majority: America's Best Kept Secret*. Ithaca, NY: Cornell University Press.

CHAPTER 18

'The Thing Is I'm Actually from Bromley': Queer/Class Intersectionality in *Pride* (2014)

Craig Haslop

Introduction

It is almost axiomatic that we dare not speak of class in the UK. Despite this, I am still surprised by the dearth of academic inquiry around the intersections between LGBTQI+ identities and class background (Taylor 2010). Given that all queers[1] are from a classed background, and even today, in the era of gay marriage and increasingly liberal views around sexual orientation, it is more difficult to come out if you are from a working class background (McDermott 2010)-it is surely an important intersection to consider. After all, in media studies there has been something of a renaissance in the broader area of class, partly driven by the rise of reality TV, its poverty porn and denigration of anything other than middle class identity (Morley 2009; Skeggs 2009 and Smith 2014). Indeed, there is a considerable body of work on class more broadly in film studies (see Hill [1986] *and* Nystrom [2009] as just two examples). And yet, the class/queer intersection is a rare explicit focus in film studies and beyond academically (Taylor 2010). This is partly due to the smaller number of films dealing with this specific intersection, a point I want to return to, but also perhaps because academia itself is a classed field (Medhurst 2000) where middle class identity is normalised.[2] Added to this a postmodern queer studies, where

---

1 'Queer' as a political identity, and 'queer theory' as an academic project are both contested and disputed in terms of how meaningful they are, in relation to both academic analysis and wider political change (Dean, 2015). In a special issue of *Social Text* ten years ago, Eng et al. reasserted their commitment to the notion that queer studies "has no fixed political referent" (2005, 3), despite continued critique that this leaves Queer 'subjectless', they saw this as a strength; queer for them is able to represent marginal identities and challenge the status quo from race to age to nationality. While queer has been used in wider contexts, in this chapter, I want to be clear that I use 'queer' as a term that refers to an approach that represents the interests of the LGBTQI+ communities, while academically maintaining a focus on 'queer theory' as a project critiquing heteronormativity.
2 I use the terms, working, middle and upper classes throughout this chapter for consistency, although the nature and make-up of these groups is potentially fragmenting (see Savage 2013).

fluidity is the dominant identity paradigm, leaves less room for the realities and necessary classifications of class (Taylor 2010). Whatever the causes, in this chapter I join a few others in media and film studies (Halberstam, 2001; Henderson 2001; Jennings 2006; Clare 2013), who have paid sustained attention to this intersection in film, to consider representations that highlight the subjectivities in privilege/disadvantage, that your place in the class hierarchy brings about in terms of your queer experience.

My interest in this area was sparked by seeing the film *Pride* (2014), the focus for this chapter. *Pride* was a critical and box office success. It recounts the true story of the Lesbians and Gays Support the Miners (LGSM) campaign in the UK in the 1980s and the struggle of the National Union of Mineworkers, in a period of taken-for-granted homophobia, to accept and receive help from the Lesbian and Gay community. Much has been made of the 'feel good' factor of the film evoked by the solidarity of the two groups (Bradshaw 2014; Roddick 2014). The film received praise from the LGBTQI+ media for its portrayal of life as an out gay man or lesbian at the start of the AIDS crisis (Fraser 2014). Indeed, as a queer man who grew up in the 1980s, this untold story of unlikely allies, aware as I was of the level of homophobia at the time, certainly did touch me. However, I was curious to understand why the film moved me so much, why it seemed to strike such a particular chord with me. I realised that it was *Pride*'s close attention to class politics, but from a queer perspective, that really spoke to something from my own past. It resonated with me as someone whose class identity has shifted, from that difficult to define working to lower middle class background, to my undeniably middle class academic life today, but all experienced through the particular lens of becoming an out gay man. This process provided me with the very specific subjectivity of noticing what it's like when these two intersecting facets of identity shift all at once, as they once did, for me.

Of course, intersectionality in *Pride* is not without its problems. Kelliher (2015) cites its lack of complexity and poor attention to lesbian class intersectionality as two key issues. Nevertheless, in terms of a prolonged focus on classed queer identity, it is still rare. In this chapter, I want to contextualise *Pride* within filmic history to consider how significant it is in terms of foregrounding class and queer intersectionality. Intersectionality considers subjectivities across a range of identity groups, beyond class and queer categories and remains a healthily contested term (Taylor 2009). By way of helping to

---

Nevertheless its divisions are still real and they affect people's life chances (Morley, 2009). Here I use the terms in their broadest sense in relation to morphing, but still-present, cultural understandings, representations and subjectivities.

make clear my approach and use of the concept, I want to start by returning to the roots of intersectionality.

The Intersectional Turn

Intersectionality, "the interaction of multiple identities and experiences of exclusion and subordination" (Davis 2008, 67), has become an academically fashionable term with multiple meanings (Taylor 2009). Originally, it was intended to address the absence of attention paid to women of colour where their interests were falling between feminist and anti-racist thinking. Crenshaw (1991) argued that there was a need for theorists to think about the lived experiences of women of colour from both perspectives; how both facets of these identities interact to create subjectivity and its related outcomes for privilege or potential multiple oppressions. Since then, there have been many attempts to 'pin down' intersectionality, but it remains elusive in the sense that some see it as a theory, others an approach for political institutional change, and still others a means of analysis (Davis 2008, 68). Indeed, not only is the epistemological structuration of the theory flexible in its multiple conceptualisations and applications, but ontologically it also reaches across and builds knowledge in a range of academic disciplines from gender to sociology to postcolonial studies. This has also created theoretical challenges for intersectional studies, leading to less rigour. As Taylor (2011, 6) has noted, it "often appears as an over-burdened term, where the promise of an 'intersectional' focus has not delivered in relation to specific interconnections, such as those between class and sexuality". To be clear, in this chapter, I want to think about intersectionality in terms of how multiple facets of identity, particularly across the queer/class axis, create specific subjectivities and how this is foregrounded in film to make intersectionality explicit, to add force to its political cause, and in particular that of a classed queer politics.

Although not always clearly defined, intersectionality can make obvious that privilege can completely alter one's experience of being part of an oppressed group. It can disrupt political discourses to remind us that a cause has to cater for different needs and circumstances. Class has very real implications on your experiences as a queer person, creating more hostile conditions or reducing your financial ability to 'get out' if you need to move away from home, for example (Taylor 2010). The absence of analysis along the queer/class axis in general, but specifically in relation to media and film, is even more important when we consider that class differences are being elided through an increasingly neoliberal, commodified and depoliticised LGBTQI+ culture. Duggan has theorised that this is part of what she calls 'homonormativity' (2003) where certain expectations of identity have come to dominate queer lives, creating cultural pressures to live up to a new set of 'standards'. The assumption of homonormative pressure is that an openly queer lifestyle is available, and a way of life to be freely styled. Whereas for many from poor or working class backgrounds, even being out and queer could be, at the very least difficult, and emotionally intensive; an experience dominated by other challenges before the luxury of shaping and styling identity can be indulged.

Homonormativity, as an assumption of a classed version of living an LGBTQI+ lifestyle, is refracted through a mainstream media that is most interested in the best presented and 'marketable' aspects of LGBTQI+ culture. The parts that most easily fit into a media culture that often 'normalises' middle class culture while ridiculing or shaming working class or resource poor backgrounds (Biressi and Nunn 2008; Morley 2009; Skeggs 2009 and Wood and Skeggs 2011). In relation to LGBTQI+ culture in the UK, we can see this through the imagery that circulates of gay men, lesbians and trans people, in online and mainstream magazines. *Attitude* and *GT* (*Gay Times*), the leading gay male magazine titles in the UK, are replete with images of men with perfect physiques in designer clothes, both of which require economic and (middle/elite class) cultural capital to obtain. As Hennessy notes, in her writings on the relationships between queer culture and capitalism: "The increasing circulation of gay and lesbian images in consumer culture has the effect of consolidating an imaginary, class-specific gay subjectivity for both straight and gay audiences" (2002, 113). Indeed, the same can be said for American and British film, where a focus on working class lives or the differences between classed lives for queer people has been rare.

Locating the Classed Cinematic Queer

In the mainstream of Hollywood film, LGBTQI+ characters are still few and far between. Even more so in relation to poor or working class queers, perhaps with the exception of Ennis Del Mar (Heath Ledger) in *Brokeback Mountain* (Ang Lee, 2005). If we think of wider American 'independent' cinema there are a few more examples worth highlighting. *My Own Private Idaho* (Gus Van Sant, 1991) is significant in terms of its taken for granted approach to sexuality but in the context of the story of a narcoleptic hustler, who both starts and ends the film on the roadside and at the mercy of those using it. Here intersectionality is more implicit. Conversely, *Boys Don't Cry* (Kimberley Peirce, 1999) is much more explicit in its intersectionality and rare in its focus on FTM transgender issues through the retelling of the tragic story of the murder of Brandon Teena (Hilary Swank). Halberstam, (2001), in her now seminal essay on the film and the transgender gaze, touches briefly on an intersection with class noting that in one scene where Lana (Chloe Savigny) is supposed to check Brandon's sex by inspection, she instead chooses to misrecognise him as male, while he sees past her classed based social alienation to recognise her as special and beautiful. More recently, films of note include Araki's dark tale *Mysterious Skin* (Gregg Araki, 2004) of a teenager who turns hustler in New York to uncover the truth behind the mystery of why he blacked out as a small child. The recent visceral experience of *Tangerine* (Sean Baker, 2015) has to be mentioned, throwing the audience into a day in the life of two transgender working girls on the streets of LA.

British cinema has often been more willing to be explicit about the social realities of class in the UK. Films including *Brassed Off* (Mark Herman, 1996), *The Full Monty* (Peter Cattaneo, 1997) and *Billy Elliot* (Stephen Daldry, 2000) have championed British working class cultures through feel good stories of resilience in the face of the social and cultural upheavals of Thatcherite politics. In some ways, *Pride*, as a comedy drama with a focus on the miner's strike, follows in this tradition. However, the particular focus of sexual identity and class, has been explored less, but, where it has there are varying approaches to this intersection. *My Beautiful Launderette* (Stephen Frears, 1985) stands out in its depiction of complex intersectionality, highlighting the overlapping layers of queer, class and race identity experienced by Omar (Gordon Warnecke), British born but from a Pakistani background, from the working class side of a middle class Pakistani family. The film highlights the dark side of the raced subjectivity of class where Jonny (Daniel Day Lewis), Omar's working class lover, is asked by his white friends why he would work for a Pakistani family; "they came here to work for us". But, the film also metaphorically champions working class culture through the symbolism of the revamp of the launderette, a place traditionally associated with low incomes (not having a washing machine) but here made glamorous (and queered through camp, and its close relationship to gay politics, particularly in the more closeted 1980s) by the revamp of the launderette to make it a vibrant outpost in the inner city landscape of South London.

More recently however, this kind of complex intersectionality is harder to find. There are some stand out texts worth mentioning. *Beautiful Thing* (Hettie Macdonald, 1996) with its frank depiction of the realities of being gay as a young working class man in the 1990s, was critiqued by many at the time for falling back into an old style of identity politics through the use of the coming out narrative as a central plot device. However, the film is interesting in intersectional terms, in the way it foregrounds the 'everyday' of working class culture in relation to coming out experiences, and those in the community coming to terms with those revelations. In terms of recent British films, *Weekend* (Andrew Haigh, 2012) tells the story of a middle, and a working class guy, getting together over a weekend, focusing on 'escapism' from the realities of working life.

Although the list of British films that deal with the class/queer axis is short, *Pride* can be seen as one of the latest additions to this oeuvre. How does *Pride* fit into this body of films, in what ways does it sit alongside or stand out from these films? In the following analysis, I want to contextualise the film in its particular approach to the class/queer axis and suggest that the film has a very specific structure and narrative content in relation to intersectionality. Theoretically, I draw on early (but I want to highlight, still relevant) thinking about class in cultural studies through Andy Medhurst's writings on class 'transitions' (2000) and Richard Hoggart's earlier work on working class cultures (1957).

Pride's Class/Queer Intersections and Transitions

Pride opens with a series of scenes proposing queer/class intersectionality as a core theme that the film will pivot upon. In the first of these, following initial sequences of archive news footage of the miner's strike, we are introduced to Mark Ashton (Ben Schnetzer), a character based on the real-life firebrand activist of the same name. Mark watches Arthur Scargill on television speaking about the miner's strike, in his flat, while he makes breakfast. The flat is located in a high-rise block in London, suggestive of an inner-city council estate. Mark's representation as an intersection between class and queer politics is made clear quickly, in a scene where the camera pans around the flat showing a number of symbols of his role in the Communist Party League. The camera rests on Mark's lover of the previous night, who interjects that he would see him at the march, referring to the London Gay Pride march. This is followed by a scene where his neighbour declares that he has spoken to the council about Mark's 'deviant parties'. Mark's inner city community and life is portrayed as one that is economically restrictive, but allows him room to resist, even if he encounters homophobia through his neighbours.

Directly after the scenes featuring Mark, a further juxtaposition of sexual identity with class is made, but in a different class context, when we meet Joe, a fictional character created for the film who was not part of the original LGSM. This scene shows Joe sitting in what is immediately portrayed as the much more reserved, tidy and drab surroundings of a lower middle class (as Medhurst [2000] notes that most anxious of all class groups) suburban family home, devoid of the markers of youth, resistance and campery present in Mark's flat. Joe, a character we will soon discover is currently still not out as gay, is opening a camera, a present from his Dad, who Joe thanks; his father responds with a limited emotional response, one which later we will come to understand is part of his version of a traditional hegemonic masculinity (Connell, 1985) that features emotional suppression and homophobia. Eventually we will realise that this rather sterile and grey family home and life, represents a classed prison of sexual identity for Joe.

It is not just the film's opening statement that makes intersectionality implicit in the film, but also the film's *modus operandi*. A repetitive trope in the film is set up in the first scenes through the use of transitions between different types of classed, queer and non-queer spaces. In the opening sequence, this is proposed through cross-cutting the two young men's excited departures from their respective surroundings, both from non-queer spaces of differing class origins, and both towards the utopian queer space of the *Pride* march in London. This transition trope becomes a regular feature of the film, as we follow Joe and Mark's journey and the development of the LGSM through a series of relocations. From their suburban homes into the relatively queerer space of central London (the *Pride* March, followed by a party full of queers, the meetings at the HQ for the LGSM in the bookshop 'Gay's the Word'), then from that queer space into the predominantly heterosexual space of a Welsh village, and then back to the queerer space of the bookshop and Central London. The film makes obvious that its two main locations of London and rural Wales are not clear-cut, in terms of their queerness or heteronormativity (there are homophobic attacks in London and we find out that a key Welsh character, Cliff [Bill Nighy], is a closeted gay man).

The feelings of crossing these (blurred) boundaries, of being made aware of your identity by placing it into a different less familiar context, are foregrounded by the film. While much of the focus of the film is around homophobia and the feelings experienced by those moving from a queerer space into a less queer space (and vice versa), it is also about how gender and sexuality is experienced in different class settings. For example, the importance of class is made clear early on when Joe first arrives into the queer location of the *Pride* march. Joe announces 'The thing is I'm actually from Bromley', invoking the notion that the reason he is shy and fearful about being open is not his current closeted queer status, but his roots in the reserved, surburban, quiet and predominantly (lower to) middle class area of Bromley.

The core intersection of class and queer identities is made clearer through the second but most significant geographical transition in the film, when the LGSM make their first journey to Wales. Class difference is foregrounded in the scene through the setting; the LGSM leave a London book-shop with its associations to a metropolitan educated middle class, and arrive at a working men's club in the Welsh village of Onllywn. Regardless of differences around sexuality, this is a transition from one classed space to another. The men's union and women's support group committee greeting the LGSM, on the whole provide a positive welcome, but the difference of the environment for the LGSM is made clear by their expressions of concern about entering a working men's club.

The reasons for their concern are made clear by the narrative in the first transition of the LGSM to the Welsh community, in the way a number of men find the LGSM's arrival difficult to handle. This is visualised when Mark gives his opening speech to the working men's club to declare the LGSM support for their mining community, to be greeted by a mass walkout by mainly men (although led by Maureen [Lisa Palfrey]). Further resistance by the men to being associated with the LGSM is shown later when Carl Evans (Kyle Rees) is seen to be drinking with the other men in the working men's club rather than talking to the LGSM. It is left to the leadership of Hefina (Imelda Staunton) to challenge him, compelling him to make a further effort and speak to the LGSM again, despite his earlier peace offering of buying drinks for the LGSM.

Implicit then, in the coming together of these two groups, creating solidarity in the film, is not only overcoming homophobia but also the classed differences that drove and created particular conditions of gendered sexual identity. The LGSM meet a rural community less exposed to the diverse communities of the cities and masculinities more entrenched in a traditional hegemonic (homophobic) version and less fragmented than the plural versions of masculinity becoming available in metropolitan spaces (Mort 1996, 15). The transition of the LGSM into Wales, serves to highlight movement from the metropolitan and middle classed space of the bookshop into a regional working class space. But also from the, perhaps reluctantly, more queer urban geography of London. The LGSM's arrival in rural Wales disrupts the assumed homophobia of the Welsh men, but it also disrupts class, and in ways that are closely tied to sexuality. For example, Jonathan Blake (Dominic West) 'teaches' two of the local men to dance, in a narrative move that all at once reproduces a classed cultural hierarchy where the sophisticated metropolitan visitor teaches the less well educated men to dance, and a gay male stereotype where queer men have natural dance ability, that straight men do not.

The film is, however, careful not just to foreground the intersection of classed and gendered sexual identities for men. Indeed, it is through the intersection of class, gender and sexuality that the film positions women as anything but powerless in the Welsh community. The women's group (portrayed mainly through the committee members in the film) is depicted as standing out in their support for the LGSM, and demonstrates their power through their ability to coerce and influence the men in the community to eventually change their minds and be friendly to the LGSM. Moreover, the film puts two women at the heart of the moral battle over whether the miners should work with the LGSM; Hefina and Maureen (Lisa Palfrey) who clash on several occasions. Both of the women bully men into taking action that supports their opposing views in relation to how closely they should work with the LGSM.

The film continues its intersectional commentary on class, gender and sexuality through women, by juxtaposing the women of Onllwyn with Marion Cooper (Monica Doolan), Joe's Mother. The women of Onllwyn, despite their differences, are shown to be a tight knit community, interdependent and supportive. Marion in stark contrast, is always shown to be on her own or with her family, a lonely figure operating in the context of an atomised suburban estate in Bromley. These two classed landscapes offer different freedoms and restrictions to the women in their respective areas. For the women of Onllwyn, there is a sense that while heteronormativity dominates, their sense of togetherness as women allows them to discuss their desires and curiosities, demonstrated in another transitional scene when the women travel to London to support the 'Pits and Perverts' gig and go out on the town together, barging their way into a men-only leather bar, dancing with the clientele and cross-questioning them about their sex lives. Although potentially romanticising working class culture, the women's open and forthright nature, and willingness to be playful, carnal and carnivalesque, is shown to allow greater freedom to explore their sexuality. In contrast, Joe's Mum Marion is depicted as performing a middle class version of femininity, distanced from the pleasures of the body. Instead, she becomes a gatekeeper of heteronormativity, following a scene where Joe's parents find out he is gay, Marion tells Joe in the next scene; "I know you think you know what you want" and then later says "I didn't know what I wanted when I was your age", discursively extending her own disciplined version of gender and sexuality to Joe. Marion's final scene in the film, when Joe leaves home, acts as the crescendo that finally reveals the extent of the performed and classed nature of sexuality and gender for Joe's family. Joe arrives home in the LGSM van, returning after he has run away to Wales, to find his sister's wedding party taking place at his house. The family is formally dressed, standing at the front of the house, on display to the neighbourhood for the wedding. Joe's arrival in the van with Sian interrupts this scene in class and sexual terms, the van representative of the working class miners crashing a formal middle-class occasion. Joe symbolic of an alternative sexual lifestyle making its presence known at the wedding ritual; one that is at the heart of heteronormative family life. Marion defends the middle class heteronormative family home a final time, asking

Sian to move the van from her property and then challenges Joe, asking where he is going. Marion is portrayed as a woman unravelling, underneath her anger she knows that on some level what she is trying to hold on to, is artifice.

Feeling Class and Sexual Identity

In all these cases in the film, the transitions across these spaces, cause disruptions to the classed sexual status quo, that makes obvious the 'feelings' of classed sexual identities. Andy Medhurst (2000) has written on the feelings of class (dis)location based on his own experience, and in defence of Hoggart's autobiographical work against a barrage of academic attacks designed to defend the cultural studies move to 'theory' and denounce experienced-based work on class as nostalgic. As Medhurst notes:

> Anyone who speaks about a working class upbringing, certainly in a British context, is liable to find themselves accused of sentimentality. This is hardly surprising since class is an emotional business. Class privilege and prejudice are not reducible to dispassionate debate or the algebra of abstracting. Class is felt, class wounds, class hurts, and those on the cusp between classes bruise particularly easily (2000, 21).

Medhurst highlights here that class is more than its economic or social outcomes, it is an experience that we feel, and particularly so once we start to move between or straddle classes. In this way, class movement is an intersection in itself. We think of intersectionality as the experiences of belonging to several groups, as oppressions that can be doubled or multiplied as was the case in Crenshaw's original meaning for the word, in relation to black women. However, *Pride* makes obvious that being working or lower middle or middle class is an identity itself, and when you start to crossover into different class groups, you are experiencing an intersection; you start to become part of another classed identity, but retain some of the sensibilities of your roots. As Medhurst notes of his own adapted middle class identity as an academic from a working class background: "my sense of class identity is uncertain, torn and oscillating—caught on a cultural cusp" (21). Of course, this type of intersection is not the same as the intersection of being black and a woman, your class roots are not necessarily obvious to others (although they often are, and that can be one of the feelings evoked, of not quite fitting in) and eventually you will probably become mostly middle class. Indeed, a transition into middle class culture, although confusing and maybe 'bruising', is one that starts offering more privilege, changing perceptions of class and of being queer, reducing the ability to know what it is like if you're queer with less resources. This intersection is not the same as the potential double oppression experienced if you're a black woman in quantitative or qualitative terms. However, the intersection between class groups is particular in the way that you are likely to experience it as part of your developing life, it has commonalities with sexuality for many, where there is a transition from identifying as straight to gay, bi or queer. There is a potential that, if like me, you went to university from a working to lower middle class background and then come out as gay, you are experiencing two sets of transitions. One intersection is the subjectivities of experiencing class and sexual identity at the same time. I was part of a new sexual subculture, naïve but excited with discovery; while retaining links to the old, straight friends who still assumed I would get a girlfriend. I was also part of a new class group, my love for ketchup on everything a joke with new friends, while old friends called me a snob, noting I returned from university with new ideas and a changing set of interests; garlic with everything. Moreover, like Joe in *Pride*, I embodied two other intersections, between old and new class and sexual cultures, straddling across them, while negotiating the changes from old to new, within each.

Pride makes this type of intersectional complexity more obvious than most films. It highlights the intersections within identity groups through the disruptions felt when experiencing classed and sexual identities in the context of different classed and sexual subcultures. *Pride* is always 'on the cusp'. A film that shows solidarity across margins, but that does so by hanging around the margins, and making obvious the feelings of uncertainty which it brings to those crossing boundaries, traversing class, sexual and regional borders. When Joe leaves home, he rejects his mother and father's restrictive, sterile and performed version of middle class heteronormativity, by channelling the power to resist and fight, which he learnt from Mark Ashton, an activist who represented both a fight for workers as well as queer rights. Joe also held on to a sense of acceptance through community that he had been exposed to in the working class culture of rural Wales. The film offers a Hoggartian reminder that a working class community, and one under siege, can create conditions that offer a 'live and let live' tolerance. As Hoggart notes it is:

> bred from charity, in that all are in the same lower situation together, and from a wider unidealism which that situation creates. The larger unexpectancy encourages a slowness to moral indignation, after all, it's no good creating problems; there are plenty as it is; anything for a quiet life (1957, 93).

As such it is an antidote to the poverty porn, denigration and stigmatisation of the poor and working classes that seems almost to be taken for granted in recent British television (Morley, 2009); one that serves to remind Joe of the possibilities and power of community, in his own queer politics.

Conclusion

To draw the points made in this chapter together, I want to return to *Pride*'s place in the canon, if we can call it that, of British queer intersectional films. There is no doubt, as Kelliher has argued, there are problems with *Pride*'s intersectionality. It is fair to say that the film focused mostly on the intersection of gay male queer and class politics, although often through gender politics, to the detriment of the intersection of lesbian and class politics. However, I have suggested here that it is *Pride*'s particular approach to the intersectionality of queer and class politics that make it important. Ros Jennings (2006) writes about *Beautiful Thing*, that while it might not have the art film credentials associated with other queer film directors of the time including Derek Jarman and Isaac Julien, the film still has value precisely because it is a 'comfort food' of a film, that focuses on everyday struggles and small triumphs: "The politics of the film are lived and personal, taking place on a very human scale" (183). *Pride* stands out in this way too; its intersectionality might not be the most complex or historically accurate, but it brings to life the very real lived experiences of class and queer disruptions in the 80s, the feeling of intersections between class groups and queer and non-queer spaces and communities.

Pride highlights that class in the UK existed (and of course still does), and more than its economic and social consequences. Class is cultural, has its own norms and pressures that we may only realise we are aspiring to, or are confined by, when they are interrupted; when we try to move 'up' or are pushed 'down' the class spectrum. Moreover, its focus on the intersection of sexuality with class provides an interesting perspective on sexual liberation, challenging assumptions that have developed of a metropolitan liberal middle class as the arbiters of gay culture. The film celebrates a working class community as a place that a middle class gay man can run to, turning on its head a very real experience for many working class queers, currently trying to fit into the pressures of an increasingly middle class, homonormative sub-culture. A sub-culture, that the film reminds us, can still be a place beyond neoliberal commodified consumption, a space to draw strength and unity as a community and fight for the struggles of those across the LGBTQI+ spectrum. Its message is perhaps even more important now, at a time when despite years of improvements in the social, cultural and legal circumstances for LGBTQI+ people, there are signs of a backlash to this progress, with reports of renewed homophobia in post EU exit Britain (Stone, 2016) and a backdrop of rising far right politics in Europe and the US. Moreover, linked to the film's reminder of the possibilities of a radical queer politics, the film celebrates the solidarity between the LGSM and the miners, who seem so diametrically opposed in terms of their attitudes and views about sexuality; a reminder for the queer politics of today, that intersectionality is not only a way to theorise the subjectivities of multiple oppressions, but also a practice, that can, and should, bring different identity groups and those from different class backgrounds together to fight for each other's causes.

References

Biressi, A. and Nunn H. (2008) Bad Citizens: The Class Politics of Lifestyle Television. Gareth P. (Ed) *Exposing Lifestyle Television: The Big Reveal*. London: Ashgate. 15–24.

Bradshaw, P. (2014) Pride review—when gay activists struck a deal with miners. *The Guardian*. Available at http://www.theguardian.com/film/2014/sep/11/pride-film-review-miners-strike-gay-people-1984.

Clare, S.D. (2013) (Homo)normativity's romance: Happiness and indigestion in Andrew Haigh's Weekend. *Continuum*, December 1, 2013.

Connell, R. (1985), Theorising Gender. *Sociology* 2: 260.

Contemporary British Television. *European Journal of Cultural Studies* 12 (4): 487–508.

Crenshaw, K. (1991) Mapping the Margins: Intersectionality, Identity Politics, and Violence against Women of Color. *Stanford Law Review* 6: 1241.

Davis, K. (2008) Intersectionality as buzzword: A sociology of science perspective on what makes a feminist theory successful. *Feminist Theory* 9 (1): 67–85.

Dean, T. (2015) No Sex Please, We're American. *American Literary History* 27 (3) 614–624.

Eng, D. Halberstam J. and Muñoz J.E. (2005) What's queer about queer studies now? *Social Text* 84–85; 1–17.

Fraser, A. (2014) 'Pride': The first gay press review by Attitude's Andre Fraser. *Attitude*. Available at http://attitude.co.uk/attitudes-deputy-editor-andrew-fraser-reviews-pride/.

Halberstam, J. (2001), The transgender gaze in Boys Don't Cry. *Screen* 42 (3): 294–298.

Henderson, L. (2001) The class character of Boys Don't Cry. *Screen* 42 3: 299–303.

Hennessy, R. (2002) *Profit and Pleasure: Sexual Identities in Late Capitalism*. London: Routledge.

Hill, J. (1986) *Sex, class and realism: British cinema, 1956–1963*. London: British Film Institute.

Hoggart, R. (1957) *The Uses of Literacy: Aspects of Working class Life with Special Reference to Publications and Entertainments.* Harmondsworth: Penguin in association with Chatto and Windus.

Jennings, R. (2006) Beautiful Thing: British Queer Cinema, Positive Unoriginality and the everyday. In: Griffiths R. (ed) *British Queer Cinema.* London: Routledge, 183–195.

Kelliher, D. (2015) *Pride*: What's left out and does it matter? BIMI presents PRIDE Screenings, Symposium and Roundtable, 6th Nov.

McDermott E. (2010) 'I wanted to be totally true to myself': Class and the making of the sexual self'. In: Taylor Y. (ed.) *Classed Intersections: Spaces, Selves, Knowledges.* Aldershot: Ashgate, 199–216.

Medhurst, A. (2000) If Anywhere: Class identifications in Cultural Studies. In: Munt S (ed) *Cultural Studies and The Working Class.* London: Cassell.

Morley, David G. (2009) Mediated Class-ifications: Representations of Class and Culture in Contemporary British Television. *European Journal of Cultural Studies*, 12(4), pp. 487-508

Mort, F. (1996) *Cultures of Consumption: Masculinities and Social Space in Late Twentieth-Century Britain.* London: Routledge.

Nystrom, D. (2009) *Hard hats, rednecks, and macho men: class in 1970s American Cinema.* New York: Oxford University Press.

Roddick, N. (2014) Pride, Cannes Film Festival—film review. *Evening Standard.* Available at http://www.standard.co.uk/goingout/film/pride-cannes-film-festival-film-review-9437759.html.

Savage, M. (2013) A New Class Paradigm? *British Journal of Sociology of Education* 24 (4):535–541.

Skeggs, B. (2009): The Moral Economy of Person Production: The Class Relations of Self Performance on "Reality" Television. *The Sociological Review* 57 (4): 626–44.

Smith, D. R. (2014) The Gent-Rification of English Masculinities: Class, Race and Nation in Contemporary Consumption. *Social Identities* 20 (4-5):391–406.

Stone, J. (2016) Brexit vote driving anti-LGBT hate crime as victims told: 'You're next', 15th November 2016, http://www.independent.co.uk/news/uk/politics/brexit-lgbt-hate-crime-rise-galop-home-affairs-youre-next-a7419111.html.

Taylor, Y. (2009) Complexities and Complications: Intersections of Class and Sexuality. *Journal of Lesbian Studies.* 13 (2): 189–203.

Taylor, Y. (2010) Introduction. Taylor Y. (ed). *Classed Intersections: Spaces, Selves, Knowledges.* London: Routledge.

Taylor, Y. (2011) Sexualities and class. *Sexualities*, 14 (1): 3–11.

Wood, H., & Skeggs, B. (2011) *Reality television and class.* London; Palgrave Macmillan.

Index

Africa   84, 86, 102, 103, 125, 128, 149–162, 207
Allman, P   46, 153–154, 157
Althusser, L   31, 34, 42, 44–45, 125, 127, 151, 219
Anderson, P   135
Andrejevic, M   281–282, 282
Apple, M.W   45–46
Argentina   5, 134, 137, 140–146
Ashley, M   39
Australia   8, 217–231

Bales, K   142
Ball, S   24, 43
Battle of Orgreave   241
Bauman, Z   298
Beautiful Thing   307
Benefits Street   189, 196, 289, 294
Benjamin, W   182
Bernstein, B   31, 41, 44, 47
Bhaskar, R   53–54
Big Bang Theory   276–277
Big Brother   282
Billy Elliott   307
Biressi, A   9, 10, 269
Black, C   240, 247
Blair, T   47, 204, 223
Bourdieu, P   31, 41–43, 45, 188, 228
Bowles, H   31, 42, 44, 45
Boys Don't Cry   306
Branson, R   39
Brassed Off   307
Brazil   83, 84, 86
Breaking Bad   10, 11, 288–295, 298–299
Britain   6, 21, 32, 38, 40, 43, 68–91, 178, 185–187, 195, 196, 224, 239, 241, 274–275, 278–280
Britain's Got Talent   283
Brokeback Mountain   306
Brown, G   47
Brown, W   291
Butler, J   213

Callinicos, A   57, 58
Cameron, D   37, 298
Capital   16, 55, 99, 117, 125

Capital in the Twenty-First Century   218
Carchedi, G   25
Carter, B   24
Castells, M   16, 18
Charlie Hebdo   208
Children of Golzow   251
China   84, 85, 86, 94, 105, 106
Chomsky, N   173, 174
Choonara, J   2, 9
Clinton, B   204
Cole, M   46
Collins, S   280
Communist Manifesto, The   15, 34–35, 198, 202
Condition of the Working Class, The (film)   9, 237, 243–252
Connell, R.W   213, 219, 225
Conservative   37, 46, 47, 75, 77–78, 88–89, 187
Couldry, N   269
Crenshaw, K   305
Crocodile Dundee   217
Curthoys, A   224, 225

Daily Mail   195, 239
Daily Mirror   195
Denmark   7, 72, 83, 201–204, 207–08
Devine, F   228
Devoto, F   140
Dogs of the Dole   189
Donato, M   4
Doogan, K   26–7, 52, 63
Dorling, D   3, 4
Draper, H   19, 21, 22, 23
Duffield, S   31, 43
Duncan, J   156, 158
Dylan, B   78

Eccleston, C   279–280
Eckersley, R   222
Ehrenreich, B   56, 289
Ehrenreich, J   56, 289
Eighteenth Brumaire of Louis Napoleon, The   35
Ellis, J   259

Engels, F   198, 237, 241, 242, 244, 245, 248, 251
England   7, 43, 46, 47, 78, 81, 82, 123, 237, 243, 245
Ensenzberger, H.M.   167
Equity   279
Europe   7, 68, 84, 85, 86, 102, 125, 152, 184, 185, 195, 198, 200, 203, 204, 205, 207, 212, 218, 224, 227, 256, 266, 275, 237, 241, 242, 244, 245, 248, 251

Fine, B   25–26
Ford, H   172
Foucault, M   251, 293
Frazer, N   6
Frey, C.B   107
Full Monty, The   307

Game, A   225
Gay Times   306
Gender at Work   225
German Ideology, The   16, 166–167, 176, 199
Germany   83
Gibson, M   228
Gillard, J   224
Gintis, H   31, 42, 44, 45
Golding, P   275
Goldthorpe, J   56
Gonski, D   224
Gramsci, A   6, 22–23, 44, 156, 160, 166, 169–174, 176, 181, 204–205, 219
Green, P   39
Guardian, The   87, 179, 195, 240
Gubbay, J   55

Habermas, J   168, 169
Halberstam, J   307
Hall, S   207
Hardt, M   15, 19
Hart, G   155
Hartley, J   278
Haslop, C   11
Hawke, B   221, 222
Hegel, GWF   167
Hegemony and Socialist Strategy   214
Heinzen, K   17
Hennessy, R   306
Hill, D   2, 3, 46
Hills, J   195
Hobsbawm, E   16, 135, 136

Hogan, P   217
Hoggart, R   225, 229, 308, 312, 313
Holy Family, The   28
Howard, J   223
Howe, B   221

Independent, The   32
India   84, 106, 199

Jakobsson, P   9, 10, 11
Japan   72, 84, 85, 91
Jennings   314
Jobs, S   172
Joseph Rountree Foundation   32

Kabat, M   5
Karabarbounis, L   107
Kazin, M   211
Keating, P   217, 221, 222, 223
Keilliher, D   304, 314
Kelsh, D   45
Krarup, S   207–208

Labor Party (Aus)   8, 217, 218, 220–224, 226
Labour Party (UK)   8, 24, 46, 81, 88–89, 187, 193, 196, 204, 223
Laclau, E   16, 134, 137, 215
Latham, M   223, 224
Lenin, V.I.   138
Lesbian and Gays Support The Miners   11, 179, 304, 308–311, 315
Lewis, H   4, 5
Lipsitz, G   210
Littlewood, J   250
London   6, 7, 11, 20, 33, 72, 81–82, 84, 91, 187, 190–191, 196
López, C   136, 137
Lukács, G   126
Lumby, C   8
Luxemburg, R   138

Macbeth on the Estate   251
Macri, M   142
Madmen   289
Major, J   37
Making a Difference   225
Making of the English Working Class, The   135–136

INDEX 319

Marx, K 2, 4, 6, 15, 16–17, 19–20, 21, 24, 28, 34, 35–36, 37, 51, 53, 99, 104, 106, 108, 111, 120, 121, 123–125, 126, 138, 166–169, 172, 175, 177, 181, 198, 199, 211, 242, 283, 284
Mason, P 16
Mathiesen, T 293
McKenzie, L 6, 7
McLaren, P 46
McNally, D 159
Medhurst, A 308, 312
Meiksins-Wood, E 15, 135, 136, 161
Mills, C.W. 24
Mondon, A 209–210
Moore, T 8, 9, 222
Morley, D 257
Mouffe, C 16, 214
Murdoch, G 275
Murray, A 5
Muslim 202–204, 206, 207–209, 213
My Beautiful Laundrette 11, 307
My Own Private Idaho 306

Negri, A 15, 18, 19
Neiman, B 107
Netherlands 72
Nilsen, A 157
Norway 72, 83
Nottingham 6, 189, 192, 194
Nunn, H 269

O'Hara, M 195
O'Neill, D 6, 9, 237, 238, 240, 243–246, 249, 251
Obama, B 214, 288
Occupy 118, 176, 218
Osborne, M.A. 107

Pannekoek, A 36
Panse, S 251
Paris 20
Picketty, T 218
Pini, B 228
Policing The Crisis 207
Portello, A 210
Poulantzas, N 57
Poverty of Philosophy, The 35, 124
Pratschke, J 3, 4, 171
Previte, J 228
Pride 11, 304, 307–314

Pringle, R 225
Puar, J 213

Raphael, C 277
Reid, J 178
Renner, K 56
Resnick, S 125
Riddell, S 43
Rikowski, G 46
Rock, D 139
Romero, L 138–139
Rotha, P 249
Rustin, M 291

Sábato, M 138, 139
Said, E 172
Sartelli, E 5
Savage, M 227
Schwartz, J 174, 177
Scotland 43
Seddon, D 165
Seltzer, M 10, 11
Sen, A 223
Shakespeare on the Estate 251
Shameless 289, 294, 299
Sheffield 69
Shildrick, T 189, 194
Skeggs, B 7, 187, 188, 227, 228, 239, 268
Skint 196
Sopranos 289
Standing, G 16, 18, 27
Steedman, C 239
Stevenson, H 24
Stiernstedt, F 9, 10, 11
Strangleman, T 251
Sun, The 195
Surplus Value 4–5, 18–20, 25, 35, 36, 55, 57, 61, 62, 93, 99–100, 108, 110–111, 116, 119, 120, 121, 122, 124, 180, 281–284
Survivor 275–276, 280
Sweden 9, 10, 255, 258, 259–268
Swindon, R 181

Taddeo, R 4
Taylor, I 269
Thatcher, M 78, 110, 204, 240, 274, 290
Thompson, E.P. 5, 127, 133–137, 139–140, 150, 152–153, 156, 161, 225, 229, 230, 242
Thorborn, G 258

Tirman, J 293
Trump, D 8, 185, 198, 206, 210–211, 214
Turner, G 281
Tyler, I 269

USA 7, 10, 21, 32, 47, 68, 78, 83–4, 89, 101–102, 103, 105, 107, 110, 114, 115, 125, 199, 210–211, 212, 224, 227, 266, 274–278, 280, 288–299

Wales 46
Wayne, M 6, 9, 237, 238, 239, 240, 243–246, 249, 251
We Pay Your Benefits 189
Weekend 308

Whitlam, G 219
Wilby, P 87
Williams, R 225, 229
Williamson, M 10, 11
Wolff, R 125
Wood, H 268
Woolcock, P 251
Wright E.O. 24, 36, 57, 58, 59, 125

X-Factor 279

Yılmaz, F 7, 8, 9

Zeilig, L 151
Zizek, S 16

CPSIA information can be obtained
at www.ICGtesting.com
Printed in the USA
LVHW030120071218
599536LV00003B/4/P